*Acadia, Maine, and
New Scotland*

As jurors,
we have unanimously selected the manuscript
'Acadia, Maine, and New Scotland:
marginal colonies in the seventeenth century'
as the winner of the 1976 Sainte-Marie Prize
for its original contribution to the study of
seventeenth-century Canadian history.

JOHN MOIR
University of Toronto

BRUCE TRIGGER
McGill University
Montreal

MARCEL TRUDEL
University of Ottawa

JOHN G. REID

Acadia, Maine, and New Scotland

MARGINAL COLONIES IN THE SEVENTEENTH CENTURY

Winner of the Sainte-Marie Prize for History, 1976
Huronia Historical Parks
Ontario Ministry of Culture and Recreation

Published in association with Huronia Historical Parks,
Ontario Ministry of Culture and Recreation
by University of Toronto Press
Toronto Buffalo London

Printed in Canada

ISBN 0-8020-5508-7

Canadian Cataloguing in Publication Data
Reid, John G.
Acadia, Maine and New Scotland

Bibliography: p.
Includes index.
ISBN 0-8020-5508-7

1. Acadia – History – 17th century.*
2. Maine – History – 17th century.
3. Maritime Provinces – History – 17th century.*
I. Huronia Historical Parks (Ont.).
II. Title.

FC2043.R44   971.01′6   C81-094133-3
F1038.R44

For J.H.R. and G.M.R.

Contents

Foreword / ix

Preface / xi

Acknowledgments / xvii

PART I

INTRODUCTION

1 Beginnings, to 1630 / **3**

PART II

THE FORMATIVE YEARS, 1630–1650

2 Relationships with Europe / **37**
3 Relationships with Native Peoples / **58**
4 Relationships with Other Colonies / **80**
5 Internal Relationships / **103**

PART III

THE INTERPLAY OF FORCES, 1650–1690

6 Euramerican Adjustment, 1650–1660 / **127**
7 European Reassertion, 1660–1675 / **144**
8 Violent Dissolution, 1675–1690 / **164**

Conclusion / 184

Maps / 191
Notes / 195
Bibliography / 263
Index / 279

Foreword

This book exemplifies in superlative degree the author's ability to take account of the many diverse and interacting factors which help explain the hazards and fortunes of colonial enterprise in northeastern North America in the seventeenth century. His reader thus can appreciate the congeries of forces and conditions that impinged upon and determined the outcome of the distinct but interrelated aspects of a constantly changing scene that opened with the halting attempts to plant colonies early in the century, and concluded with the first of the great colonial wars that broke upon them in 1689.

As all scholars must, Dr Reid has absorbed, with a commendable degree of thoroughness, existing knowledge of his subject which, in this case, has been explored in considerable depth over the last twenty-five years. Because of his acquaintance with new approaches, he has succeeded in penetrating to the heart of complexities not clearly elucidated before. For example, the persistent establishments of the French and English differed markedly in their impact on Amerindian cultures, and Dr Reid has sought to explain this difference in all its complexity. He does not reject altogether the long-standing belief that King Philip's War resulted from the influence of 'racist' bias and Calvinist exclusiveness but he emphasizes the effect of the diversity of practical circumstances among the French and the English settlements. In particular, the engrossment of Indian land in the Maine towns contrasted with the lack of encroachment on Indian territories by the French agricultural communities to the eastward.

Although Dr Reid may not go all the way with such scholars as Innis and Creighton in attributing the expansion of English settlement in this part of the New World to a more intensive development of the dry fishery, as opposed to the limitation of French communities because of the French concentration on the green fishery, he nevertheless recognizes the importance of the fishery and the fur trade in the early colonial economy. He sees too their importance in what became the development of first importance as the century advanced: the rise of the Massachusetts Bay Colony, and the extension of its influence over the northeastern settlements. Although the French early in the century shifted their principal fur-trading operations to the *pays d' en haut* to which the St Lawrence gave access, the Acadian region was never entirely abandoned, and French concern for it was enchanced as imperial rivalries became intensified. The fragmented settlements of Acadia and Maine were thus caught up in what became a world-wide struggle pursued by France and England for reasons that were at bottom very similar.

One is here reminded of the author's insistence that French and English colonial policies were similar, having been formulated for the pursuit of objectives commonly held throughout western Europe. As is well known, the governments and mercantile communities of both states were initially bemused by the aim of finding untold wealth in the form of gold and silver comparable with the fruits of Spanish exploitation of the Indies. While fish and furs proved to be of more enduring worth, the dream of acquiring large quantities of the glittering metals never entirely faded from the minds of the colonizers of England and France.

Dr Reid stresses the way in which metropolitan intentions failed to conform to American realities, but the persistence of such cross purposes was only one of the retarding conditions of colonization in the northeastern region of the continent. Small-scale enterprise, insufficiency of material incentive, fragmentation and scatter, all give point to the concept of marginality which he appropriately enshrines in his subtitle. It was such inhibiting circumstances as I have just enumerated that persisted in varying degree throughout seventeenth-century Acadian history, favouring, as they did in the long run, the English colonial interest over the French. On the other hand, it was a tribute to a *ci-devant* Scottish reality that when Acadia's stronghold was taken in 1710 by a largely New England force, the territory was ceded three years later as New Scotland in the Latin form of that name, thus testifying to the endurance of a tradition that would in the fullness of time be strengthened by the arrival there of thousands of Lowland and Gaelic-speaking Scots. Many of these were destined to achieve distinction in their adopted country, not least, as a late arrival, the author of this book. He wrote the first doctoral dissertation in the field of history to have been approved by the University of New Brunswick, and his efforts have been crowned by having had it accepted for publication as the winner of the much coveted prize that bears the name of Sainte-Marie among the Hurons.

Alfred G. Bailey
Professor emeritus of history
University of New Brunswick

Preface

This is a study in comparative North American colonial history. As such, it has two aspects. In the first place, it is an examination of three colonies – Acadia, Maine, and New Scotland – which originated from three different European countries – France, England, and Scotland. Secondly, it is an account of the interaction of Europeans with the native peoples and physical environment of a region of North America. The two aspects, while separable, are closely related: comparison of the three colonies is facilitated by their location in a region which contained native cultures of a generally similar kind and which had similar geographical characteristics; the concept of 'Europeans' presupposes the existence of a degree of unity among the three national cultures in their approaches to colonization. Thus, what follows is an investigation both of colonies and of a region.

This comparative approach implies an effort to move beyond the purely national interpretations which have tended to dominate the colonial history of the Americas. For some historians, the importance of the colonial period has stemmed chiefly from the search for the beginnings of the American nations which emerged in the late eighteenth and nineteenth centuries: Canada, the United States, the Latin American countries. Others have preferred a different kind of national approach, stressing the distinctive influence of the several European nations upon their American colonies. Neither of these approaches is necessarily invalid. To trace the origins of modern societies is a perfectly legitimate historical goal, as is the exploration of the particular characteristics of Spanish, Portuguese, English, French, Swedes, Scots, or Dutch in America. Yet both approaches leave important questions unanswered, especially in regard to the seventeenth century. Why should we suppose that seventeenth-century American history can be neatly classified either according to the terminology of modern North or South America or according to that of seventeenth-century Europe? Surely the turbulent human experience of the invasion of a continent by colonizers – sometimes successful, sometimes not – deserves more subtle treatment by historians?

As always, though, it is easier to diagnose the faults of past scholarship than to find new perspectives. Fortunately, a widened vision of colonial history has recently been approached from a number of directions. One of these has been the development of the study of first European contacts with America, and indeed with the other parts of the world explored by Europeans concurrently. J.H. Parry has illuminated in rich detail the interdependence of the various aspects of European expansion in the fifteenth and sixteenth centuries, while Immanuel Wallerstein has persuasively interpreted this expansion as the beginning of a European 'world-economy' of which America formed part.[1] Another contribution of great importance has been made by the Mexican historian Edmundo O'Gorman, whose discussion of the 'invention' of America carries the implication that the expansion of Europe into American colonies was not only a physical process but also an intellectual and conceptual one.[2] Furthermore, certain recent studies of European national efforts at colonization, although not explicitly comparative in purpose, have sought to appraise the problems encountered by the separate nationalities in a radical way which invites and facilitates comparison. One example is Charles Gibson's work on the Spanish. Another is the examination of English colonization by Clarence L. Ver Steeg; W.J. Eccles has performed a similar function for the French, and Thomas J. Condon for the shorter period of Dutch interest in North America.[3]

Comparative study has also been approached from the standpoint of the historical geographer. Although it is not necessarily the avowed intent of the historical geographer to comment upon the similarities or differences between colonists of different European nationalities, the detailed study of the colonists' interaction with the physical environment of America inevitably reveals adaptations which were forced upon colonists regardless of nationality. Particularly suggestive in this regard have been the works of R. Colebrook Harris, James T. Lemon, Andrew Hill Clark, and Douglas R. McManis.[4] Closely connected has been the growth of schools of historical interpretation that have examined the minute details of European adaptations. Community and demographic histories of New England towns, for example, might be thought to offer too narrow a focus to be of use to the comparative historian; yet detail of this kind has great importance in assisting the comparative historian to substantiate his generalizations.[5] The same may be said, to take further examples, of the work of the Quebec historians Marcel Trudel and Robert-Lionel Séguin, with their exhaustive study of specific aspects of seventeenth-century Canadian society, or of the enquiries of the American historical sociologist Sigmund Diamond into the inner dynamics of the earliest colonial organizations.[6]

Of the recent approaches, one of the most fruitful has been in Indian history. The native peoples of America were long treated by most historians as mere adjuncts to a central process, the colonization of an empty wilderness by Europeans. That such a view is no longer possible for a serious historian is a testimony to recent developments in Indian history, which have revealed the process as one of interaction between human cultures that were different but not intrinsically unequal in significance. It has been demonstrated that the reasons for the profound changes in Indian society that accompanied European contact must be sought in the nature of the Indian culture and its environment, rather than in facile assumptions of European superiority, and this insight has been applied to the northeastern Algonkian peoples in such works as the pioneering ethnohistory of A.G. Bailey and the more recent studies of Cornelius J. Jaenen and Calvin Martin.[7] Among the most important general insights offered by Indian history to the comparative historian has been the obvious but neglected truth that the Indian-European interaction was one between cultures that combined unity, though not uniformity, and complexity. Just as the complexity of the vastly diverse Indian cultures has generally been underestimated by historians, so the cultural unity of the various European nations has also been overlooked. Wilcomb E. Washburn has set out to redress this balance in a general sense, and Francis Jennings' study of 'the invasion of America' has led him specifically to comparative analysis of European colonizing methods.[8]

With all of these tendencies leading towards, or at least facilitating, the development of comparative colonial history, it is not surprising that directly comparative works have appeared, though as yet in small numbers. A forerunner was Herbert Bolton earlier in the present century, who argued that differences of nationality and religion should not be allowed to obscure the common perceptions and desires which were characteristic of Europeans who colonized America.[9] More recently, a renewed impetus has been given by the important works of the Mexican historian Silvio Zavala, the British historians K.G. Davies and David B. Quinn, and the American historian Max Savelle. All of these, as well as working in more specific non-comparative fields, have produced comparative overviews of American or North American colonization over lengthy periods, and have identified concepts, problems, and experiences common to European colonizers.[10] But what does all this mean for the history of particular parts of the Americas? Only more detailed comparative studies can provide answers, as this one seeks to do for the colonies of Acadia, Maine, and New Scotland. These three colonies were all originally conceived as major colonial thrusts of their respective parent countries, though each failed to

develop as its European promoters had envisaged. All three were situated in the
region bounded by the St Lawrence river and gulf, the Atlantic Ocean, the
Piscataqua River, and the western fringe of settlement: the northeastern maritime region. All three had a tenuous existence from their beginnings in the early
seventeenth century until they faced near-devastation by warfare in 1690.

One central characteristic of this period was the existence of tension between
the original European concepts of the respective colonies, on the one hand, and
the exigencies of actual survival in America on the other. From the beginning,
colonization was a conceptual as well as a physical process. The first sighting of
the new western lands by Europeans of the Renaissance period had to be
accompanied by recognition and intellectual accommodation before 'America'
came into being. Similarly, 'Acadia,' 'Maine,' and 'New Scotland' had to be
conceived in European minds before colonies of those names could exist. The
problem, however, was to reconcile the European concept – in terms not just of
a name, but of the extent and nature of the projected colony – with the realities
of the American peoples and geographical environment upon which its physical
existence and survival would depend. For France, England, and Scotland, this
problem was complicated by their relatively late appearance as colonizing
nations. Inevitably, the concepts entertained in these countries in the late
sixteenth and early seventeenth centuries were profoundly influenced by the
known colonial achievements of Portugal and Spain, and especially by the
spectacular success of the latter in Central and South America. In North
America, including the northeastern maritime region, the European colonies
were founded in the early seventeenth century, therefore, primarily in the hope
of large finds of precious metals, along with the profitable exploitation of native
labour, and of the discovery of a sea passage to Asia.

Implied in these hopes was the intention to emulate Spain in establishing
extensive areas of colonization which would bring national prestige and personal prestige to those directly involved. The reality, however, proved different, owing to the totally different conditions obtaining in North America from
those found by the Spanish conquistadores further south. Consequently, Europeans of various nationalities in North America found themselves unable to
respond satisfactorily to their environment, and thus confined to tiny communal
settlements on the fringe of the continent. Such settlements existed only so long
as they were tolerated by the native inhabitants, and furthermore had little
useful purpose in European terms: as instruments of colonization they were
clearly defective, and what they achieved by way of commercial activity could
be pursued more cheaply by annual voyages from Europe.

The result of this early disjunction between European concept and American
reality was a refinement of the former. In England, Scotland, and France,
efforts were made by colonial promoters both to assess the potential benefits

offered by North America more realistically and to search in European precedents and customs for ways in which to implant colonies. By 1630, the
organization of colonies had become more sophisticated. Yet the following
twenty years saw the colonies of Acadia, Maine, and New Scotland, as they
were conceived in Europe, still failing to harmonize with the northeastern
maritime region in which they were intended to take root. It was during these
formative years that the three emerged as 'marginal' colonies. Small populations were established in Acadia and Maine but were insufficient to give either
colony a firm identity in America. To be successful, any colony required not
only a conceptual existence, but also a political and an economic basis upon
which to support a community of settlers in America itself. Clearly there was no
one formula for success, but colonies were relatively securely established in
America in various ways at different times in the sixteenth and seventeenth
centuries. The mineral wealth of New Spain, the tobacco trade in Virginia, the
Hudson Valley fur trade in New Netherland, the agricultural development in
Massachusetts (facilitated by the large numbers of colonists in the initial
decade of settlement), the combination of the fur trade and royal subsidy in
Canada: all of these were realistic supports for colonies. None had any real
parallel in the colonies of the northeastern maritime region.

The colonies were marginal too in other respects. They remained dependent
upon Europe, and were exceptionally sensitive to European national and
international politics. The colony of New Scotland, for example, was jeopardized in 1632 by the withdrawal of royal support from the small settlement
which had been established. These colonies were also susceptible to the
interventions of the native societies upon whose tolerance successful settlement
depended throughout the region. Settlement in Acadia was literally marginal,
in that it was based largely on coastal marshland which was of little use to the
native population. In Maine, larger appropriations of uplands were made, but
they remained subject to Indian influence and potential Indian reclamation, as
the wars fought in 1675–78 and after 1688 demonstrated. Increasingly as the
seventeenth century went on, the northeastern maritime colonies were marginal
also with regard to other European settlements, and particularly in relation to
the large and populous colony of Massachusetts, which had extended its
economic influence northeastwards by 1650 and thereafter intermittently held
political sway.

In short, the marginality of the northeastern maritime colonies implied that
they were dependent upon external forces for their characteristics and their very
existence. The interplay of these forces continued in the second half of the
century, leading eventually to the outburst of violence which gained full force
by 1690 with dire consequences for all the peoples who inhabited the region.
Colonization in the seventeenth century was not a simple, clean, or inevitable

process; it was complex, bloody, and unpredictable. The northeastern maritime region was one part of America where the Europeans did not carry all before them, and this study focuses on the reasons why.

A Note on Form

Quotations have been rendered in the original language and exactly as written, with the following exceptions: quotations in languages other than English, French, or Scots have been translated into English; standard abbreviations have been expanded; the thorn has been changed to 'th' and the ampersand to 'and' or 'et' as appropriate; where they are interchangeable, the letters 'v' and 'j' have been changed to 'u' and 'i'; superscript letters have been lowered. Translations of French quotations of more than a single phrase have been provided in the notes.

During the seventeenth century, the Julian (Old Style) calendar was in force in England and the year was reckoned from 25 March to 24 March; France had adopted the Gregorian (New Style) calendar and reckoned the year from 1 January to 31 December; Scotland retained the Julian style of dating but had also adopted the practice of reckoning the year from 1 January to 31 December. In all references in this study, the appropriate respective calendar style has been used, with the following exceptions for the sake of clarity: the years have been modernized in all cases to begin on 1 January; calendar references to international negotiations and agreements involving France have been given in New Style.

Place-names have normally been given in accordance with seventeenth-century rather than modern usage, though a single consistent spelling has been adopted in each case. Acadian place-names have been given in their French form, with the exception of certain well-known geographical designations – such as Cape Breton Island, the Bay of Fundy, and the St John River – which describe features familiar to all nationalities in the region and have been cited in English throughout.

Acknowledgments

Over the years of its preparation, this study has benefited from assistance and co-operation from many quarters. My warmest thanks are due to Dr Thomas J. Condon, under whose supervision the work was originally completed as a dissertation; without his sure guidance and constant encouragement, it probably would never have been started and certainly would never have been finished. Valuable assistance was also provided by the other members of the history department of the University of New Brunswick, and in particular the manuscript was reviewed at various stages by Professors A.G. Bailey, Wallace Brown, Stephen E. Patterson, and Peter M. Toner. To all of them, and to others in Fredericton and elsewhere who gave their support and their friendship, I extend my thanks. I am grateful too to the jurors of the Sainte-Marie Prize series – John Moir, Bruce Trigger, and Marcel Trudel – all of whom offered advice on the revision of the manuscript. The faults that remain, of course, are mine.

The research for the study was carried out at a variety of libraries and repositories, and I am much indebted to the staffs of all of these. I thank especially the staff of the Centre d'études acadiennes of the Université de Moncton, the Maine Historical Society Library, the Massachusetts State Archives, and of course the Harriet Irving Library of the University of New Brunswick. My thanks are due also to the Maine Historical Society, the Société historique acadienne, and the journal *Acadiensis*, as the publishers of my earlier endeavours in colonial history upon which I have drawn in some portions of this study.

The publication process was greatly eased by the expertise of the University of Toronto Press, and in particular that of Mary McD. Maude as editor, and by the indexing skills of Mark and Lorna Davis, all of which I much appreciate. I thank the University of New Brunswick and the Canada Council for financial support while the study was in preparation; publication was assisted by grants from the Publications Fund of the University of Toronto Press and the Humanities and Social Sciences Research Fund of Mount Allison University, as well as by the sponsorship of the Ministry of Culture and Recreation of the Government of Ontario.

Part I
Introduction

CHAPTER 1

Beginnings
to 1630

The Northeastern Maritime Region

The colonies of Acadia, Maine, and New Scotland were not planted in an empty wilderness but were established in a region already occupied by Algonkian-speaking peoples. The territory of the Micmac included present-day Nova Scotia, Prince Edward Island, eastern and northern New Brunswick, and the Gaspé. The Malecite, or Etchemin, occupied the St John and Ste Croix river valleys and thence perhaps as far southwest as the Penobscot. The adjoining lands of the Abenaki reached further down the coastline to the southern part of present-day Maine, and bordered with those of the Penacook somewhat to the north of the Piscataqua River.[1] The first human habitation of these territories can be dated back at least 10,600 years (as shown by the excavation of a paleo-Indian camp at Debert, Nova Scotia), and the direct ancestors of the Algonkian cultural tradition can be identified some 3,000 years ago, or more than 2,500 years before the coming of the European.[2] The term 'Algonkian' refers to language. In terms of economy and material culture, the peoples of the region between the Gaspé and southern Maine – the northeastern maritime region – represented a variant of the more general eastern woodland grouping. They shared distinctive characteristics which arose from such influences as the location of most of their settlements by the sea and by rivers and the patterns of resource exploitation that resulted.[3]

The Indian economy of the region was based on hunting, gathering, and fishing; only in the southernmost areas, chiefly southwest of the Saco River, was agricultural cultivation practised to any extent.[4] Seasonal migration was characteristic of these activities as a means of exploiting all available food resources, and villages and camping sites were established and often occupied repeatedly by the same band. A yearly cycle might involve spending spring and early summer on the coast, late summer and autumn travelling inland, and winter in hunting camps deep in the woods, before returning to the coast along a river valley for fishing and planting. There was no one migratory cycle, however; patterns would vary through time and from band to band. Normally, the resources of the coast provided a great proportion of the food and raw materials needed, but inland hunting for such animals as moose, bear, and beaver was also essential. In winter survival depended almost exclusively upon the hunt. What was constant was the attunement of each band to its environment, an attunement that depended upon mythology and religious observance: any form of wasteful killing or destruction was regarded as a spiritual offence and consequently liable to bring bad luck upon the offender.[5] The importance of spiritual restraints was shown in the prominent position held within the band by the shaman – the interpreter of the spirit world. The importance of ecological adjustments was also reflected in social organization. The size of a band, for example, would fluctuate seasonally: a large band which assembled in summer for fishing and agriculture might divide into smaller and more practical groups for winter hunting. Even the size of hunting and gathering territories, and their allocation by the band leader – the sachem or sagamore – was subject to change from year to year according to the exigencies of subsistence.[6] Resilience was thus maintained.

By the time that European colonies were established in the region in the early seventeenth century, the traditional organization of the native peoples had already been changed by intermittent contacts with visiting Europeans over the previous hundred years. Especially disruptive, and at times devastating, was the impact of European diseases such as smallpox and typhus. Many Europeans recorded Indian complaints that the coming of the white man had been accompanied by disease and degeneration; as the Jesuit missionary Pierre Biard reported from Acadia, 'ils s'estonnent et se plaignent souvent de ce que dès que les François hantent et ont commerce avec eux, ils se meurent fort et se depeuplent.'[7] Thomas Dermer, an English captain who visited the coast of northern New England in 1619, saw Indian villages 'not long since populous, now utterly void' on account of a recent epidemic, and later in the century a Recollet missionary wrote of 'la décadance de la Nation Gaspesienne [Micmac], autrefois l'une des plus nombreuses et des plus florissantes du Canada.'[8] More subtle were cultural changes induced by European contact, to which Indian societies were particularly vulnerable because of being weakened by disease. The fur trade led to an unprecedentedly heavy emphasis upon hunting and thus changed migration cycles; most importantly, it had its effect upon traditional values, undermining customary restraints on wasteful hunting and stimulating competition among individual Indians for a form of economic status based on the exchange value of furs. Such actions would have been inconceivable previously. The new individualism also had a detrimental effect upon band authority, which was traditionally based upon persuasion rather than force and so depended ultimately upon the clear perception of a common interest.[9]

Thus the Indian peoples encountered by colonists were not the same as they had been a century before. Nevertheless, the resilience of Indian culture had not yet been stretched to the breaking point, and pride and self-reliance remained. It was the colonists who often found themselves regarded, with good-humoured patronage, as the inferiors of the natives. Biard reported with some annoyance in 1611 that 'ils s'estiment plus vaillans, que nous, meilleurs que nous, plus ingenieux que nous, et, chose difficile à croire, plus riches que nous.' Much later, in the Gaspé, the Recollet Chrestien Le Clercq noted that 'ils sont si infatuez de leurs manieres de s'habiller et de leurs maximes de vivres, qu'ils méprisent les nôtres.'[10] In their more reflective moments, and with suitable reservations for the benefits of the Christian religion, the two missionaries were inclined to agree that the Indians had a case, Le Clercq commenting that 'leur vie n'est pas traversée de mille chagrins comme la nôtre ...'[11] Even less spiritually minded Europeans were forced to recognize the value of Indian technology in the North American environment, particularly in regard to travel. 'You would think it strange to see,' wrote the English traveller John Josselyn, 'yea admire if you saw the bold Barbarians in their light Canows rush down the swift and headlong stream with desperate speed, but with excellent dexterity.'[12]

For all that, there were great differences between Indian and European, even in the way in which they perceived the physical environment of the northeastern maritime region. The most obvious and pervasive feature of that environment was the forest. Though subject to local variation, the forest of this region represented a transitional zone between the great boreal forest which spread across the top of the North American continent, and the deciduous forests further south. Thus, although particular stands could be predominantly composed of either coniferous or deciduous growth, the bulk of the region supported a mixture of both. The variety ranged from such characteristically northern species as balsam fir and white spruce to more southerly ones such as beech and ash, also including hemlock, pine, birch, and maple.[13] For the Indian, the forest was a fundamental basis of life. Wood was the essential raw material of technology, used in housing, for canoes, for cooking utensils, and in an infinite variety of other uses. The animals of the forest, of course, were also crucially important sources of food, clothing, and raw materials, such as bones and thongs. The forest, or rather patches of land cleared from it, was also the site of Indian agriculture in the more southerly parts of the region. Samuel de Champlain noted increasing signs of cultivation of corn, beans, squash, and tobacco as he coasted southwards from Île Sainte-Croix in the summer of 1605.[14]

The Indian's relationship with the forest, however, is not defined simply by cataloguing activities which depended upon certain forest materials. For the Indian, the forest and all of its inhabitants – human beings, animals, and objects – existed as part of a spiritual unity. For the European, the forest was seen as a repository of exploitable resources. Not all Europeans who came to the northeastern maritime region did so for commercial reasons, but the commercial impulse was especially strong in the early years of contact. Even those Europeans whose chief motivation was to colonize for the sake of national prestige or Christian evangelization, or simply to gain land, recognized the need to relate America and its commodities to the market economy of Europe. Indeed, the first European settlers saw the region as a quarrying ground. Champlain's accounts of Acadia are full of references to the possibility of mining precious metals, for example, at 'une mine d'argent tresbonne' on Digby Neck. The Englishman John Brereton reported in 1602 his opinion that the Indians of what was to become New England were possessed of 'Mines and many other rich commodities.'[15] The endurance of this hope was shown in the continuing practice of reserving, under colonial charters of the English, Scottish, or French crowns, a certain part of the proceeds of such mines to the crown.

In this region, however, as in eastern North America as a whole, the search for precious metals was doomed to failure. Thus there was no prospect of emulating the glittering achievements of the Spanish in South America, and the persistence of the European presence would depend upon an appreciation of what resources were in fact available. Marc Lescarbot, a Paris lawyer who had visited Acadia during 1606 and 1607, later remarked with some justification that 'l'avarice des hommes a fait qu'on ne trouve point un pais bon s'il n'y a des Mines d'or.'[16] One counterweight to the view of America purely as a source of precious metals was the potential of the fur trade, which had probably originated about 1500 in occasional visits to land of fishermen. In 1524, Giovanni da Verrazzano found Abenakis willing to trade in the Casco Bay region, and Jacques Cartier in 1534 conducted a ceremonious exchange with Micmacs on the coast of the Gaspé.[17] Expansion of the trade was temporarily hindered by the lack of a ready European demand, 'car au temps de Jacques Quartier,' as Lescarbot observed, 'on ne soucioit point de Castors. Les chapeaux qu'on en fait ne sont en usage que depuis ce temps-là.'[18] By the late sixteenth century, though, the demand was rapidly increasing, and the fur trade was to become a major attraction for all Europeans, for English and Scots as well as for the French. The English colonial propagandist, Captain John Smith, visiting New

England in 1614, claimed that 'of Bevers, Otters, Martins, Blacke Foxes, and Furres of price, may yearely be had 6 or 7000,' and Sir William Alexander, the grantee of New Scotland, was confident in 1624 that the furs of his colony would enrich Scotland and its merchants.[19]

The timber resources of the forest were also powerful inducements to European interest, especially because the mixed nature of the forest allowed for a variety of both hardwood and softwood products. As Smith remarked, there was 'plenty of all sorts.'[20] In the expanding European economy of the sixteenth century, the need for wood and wood products was putting great strain on the available supplies. In England particularly, this situation had reached crisis proportions by the latter part of the century. Efforts at conservation were ineffective; the substitution of coal as a fuel tended to aggravate the shortage because of the wood required in its production; and the importation of timber and naval stores from the Baltic, while inevitable, was of doubtful reliability for political reasons. Scotland and France, with their greater area in relation to population, were better off. The Scottish Highlands supported both hardwood and coniferous timber, and the royal and private forests of France were still sufficiently well stocked in the later seventeenth century to be successfully managed under a royal ordinance. Nevertheless, Scotland and France continued to supplement their own resources by conducting an extensive timber trade with the Baltic nations. In practice, North American timber was never able to compete as successfully with the Baltic as was hoped by such optimists as Smith and Lescarbot, but in time the production of planks, masts, hardwood products, and naval stores was to become an important part of the economy of each of the northeastern maritime colonies.[21]

Agricultural potential was a different matter from furs and timber, since agricultural products of the northeastern maritime region could not be expected realistically to fulfil European demand in the same way that sugar, indigo, and tobacco did further south. None the less, agriculture was seen as essential to the survival of any settlement, even where the exploitation of marketable resources was an important aim. The sheep which found immortality by drowning in Port Mouton harbour, during the colonizing voyage of de Monts to Acadia in 1604, is a testament to the perceived need for livestock. Further, one of the first activities of that expedition, after the making of a settlement, was the planting of 'quelques jardinages ... où on sema plusieurs sortes de graines, qui y vindrent fort bien ... '[22] In the same way, the manager of a later English fishing enterprise on the Maine coast recorded: 'I do not sett nor sow any seed but doth prosper very well, and hodges [hogs] doth prosper well, and I thinke so will Cattell also, yf they weare heare.'[23] The soil of the northeastern maritime region was varied, but the potential of certain areas of Maine had already been shown by Indian agricultural pursuits, and there were also fertile areas in

Acadia. Taken together with the climate – moderated throughout the region by the influence of the ocean although still retaining the continental features of hot summers and cold winters as compared with Europe – the land certainly permitted agricultural pursuits as they were known to Europeans from the British Isles or France although it was not ideal for them.[24]

Throughout the northeastern maritime region, however, cleared land was not the only recourse of the farmer; tidal marshland was often the key to successful agriculture. Formed by the action of tides, through the inundation of vegetable material exposed to the sea by progressive sinking of the land, and the deposit of silt, these marshes were and are found along most of the Atlantic coast of North America. In the region itself were two types: the New England type, extending northeastward to the Bay of Fundy, and the Fundy type, extending around the bay. The two types are distinguished by the presence of more peaty deposits of vegetable material in the New England type and the greater quantity of silt material around the Bay of Fundy.[25] What all the salt marshes had in common was their agricultural potential. Covered by coarse grass, the marshlands were suitable for the cultivation of grasses and grains, whether for hay, pasture, or grain crops.[26] Thus the region could support a European population on the margins of sea and rivers, and the salt marshes did indeed become the basis of Acadian agriculture. The evidence of use of salt marshland in Maine is less extensive, perhaps because of greater concentration upon freshwater meadows along river banks, but the Maine salt marshes were of sufficient importance by the mid-seventeenth century that their control became a factor in New England politics.

The salt marshes are one example of a resource depending upon the sea; however, there is no doubt that the first Europeans to visit the region thought of the sea far more as a source of fish. The Atlantic fishery was, of course, long established before the beginning of the seventeenth century. Whether or not the English fishery off Newfoundland preceded the first voyage of Columbus, it was well under way by the turn of the sixteenth century.[27] By that time the fishery was an international affair, involving Spanish and Portuguese vessels as well as English and French; as well as the cod fishery on the banks, a large-scale whaling operation was carried on by Basques further north and off the coast of Labrador for much of the sixteenth century.[28] In the cod fishery, two basic techniques were used: the 'green' fishery, involving the salting of wet cod in barrels on board ship, and the 'dry' fishery, which depended upon shore installations for drying the catch. Both had their advantages. The green fishery required few men and little equipment, and the relatively short distances from Europe to the banks, as opposed to the shores of America, allowed two voyages each year. The dry fishery demanded less salt, allowed carrying a greater number of fish per ship, and provided a non-perishable product which could be exported over longer distances. Both techniques were practised by French and English, but the easier availability of salt in France, and the demands of the large French domestic market, led them by the end of the sixteenth century to concentrate on the green fishery, as opposed to the primary importance for the English of the dry fishery at Newfoundland.[29]

Certainly fish could be found in abundance on the great fishing banks and submerged continental shelf of the North Atlantic, which provided an ideal feeding and spawning ground for cod. Thus, while the Grand Banks off Newfoundland were conveniently close to Europe and provided the largest fish, a profitable fishery could also be pursued closer to the continental shores.[30] This was especially true when European markets expanded in the latter part of the sixteenth century with the decline of Spain as a maritime power and the opening of the Mediterranean market to the fishing fleets of both France and England; the price rise in Spain, which accompanied the import of bullion from New Spain, made it an even more attractive export market. By the end of the sixteenth century, the Newfoundland fishery had become an important aspect of both the French and the English economies.

The use of the American mainland for the pursuit of the cod seems to have occurred earlier on the coast of what was to become Acadia or New Scotland than on that of Maine. Lescarbot reported that on a voyage from Port Royal to France in 1607 he met a certain Captain Savalet of Saint-Jean-de-Luz, who was engaged in the dry fishery near Canso, on the coast of present-day Nova Scotia, and who was making his forty-second annual visit to the same harbour. That the fishery could be vastly expanded was emphasized by Lescarbot in his affirmation that 'en passant le temps és côtes de ladite Nouvelle France j'en prendray en un jour pour vivre six semaines és endroits où est l'abondance des Moruës (car ce poisson y est le plus frequent) et qui aura l'industrie de prendre les Macreaux en mer, il en aura tant qu'il n'en sçaura que faire.'[31] English explorers of what was to become northern New England reacted in similar fashion to the plentiful fish stocks they found. In 1603 the Bristol captain Martin Pring recorded that he had found at Penobscot Bay 'an excellent fishing for Cod, which are better then those of New-Found-Land, and withall we saw good and Rockie ground fit to drie them upon.'[32] Similarly, James Rosier reported, following the voyage of Captain George Waymouth to the Maine coast in 1605, 'how great a profit the fishing would be, they being so plentifull, so great and so good.' Rosier noted also that nowhere had he found signs that 'ever any Christian had beene before; of which either by cutting wood, digging for water, or setting up Crosses ... we should have perceived some mention left.'[33] Shortly after Waymouth's voyage, however, the New England fishery was certainly well under way.[34]

The fishery on the coasts of the northeastern maritime region was a greater attraction to Europeans because of the abundance of good harbours which could serve as fishing bases. The same physiographic characteristic of the submerged coastline which had produced the fishing grounds had also produced innumerable rocky coves and indentations. As Sir Ferdinando Gorges, later proprietor of the Province of Maine, remarked in 1620, 'the coast doth abound with most convenient havens, and harbours, full of singular islands'; more sombrely, Champlain shrewdly observed that Acadia would be 'mal aisée à conserver, à cause du nombre infiny de ses ports, qui ne pouvoient garder que par de grandes forces ... '[35]

Yet such analyses of particular aspects of the configuration of the region also re-emphasize the difference in perspective between European and Indian. Long before the beginning of the European fisheries, fishing had been an important Indian activity. As with other natural resources, the Indian hunted fish as part of an integrated harvest of food. Nor was any one fish predominant among the catch; all available fish and sea mammals could be utilized. The seal and the walrus were hunted on land as sources of food and of raw materials for implements. River fish such as salmon, trout, and lamprey were caught by means of nets or spears; lobsters, clams, and other shellfish were taken on the beach at low tide; inshore and deeper water fish such as bass, bluefish, sturgeon, and cod were harpooned from canoes; and whales were hunted at least as far south as the Penobscot River.[36] Since the diet of the Indian was so varied, it is not surprising that a Micmac chief observed to the missionary Le Clercq and certain French fishermen that 'nous voïons même que tous vos gens ne vivent ordinairement, que de la Morüe que vous pêchez chez nous; ce n'est continuellement que Morüe, Morüe au matin, Morüe à midi, Morüe au soir, et toûjours Morüe, jusques là même, que si vous souhaitez quelques bons morceaux, c'est à nos dépens ... '[37]

This exasperated outburst illustrates more than the monotony of the cod fishery. Those Europeans who came to the northeastern maritime region only to exploit resources hardly perceived the natural environment at all, except insofar as it related to the specific activity in hand. Yet even the Europeans who came to stay, or who took time to look around them, could hardly avoid seeing nature in its American forms as an alien force: hence the concept of the 'wilderness.' The settlers of Massachusetts, for religious reasons, were especially prolific in articulating 'the hard labours this people found in Planting this Wildernesse,' but their experience was common also to the more northerly region.[38] Even after almost a century of colonization, a French visitor to Port Royal disconsolately described Acadia as a 'Pays Sauvage ... Rien ne s'offre à mes yeux que des Bois, des Rivieres, Des Masures et des Chanvieres ... ' Other Europeans saw the wilderness as a challenge – such was the view taken, for example, by the Scottish colonial promotor Sir Robert Gordon towards the 'hudge and so waste a tract' of Cape Breton Island.[39] Here, as in other parts of North America, a well-adapted native culture (albeit one suffering the effects of disease and acculturation) was confronted by Europeans who regarded both the culture and the environment as alien, and whose instincts were to exploit available resources and to change the environment to make it conform to European expectations. Except in European perceptions, the wilderness did not exist, but European efforts to replace the wilderness with the colonies of Acadia, Maine, and New Scotland would dominate the lives of all those who lived in the northeastern maritime region throughout the seventeenth century.

Initial European Attempts

The European colonization of the northeastern maritime region, while it did not begin until the seventeenth century, had its conceptual roots in earlier expansions of Europe. Spain's conquest of much of Central and South America was particularly attractive as an example and a model, involving as it had the subjugation of a native population of some twenty million. This remarkable and, to European eyes, admirable achievement had been followed by the setting up of a successful pattern of colonization, based on the use of Indian labour to produce vast quantities of precious metals. The Indians, remnants of the great conquered empires, were demoralized both by the conquest itself and by the ravages of European disease; they were effectively exploited by a series of regimes ranging from slavery to forced labour, often ruled by their own chiefs as subordinates of the Spaniards. With labour thus provided, the Spanish culture of the colonists was perpetuated in numerous towns which replicated the urban and rural pursuits of Spain, while political power was firmly retained by the Spanish crown and government financed by the profits of the bullion trade. Not all, of course, was success and stability in New Spain. Resistance by unsubjugated peoples, and conflicts between church and secular colonists existed from the beginning. Furthermore, the seventeenth century would bring economic and political upheavals which would reveal that the initial coherence of New Spain, like Spanish ascendancy in Europe, had been temporary. Nevertheless, other Europeans watching the Spanish colonizing efforts of the sixteenth century perceived the building of an awesomely successful empire, a fit object for their own envy and emulation.

Another possible model was that of the Portuguese. The treaty of Tordesillas, signed by Spain and Portugal in 1494, had divided the world according to a line drawn at 46° 37' west; everything west of the line, including supposed trading routes to Asia, was to be a Spanish area of exploration, while Portugal was to control eastern routes and, though not known in 1494, the American territory of Brazil. Although the settlement of Brazil was under way by the end of the sixteenth century, it was the eastern trade to Africa and Asia which was given more initial attention. For Portugal, conquest had little part in the building of empire; the object was rather to establish an extensive network of trading posts which could harness the trade in spices, both African and Asian (and later in slaves from Africa), and in gold and other precious metals where possible. The typical Portuguese settlement was the isolated fortress and trading house; any attempt to conquer any large area of Asia or Africa was precluded by the small population resources of the Portuguese. Thus, while Portugal did fight wars in the east – the relationship between Portuguese and Moslem traders in the Indian Ocean was one of outright enmity from the start – they were limited wars, designed to fulfil particular trading objectives. By the mid-sixteenth century, Portuguese forts had been established on the coasts of India and Ceylon, in Burma, the East Indies, China, and even Japan.

The Spanish and Portuguese empires thus provided alternative patterns to be observed by other European nations. What both shared was the effort to make alien lands and peoples serve European needs. Whether by the Spanish method of conquest and reconceptualization – the metamorphosis of large areas in such a way as to make the natives into aliens on their own land – or by the Portuguese method of concentrating on commercial exploitation, both empires enjoyed great success. When John Smith, in the same paragraph of his description of New England in 1614, recalled both the 'admirable adventures and endeavours' of 'the industrious Portugales' in Africa and the 'most memorable attempts' of the Spanish 'brave spirits' in the West Indies and South America, he recognized both the diversity and the unity of early European empires.[40] For the nations of northern Europe, however, as Smith well knew, the sixteenth century had not seen expansion comparable with that of the Iberian empires. The crowns of England and France had shown an interest in the New World in their early patronage of the voyages of John Cabot and Giovanni da Verrazzano respectively, and both countries had sent out several colonizing attempts, without lasting success. Inexperience in dealing with the American native peoples and environment, the lack of precious metals, and insufficient capitalization combined to frustrate these attempts before any had properly begun.[41] Furthermore, the governments of the two countries were too preoccupied with internal strife and European affairs to give any sustained support to colonization, while private enterprise had other ways of exploiting America which had little or nothing to do with the founding of colonies: illegal trade with New Spain, privateering off the Spanish Main, and, of course, the fishery. Thus, efforts at colonization had little incentive.

Nevertheless, the Newfoundland fishery did have potential, if not yet actual, connections with colonization. The fishery had quickly become an integral part of the economies of both England and France, and assumed special importance for the port towns in which the fishing fleets were based. Major centres of the French fishery were located at Rouen and other Norman ports; at a number of Breton ports, notably Saint-Malo; and on the Bay of Biscay, at Nantes, La Rochelle, Bordeaux, Bayonne, and others. The English fishery was centred in the West Country, at such ports as Barnstaple, Falmouth, Plymouth, Dartmouth, and Exmouth, with much of the financial support and organization coming from London. The fishery, like the fur-trading voyages to the St Lawrence which started from Saint-Malo as early as 1581, had no immediate connection with colonization as such, since temporary bases at most were set up on shore, but it did bring about an awareness of North America and of the possibilities of extended landings there. The fishery and the fur trade also provided pools of expertise and manpower for future voyages, as well as a mercantile network which would provide a basis for the financing of colonization in later years. It was no accident that many of the seventeenth-century colonial voyages went from such ports as Plymouth, Rouen, and La Rochelle, nor that merchants of these towns, as well as others from London and Paris, were deeply committed to such schemes.[42]

A further precursor of northern European colonization of America involved the action of royal governments in England and Scotland. Both crowns laid claim to large areas of Celtic territory which were only nominally under the royal sway: the English crown in Ireland, the Scots crown in the Highlands and Islands. Centuries of efforts to solve these problems by a variety of expedients had failed to bear fruit, and both crowns attempted during the sixteenth century to plant colonies of reliable subjects in the midst of the Celtic lands. First mooted in the reign of Mary, efforts to settle English colonists in Ireland were put more seriously in hand under Elizabeth, when the offer of estates to be won, held, and populated with tenants was made to attract the younger sons of noble and gentry families. James VI of Scotland was concurrently encouraging the colonization of the western isles, such as 'the hitherto most barbarous Isle of Lewis,' through colonists and capital from lowland burghs.[43] Despite the failure of major schemes in Lewis and in Munster, in the face of strong local resistance, the two crowns persisted. Co-ordinated efforts were facilitated by the union of the crowns in 1603 and lasting results (for better or worse) were achieved in Ulster, in Orkney and Shetland, and in Kintyre.[44]

The use of land as an incentive to colonization of the Celtic areas, especially through the promise of baronial estates to successful colonizers, foreshadowed later styles of American colonization, as indeed did the efforts of the Scots crown to mobilize the capital of urban merchants. Also significant is the extent to which the same individuals were involved in Celtic as in American colonization. In the reign of Elizabeth, Sir Humphrey Gilbert and Sir Walter Raleigh were concurrently prominent in both; among the other West Country gentry so involved was Sir Arthur Champernowne, whose son was to become one of the first land grantees of Kittery, in the Province of Maine, and whose grandson would become a long-term resident of Maine in the seventeenth century.[45] In the plantation of Ulster under James VI and I, Andrew Stewart, Lord Ochiltree, was among the first applicants for land and had planted 80 people by 1619 on his 3,000-acre estate there. In 1615, deciding to devote himself to his Irish lands, Stewart made over his title to his uncle, James Stewart of Killeith, who thus became the fourth Lord Ochiltree and in 1629 was to start a short-lived Scottish colony on Cape Breton Island.[46] Another future colonizer of New Scotland was Sir George Home, commander at Port Royal in 1630 and 1631, who obtained 1,000 acres in Ulster which he planted with tenants, albeit as an absentee proprietor.[47]

The sixteenth century had thus revealed to the nations of northern Europe two rather different forms of contact with alien lands: exploitation of natural resources for private gain, and colonization for reasons of state. The two were by no means mutually exclusive, and indeed the difference is better expressed by a continuum rather than by an absolute distinction. The Spanish and Portuguese empires, for example, had elements of both, and no colony could survive unless it eventually became both a body politic and an economic unit. By the end of the century political stability was returning to England, France, and Scotland, and the respective governments were able to turn their attention to an America which was gradually coming to be recognized as a potentially significant factor in European international competition.[48] The time when royal governments would take actual control of colonies was still far in the future, but the early years of the new century did witness efforts by the crowns of France and England to encourage and harness the commercial impulse. The result was the founding of two colonies in the northeastern maritime region: Acadia and north Virginia.[49]

The northeastern maritime region was not yet known, as it would be later in the century, as an area of marginal, unstable colonies. Although neither the French colony of Acadia nor the English colony of north Virginia was able in early years to live up to European expectations, both began as conscious efforts to emulate the imperial successes of southern Europe. The royal patent granted in 1603 to Pierre Du Gua, Sieur de Monts, prescribed that one hundred French colonists should be transported annually to Acadia (the figure was later reduced to sixty at the request of de Monts), and the royal aims were further elaborated in a commission to de Monts as lieutenant general in Acadia, generously defined as extending from the 40th to the 46th degree of latitude. Within that area de Monts was to rule, with powers of government, war and peace, regulation of commerce, and allocation of lands, in all of which he was to be responsible to the crown. The stated object was 'la demeure, possession, et habitation' of the territory in question, which would not only bring glory and spiritual rewards through the conversion of native people to Christianity, but would also stimulate the commerce of the mother country.[50] These were also the stated aims of the north Virginia colony in the Virginia charter of 1606. The northern part of Virginia, defined as lying between the latitudes of 38° and 45° and thus including what was later to be known as New England, was granted to a group of promoters centred in Plymouth, who were accorded powers of war and peace, regulation of commerce, and allocation of lands. In this case, government was to be in the hands of a council, to be formed according to subsequent royal instructions, and a single superior council was to be ultimately responsible both for north Virginia and for the sister colony of south Virginia.[51]

Both French and English colonies thus involved the assertion of the respective royal authorities over vast areas of America, and both included provision for the gathering of the colonies under royal authority. Here as in so many other European colonizing schemes, however, concept was widely at variance with practice. The English government, faced with debts which had been one part of the legacy of Elizabeth, was unable to fund any active involvement in ruling colonies, and even the projected royal council for Virginia never in fact functioned. In France, funds were also at a premium, and the opposition of the Duc de Sully, Henri IV's chief minister, to colonizing projects in the northern part of North America ensured that the crown's involvement would not go beyond permissiveness.[52]

In this situation, the onus for all aspects of colonization tended to fall upon the colonial promoters themselves, and upon their commercial backers. The commercial aspects of the colonies, however, presented their own problems. The promoters of both colonies were thinking in terms of permanent, extensive colonies. Lescarbot remarked in describing the first voyage of de Monts that 'il y a beaucoup d'autres secrets et belles choses dans les terres, dont la conoissance n'est encore venuë jusques à nous, et se découvriront à mesure que la province s'habitera.' Sir Ferdinando Gorges, one of the promoters of the north Virginia colony, revealed a similar concern for extensive and progressive colonization when he wrote in late 1607 to the secretary of state, the Earl of Salisbury, of the 'greate newes [from the first north Virginia settlement at Sagadahoc] of a fertill Contry, gallant Rivers, stately Harbors, and a people tractable ...'[53] What was not clearly appreciated was the vast amount of capital which would be necessary to realize any such dreams, especially since the promoters' concepts of America and its nature were inaccurate. Neither mines of precious metals, nor a lucrative trading route to the Far East were to be found, despite the bland assurance given by George Popham, president of the Sagadahoc settlement, in a letter of 1607 to James I, that 'the Southern ocean, reaching to the regions of China ... unquestionably cannot be far from these regions.'[54]

Thus, the colonists had extensive plans for a continent which they knew only slightly, and if their conceptions were to have any chance of realization, a commercial organization would be required with the means to generate large sums of capital without requiring quick profits. Such capitalization was not forthcoming. Neither the Acadian colony nor that of north Virginia operated even on the lines of a joint-stock company. Instead, they were based upon private subscriptions obtained by private invitation, an arrangement which resembled the joint-stock principle in that the object was to raise and combine investments from a variety of sources, but the result was inevitably less formal and smaller in scale. This semi-joint-stock principle was already familiar by the late sixteenth century as a means of sending commercial voyages to the fishery or the fur trade. As an instrument of colonization, however, it was hardly adequate. The capital sums thus raised were small; furthermore, the investors were conditioned by their experience with commercial voyages to expect a significant profit in a single season.

For the moment, however, these inadequacies were not appreciated. Like his predecessor Pierre Chauvin, Sieur de Tonnetuit, who had in the winter of 1600–1 planted a small and unsuccessful colony at Tadoussac on the St Lawrence, de Monts was granted a ten-year monopoly of the fur trade; indeed, de Monts' monopoly, including both the Atlantic coast and the St Lawrence, was even more extensive than the previous one. Despite initial reluctance on the part of the merchants to venture capital, the monopoly was finally closed in early 1604 with subscriptions amounting to 90,000 *livres*; the subscribers, as de Monts formally acknowledged on 10 February, were 'marchands tant de cette ville de Rouen [the headquarters of the venture], Saint-Malo, la Rochelle et Saint-Jean-de-Lux ...'[55] As a structure for the sending of commercial voyages, this arrangement was promising enough. For colonization on the scale envisaged, however, the capital sum was inadequate; the diversity of the subscribers ensured division if expected profits did not materialize, and the exclusiveness of the monopoly ensured continuing opposition from those excluded.

In the case of north Virginia colony, capitalization was again the concern of an individual promoter who set out, like de Monts with royal encouragement but without royal investment, to raise subscriptions in the various towns which already had commercial connections with America. Here, the individual was Sir John Popham, lord chief justice of England, and the towns were the West Country sea ports. Despite disagreements among the towns and the failure of one of two reconnaissance voyages in 1606, Popham raised funds with the aid of Gorges for a further voyage in 1607. This expedition was to found the

Sagadahoc colony. While exact details of the financing of the venture have not survived, the adventurers were described as 'divers gentlemen and Marchaunts of the Westerne parts,' and the organization was on a private, semi-joint-stock basis.[56] Both the French and the English projects, therefore, started from large-scale concepts and small-scale financing, and the results in each case were similar. First, the colonies so founded never developed beyond very small, communal establishments. Secondly, the colonies continued to be totally subservient to the exigencies of commercial backing in the respective mother countries in Europe. The communal colony was the quintessential unit of North American colonization at this time, not only in the northeastern region, but also at Quebec and Jamestown. At first intended simply as a base for the more extensive exploration and settlement of a colony such a habitation tended to remain the only settled portion.

Confronted with an alien environment, one of the first thoughts of the European was naturally defence, and one important characteristic of the communal colony was its defensive function. Champlain recorded, regarding the decision by de Monts to settle the first Acadian colony on Île Sainte-Croix, that 'n'ayant trouvé lieu plus propre que ceste Isle, nous commençames à faire une barricade sur un petit islet un peu separé de l'Isle, qui servoit de platte-forme pour mettre nostre canon.' When the Acadian settlement was moved to Port Royal in the following year, this concern was repeated.[57] The Sagadahoc colonists, for their part, chose their site on 19 August 1607; on the 20th, as one of the colonists recorded, 'all our Companyes Landed and thear began to fortefye ...' Indeed, the colonists habitually referred to their settlement as 'the fort.'[58] As well as being a fortress, the communal colony was the centre for all activities of the colonists. Emphasis was laid upon the gathering of all buildings, whether dwelling houses, storehouses, workshops, or chapel, into a small space. The building of such a settlement could clearly take place only through planning and disciplined work, which indicates a further important characteristic of the communal colony: it was an organization rather than a body politic, in which the gentlemanly promoters stood in relation to the labour force – 'les ouvriers,' as Lescarbot described them – as employers to employees.[59]

Having established a settlement, it was then necessary to set about forming trading relationships with the Indians. The communal colonies depended upon the natives for trade goods, especially furs, with which the colonies could satisfy mercantile investors in the absence of mines of precious metals. As William Strachey ruefully pointed out in regard to Sagadahoc, such mines had been 'the mayne intended benefit expected to uphold the charge of this plantacion.'[60] In trade, the Sagadahoc colonists had mixed success, and on at least one occasion an attempt at trading led to armed conflict with the Indians. Although Strachey reported that during the winter of 1607–8 'many kinds of

furrs [were] obteyned from the Indians by way of trade,'[61] Sir Ferdinando
Gorges was writing to Lord Salisbury in February 1608 that the Abenaki 'shew
themselves exceeding subtill and conninge, concealing from us the places,
wheare they have the comodityes wee seeke for.' Gorges went on to complain
that 'these often returnes without any comodity hath much discouraged our
adventurers.'[62] This discouragement of high commercial hopes, together with
the death of George Popham, the president of the colony, the determination of
Raleigh Gilbert, another of the leaders, to return home to take up an inheritance, and the fears of a repetition of the severe winter of 1607–8, led to the
abandonment of the Sagadahoc colony. The colony had failed both to move out
of its communal bounds and to fulfil its commercial obligations to its English
backers.

The colony of de Monts had rather greater success in its trading activities, at
least in its first two years.[63] It was, however, plagued by infractions of its
monopoly by other Frenchmen and by foreigners, such as the Dutch. 'Voila les
effets de l'envie,' lamented Lescarbot, 'qui ne s'est pas glissée seulement és
coeurs des Hollandois pour ruiner une si sainte entreprise, mais aussi des nôtres
propres, tant s'est montree grande et insatiable l'avarice des Marchans qui
n'avoient part à l'association du sieur de Monts.'[64] Indeed, there may well have
been fraudulent dealing even by participants in the monopoly. A rise in the
price of beaver skins in France of perhaps 150 per cent between 1604 and 1607
further exacerbated pressures for the revocation of the monopoly, and a complaint by the hatters' corporation of Paris to the receptive ear of the Duc de Sully
eventually led to revocation. News of this was brought to Port Royal on 24 May
1607, and of the consequent order by de Monts, who had been in France since
the previous year, for the abandonment of the colony. The dissolution of the
monopoly, which in theory had had seven years to run, had been the last straw.
'Mais d'ailleurs,' reflected Lescarbot, 'le sieur de Monts et ses associés étans
en perte, et n'ayans point d'avancement du Roy, c'étoit chose qu'ilz ne
pouvoient faire sans beaucoup de difficulté, que d'entretenir une habitation
pardela.'[65]

Thus ended the first two seventeenth-century colonizing attempts in the
northeastern maritime region. For the English, the setback was, as Sir Ferdinando Gorges put it, 'a wonderful discouragement to all the first undertakers, in
so much as there was no more speech of settling any other plantation in those
parts for a long time after.'[66] The Popham family, despite the death of the lord
chief justice, continued to interest itself in voyages to exploit the fishery and the
fur trade, as did Gorges, but colonization as such was abandoned until the
foundation of the Council for New England in 1620.[67] The French continued to
inhabit Acadia, though the capitalization of the de Monts colony was never
equalled by any of the colonizing projects until the formation of the Compagnie

des Cent-Associés in 1627.[68] When Port Royal was re-established in 1610, it was at the hands of de Monts' former lieutenant, Jean de Biencourt de Poutrincourt, who had early received a grant of Port Royal in seigneury and had formally taken over de Monts' remaining rights there in 1608. Poutrincourt quickly ran into the same financial difficulties as had de Monts. He attempted to secure private patronage, on the grounds of the colony's religious function, by enlisting the support of a leading patron of the Jesuit order, Madame de Guercheville, but succeeded only in provoking quarrels which led to the foundation of a rival colonial establishment. The colony of Saint-Sauveur, established by the Jesuit father Pierre Biard and three other Jesuits in 1613 on a site opposite Mount Desert Island, near the Pentagouet River, lasted only a few weeks before it was destroyed by a devastating English attack from Virginia under Samuel Argall.[69] Later in the summer of 1613, Argall also attacked Port Royal but failed to destroy it since the few colonists were not in the habitation at the time. The colony also survived the death of Poutrincourt in 1615 – his son Charles de Biencourt de Saint-Just remained in charge – and was able to continue by engaging in the dry fishery, in close co-operation with La Rochelle merchants Samuel Georges and Jean Macain, who had been associated with de Monts from the beginning of his colonizing attempts and before that with the Newfoundland fishery. The increased importance of the fishery to Biencourt's enterprise was reflected in his removal to the southern part of the Acadian peninsula during the winter of 1617–18: rather than Port Royal, the harbours of Cap Nègre, Cap de Sable, Port Lomeron, and later La Hève would be the chief centres of the French presence in Acadia for the next seventeen years.[70]

The surviving Acadian colony was certainly not totally disorganized; but it continued only on the smallest of scales, and there was little prospect of a breakthrough to the more extensive form of colonization which had originally been envisaged. Biencourt himself gave vent to his frustration in a written appeal to the town authorities of Paris in 1618 for support in efforts to break the bonds of the communal colony. All that was required, he argued, was a small initial subsidy for transporting colonists and for feeding the poorest of them; 'si ce païs a esté méprisé jusques icy, ça esté par ignorance et par la malice des marchans.'[71] In reality, the problems ran deeper than Biencourt implied. Between colonizers and merchants there was a basic difference of interest. If the colonies had contained mines of precious metals requiring inland establishments for their exploitation, if the colonies could have become staging posts for the Far Eastern trade through a northwest passage to the Pacific, they would have been unquestionably valuable. As it was, the commercial value of large-scale colonization was dubious. The fur trade and the fishery could be carried on by single voyages, or at most by using a small communal habitation as a base. The communal colony, for the merchant, was the most that could be justified. But for those who believed in colonization for reasons other than commercial – for personal or national prestige, or for evangelization – the communal colony was a creation of necessity rather than choice, a product of the gap between vast conceptions and inadequate techniques and resources. Both French and English had hoped to emulate Spain, but all they had accomplished was a series of tenuous and unanticipated imitations of the Portuguese factory: small pockets of Europeans perched on the edge of what Biard described as 'un horrible desert.'[72]

New Approaches

Not surprisingly, the failures of these early years prompted much reflection among those involved in colonial attempts, whether as theorists or practitioners. Marc Lescarbot lamented the avaricious mentality that could see value in colonies only if they yielded precious metals and advocated the adaptation of colonization to the known resources of the land. For him, 'celui qui a du blé en son grenier, du vin en sa cave, du bestail en ses prairies, et au bout des Morües et des Castors, est plus asseuré d'avoir de l'or et de l'argent que celui qui a des Mines d'en trouver à vivre.'[73] John Smith remarked in 1624, in regard to the territory which he had named 'New England,' that 'the Sea is better than the richest Mine knowne.'[74] Smith and Lescarbot looked to American colonies as sources of national power and prestige and as a means of expanding the Christian religion, and along with others they put forth their vision to a growing audience of literate Europeans who read colonial propaganda works.[75] Yet the question still remained as to how such a vision could be put into practice. One of the few who grappled directly with this question was Pierre Biard.

Biard's perception of American colonization was influenced by his adverse experiences at Port Royal and Saint-Sauveur but was based on a firm conviction that colonization was necessary to facilitate the conversion of Indians to Christianity. Turning a sceptical eye on the 'imaginatives attentes' of his pesonal enemy Biencourt, Biard poured scorn on those who would seek quick profits in colonization or who thought that large, prestigious colonies could easily be established.[76] Such misconceptions had ensured, he believed, 'que nous autres François y allons volontiers à yeux clos, et teste baissée,' and in future a more careful approach would be needed.[77] The basis of such an approach would be careful choice of a source of private and non-commercial financing in order to offset dependence upon mercantile investors: 'il y a plusieurs maisons particulieres dans Paris, et autre part, qui ont les moyens esgaux à l'entreprinse.' Along with this Biard advocated a painstaking selection of a colonial site, ensuring that the proposed location had a wide variety of natural resources in as small as possible an area: 'lotir une place où toutes les qualitez desirables uniment se r'assemblent ... [c'est] le project et idee d'un sagement enquerant.'[78] Thus, to the basic problem of the gap between great aspirations on the one hand, and small resources and achievements on the other, Biard returned a logical answer: scale down the aspirations and make a virtue of small, solid achievements. Biard still believed that the whole of New France would eventually be settled, but for him this was a goal to be approached cautiously and in gradual stages.[79]

Yet Biard's response to the seeming impasse which had been reached by European colonists of the northeastern maritime region (and other parts of North America) was not the only logical one. As the 1620s began, an approach was developed which was equally logical but diametrically opposite: to retain the concept of large-scale, extensive colonization, frankly to recognize that there existed neither mines of precious metals nor a passage to the Far East, and to raise the necessary resources through bigger and better organization. What this approach inevitably implied was the active participation of the state. In England, Sir Ferdinando Gorges persuaded the crown in 1620 to interest itself in the colonization of New England and wrote an elaborate justification of American colonies in the *Brief relation of the discovery and plantation of New England*, which was published in 1622 by the newly created Council for New England. In dedicating the work to Prince Charles (the future Charles I), Gorges naturally enough stated the primary aim of New England as being 'to serve his majesty with honour and profit,' and once again the honour was to lie largely in the aim 'to advance the cross of Christ in heathen parts.' Mention was also made, however, of competition with France, a strategic argument which was further developed in the suggestion that timber and naval stores could be obtained from New England. Gorges thus emphasized the public usefulness of the projected colony – 'what benefit our country is like to receive by it.'[80]

Gorges sought also to link colonization to one of the English crown's political priorities, the consolidation of the two kingdoms of England and Scotland; hence his encouragement of the foundation of a colony of New Scotland to the north of New England.[81] Sir William Alexander, a member of the Scots Privy Council and future proprietor of New Scotland, acknowledged Gorges's role, but stressed in his own propaganda work, *An encouragement to colonies*, that New Scotland was not merely an English scheme under a Scottish figurehead. 'I shew them,' he wrote, 'that my Countrimen would never adventure in such an Enterprize, unlesse it were as there was a New France, a New Spaine and a New England, that they might likewise have a New Scotland.' Like Gorges, Alexander emphasized the prestige which would accrue from such a venture, and the strategic benefits. Furthermore, the colony would be a productive alternative for that part of Scotland's population which had been

accustomed to serve in foreign armies, 'Scotland by reason of her populous-
nesse being constrained to disburden her selfe.' Scotland was generally agreed
at this time to have an abundance of labour, and, as Alexander observed, the
demands of Irish colonization had now slackened.[82] Moreover, although this
was probably a later development, Alexander was in 1629 negotiating with
Highland clan chieftains with a view to encouraging emigration to New
Scotland. This met with the enthusiastic approval of the crown as a means of
'debordening ... our kingdome of that race of people which in former times
hade bred soe many trubles ther ... ,' but the scheme was never carried into
practice.[83]

   Gorges and Alexander, in their efforts to base colonization squarely upon
reasons of state, soon found a French counterpart in the person of Isaac de
Razilly. Razilly, an experienced naval commander and a knight of Malta,
presented an important memorandum in 1626 to Cardinal Richelieu, newly
emerged as chief minister of Louis xiii, in which he advocated that France
respond to foreign initiatives in North America, and especially those of the
English. 'Quy entreprendroyt de planter une colonye en ce pays-là,' he wrote of
New France, 'il fauldroyt borner les Angloys le plus proche qu'on pouroyct.'
More generally, Razilly explored the question of sea power in a world context
and found the French position unduly weak. If necessary changes were made,
he suggested, benefits could be derived from trade with Asia and the East
Indies, as well as colonization in Africa and America. Coming specifically to
America, he impugned – like Biard before him – the preoccupaion of merchants with immediate profit. Had colonization been seriously pursued in New
France, 'il y pouroyt avoir à présant plus de quatre mil ames, et néantmoings il
n'y en réside pas plus de vingt-cinq.' Razilly proposed that royal resources
should be deployed, and merchant investors should be deprived of any active
control over the colonies; both of these aims would be accomplished through
the foundation of a royal company. Thus Razilly sought to put colonization in
France on a public basis, as had already been effected in England and
Scotland.[84]

   Sir Ferdinando Gorges' approach to the English crown had taken the form of
a petition of March 1620 for a new charter of incorporation which would accord
to New England all the equivalent rights and privileges to those belonging to the
'first colony' of Virginia by virtue of its charters of 1606, 1609, and 1612. The
result was a patent of 3 November which incorporated 'the Councill established
at Plymouth, in the County of Devon for the planting, ruling, ordering, and
governing of New-England, in America.'[85] The council was assigned territory
delimited by the latitudes of 40° and 48°, and was equipped with a series of
powers designed to ensure successful colonization: the power to convey land to
prospective colonizers, a monopoly of trade and the fishery, and customs

concessions on goods going to and coming from New England.[86] Composed of forty royal nominees, the council had a characteristic which was at the same time its greatest theoretical strength and its greatest practical weakness. It was essentially an organ of government rather than of capitalization, a council rather than a company. The forty members, drawn from the ranks of the nobility and gentry and including seven privy councillors, were equipped with no provision for the formal association of merchants to provide capital. In contrast to the large and various membership of the Virginia Company, the Council for New England was to be a small, working, governmental council; it would rule New England through a governor, who in turn would be assisted by those recipients of land patents who had taken up residence in the colony and by a variety of subordinate officers.[87]

Even allowing for Gorges' assumption that individual patentees would send particular expeditions, the initial launching of New England would clearly require large investments, especially in settling the one-third of the colony's territory which the council intended to retain as a 'public plantation.' Gorges and his colleagues were aware of this necessity and evolved schemes to deal with it, but their casual approach to the problem stemmed in part from complacency arising from their close connections with the crown. The payment of £110 by each councillor was inadequate to finance anything beyond an initial voyage, and a scheme to raise capital through the issuance of joint stock among West Country fishing merchants foundered on the familiar shoals of mercantile distrust and inter-town rivalries. A scheme to tax the fishery through the licensing of vessels by the council was frustrated by western interests in parliament in late 1621.[88] The council continued to meet and make its plans; at a meeting in February 1623, for example, the public plantation was allocated forty square miles of territory at Sagadahoc, and consideration was given to obtaining supplies of poor children as colonists. Later the same year, a circular letter was directed by the crown to the lords lieutenant of the three western counties and the cities of Bristol and Exeter, exhorting that 'persons of quality' should be found to go to New England.[89] Also in 1623, a governor was sent to New England in the person of Robert Gorges, son of Sir Ferdinando. This privately financed expedition failed to assert the authority of the council, however, even over the struggling Pilgrim settlement at New Plymouth, and this failure, allied to the threat of renewed controversy over the fishing monopoly, discouraged future efforts by the council for some years.[90]

In Scotland, meanwhile, Sir William Alexander was attempting to promote his colony. By charter of 10 September 1621, he had been granted lands extending north and east from the length of the Ste Croix River as far as the St Lawrence River, comprehending the modern Maritime provinces and the Gaspé. Since the territory was defined by landmarks rather than by latitudes,

Alexander claimed with some justification 'that mine be the first National Patent that ever was cleerly bounded within America by particular limits upon the Earth.'[91] These lands were to be held by Alexander and his descendants as 'one entire and free lordship and barony which shall be called in all future time by the ... name of New Scotland.' As in the New England charter, Alexander was granted a number of powers and privileges to facilitate the work of colonization, including the right to grant lands, a monopoly of fishery and trade, and total freedom from customs payments for three years, followed by the payment of a minimal duty of 5 per cent. Provision was also made for government, not in such an elaborate form as in the case of New England, but through Alexander, as hereditary lieutenant general and lieutenant of justiciary and admiralty.[92] As with New England, lack of capital was to prove a grave obstacle. Despite the charter's recognition that the expenses of colonization 'exceed the means of any private man,' lack of investment was the major reason for the failure of an expedition sent out by Alexander in 1622; many of its potential colonists were lost to the Newfoundland fishery when supplies from Scotland failed to arrive.[93] Indeed, this first New Scotland scheme suffered from the same defects in theory and practice as had that of de Monts some eighteen years earlier; the granting of a large colonial area to a single promoter offered little chance of effective colonization.

Adjustments to the scheme came about in 1624 with the institution of an order of knights-baronetcies, a measure consciously modelled upon the Ulster baronetcies, and one which by its very nature overhauled and updated the New Scotland project.[94] The baronetcies had three principal purposes, the first of which was to raise capital for colonization. Each baronet would be obliged to make a payment of 1000 merks Scots (about £50 sterling) to Alexander 'for his past chargeis in discoverie of the said cuntrey and for surrandering and re-signing his interest to the saidis landis and barronies.' In addition, the baronet would have the choice of sending and supporting 'sex sufficient men, artificeris or labourers' to the colony or paying a further 2000 merks in lieu. Had the anticipated 150 baronetcies been created, the scheme could have brought in some 450,000 merks or £22,500 sterling. Secondly, the baronies were intended to help in breaching the bounds of communal colonization, since each contained 30,000 acres of land, of which 16,000 would be held by the baronet himself directly from the crown, with the remainder reserved for public uses. Thirdly, resident knights-baronets, like resident patentees of New England, would give counsel in matters of government.[95] Thus the new order, at least in intent, strengthened the New Scotland colony, and a new charter was issued in 1625 by Charles I, substantially unaltered from that of 1621.[96] In practice, there were difficulties. Although opposition to the new order by small barons (whose status was threatened) was overcome, under-subscription of the order was a basic problem.[97] Whether through scepticism regarding the colony, dislike of the parvenu Alexander, who had recently become royal secretary for Scotland, or both of these, the knights-baronetcies were little in demand. Despite a deliberate easing of the procedural formalities associated with the order, rather defensive assertions that Alexander had used the colony's funds honestly, and threatening letters to individuals implying that their future advancement would depend upon their accepting the title of knight-baronet as 'a nixt steppe to a further title,' relatively few knights-baronetcies were ever conferred, and none was ever effectively taken up in New Scotland.[98] The scheme, like that of New England, was a real attempt to reconcile colonial concept and reality, but one which was less than successful.

While Alexander was struggling to find ways of developing New Scotland, Cardinal Richelieu was formulating new colonial approaches on behalf of the French crown. Under pressure from the Jesuit order to provide security for its mission on the St Lawrence, and in accordance with the suggestions of Razilly, a far-reaching overhaul of French governmental involvement in commerce and marine affairs included the organization in 1627 of the Compagnie de la Nouvelle-France, or Compagnie des Cent-Associés.[99] The company was granted lands which were even more extensive than either New England or New Scotland: 'tout le ... pays de la Nouvelle-France, dite Canada, tant le long des costes, depuis la Floride ... jusqu'au Cercle Arctique.' This territory, including though not naming Acadia, was to be held by the company from the crown 'en toutte proprieté, Justice et Seigneurie,' with the right to make allocations of land. Government would be exercised by a governor selected by the crown from three nominees of the company.[100] In matters of capitalization and trade, the company was clearly intended to operate on a large scale. The projected capital was 300,000 *livres*, divided into 100 shares of 3,000 each; this amount in itself made the company the largest North American colonizing venture ever attempted. No profits would be distributed for the first three years and only a limited proportion thereafter, the balance being added in each year to the capital investment of each associate. The headquarters of the company was to be in Paris, rather than in any provincial port, and Parisians were prominent among the approximately one-third of the associates who were merchants. The company was obliged to transport 4,000 colonists to New France by 1643; in return, it was accorded a perpetual monopoly of the fur trade, a monopoly of all other commerce except the fishery until 1643, and an exemption from customs duties for the same period. As an additional inducement to investment, nobles and clergymen were permitted to become full members of the company without compromising their rank, and the majority of the associates were drawn from the *noblesse de robe*. Further, it was promised that up to twelve of the associates who were commoners would be ennobled, and as an attraction to humbler colonists it was prescribed that artisans who practised their trade in New France for six years would be reputed masters of their craft in the event of their return to France.[101]

Although it was much more thorough in setting out arrangements for capitalization, the Compagnie de la Nouvelle-France was a response to needs similar to those that led to the Council for New England and the Alexander colony of New Scotland. Circumstances, however, did not favour the success of the company. The grant to the Cent-Associés was in conflict not only with New England and New Scotland, but also with Virginia and New Netherland. In this early period of tiny settlements, such conflicts did not necessarily have practical significance. In 1627, however, war broke out between England and France. In the same year in London, a company, which included the London and Dieppe merchant Gervase Kirke, was formed, with the object of capturing the St Lawrence settlements and monopolizing the fur trade there. In the course of the next three years, Quebec and Tadoussac were indeed seized by Kirke's five sons, and, in co-operation with that venture, a colony was founded in New Scotland by Sir William Alexander.[102] Thus, the Compagnie de la Nouvelle-France, however well conceived, suffered from circumstances which ensured that it would have to struggle for survival just as hard as its English and Scottish counterparts.

Aside from the practical difficulties encountered by the French, English, and Scottish colonial projects, all three had arrived by the late 1620s at concepts of colonization which stressed large-scale occupation of American lands for reasons of national power and prestige. The Council for New England was a governmental council, New Scotland a baronial estate, and the Compagnie de la Nouvelle-France a commercial company. Fundamentally, all three had elements of these three important characteristics. All three arose from the recognition that to facilitate the process of settlement and the permanence of colonies, a government, a land structure, and a trading economy were needed. Not that all questions raised by colonization had been answered. Confusion remained, especially in the English and Scottish cases, as to what amounts of capital would be required and how they could be raised. Confusion remained as to how rigorously the religious function of the colonies should be pursued. All three colonies professed conversion of the Indian to be their primary function; yet only the Compagnie de la Nouvelle-France had formal obligations in this regard.[103] Confusion remained also as to the exact status of the colonies in relation to the respective mother countries. The individual colonists were well enough defined: in all three cases they were obliged to be of proven acceptability to the crown in terms of religion and allegiance, but having satisfied these conditions they were deemed in each case to enjoy the full rights and privileges of their nationality; in the French case, though not in the English and Scottish, even Indian converts were included.[104] As to the relation of the colony as a whole to the mother country, however, little was said beyond undefined professions of unity.

One matter which had been confronted more directly was the structure of landholding in the three projected colonies. In each case, conventional European structures were to be exported to America, involving the introduction of *féodalité* and the prevailing assumption of 'nulle terre sans seigneur.'[105] That there was no intention for New England to depart from traditional institutions of landholding was early shown in the 'Brief relation' of Gorges, in which Gorges reviewed the English forms of territorial division into 'counties, baronies, hundreds, and the like,' and declared that 'this foundation being so certain, there is no reason for us to vary from it, and therefore we have resolved to build our edifices upon it ...' Counties would be subdivided into 'manors and lordships ... giving to the lords thereof power of keeping of courts, and leets, as is here used in England, for the determining of petty matters, arising between the lords, and the tenants, or any other.'[106]

An example of one of the earliest large-scale land grants of the Council for New England is that of the Province of Maine, made in 1622 in favour of Gorges and his partner John Mason. This grant – which introduced the name of Maine, though it was differently bounded from the future Province of Maine which would be granted to Gorges in 1639 – comprehended the sea coast from the Merrimack to Kennebec rivers, and extended westward as far as sixty miles inland from the head of each river. The territory was to be held directly from the crown, on the same tenure as that of the Council for New England as a whole, although a token annual rent of ten shillings was reserved to the council. Mason and Gorges were obliged to erect a government and to populate the province with tenants, including at least ten families within the first three years.[107] In its early years, the Council for New England experimented with a variety of sizes and tenures of grants in its efforts to promote colonization, including such large grants as that of Mason and Gorges, smaller grants to be held from the council itself, and municipal grants. For the most part these were not taken up, but the intention of establishing a conventionally structured English land-owning society in America was clear.

A similar aim lay behind the knights-baronetcies of Scotland. Sir William Alexander had envisaged in 1624 the division of New Scotland into two provinces: Alexandria, comprising the modern New Brunswick and the Gaspé, and Caledonia, comprising the modern peninsular Nova Scotia.[108] The letter of the Scots Privy Council accepting the institution of knights-baronetcies elaborated further, dividing the provinces into dioceses, counties, baronies, and parishes. Each knight-baronet was to enjoy 'ten thowsand aikeris of propertie besydis his sax thowsand aikeris belonging to his burgh of baronie [a town to be set up in each baronial holding], to be holden free blanshe [without payment of a quitrent], and in a free baronie of your Majestie as the barronies of this kingdome.'[109] In accordance with this detailed plan, knights-baronetcies conferred up until 1638 carried with them a named and precisely bounded area of land in New Scotland, along with conventional rights of barony which included powers of jurisdiction. Overall rights of government remained to Alexander as lieutenant general. Thus, the baronies of New Scotland, like the Province of Maine granted in 1622, were held directly from the crown. Somewhat different, though similar in intent, were the powers granted to the Cent-Associés to distribute lands 'à ceux qui habiteront ledit pays et autres en telle quantité et ainsi qu'ils jugeront à propos.'[110] Here the company itself was empowered to subinfeudate land in creating seigneuries to be held of itself rather than the crown, a power that would be exercised in 1632 in granting a concession to Razilly on the Ste Croix River in Acadia, and then in the creation of large numbers of seigneuries in the St Lawrence region in later years.[111]

The privilege granted to the Compagnie de la Nouvelle-France of creating seigneuries and receiving homage was an exceptional one for the French crown to make and one which superficially resembles the powers enjoyed by medieval barons. Indeed, the introduction of *féodalité* to America has sometimes been seen as an attempt to recreate medieval feudalism, to turn the clock backwards. In no way, however, was this the intent. In so far as the term has meaning, medieval feudalism was the complex outgrowth of particular social circumstances and was characterized by the weakness of the state and fragmentation of authority. Each of the crowns of France, England, and Scotland had gradually liberated itself from the constraints of such weakness, and none of the three intended to recreate their problems in the New World. The *féodalité* which was projected for North America was shorn, for example, of the military trappings of feudal tenure, and governmental authority was carefully defined. When exceptional privileges were given, they were given to such a body as the Cent-Associés, which could be kept under the direct supervision of the crown. Where fragmentation of authority occurred in the colonies – as it would in the northeastern maritime region – it occurred in spite of the original concepts of colonization, and certainly not because of any intention to recreate an outmoded form of society. The true intent of *féodalité* was much simpler. Colonization on an extensive scale required a suitable structure of granting and holding land. Not surprisingly, conventional European structures were selected, along with the basic principle of 'nulle terre sans seigneur.' What remained to be seen, however, was whether this concept could be successfully reconciled with American reality.[112]

Settlements by 1630

The decade of the 1620s was fertile in concepts of colonization but less successful in the practical task of establishing colonies. Settlements were established by French, English, and Scots colonists, but nowhere were the constrictions of communal colonization effectively broken. Complication was introduced by the element of competition among the three nations, which often took the form of armed conflict. By 1630, the European had undoubtedly made an impression upon northern North America, but not a profound one.

Of the three future colonies of Maine, Acadia, and New Scotland, Acadia in 1620 was not only alone in having been conceived and named, but was also the only one with European settlement. English fishermen had occasionally wintered on the coast of what was to become Maine but without any colonizing intent. In Acadia, the Biencourt settlement continued its tenuous, but ordered, existence. It was accompanied from 1620 by a Recollet mission on the St John River; in 1623, it survived the death of Biencourt, whose brother and heir Jacques entrusted the direction of the colony to Charles de Saint-Étienne de La Tour. La Tour, a close associate of Biencourt, had already been in Acadia for many years, claiming in a letter of 1627 to have moved there some twenty years previously.[113] La Tour, however, faced major problems. A memorandum addressed by the French ambassador in London to the English government in 1624 complained of the aggressions of the subjects of 'Sa Majestie de la Grande Bretagne' in New France, 'tant envers le Sieur de Poutrincourt habitue audit pays qu'envers les autres François qui y navigent.' The English segment of America, the memorial went on, stretched from Virginia to the Gulf of Mexico (a concession which was withdrawn three years later in the inauguration of the Compagnie de la Nouvelle-France), and the king was invited to bring this to the attention of his unruly subjects, so as to 'les convyer a se contenir dans leurs bornes pour n'estre obliger les uns et les autres a en venir aux extremites d'une petite guerre.'[114] The English reply was not conciliatory, reminding the French of the New England patent extending from 40° to 48°, and further affirming that the land claimed by 'Poutrincourt' was held by Alexander 'comme de la Couronne d'Escosse, afin que ses [the king's] sujets de cette Nation la puissent semblablement avoir l'oportunite d'establir une Plantation en ces Parties la.' The reply suggested a conference to be held 'pour la meilleure confirmation d'un cours civil entre eux et nous pour le temps a venir,' but the implication was that 'une petite guerre' would be preferable to compromise.[115] By 1627 La Tour was writing to Louis XIII, from Port Lomeron in the southern part of the Acadian peninsula, that 'j'ay esté contrainct par le mauvais traictement que nous avons receu des Anglois de vivre ainsy que les peuples du pays et vestus comme eux, chasser à force les bestes, et pescher les poissons pour vivre ... ' Among La Tour's purposes in this letter, and in one written on the same day to Richelieu, was to recall his existence to the government, presumably because he had heard of the formation of the Compagnie de la Nouvelle-France, and to propose that he be given a commission 'pour la conservation de la Coste de l'Acadie avec defense à tout autre de me troubler.' It was in his interest, therefore, not to underestimate the chaos which prevailed. He was certainly correct, however, in stressing his vulnerability to outside attack, since he had only '[une] petite troupe de Françoys avec trois moyenne barque.' Such in 1627 was the extent of the colony of Acadia.[116]

The English also had their troubles. The most significant colony to be settled in New England during the 1620s, that of New Plymouth, had no initial connection with the Council for New England, and no ambition to fulfil the council's grandiose aspirations. The failure of Robert Gorges' expedition of 1623 has already been mentioned: despite receiving a personal grant of 300 square miles on Massachusetts Bay from the Council for New England, Gorges soon ran out of both money and enthusiasm and left New England, as William Bradford of New Plymouth wryly observed, 'having scarcely saluted the country in his government ... '[117] With Gorges came Christopher Levett, a member of the Council for New England who had a patent for 6,000 acres of land at Casco Bay. Levett evidently lingered at Casco long enough to establish friendly relations with the Abenaki inhabitants and to write a detailed description of the area, but his settlement had no lasting results after his departure in 1624.[118] More tenacious was David Thomson, a Scot in the employ of the Council for New England who had also obtained a patent for 6,000 acres and established a settlement at the mouth of the Piscataqua River. Having obtained the support of three West Country merchants for the transportation and support of himself and seven other colonists, Thomson lived at Piscataqua for some two years on the fishery, the fur trade, and small-scale agriculture, then moving to an island in Massachusetts Bay before his death in 1627 or 1628.[119]

Thus, New England failed to develop along the lines envisaged by its promoters during the 1620s, and the attempts at colonization within the territory of the future colony of Maine failed to make any lasting impression. The end of the decade saw the beginning of the Massachusetts colony and also that of the Laconia Company. The latter, an attempt by Gorges and Mason to divert the interior fur trade away from the French by finding a route towards Lake Champlain from a base on the Piscataqua River, did eventually bring settlers to Maine, but in the meantime English achievements in colonizing the northeastern maritime region remained slight.[120]

Sir William Alexander, renewing in late 1626 his efforts to populate New Scotland, enjoyed success rather sooner. By the summer of 1627 Alexander had assembled a fleet at the Scottish port of Dumbarton, under the command of his son, the younger Sir William Alexander. Long delayed by financial difficulties, and hampered by desertions among the potential colonists, the fleet eventually set sail for America in the spring of 1628.[121] The specific details of the planting of two New Scotland settlements – one under the command of Lord Ochiltree on Cape Breton, probably with a connection to the old New Galloway grant of the now-deceased Gordon of Lochinvar, and one under Alexander the younger at Port Royal – are not entirely clear from surviving records.[122] The most confusion arises from the existence of evidence which apparently makes 1628 a likely date for the foundation of the Port Royal settlement and 1629 the most probable for that on Cape Breton, whereas it is clear that both were established in the same year; on balance, 1629 seems the more probable.[123] It is certainly true that Sir William Alexander wrote on 18 November 1628 that 'my sone, praised be God, is returned safe, haveing left a colonie neare Canada behind him'; however, as one historian has persuasively argued, it is probable that this initial settlement wintered elsewhere in America, perhaps on the Gaspé coast or at Tadoussac. Subsequently, in 1629, the younger Alexander returned to supervise the transfer of the colony to Port Royal, leaving Lord Ochiltree in command of '60 or 80 English' at Port aux Baleines, on Cape Breton, as the elder Alexander later stated.[124]

These New Scotland colonies (albeit that it seems that the colonists on Cape Breton were chiefly English) were, however, vulnerable both to English and French. As William Maxwell of Edinburgh remarked in a letter of 23 November 1628, 'the Englische men ar suiten of his Majestie a patent to plant and possesse quhatsumever lands thairof quhilk they please, and these to be halden of the Crowne of England.'[125] The reference was to the brothers Kirke, who had been active in their efforts to capture the St Lawrence settlements, in which they were to succeed in 1629. It is probable that the Kirkes' previous expedition in 1628 had sailed with Alexander, but that the friendship was only one of convenience was shown in the winter of 1628–9, when claims and counter-claims were made by the Kirkes and the Alexanders to both Canada and New Scotland. The quarrels were eventually settled by the formation of a new company in 1629, the English and Scottish Company, to trade on the St Lawrence in a separate but co-operative relationship with New Scotland.[126]

Vulnerability to French attack proved to be a more dangerous menace, especially to the Cape Breton settlement, which was attacked on 10 September 1629 by Captain Charles Daniel, one of the Cent-Associés who was on a voyage to Quebec when he learned of Ochiltree's establishment. Accompanied, as Ochiltree later complained, by 'threescore sojours and ane certaine number off savages,' Daniel obtained entry to Ochiltree's fort by peaceful means, since the treaty of Suza had recently been signed between France and the British kingdoms; he thereupon seized the fort, transporting some of the colonists to England and taking others prisoner to France.[127] From Daniel's description, Ochiltree's settlement was very much a fortified communal colony: 'Il n'eust pas este possible de le tirer de sa Citadelle: car il avoit des vivres pour plus de deux ans ... [et il avait] toute sorte de comoditez, d'outils, d'instruments et d'ouvriers.'[128] Ochiltree had evidently found a means of obtaining supplies by taxing French fishermen 10 per cent on their catch. The colony had not proceeded beyond the communal habitation, however, and its fall was a further illustration of the vulnerability of such a settlement.

Alexander's colony at Port Royal was longer-lived, but still operated within a communal framework, and was subject to the hazards of such a settlement. In the winter of 1629–30, for example, Claude de Saint-Étienne de La Tour, the father of Charles, reported (according to Champlain) that 'il estoit mort trente Escossois, de septante qu'ils estoient en cet hyvernement, qui avoient esté mal accommodez.'[129] The problem of dependence upon the mother country was also as acute as ever. In early 1630, Sir William Alexander the elder became progressively more agitated in London as he attempted to find capital with which to send out relief. On 21 January, he wrote to the Earl of Menteith that 'I can lift no monie here in hast; the English marchants never taking Scottish securitie, and the Scotish factours not haveing monie.' By 9 February he was even more worried 'concerneing my sone's supplie, whereupon his saftie or ruine doth depend ... there is no monie to be had here ... and therefore whatever happen, I wold the ship that is fraughted at Leith [the Scottish port] were hasted away with some twentie or threttie good fellowes, and so much for provisions as she may carrie ... ' Apparently this broad hint was heeded, but the urgency of the need for Menteith's help illustrates the dependent position of the colony; indeed a similar request was made again by Alexander the following winter.[130]

To be sure, not all was gloomy in the New Scotland settlement. Harmonious Indian relations, essential to the survival of a communal colony, seem to have been early established. The colonists were visited shortly after their arrival by '2 savages in a Canou,' and this was followed a few weeks later by a trading visit by a larger party.[131] Furthermore, a contemporary reported in a letter of February 1630 that Charles I had been visited by the Micmac chief Segipt and his family, who had come 'to be of our king's religion, and to submit his kingdom to him ... '[132] Even among the French who remained in Acadia, there were indications of a possible willingness to convert to the Scottish allegiance in return for certain guarantees. Captured by the Kirkes at sea in 1628, Claude de La Tour had been carried to England where he had met with Alexander. The subsequent episode is the subject of conflicting evidence, but it seems clear that Alexander made an agreement with La Tour that he and his son would be made knights-baronets, an agreement which Alexander fulfilled on 30 November

1629 and 12 May 1630 respectively.[133] By the agreement, the La Tours would hold an area in the southern part of the New Scotland peninsula from the Ingogon River, near Cap Fourchu, to Mirliquesh (in modern terms, from Yarmouth to Lunenburg, N.S., and thus including both Port Lomeron and the La Tours' settlement at Cap de Sable), would divide the fur trade with Alexander, and would be free to make settlements in their territory. In return, the La Tours must undertake to be 'bons et fideles sujets et Vasseaux dudit Roy [of Scotland], et luy rendre toute obeïssance et assister vers les Peuples a la reduction dudit Païs et Coste d'Accadie.'[134] The elder La Tour was unable to convince his son to endorse this agreement, and he himself abandoned the Scottish allegiance later in 1630, after supplies had been sent to his son by the Compagnie de la Nouvelle-France.[135]

The fact that such an agreement was seriously considered on both sides, however, indicates the weakness of the European hold on the northeastern maritime region. The Scottish colony was sufficiently well rooted to be impressive even to its enemies, and the elder La Tour temporarily changed his allegiance accordingly. Yet even the New Scotland colony had failed to break free of the constraints of communal colonization, and remained small, isolated, and dependent upon Indian goodwill as well as upon the prompt succour of European supplies. All three of the colonies of Acadia, Maine, and New Scotland had been named by 1630, though only New Scotland had been precisely defined. All three were the subject of, or were included in, elaborate quasi-governmental schemes for large-scale colonization. Yet the fact was that the northeastern maritime region remained Indian territory. European trade had already had a profound effect upon Indian culture, but European colonization had made only the faintest of imprints upon the land. Acadia had a tiny population, had had one of its principal ports taken over by the New Scotland colonists, and was only beginning in 1630 to obtain support from the Compagnie de la Nouvelle-France. Maine was not yet conceived as such, though the Laconia Company again provided some hope for settlement in the future, just as the Massachusetts Bay Company did further south. New Scotland survived, narrowly. Of the three, it perhaps seemed in 1630 to be the one most likely to succeed; but conception and reality, even in New Scotland, were still far apart. Despite more than twenty-five years of attempts, the real struggle to establish European colonies in the northeastern maritime region was only beginning.

Part II
The Formative Years, 1630–1650

✳✳✳✳✳✳✳✳✳✳✳✳✳✳✳✳✳✳✳✳✳✳✳✳✳✳✳✳✳✳✳✳✳

CHAPTER 2

Relationships with Europe

✳✳✳✳✳✳✳✳✳✳✳✳✳✳✳✳✳✳✳✳✳✳✳✳✳✳✳✳✳✳✳✳✳

Settlement: The Permissive Function of the Crown

For the colonies of Acadia, Maine, and New Scotland, the period between 1630 and 1650 was one of adjustment and definition, as European concept and American reality began to be reconciled in the existence of colonial populations. Survival was still perilously tenuous and colonies could and did disappear. The New Scotland colony did so for a considerable time, and when it was revived after 1650 its form was very different from that of 1630. Maine and Acadia reached 1650 in a state of some internal disorder, but well defined, and containing permanent populations. All three colonies developed, or failed to develop, as the result of an interconnected series of external and internal relationships, the external including relationships with Europe, with native peoples, and with other colonies. Relationships with Europe were of especial importance in the early stages. Each colony was dependent upon its crown for the charter, or other such instrument, which created it, as well as for essential support and encouragement. What the crown gave it could take away, and the crown was thus at the same time an important prop and a grave threat to each colony. Should the crown withdraw its support or, most destructive of all, its permission for settlement to be made and maintained, the colonies and their promoters had few resources with which to attempt survival. In the early history of the northeastern maritime colonies, both sides of the royal influence are in evidence, and the New Scotland colony in particular found out how crushing the withdrawal of royal support could be.

On 13 May 1630, Charles I addressed an encouraging letter to Sir William Alexander the younger, complimenting him on his work 'for planting of a colonie at Port Royall, which may be a means to setle all that cuntrie in obedience' and expressing the hope 'that the wark may be brought to the intendit perfectione, which wee will esteem as one of the most singulare services done unto us.'[1] This was an emphatic endorsement of the Alexanders' progress. Yet in private, the king was considering the return of Port Royal to the French. The war between France and the kingdoms of Charles I, which had begun in 1627, had been brought to an end in 1629 by the interim treaty of Suza. It remained to negotiate the final terms of peace, and one of the first demands of the French was for the restitution of 'les places de la Cadye' in addition to Quebec and Canada.[2] A year later, when serious negotiations were getting under way, this demand was pressed firmly by the French chancellor and special ambassador in London, the Marquis de Châteauneuf. On the question of Canada, agreement was quickly reached. As Viscount Dorchester, the English secretary of state, admitted, the French had been expelled from Quebec 'by strong hand,' and this action of the Kirkes had taken place after the treaty of Suza. Therefore, restitution would be made without demur. The question of Acadia was more complex. Châteauneuf, as Dorchester informed the English ambassador in France, was 'ill satisfyed, that he could not obtayne a direct promise from His Majesty for the restoring of Port Royall, joyning to Canada, where some Scottish men are planted under the title of Nova Scotia.' Although Charles I had promised in a personal meeting with the French ambassador 'thus much that unles he found reason as well before, as since the warre, to have that Place free for his Subjects plantation, he would recall them,' Dorchester reflected that the Scots had 'there seated themselves in a place where no French did inhabite,' and furthermore expressed a belief that on this point Châteauneuf had spoken 'rather out of his owne discourse ... then by Commission.'[3]

Thus in the spring of 1630, the royal attitude was somewhat uncertain, though inclined to stand fast if sufficiently strong arguments could be found. In July, the king wrote to instruct the Scots Privy Council to investigate the whole matter, and in reply he received a series of assurances from Scotland that the New Scotland colony was legitimate.[4] These were communicated to the royal negotiators in France. Yet the French still insisted on restitution. Towards the end of the year the negotiators, René Augier and Henry De Vic, reported to Dorchester that even an attempt to have the matter postponed to future negotiation had been categorically refused by the French; Châteauneuf, by now recalled to France in his capacity of chancellor, had replied, they stated, 'que le fait dudit Port Royal estoit joint avec le reste.'[5] By the end of January 1631 the matter of Port Royal was 'the only difficulty' standing in the way of a peace treaty, and Augier and De Vic were convinced that the French would go back to war over the matter if necessary.[6] But why? As Charles I was to remark a few weeks later, 'places taken and held upon that whole continent of America have never binne drawne so into consequence by the Princes of Europe as thereupon to frame disputes for interruption of treatyes betwixte kingdomes and States ... '[7] The negotiators thought they knew the answer. In their opinion, the French (and especially Châteauneuf) were more interested in Port Royal as a point of honour than in Acadia as a colony. Augier and De Vic therefore suggested a strategy: 'if Sir William Alexander wolde exchange that Seate for some other upon the same coast, and not farr distant from the porte Royall, and some meanes were founde to indemnize him of parte of the charges hee hath beene att to make his plantation, it may bee that wolde give them satisfaction here in pointe of honour.'[8]

It was this recommendation which became the basis of a settlement by which the Scots colony of Port Royal was to be evacuated, without any renunciation of the Scots claim to New Scotland. The evacuation was agreed privately with the French in April 1631, and was ordered by Charles I in July, though it was not carried out until the arrival of a French expedition at Port Royal the following year. All of the Scottish documents, however, made it clear that evacuation did not imply giving up New Scotland, and this point was reinforced by the ostentatious showing of royal favour to Sir William Alexander, including his elevation to the title of Viscount of Stirling.[9] In early 1632, Alexander was awarded an amount of £10,000 sterling in compensation for his losses in New Scotland, with a stipulation that the grant was 'nowayes for quyting the title, ryght, or possession of New Scotland, or of any part thereof, bot onlie for satisfaction of the losses ... '[10] Later in the same year, a royal letter to the knights-baronets assured them of the continuance of New Scotland despite 'the Colonie being forced of late to remove for a tyme by meanes of a treatie we have had with the French'; only a year later, all of Alexander's patents and rights in New Scotland and Canada were specifically confirmed by the Scots parliament.[11]

The fact was, however, that the continuance of New Scotland had no basis in American reality. Despite all affirmations to the contrary, the surrender of Port Royal by the treaty of Saint-Germain-en-Laye in 1632, and the shipping of the colonists to England, where they arrived in early 1633, was a crushing blow to the colony.[12] The Scots crown had made two fundamental miscalculations, which had been exacerbated by a loss of contact between the crown and its negotiators in France for some five months in early 1632, occasioned by the illness and death of Dorchester.[13] First of all, there was no real chance that Alexander would be able to raise enough capital to recolonize New Scotland. Secondly, the Scots had consistently underestimated the importance attached to Acadia by the French.

Charles I and his advisers had never believed that the French would seriously attempt to colonize Acadia after the restoration of Quebec. This view, however, was soon belied by the power and prestige of the French expedition which

sailed for Acadia in 1632: on 16 June Stirling in a note to the crown described
the size of the expedition, observing that it had 'a desyne more than ordinarie
herein.'[14] The first hint of this had come with the selection by Richelieu of Isaac
de Razilly to take the surrender of Port Royal; this nomination in itself revealed
the importance attached to the expedition, since Razilly was one of Richelieu's
closest and most influential colonial advisers. Planning had commenced early,
and an appeal for colonists for 'le Royaume de Lacadie' had been issued in
January. Razilly was granted a fully equipped warship, *Espérance en Dieu*,
and 10,000 *livres* by the crown, on condition that he and the Compagnie de la
Nouvelle-France would contribute further equipment and men; with these
forces, which eventually consisted of three ships and 300 men, Razilly was to
take possession of Port Royal in the name of the Compagnie de la Nouvelle-
France.[15] Thus the expedition was a major one, with an unusual degree of
government participation. Razilly was also accorded a royal commission
'pour recevoir des mains des Anglois ou Ecossois en nôtre nom ledit Port
Royal,' was granted by the company a seigneury comprising the river and bay
of Ste Croix, and was further commissioned to stay in Acadia as the royal
lieutenant general in New France.[16]

Thus the French expedition which departed in July 1632 for Acadia bore
every indication of intended strength and permanence. It denoted, perhaps, the
converse of the Scottish situation. Both the Scots and the French crowns
professed to believe in the value of colonization in the abstract. The Scots
crown, however, saw the actual settlement of Port Royal as an obstacle to the
more important aim of a favourable peace in Europe; Richelieu and the French
crown, having regard to the strategic necessity to counterbalance the growing
strength of New England, gave Acadian settlement an important priority.
During the next three years, Razilly, with his lieutenants Charles de Menou
d'Aulnay and Nicolas Denys, and in partnership with his merchant brother
Claude de Launay-Rasilly, acted with vigour in establishing the Acadian
colony, the principal settlement being made at La Hève, on the Atlantic coast of
the peninsula, with at least one other at Canso. Razilly, moreover, was able to
work in harmony with the La Tours, who made efforts to attract colonists to
their bases at Cap de Sable and on the St John River.[17] Charles de La Tour had
also been in possession since 1631 of a commission as royal lieutenant general
for Acadia.[18]

Difficulties were, of course, experienced by the Acadian colony in this
period, the most pressing being the perennial problem of mobilizing sufficient
capital. Despite the grant to the Razillys of additional seigneuries at La Hève,
Port Royal, and Sable Island, and their acquisition of a trading monopoly (to be
held jointly with the La Tours) for ten years, the enterprise fell heavily into
debt. Royal permission for settlement, however, was not a difficulty. Indeed,

Richelieu himself, while unwilling to commit royal funds, entered into personal partnership with the Razillys with an investment of 17,000 *livres* in early 1635, the principal aim being to speed the peopling of the colony.[19] The positive interest shown by Richelieu in Acadia began to wane in 1635 with the death of Isaac de Razilly, but the period between 1632 and 1635 gave the Acadian colony an unprecedentedly secure basis and, whether directly or not, paved the way for the establishment of colonists. One of the first acts of d'Aulnay, who succeeded to Razilly's authority on delegation by the surviving brother, Launay-Rasilly, was to move the principal Acadian settlement to Port Royal from La Hève, and on this site a small but permanent population established itself on the fertile marshlands.[20] By 1650 it had grown to some 300 persons and was gradually becoming less a cluster of houses around a fort than a genuinely extensive settlement.[21]

The French example in Acadia illustrates the power of royal support in giving impetus to colonial settlement, just as the Scottish example in New Scotland shows conversely the destructiveness of the withdrawal of royal permission. The negative power of the crown may also be discerned in the English efforts in Maine, though with less practical effect. The colonization of New England, and the colonization of Maine from the time that province was defined in 1639 and made a proprietary province, continued to be the concern of Sir Ferdinando Gorges. After the failure of the Laconia Company in 1635 and the concurrent resignation of the patent of the Council for New England, New England had been divided among various members of the council; Gorges received an area bounded by the Piscataqua and Kennebec rivers which he named the Province of New Somersetshire.[22] This area was subsequently extended further inland to form the principal part of the Province of Maine as defined in 1639.[23] For most of this period Gorges was in high repute with the crown as a colonizer and at least between 1635 and 1637 was designated governor in a future general government for New England.[24] In these circumstances, it is not surprising that he was able to send with William Gorges, his nephew and his deputy in New Somersetshire, 'some ... craftsmen for the building of houses and erecting of saw-mills; and by other shipping from Bristol, some cattle with other servants – by which the foundation of the Plantation was laid.'[25] These preparations were clearly quite small in scale, and William Gorges provided leadership for only a short time before leaving the colony, but the effort nevertheless had been made with the approval of the crown.[26]

Shortly afterwards, however, Gorges had a taste of the negative power of the crown. Charles I and his ministers, particularly Archbishop Laud, looked with some misgiving at the Massachusetts colony, rapidly increasing its population throughout the 1630s, as a potentially powerful centre of sedition. In February

1634, early in Laud's governmental career, a 'stay' had been put on all ships preparing to leave for New England, since 'ill affected' colonists were thought to be on board. Although the ban was shortly lifted on certain conditions, including the use of the Book of Common Prayer on board ship, the incident signalled a series of efforts to bring New England more directly under royal authority.[27] In 1638, a stay of shipping was again employed: a limited ban on 30 March was extended two days later to a general prohibition of all ships bound for New England. Although the measure was relaxed on 6 April on petition from merchants whose trade was adversely affected, New England was declared to be 'unfitt and unworthie ... of any support or Countenance from hence,' and a special licence would henceforth be required for any voyages bound for that region.[28] Here was an exercise of negative royal power, and Gorges felt the effects, despite the fact that his own conduct had always been in conformity with Laud's aims. A petition by Gorges for exemption from the restraints upon shipping, on the basis that his colony was impeccably loyal and was in dire need of supply, was curtly rejected by Laud.[29] This royal measure was not successful in curbing Massachusetts, and efforts to do so were soon lost in the chaos of English political conflicts, but as a threat to the embryonic colony of Maine it was clearly considered by Gorges to be very real.

Alexander, Razilly, and Gorges had made successful efforts to convince their respective crowns that American colonization should be considered to be of national significance, hoping thus to facilitate the process of settlement. Just as the royal favour in political matters had both its positive and its negative sides, however, so too did the royal countenancing of colonization. Once the concept of American colonies had entered the sphere of royal consideration, it was subject to all the exigencies of government and diplomacy. Thus, when America was unwontedly brought into the negotiations for the treaty of Saint-Germain-en-Laye, the well-being of New Scotland was sacrificed to European considerations; when the Massachusetts colony was seen as a danger to the security of the realm, all New England colonization was put in jeopardy. In the settlement phase, the colonies were particularly vulnerable to such forces: Alexander and, to a lesser extent, Gorges found out that by portraying the colonies as matters of national and strategic importance they had forged a double-edged sword.

Economy: Trade Relations with Europe

In order for American colonies to survive, they clearly needed economic functions that would support, as far as possible, the capital outlays of their promoters and the subsistence of their inhabitants. In the earlier years of colonization, a direct dependence upon the resources of the mother countries in

Europe was inevitable. The economy of the northeastern maritime colonies in the period 1630–50 remained one predominantly based upon trade – more precisely, upon the exploitation of natural resources through export. The fishery, the fur trade, and, to a lesser extent, the timber trade provided the principal export commodities. None of these, of course, was necessarily connected with colonization, and all continued throughout the period to be exploited also by seasonal voyagers who would have no permanent establishments on the soil of America. Nevertheless they were also the resources upon which colonies had to depend for their economic welfare. Both colonization and the systematic exploitation of natural resources by colonies required large capital investments, and in this lay one of the major links of dependency between the colonies and Europe.

An association with mercantile supporters in Europe remained essential for colonial promoters. Charles de La Tour, whose association with Acadia had begun with the Poutrincourt/Biencourt colony, maintained links with several of the La Rochelle merchant families who had been associated with that colony. Samuel Georges, his kinsman Daniel Lomeron, and the latter's son David Lomeron, are examples of those who in 1633 were acting as La Tour's agents in his colonizing and trading efforts.[30] Also in the 1630s, La Tour was acting in association with a number of the Cent-Associés in prosecuting the Acadian fur trade, and by 1636 he was represented by a permanent agent at La Rochelle, Guillaume Desjardins Du Val.[31] La Tour thus maintained cordial relations with the Compagnie de la Nouvelle-France and also pursued his own trading activities. Also maintaining close relations with the associates was Nicolas Denys, a colleague of Charles d'Aulnay in the Razilly company who severed that connection when d'Aulnay acquired control of the Razilly interests. Denys's early activities in Acadia culminated in his acquiring in 1645, in partnership with his brother, a trading concession at Miscou under the Compagnie de la Nouvelle-France, although he was shortly afterwards expelled by d'Aulnay.[32]

The Razillys and d'Aulnay, however, were able to operate virtually independently of the Cent-Associés. Claude de Launay-Rasilly was a Paris merchant and one of the associates; he was thus in a position both to organize funding and to deal with the Compagnie de la Nouvelle-France. The result was that the Razillys were able to form a private company which replaced the Compagnie de la Nouvelle-France on their territory, and it was from this company that d'Aulnay drew the origins of his financial interest in Acadia, first as an aide to the Razillys and from 1641 as a shareholder. In 1642, Launay-Rasilly ceded his interest in the company to d'Aulnay, thus giving him effective control. D'Aulnay continued to have little to do with the Compagnie de la Nouvelle-France, and indeed his rivalry with the associates led to acts of violent hostility in 1646 and 1647.[33] D'Aulnay was still, however, dependent upon French mercantile backing, chiefly in the person of Emmanuel Le Borgne, another prosperous and influential La Rochelle merchant. D'Aulnay had dealt with Le Borgne at least as early as 1634, when the latter had been one of two merchants lending 900 *livres* to the Razilly company to buy trade goods for Acadia.[34] In 1642, d'Aulnay and others interested in Acadia nominated Le Borgne as their *procureur-général* at La Rochelle, whereupon Le Borgne advanced 16,000 *livres* for the Acadian trade; the association continued until d'Aulnay's death in 1650, by which time the latter's debts to Le Borgne had risen to some 260,000 *livres*.[35]

The close links maintained by Acadian colonizers with European merchants were paralleled further south, in Maine. In the Laconia Company, for example, Gorges and Mason were associated principally with a group of London merchants; the partnership was able to raise sufficient capital to send sixty-six men and twenty-two women to the colony, though lack of profits led the merchants to withdraw from the scheme by 1634. Without mercantile backing, Gorges and Mason were unable to continue.[36] A longer-lived project, and one which was more successful than most English efforts on the Maine coast, was the plantation made at Richmond's Island, under the terms of a grant by the Council for New England in 1631 to two Plymouth merchants, Robert Trelawny and Moses Goodyear. Funded from Plymouth, the colony (which in this case had an avowedly commercial purpose and a straightforwardly communal structure despite its relation to the Council for New England, which supposedly had aims very different from these) was administered by John Winter, Trelawny's son-in-law, and continued to operate until 1642, when it succumbed to the joint pressures of disruption of trade in England owing to the incipient civil war and economic depression in New England.[37] Here was an operation in which the essential need for capitalization was expressed in a particularly strong control from Europe, since in the Trelawny case the American representative of the association was not a partner but an employee.

The close connections maintained with European merchants implied also that markets for raw materials exported from the northeastern region would be determined accordingly. Commercial ties in this period being essentially personal in nature, colonizers, whether French or English, tended to trade with those whom they knew by kinship or by close acquaintance in Europe. In 1634–5, for example, efforts by Nicolas Denys to export to Oporto were put in hand through Denys's brother; this was hardly a successful example, however, since the export failed disastrously owing to an outbreak of war between Spain and France and was one of the principal occasions of the failure of Denys's sedentary fishery at Port Rossignol. The dried cod from Richmond's Island was also directed in large part at the Mediterranean market, through the contacts of the island's co-owner, the Plymouth merchant Robert Trelawny.[38] Furs, although Winter found this trade disappointingly unproductive, were directed to Bristol on Trelawny's account.[39] Charles de La Tour also worked within a network of merchants with whom he and his agent Desjardins were connected for purposes of both capitalization and marketing of furs.[40] Timber, in so far as it was exported from the northeastern region, was also marketed chiefly through merchants whose interest in America also included direct investment. In early 1633, for example, d'Aulnay marketed a cargo of masts through Jean Tuffet, a La Rochelle merchant who traded for many years to Acadia on his own account and in partnership with others, and in 1639 Winter was directing a cargo to pipe staves to Trelawny in Plymouth.[41] Capital and marketing were closely tied to each other and to Europe.

Capital and marketing were not, however, the only respects in which the northeastern maritime colonies had to call upon European resources on a continuing basis. Labour, too, was continually in short supply, and it was necessary to import indentured labourers on a more or less temporary basis. The sedentary fishery plant at Richmond's Island, for example, in July 1637 had a total complement of 47 persons and was perhaps rather larger than that of Nicolas Denys at Port Rossignol in 1633; each required both a nucleus of long-term residents and a shifting population of short-term fishermen and labourers.[42] Labour was also needed by fur-trading enterprises, such as the Laconia Company, as well as logging operations, such as that briefly run at La Hève by Nicolas Denys in 1635 with a work force of twelve men.[43] It is not surprising, therefore, to find considerable use of short-term indentures to bring both skilled and unskilled workers from Europe. A series of indentures in 1642, for example, bound Edmond Andrewes, described as a blacksmith, Robert Saunders, a husbandman, Benjamin Stephens, also a husbandman, and John and Avis Burridge, a husbandman and his wife, to go to Richmond's Island for a period of three years to work 'in planting, fyshing, and in other labour' for a variety of wage agreements.[44] Many similar contractual arrangements may be found in connection with Acadia; in the year 1636, for example, Jean Tuffet recruited men to work at Cape Breton, on a concession made to him and his partner Pierre Desportes by the Cent-Associés. Among those indentured on the prevailing three-year contract were Jean Bourgeois, a carpenter, Pierre Bonnèfre, a stonemason, Jacques Bouildron, a baker, and Jean Sauvaget, a labourer; also recruited were mariners contracted for single voyages.[45]

Labourers moved back and forth across the Atlantic between Europe and the northeastern colonies with some regularity and in sizeable groups. In 1639, for example, twenty-five men were sent by Launay-Rasilly to the aid of d'Aulnay. The labour market was not an easy one on either side – both the Laconia Company and the Razilly/d'Aulnay company were backward in the payment of wages and shares, the Laconia Company still having such debts outstanding as late as 1639.[46] This problem occasionally led to desertions at Richmond's Island, especially in view of the available opportunities for private fishing; in 1636 Winter reported to Trelawny that 'som of them fell into such a mutany, and they ar gon away from the plantation, and do purpose to fish for them selves.'[47] The employment of men in Europe to work in the colonies, therefore, had its disadvantages, but since labour was constantly in short supply such recruitment was necessary. As Winter recommended to Trelawny in 1634, 'yf you do resolve to keepe forth fishinge heare you may please to agree with men at home, for I thinke they are to be hired better Cheepe at home then the[y] will be heare ...'[48]

A further striking aspect of the colonies' economic relationship to Europe was their dependence upon the various parent countries for basic supplies of food and clothing. The predominant concept held in this regard by colonial promoters was that of 'relief': a colony which was unrelieved would perish. In the case of New Scotland, Sir William Alexander had addressed an urgent appeal to the Earl of Menteith in February 1630 for assistance in dispatching 'my sone's supplie, whereupon his saftie or ruine doth depend'; Sir George Home, an employee of Alexander, had been active in Scotland at this time in gathering provisions for New Scotland before sailing for Port Royal in the spring.[49] The necessity of supply from the mother country was certainly seen as paramount, and rightly so. In the following year, the English settlement at Piscataqua under the Laconia Company was shown to be in similar straits when the English Privy Council on 6 March 1631 accorded permission to one Captain Henry Keyes 'to transporte thirtie quarters of Meale, and twenty quarters of Pease, from the Porte of Portsmouth to Pascatoway in New-England, for the reliefe of his Majesties Subjects the planters there, who through want of such supply are not able to proceede to a farther discovery of those partes.'[50] The Trelawny plantation at Richmond's Island, although its limited agricultural endeavours (which in 1639 employed seven husbandmen) enjoyed consider- able success, remained dependent upon imported provisions. On 10 January 1636, Edward Trelawny, then in Boston, wrote to his brother Robert that 'The Country [meaning New England as a whole] ... is sicke in a gennerall want of provissions,' and suggested that such goods should be imported from Ireland, 'where they are Cheape.' Similarly in July 1638, Winter reported that 'vittells is very hard to be gotten heare: yf any to sell, yt is very deare, and I use all the meanes I Cann, and yett I Cannot provide Innough by much to mainetaine our people their 4 mealls of flesh a weeke.'[51]

Relief shipments were also essential to the Acadian settlements. Nicolas Denys recalled that it was he who suggested the placing of return cargoes of timber on the ships which had brought provisions to Razilly's Acadia, 'sans quoy ils auroient esté obligez de s'en retourner à vuide en France.'[52] Indeed, the necessity for relief shipments, along with capital investment, accounts for the massive debts to Le Borgne built up by d'Aulnay. As early as 1634 and 1635, d'Aulnay was obtaining both trade goods and essential provisions from Le Borgne, the plan being that these should be paid for out of the profits of the year's trading. Such voyages continued over a long period. In September 1642, for example, Le Borgne freighted a shipload of 'plusieurs marchandises et vivres' for Acadia, by order of d'Aulnay.[53] Even after the death of d'Aulnay, an agreement made in 1650 between his father, René de Menou de Charnisay, and Le Borgne provided that the latter would undertake 'la despence des envois ... pour la subsistance et gaiges et nourriture des hommes qui y [Acadie] sont à présent et qu'il sera besoing d'y envoyer pour l'entretien du négoce ...'[54] La Tour, naturally, also shared the need to obtain supplies for his settlements, albeit for a much smaller resident population. In late 1632, he was dealing at La Rochelle with Pierre Martin, a ship's captain who agreed to supply provisions for a fishing settlement for the coming season.[55] The function of finding such supplies was shortly delegated to La Tour's agent, Guillaume Desjardins, and it is significant that in the years 1640–5, during which there was open conflict between d'Aulnay and La Tour, one of d'Aulnay's prime tactics was to induce the French government to forbid the sending of supplies to La Tour by Desjardins. On 18 July 1643, for example, the royal Conseil des Finances confirmed and reiterated previous orders that any 'navires, hommes, vivres, munitions ou marchandises' sent by Desjardins to the rebel La Tour were to be treated as contraband and seized accordingly.[56]

The imposition of sanctions upon La Tour's supplies is evidence of the dependence of the Acadian settlements upon Europe, in that such a measure was expected to bring about economic strangulation. La Tour's response, however, illustrates that this dependence upon Europe was not as absolute as it once had been: La Tour sent to the English colony of Massachusetts for help. Arriving in Boston in November 1641, an envoy from La Tour proposed free commerce between him and Massachusetts, which was agreed. Upon a request for aid against d'Aulnay and one 'that he might make return of goods out of England by our merchants,' the Massachusetts authorities procrastinated, but a further mission from La Tour in September 1642 resulted a short time later in a number of Massachusetts merchants sending a pinnace 'to trade with La Tour in St. John's river.'[57] A third embassy in June 1643, this time by La Tour himself, resulted in a prolonged debate within the Massachusetts colony as to whether to give him aid. Eventually, much to the displeasure of certain interests chiefly centred in the northern counties of Essex and Norfolk, permission was granted La Tour to seek private assistance from Massachusetts merchants.[58] Such assistance was quickly given, notably by Edward Gibbons and Thomas Hawkins, and thus was created the nucleus of an interest group in Boston which sought to exploit Acadian trade. Many and various as were Gibbons' trading interests, his investment in Acadia was a major one: La Tour's account with Gibbons showed an outstanding debit balance of £2,084 by May 1645.[59] La Tour's association with Massachusetts did not long continue to be a happy one; in 1646 he fled to Quebec to escape the victorious d'Aulnay and defaulted on his debts as well as forcibly seizing a Massachusetts trading vessel.[60] The fact remained, however, that trade relations had been established and the Massachusetts colony was able to offset Acadian dependence upon France for both capital and supplies.

In Maine also, the expanding economic power of Boston was making itself felt. As early as 1636, John Winter found a market in Massachusetts for the poorer quality fish from Richmond's Island: 'I do purpose,' he reported on 28 June, 'to send the fish that we save now in the hott weather into the Bay.'[61] This marketing arrangement, particularly in view of the shortage of currency prevalent in New England at this time, was also a means of obtaining supplies for the Trelawny plantation, as Winter noted in July 1638 in reporting that 'I have not Received the Cout [account] out of the Bay for the fish that hath bin sold their ... but I thinke I have payment for the most part in goats and Cloth and beads ...'[62] As the fur trade began to decline in southern New England owing to extinction of the beaver, and with the expansion of the New England-based fishery as traditional fishing patterns were disrupted by the civil war in England, Massachusetts merchants were further encouraged to turn their eyes northeastward.[63] In July 1641, when Winter heard that Trelawny was considering selling the Richmond's Island plantation, he commented that, while 'I take yt to be the best plantation in the land,' yet 'I thinke this Country will hardly afford a Chapman [buyer] for yt, except the gentell men in the Bay will Joine togeather to buy yt; yt would be a very good Commodious place for them now they do fall into fishing trade.'[64] Massachusetts, with a population of some 14,000 by 1650, was by far the largest New England colony and was by that time showing signs, greatly intensified by the English civil war, of taking over many of the economic functions in Maine which had previously been fulfilled by England.[65]

At their outset the northeastern maritime colonies were dependent upon Europe for all the most basic elements of survival. Old problems, particularly those stemming from the conflict of interest between trade and colonization, were not easily solved. In the early 1640s, for example, d'Aulnay wrote a memorandum to the king of France in which, after castigating his colonizing rival La Tour, he complained of the large number of interloping traders in Acadia who were depriving him of his due means of subsistence.[66] Indeed, the magnitude of d'Aulnay's debts in France at the time of his death in 1650 is proof in itself of the financial losses which were still inherent in colonization. Nevertheless, the dependence of the colonies upon Europe and European merchants did in a sense contain the seeds of its own destruction; the various commercial ventures, together with the more overtly colonial efforts, brought a shifting but significant population to the colonies, some of which became permanent. This was especially true in Maine, where the single coastline encouraged the prosecution of agriculture in the same areas where the fishery and the fur trade were centred: for example, of thirty-eight persons known to have been sent to New England by the Laconia Company, at least seven were included in official lists of Maine inhabitants compiled in the 1650s.[67] The increasing power of the Massachusetts colony was also beginning to take over a certain amount of Europe's traditional role, and so the period up until 1650 may be seen as one in which European domination of the northeastern maritime colonies decreased. This did not mean any great degree of economic independence, nor did it mean that previous problems had been solved – many of the colonial promoters of Maine, for example, were described by a contemporary in 1646 as having 'manifold debts to people in the [Massachusetts] Bay and else wher' – but it did signify that the context of economic relationships was shifting from an exclusively European towards an increasingly American one.[68]

Government: Assertions and Abdications

The problem of providing effective government for distant American colonies was a novel and perplexing one for the crowns of northern Europe. The monarchs of France, England, and Scotland had expended much effort in the previous centuries to consolidate their authority within their European realms, but the addition of colonies brought a new dimension to the old danger of fragmentation. Although American colonies as such were at this time of small import to their parent countries, the existence of agglomerations of subjects outside the normal confines of the realm could never be entirely ignored by a European government. It is not surprising, therefore, that a variety of solutions was attempted, with widely varying results. In general, the period from 1630 to 1650 was not one in which European authority was able to find satisfactory expression, and this tendency was accentuated by internal struggles within the European countries themselves.

The question of government in New Scotland did not attain the same dimensions as its equivalents in Maine and Acadia, because New Scotland was never in a position to develop as a community under the Scots crown after 1632. There are indications that the Scots crown as such was by 1635 considering abandonment even of its remaining responsibilities through the device of consolidating New Scotland with New England. On 5 January 1635, Charles I wrote to Sir Ferdinando Gorges of his desire 'that some good course be establisched for right prosecution of the work of the Plantation of New Scotland,' mentioning that he had 'bene pleased to mak choyse of yow for undertaking the cheiff charge in manageing of such things as shalbe for the good of that cuntrie,' and requiring Gorges to come to court to receive instructions.[69] On 29 January, presumably as a result of the royal instruction to Gorges, Stirling and his son, now Lord Alexander, were admitted as members of the Council for New England, and participated in a division of the land of New England early in February. In the division, Alexander received a grant of the northeasternmost area of New England, between the Kennebec and Ste Croix rivers, to be held in the same manner as Gorges' province of New Somersetshire, granted at the same time.[70]

Whether New Scotland was intended to be included within the area to be governed by Sir Ferdinando Gorges, who was by March designated as future governor of New England, is not clear. The grant of New England land to Lord Alexander, formalized on 22 April 1635, described the land as 'next adjoininge to Newe Scotland,' thus implying a continuing separation of identity, but the royal letter to Gorges of 5 January would suggest that his government was to include the Scottish colony. The Alexanders' New England grant may well have been intended as a compensation, as may an order of 28 January that Stirling might display the arms of New Scotland with unique prominence, 'considering that he hath in particular and singular manner deserved the said augmentation of the Armes of New Scotland.'[71] No commission was ever in fact issued to Gorges as governor, and in 1636 Stirling was still describing himself as the royal lieutenant of New Scotland; in short, neither Gorges nor Stirling had any real authority to govern there.[72] Stirling continued to take an interest in America – he occasionally played host to meetings of 'the late Council for New England' and as late as April 1639 was still hoping that his interests in the fur trade might be a means of rescuing his ruined finances – but he lacked the means to settle or govern a colony.[73] New Scotland was thus subsumed into the confusion of English colonial arrangements.

Several years later, on 23 December 1644, John Winthrop the younger addressed a letter from Boston to a Scottish nobleman, Lord Forbes, in which he raised the question of what had become of the government of 'Nova Scotia, called Acadia, where my lord Starling once possessed a goodly harbour, and a fort in it called Port Royall ...' Winthrop, who had some months previously acquired an interest in the Acadian fur trade along with Gibbons and Hawkins, clearly saw Scots rule in that region as a potential benefit to the security of his investment, and put this more broadly in stating that 'the English colonies heere would be gret to have their brethren of Scotland to be their neighbours in enjoying that antient right is conceived they had of Nova Scotia.' He therefore enquired 'whether the State of Scotland hath wholy deserted that country, and disclaime all right and interest therein, and upon what ground, whether only upon my lord Sterling's surrender.'[74] Technically, the correct answer was that the Scots claim still stood, but the desertion by the state of Scotland was nevertheless a fact. A further fact, and one which was to be of great importance in the subsequent history of the northeastern maritime region, was that primary interest in the government of New Scotland now existed not in Scotland but in Massachusetts.

The history of the governmental relations of Maine and Acadia with Europe is rather more complex, since both of these colonies contained actual communities and thus could not be ignored so readily. In view of the practical shortcomings of the Council for New England and the Compagnie de la Nouvelle-France in their governmental responsibilities, it was not surprising that the crowns of France and England should seek other means with which to establish their authority. With respect to Acadia, the first sign of such a change came in early 1631, with the commissioning of Charles de Saint-Étienne de La Tour as 'lieutenant-général au pais de l'Acadie, Fort Louys, port de la Tour, et lieux qui en despendent en la Nouvelle France.' Richelieu's letter presenting La Tour to the king for this position noted that 'dans ledit pais de la Nouvelle France il y a plusieurs contrées et provinces ausquelles il faut pourvoir d'ung chef et lieutenant général de Sa Majesté pour y commander, entre autres en la coste de l'Acadie et lieux qui en despendent.'[75] This conception of New France contained elements that were markedly absent from that of 1627, when neither Acadia nor any other such province had been mentioned. In a sense, La Tour's appointment was an act of weakness by the crown, aimed at ensuring his allegiance – the concern of Charles I and his negotiators in 1631 that La Tour should come to no harm at the hands of the French government was based on an underestimation of La Tour's value, as Richelieu tacitly admitted to the negotiators in March of that year in assuring them 'that our desires were already effected by a Commission given of late by this Kinge to the said de la Tour' – but the decision to accord royal commissions of government to provincial heads within New France was an effort to assert authority.[76]

A further such effort followed in 1632 with the appointment of Isaac de Razilly as 'lieutenant-général pour le Roi, en la Nouvelle-France,' a title used to describe Razilly in his grant of the bay and river of Ste Croix in May that year. While the exact relationship between La Tour's and Razilly's authority is unclear, the two were certainly intended to be complementary.[77] Both La Tour and Razilly soon received large seigneurial grants, and were accorded the right to share the fur trade equally between them. In 1633, La Tour, in return for his share of the fur trade, agreed to assume the entire responsibility for the upkeep of the posts at Cap de Sable and on the St John River, and some two years later he received these lands as fiefs from the Compagnie de la Nouvelle-France. Razilly started his period in Acadia with his seigneury at the Ste Croix River, and in early 1634 his brother Launay-Rasilly was awarded the further concessions of the settlements at La Hève and Port Royal, as well as Sable Island.[78]

The continuing necessity for settlement had thus led the French crown to combine government with land-owning and trading privileges. The result, however, was a potentially disruptive accumulation of local power in two places. As long as La Tour and the Razillys were on co-operative terms and loyal to the crown, the situation would be stable enough, and this state of affairs did indeed prevail until the death of Isaac de Razilly in 1635. Thereafter, relations deteriorated between La Tour and d'Aulnay, who acted until 1642 under the authority of Launay-Rasilly but was recognized by the crown from 1638 as lieutenant general of half Acadia. To have two strong, rival powers, each claiming to hold authority from the crown, was clearly intolerable. On 10 February 1638, Louis XIII wrote d'Aulnay to signify his hope 'qu'il y ayt bonne intelligence entre vous et le Sieur de la Tour,' and to give instructions for the formation of two spheres of influence. Under only Richelieu, the king informed d'Aulnay, 'vous soyez mon Lieutenant general en la coste des Etchemins, a prendre depuis le milieu de la terre ferme de la Baie françoise entirant vers les Virginies, et gouverneur du Pentagouet.' La Tour, on the other hand, was to be 'mon Lieutenant général en la coste d'Acadie ... depuis le milieu de ladite Baie françoise jusques au détroit de Canceau.'[79]

There was, however, one problem which the letter recognized but could not solve. Both La Tour and d'Aulnay had strong points scattered in various parts of Acadia, so that no division of territory could be fully effective. Thus La Tour's area of government included d'Aulnay's major settlement at Port Royal, while the area allocated to d'Aulnay included La Tour's fort on the St John River. Violent conflict ensued and was ended only temporarily when the two agreed to take their grievances to France for royal arbitration. Under the influence of d'Aulnay, who himself visited France on this occasion, this agreement led to an attempt at assertion of royal power. In February 1641, a series of measures struck hard at La Tour. On 1 February, the royal Conseil privé dismissed legal action against d'Aulnay by the widow of La Tour's principal sea captain, Pierre Jamin, who had been killed in an encounter in the previous year; La Tour and his followers, declared the council, were the aggressors. On the 13th an order was transmitted to d'Aulnay, informing him that La Tour had been summoned to France to answer for his behaviour, and that in the event of his refusal to obey he, d'Aulnay, was empowered to seize La Tour: 'vous vous servirez de tous les moyens, et forces, que vous pourrez, et mettrez les forts, qui sont entre ses mains, en celles de personnes fidelles ... '

Furthermore, on 24 February, d'Aulnay was himself given command of La

Tour's fort at Cap de Sable. Thus the French crown made a first attempt at attacking the new problem of over-mighty subjects in the colonies by relying heavily upon d'Aulnay.[80]

For the English crown and government, the same problem presented itself in a rather different way. Rather than having two local powers vying with one another and thus causing an affront to the king's peace, New England was now the site of a colony, Massachusetts, which was growing so rapidly in size and strength that, as a single dominant local power, it was increasingly seen as a threat to royal authority and as a congregating point for religious and political dissent. The Council for New England, formally charged with the government of that region, was far outstripped by the new colony in power and even in authority, since Massachusetts enjoyed government by a royal charter which had been brought to America perfectly legally. Some accommodation was clearly necessary between crown and colony, and the inclinations of Archbishop Laud towards assertion of royal power ensured in what direction the crown would move.

As in the case of the French government, Laud's actions had two aspects: the coercive, aimed at cutting down the strength of the Massachusetts colony, and the constructive, aimed at establishing royal authority in the gap created. The negative aspect already had a certain amount of experience on which to draw: private attempts had been made in 1632 by Gorges and others, who felt their interests to be infringed by the Massachusetts colony, to have its charter invalidated, though a Privy Council hearing had at that time vindicated the colony.[81] Under Laud, the spirit of this unsuccessful attack was powerfully revived. Following the brief stay of emigration to New England in February 1634, a more fundamental step was taken in April that year, when a royal commission was issued appointing Laud and eleven other privy councillors as a board for plantations, with extensive powers over the internal affairs of all colonies, including powers over all patents and charters. This board was clearly intended as an agent of royal coercion.[82] Further evidence of the government's determination was given in the opening in 1635 of *quo warranto* proceedings against the Massachusetts charter. The positive side of the plan was seen in the designation of Gorges as future general governor of New England. On 25 April 1635, the patent of the Council for New England was resigned to the crown explicitly in order that New England should be taken into the king's hands.[83] Although no commission had been issued to Gorges, a manifesto of 23 July 1637 detailed the royal intent. The Council for New England, it was recalled, had proved unable to redress 'the many inconveniences and mischeifs that have growne and are like more and more to arise amongst Our Subjects allready planted in the parts of New England by reason of the severall opinions differing humors and many other differences springing up betweene them and dayly like to encrease'; accordingly, the crown would 'apply thereunto Our immediate power and authority,' in the person of Gorges as governor.[84]

Both English and French governments, therefore, responded to dangerous accumulations of local power in the colonies by attempting to assert royal authority. In the English case, the attempt was more centralized, in that Gorges, while he would also continue to hold his province of New Somerset-shire and would thus to that extent combine landholding with governmental authority, was more obviously tied to the crown and its newly created board for plantations. Both, however, endeavoured to harness the efforts of an interested party in order to coerce recalcitrant subjects, by military means in the French case, by political means in the English. It was in this use of interested parties that the strength and the weakness of both approaches lay. The advantages of so doing were obvious enough: d'Aulnay and Gorges could each use his own particular expertise in bringing La Tour and the Massachusetts colony under control. The disadvantage was that by using these interested parties the crown was involving itself in private quarrels, and the penalty for failure would in all likelihood be a serious loss of prestige and authority. Such proved to be the event both in Acadia and in New England, and the result was a virtual abdication of the more active elements of royal authority.

In New England, this situation quickly came about. The Massachusetts colony, employing a tactic of delay and evasion which was to serve it well for many years thereafter, simply refused to answer any of the charges against it. Confronted with this intransigence, the royal government failed to respond effectively, as royal governments in England would continue to fail for some forty years to come. The board created by Laud had not developed with any vigour, and the attention of all those involved in government was in any case being increasing diverted to the problems arising in the later years of Charles I's personal rule, which would shortly lead to civil war. Thus, this phase of active governmental interest in the colonies was short and exceptional. More fundamentally, though, there was deep uncertainty as to how to confront intransigence. The reduction of local power in England had been accomplished by the crown many decades previously, and even the turbulence of the Welsh and Scottish marches had been brought more nearly under control. To have this same problem recur, and to have it recur in what could not but be seen as the first genuinely successful English colony in the northern part of North America, presented the government with a novel and confusing situation.

It was in these circumstances that the proprietary charter of the Province of Maine was issued in April 1639, and this resort to proprietary government must be seen as a setback for the crown. The plan for a general government of New England was abandoned, and Gorges was instead granted both land and government, as well as certain trading privileges, in a single province.[85] The crown thus defaulted in its conflict with Massachusetts, and even in the newly created Province of Maine it delegated its authority to Gorges as lord proprietor. As such, and holding the province 'in free and common Soccage,' the easiest possible form of tenure, Gorges was entitled to all the contemporary powers of the palatine bishop of Durham, as well as other rights and privileges which went far beyond those of the Durham palatinate in the seventeenth century.[86]

The 'Bishop of Durham' clause is particularly revealing in that it exemplifies the way in which proprietary provinces were created in conscious imitation of medieval palatinates. The oldest of these great franchises in England, while originating not as conscious royal creations but as survivals or accumulations of liberties, came to be seen in the course of the middle ages as instruments for maintaining peace and order in the outlying areas of the realm, and by the reign of Edward III a royal practice had grown up of deliberately creating such units for this purpose. As the monarchy strengthened its central authority, however, royal councils, instruments of direct royal control, had superseded palatinates, and the reign of Henry VIII saw even the palatinate of Durham considerably diminished.[87] The Province of Maine was in a general sense a return to the principle of the medieval palatinate, and in the context of the recent abandonment of a plan for central government of New England, it may be taken to signal the replacement of a more modern by a more medieval style of authority. America, with its wide scope for the accumulation of local power, had reintroduced the problem of the over-mighty subject; for the moment, it had been decided that medieval ailments demanded medieval remedies, and the Province of Maine was intended as a counterweight to the dangerous strength of Massachusetts. In this sense, the proprietary government of Maine was an assertion of royal authority, and one which had the added advantage of compensating the bankrupt Gorges for his colonial endeavours. The fact remained, however, that in all practical terms it was a retrenchment and an abdication.

The French government's support for d'Aulnay in Acadia seemed for a time to have been more successful. In this case, there had been no shrinking from the prospect of confronting intransigence and d'Aulnay, assisted in 1642 and 1643 by further royal measures against La Tour and his agent Desjardins, waged open war on his opponent. La Tour was not, of course, helpless, and he too took advantage of the opportunities offered by America to withdraw himself far from opposing authority. More specifically, he gathered all his forces at his fort on the St John River, and dealt with the Massachusetts colony for supplies and aid. Eventually, however, La Tour sustained a crushing defeat in 1645, when d'Aulnay seized and demolished the fort on the St John; although La Tour was in Boston at this time and so escaped death or capture, he was forced to flee to Quebec, where he arrived in August 1646.[88]

D'Aulnay's success brought immediate letters of congratulation from the young Louis XIV and from the queen mother as regent.[89] Some time thereafter, in February 1647, there followed letters patent in which d'Aulnay was granted wide powers and privileges as 'Gouverneur et nostre Lieutenant General, representant nostre Personne, en tous les ... païs, territoire, coste et confins de la Cadye,' Acadia being generously, if somewhat vaguely, defined as extending from the Gulf of St Lawrence to '[les] Virgines.' On this territory, d'Aulnay was given essentially viceregal powers of government, land allocation, and trade. Save that no reference was made to his heirs, his grant was virtually a proprietorial one.[90] Thus, English and French practices converged once again. Both had set out to assert royal authority, and both had arrived by different routes at the same point: Gorges's grant was a result of the retrenchment of a more centralized plan, while d'Aulnay's was a logical extension of the crown's decision to support him in 1641.

Neither grant, however, succeeded as planned, and the respective royal commitments to Gorges and d'Aulnay failed in the long run to disguise the essential weakness of royal authority. This may, of course, be explained partly by the European difficulties of both English and French crowns. Although the interest taken by Laud and Richelieu in colonial affairs was real, it could not survive the competition of domestic crises. Thus, the outbreak of the English civil war totally diverted the crown from colonial matters, and the reins were only gradually and uncertainly taken up by the parliamentary authorities. In France, the minority of Louis XIV and the outbreak of the Fronde suspended in practical terms any great attention to the colonies. Even setting aside these European factors, however, the proprietorial efforts in Maine and Acadia were seriously flawed, in that they depended too heavily in each case upon a single man. D'Aulnay was indisputably the dominant figure in Acadia between 1645 and 1650, a fact which he underscored in defying the Cent-Associés by seizing their fishing and trading bases in Cape Breton and at Miscou.[91] After his death in 1650, however, Acadia fell back into chaos, as all the dammed-up forces of fragmentation again had full scope. Gorges was also able for a short time to govern his province through his kinsman Thomas Gorges, who was in Maine as governor between 1640 and 1643. Sir Ferdinando, however, never himself went to America and was never able to fulfil his complex plans for the government of his province.[92] After Thomas Gorges' departure, Maine also fell prey to centrifugal forces which effectively pulled the province apart. Both Gorges and d'Aulnay, moreover, had, like Stirling, been bankrupted by many years of expensive colonial endeavours. Neither was in any financial position to contribute significantly either to economic or political elaboration in their territories, and neither crown at this time showed signs of supplying this need. The immense powers given to d'Aulnay and Gorges were given in the name of royal authority, but the weakness of royal authority is what they most aptly illustrate.

Thus, the period from 1630 to 1650 was not an encouraging one for the crowns of England, Scotland, and France in the northeastern maritime region, any more than it was in Europe itself. To be sure, European political authority did not cease to be important in the colonies. The crown, or in England and Scotland the prevailing authority during the civil war and interregnum, continued to be the fount of all legitimate colonial authority and was recognized as such even by the Massachusetts colony. When John Winthrop the younger hoped for friendly government in New Scotland, it was to 'the State of Scotland' that he looked. When George Cleeve, a contender in conflicts within Maine, wished to erect a separate province in order to secure his land claims, it was to the English parliament that he applied.[93] When La Tour, after d'Aulnay's death, wished to reassert his claims in Acadia, it was to the crown that he went to obtain a commission as 'Gouverneur et notre lieutenant general representant notre personne.'[94] Yet, beyond this need for legitimacy, which was real and a powerful tie to Europe, no effective way had yet been found of relating America to Europe in terms of government. Massachusetts, on the other hand, the only genuinely stable and powerful colony in the northern part of North America, was quickly becoming capable of filling any vacuum which occurred. The real question was whether the European crowns would find a way to assert their authority before the Massachusetts colony developed an inclination to use its power.

CHAPTER 3

Relationships with
Native Peoples

First Contacts

In the northeastern maritime region, European relations with the native inhabitants were early associated by both sides with the fur trade. Verrazzano and
Cartier are known to have traded in the region early in the sixteenth century,
and they were certainly not the first. The trade continued sporadically throughout the century before expanding rapidly in the latter decades as demand for
furs increased in France. The English were later entrants to the trade, but the
explorers Bartholomew Gosnold and Bartholomew Gilbert in 1602 found
themselves invited to meet a group of Indians on shore to be presented with 'a
large Beaver skin'; thereupon 'we became very great friends ... [and] the rest of
the day we spent in trading with them for Furres.'[1] The voyage of de Monts
found a thriving fur trade in Acadia, and one of de Monts' first acts was to
confiscate the ship of a certain Captain Rossignol, 'lequel troquoit en pelleterie
avec les Sauvages, contre les defences du Roy,' following which de Monts
quickly established relations with the Indians on his own account.[2] Even the
Sagadahoc colonists, who eventually incurred Indian enmity, received at first a
guardedly friendly welcome.[3] The later English visitor and would-be colonist
Christopher Levett took trouble to establish good relations with Indian sagamores at Saco. 'I then told them ... that if at any time they did Trucke with mee,
they should have many good things in lieu of their Beaver: and if they did not
Trucke it was no matter, I would be good friends with them ... '[4] The New
Scotland colonists at Port Royal, in one of the rare details of the history of that
settlement, were visited shortly after their arrival by '2 savages in a Canou,'
and a few weeks later by '9 savages in a Shalles from S. Jhons River with
beaver skines and hydes [who] gave the generall a present.'[5]

The fur trade provided a means of introduction between European and Indian and a basis for good relations. Not that relations were always good: several even of the friendliest exchanges were preceded by mutual suspicion and consequent resort to armed force. The first reaction of Cartier and his men in 1534 to being surrounded by Micmac canoes was that 'nous leurs tirames deux passevollans parsur eux,' and then 'leur lachames deux lanses à feu, qui passèrent parmy eulx, qui les estonna fort, tellement qu'ilz se mydrent alla fuyte, à moult grant haste, et ne nous suyvirent plus.'[6] Although on this occasion the next day's trading was still able to take place, mutual fear and suspicion could lead to damaging skirmishes. Champlain lost a man in a clash on the coast of what was to be southern New England and concluded of the Indians there that 'il se faut donner garde de ces peuples, et vivre en mesfiance avec eux, toutefois sans leur faire apperçevoir.' Similarly, the Sagadahoc colonists in 1607 had an armed confrontation with Kennebec Indians when suspicions were raised by a series of minor misunderstandings during a trading session.[7] Nevertheless, there were good reasons on both sides to desire peace and regular trade. For the Europeans, the fur trade was of obvious importance, either as an end in itself or as an economic support for colonization. Knowledge of the hunting and trapping grounds, mobility, and ability to deal with the American environment made the Indian an indispensable part of the trade, and this in itself was sufficient to make the European seek friendly relations. In the earliest stages of colonization, moreover, Indian goodwill was essential for the Europeans' survival in America, which was clearly an incentive for peaceful contacts.

The Indian was also disposed to favour friendly relations with the newcomers. First of all, the European in the early stages of colonization was not normally perceived as a threat. Once the initial fears and suspicions had been allayed, the European in his trading ship or cloistered in his communal colony on the edge of the continent obviously lacked the power to do serious harm. Nor did the small colonial establishments of the early period deprive the Indian of any significant area of land. Trade with the Europeans was seen by the Indians as a useful means of improving their way of life without departing from a traditional framework. The trade items most in demand were those which had an obvious use within Indian society: copper kettles for cooking, iron knives and hatchets for domestic use and – along with firearms – for hunting and warfare, cloth for clothing, beads or mirrors for their aesthetic value, and so on. All of these commodities were selected by the Indians not to change their culture, but to deepen and strengthen it. As a Micmac chief remarked in 1605, the idea was 'se servir de l'amitié des François ... '; in so far as the European was useful, he was undoubtedly worth tolerating in a friendly manner.[8]

Such an attitude towards the European, however, was dangerous. First of all, contact with European traders, while apparently harmless, proved to be a powerful force for change. This was true in the direct form of depopulation, and also in the gradual erosion of the material and spiritual bases of Indian society and the upsetting of the environmental balances on which that society depended. The principal instrument of depopulation was the introduction of European disease, to which the native peoples had no immunity. Added to this was the problem of alcohol addiction, which began to affect Indian health in the earliest phases of the fur trade and became increasingly dangerous in the seventeenth century as brandy displaced wine as a trade commodity. Furthermore, the desire for European trade goods led to intensified hunting of fur-bearing animals; the restraints which religious observance had customarily imposed were thrust aside, and both the spiritual and the ecological basis of Indian society were threatened. Social organization was threatened also: as the beaver came to be the main quarry of the hunt, instead of being only one of several, the traditional division of hunting territories in the common interest by the chief of the band began to lose its purpose and the interest of the individual hunter became correspondingly more important. Moreover, as the beaver hunt absorbed more and more time, other activities were neglected; dependence upon the European trader increased, not only for manufactured items and liquor, but even for supplies of food. Thus, the process became self-perpetuating, and efforts to cope with it would influence Indian responses to European colonial attempts throughout the seventeenth century.[9]

There was also another danger posed by the presence of the European that was not immediately apparent. Initially, the Indian had no way of assessing the motives of the European and the nature of his interest in America. Although the two cultures inevitably came into contact, it is hardly true to say that they met, since neither side, in the early stages at least, had any real understanding of the other. In the fur trade the European could no more understand the Indian's lack of a sense of private property, which in turn led to an essentially non-commercial view of the trade, than the Indian could understand the European desire to accumulate possessions.[10] More broadly, the reconceptualization of America which was implicit in European colonization was as incomprehensible to the Indian as the spiritually determined bond between the Indian and his environment was incomprehensible to the European. At first, Indian observers could only conclude that the European had come to North America simply to trade and to live in small communal establishments. But the whole thrust of the colonizing activities of French, English, and Scots was to break free of such restraints and to colonize on such an extensive scale that the vast territories they claimed would be transformed from their previous 'wilderness' state. If that process were successfully put in hand, Indian-European relations would clearly enter a new phase, in which solid reasons for hostility on either side might well arise.

For the Europeans, this change would inevitably be a self-conscious one; the expansion of colonies was a deliberate endeavour. As such, it would raise basic questions as to how native peoples were to be regarded and what place they would be accorded in the new scheme. The problem was certainly not unique to French, English, and Scots, nor was it unprecedented. Indeed, the earlier contacts of Spaniards with the people of Central and South America had spawned a multiplicity of theories as to the origins and nature of such peoples, which soon became the common intellectual property of all Europe. At one extreme, the Indian was seen as a brutish creature, a cannibal, and hopelessly inferior to the European. At the other extreme, he was the 'bon sauvage' of Montaigne, tragically subjected to the corruption and greed of rapacious colonists. In between was a vast range of opinions in which the Indian was agreed to be uncivilized and unchristian, but which differed as to what extent he was susceptible to improvement, and whether violence or peaceful persuasion should be used to induce a change for the better.[11]

For the Spanish, these questions were not merely academic ones, since they impinged upon the whole conduct of Indian affairs in New Spain, and upon the justice of the Spanish conquest. Was the Indian entitled only to a place of servitude, as befitted a barbarian race conquered by a civilized one? The conquistadores who had become the colonists of New Spain had obvious reasons for supporting this view. If the Indian was assumed to be in such a degraded state that forced submission to Christianity and civilization was necessary, then the violence of the conquest was morally justified. More practically, the forced labour of the Indians so essential to the economy of New Spain was also justified.[12] If, on the other hand, the Indian was considered to be fully human, capable of accepting the Christian faith through peaceful teaching, and able to aspire to the full benefits of society and religion, the case was very different. The Spanish scholastic thinkers, and particularly Bartolomé de Las Casas, upheld this view. 'All men throughout the world,' argued Las Casas, 'however barbarian and brutal they may be, can, since they are men, attain to the use of reason and the understanding of matters pertaining to instruction and doctrine ...'[13] This form of reasoning found strong support in New Spain through the agency of the church, and a conflict ensued over its philosophical and practical implications which continued even beyond the colonial period.

The same conflict arose in the colonies of North America, including those in the northeastern maritime region. Here the conditions were different, since no conquest, or even large-scale population invasion as in Massachusetts, had taken place. But the essential problem remained that of reconciling the transformation of portions of America into colonial societies with the continuing existence of the Indian. Was the Indian to be seen as an alien, to be used when necessary and otherwise ignored? Or was the care and education of the Indian a stewardship that must be discharged with all possible humanity and diligence? These two questions represent the extreme ends of a continuum which can be observed in both the French and the English colonies of northern North America; they represent the different conclusions which could be drawn from the European assumption of undoubted superiority over the Indian culture and society.

There was, however, a further element, especially in the northeastern maritime region where the European population was sparse: the resilience of the Indian. It was in the 1670s when the missionary Le Clercq was informed by a Micmac chief that 'il n'y a pas de Sauvage, qui ne s'estime infiniment plus heureux, et plus puissant que les François.'[14] The Indians of the northeastern maritime region, despite the pressures of acculturation, were far from passive in their contacts with the colonists. Thus the interactions between the colonists and Indians in the region would inevitably be complex. They would depend not only upon the initial attitudes of each side, but also upon the ways in which the colonists would respond to the continuing power and self-confidence of the native inhabitants.

The Indian as Alien

For the English colonists in the territory which was to become the Province of Maine, the prevailing tendency from the start of colonization as such was to regard the Indian as an alien. In part this was a reflection of attitudes formed in Europe. Such attitudes alone, however, do not account for the steady embitterment of relations between English and Abenaki which led to clear hostility by 1650 and would result in open warfare by 1675. Cultural misunderstandings, particularly over land, generated mistrust, which was intensified on the English side by the accumulation of news of English-Indian conflict elsewhere in America. Furthermore, English attitudes hardened at the same time as their encroachments on Indian land increased; not only did the Indian come to be regarded as a treacherous foe of the English in general, but also as a potential intruder on the landholdings of the colonists. Among the various branches of the Abenaki whose territory lay within the settled area of Maine, resistance inevitably grew up, and so the hostility of one side strengthened that of the other. That no corresponding hostility arose in Acadia was a crucial difference between the two colonies. Yet the difference was not clear or inevitable from the beginning – English and French attitudes towards the Indian shared many of the same elements – but rather arose from the complex patterns of European-Indian relations which developed in the respective colonies during their formative years.

One initial element in both English and French attitudes was the influence of the Spanish example, as interpreted through the growing body of literature relating to America which was becoming available in all major European languages in the second half of the sixteenth century. In England, for example, the works of Las Casas were widely read, and were sympathetically received in at least one important respect. By 1583, when the first translation of the writings of Las Casas was published in English under the title of *The Spanish colonie*, Spain was an enemy nation to the English. Not only could the arguments of Las Casas be read as a crushing indictment of Spanish atrocities in America, but they also gave grounds for questioning the entire moral and legal basis of the Spanish empire. It was in 1584 that Richard Hakluyt mused on the possibilities of an alliance of English and Indians to expel the Spaniards from the New World. Although such a dream was obviously far-fetched, the portrayal by Las Casas of the Indian as an innocent victim of ruthless Spanish abuse was frequently used in England as a reproach to Spain.[15]

Yet the practice of English colonization was more directly influenced by the other side of the ambivalent Spanish example. In 1555, long before the first translation of Las Casas into English, Pietro Martire d'Anghiera's *De orbe novo* had been made available in English by Peter Eden. Nor surprisingly at a time when Queen Mary had recently married Philip II of Spain, Eden's preface to Martire's description of the voyages of Columbus took pains to praise the Spanish conquest of New Spain and to stress that the Indians' 'bondage is such as is much rather to be desired than their former liberty.'[16] While the political advantages to be derived from praise for Spain did not long survive the death of Mary in 1558, this justification of the conquest of a supposedly barbarous race was an appealing one to the colonizers of Ireland in the reign of Elizabeth. Eden himself had close personal connections with the West Country gentry who were involved in Ireland from the 1560s, and the English colonizers were well aware that they were coming close in Ireland to emulating the methods of the Spanish in America.[17] Since it was this same group of West Countrymen that was intimately concerned with the first English colonization of America, the spirit of the conquistador was undoubtedly present in the early colonizing expeditions. In the northeastern maritime region, the Sagadahoc colony provides an example. According to Kennebec Abenaki accounts given to Pierre Biard on his visit to Sagadahoc in late 1611, the English had established good Indian relations under their first commander, George Popham. When Popham died in the winter of 1607–8, however, he was succeeded by Raleigh Gilbert, a member of the Gilbert family which had been deeply involved in Irish colonization. Hereupon, 'les Anglois, soubs un autre capitaine, changerent de façon. Ils repoussoient les Sauvages sans aucun honneur; ils les battoyent, excedoyent et mastinoyent sans beaucoup de retenue.'[18]

Thus the Sagadahoc colony introduced to the region the spirit of the colonization of New Spain and of Ireland. Biard noted that the Kennebecs' experience at this time had inclined them to prefer the French to the English: '[ils] nous racontoient les outrages, qu'ils avoyent receu desdicts Anglois, et nous flattoient: disans qu'ils nous aymoient bien.'[19] Together with the apparently unprovoked attack by the visiting Henry Hudson upon a Penobscot village in 1609, the Sagadahoc colony was obviously a bad start for English-Indian relations. Nor were matters helped by the kidnapping of twenty-four Indians by the English sea captain Thomas Hunt in 1614. According to Sir Ferdinando Gorges, the action of this 'worthless fellow' led to 'a hatred of our whole nation' among the aggrieved Indians, particularly as Hunt had attempted to sell his captives as slaves in Malaga. For his part, Gorges condemned Hunt's treatment of 'the poor innocent creatures, that in confidence of his honesty had put themselves into his hands,' and rejoiced that they had been rescued in Malaga by 'the friars of those parts ... to be instructed in the christian faith.'[20]

Gorges' attitude illustrates that the perception of the Indian as an undesirable inferior was not the only tendency of the English; the desire to convert and civilize was also strong, and in this case led the Protestant Gorges to approve even of the education of Indians by Roman Catholics. Gorges, influenced by Las Casas, rejected 'war and slaughter ... [and] murther of so many millions of the natives as it is horror to be spoken of, especially being done by the hands of the Christians.'[21] Yet by the time of the formation of the Council for New England, even Gorges had moved towards the view that the Indians might be ignored by New England colonists, because of the reduction of their numbers by European disease. The epidemic that prevailed among the Indians of New England from 1616 to 1620 quickly became known in England and was believed to have led to an almost total depopulation of the region.[22] By this means, wrote Gorges later, 'in a manner the greater part of that land was left desert, without any to disturb or oppose our free and peaceable possession thereof; from whence we may justly conclude that God made the way to effect his work, according to the time he had assigned for laying the foundation thereof.' Similarly, the charter of the Council for New England remarked upon the 'utter Destruction, Devastacion, and Depopulacion of that whole Territorye,' which had been 'deserted as it were by ... [its] naturall Inhabitants.'[23] Thus, whether the Indian was considered a barbarian to be disregarded or a native removed by divine intervention, New England could be looked at as an empty land.

New England, of course, was not an empty land. On the contrary, when English visitors and settlers began to arrive in the 1620s, they discovered that there remained a substantial and organized native population.[24] At this point, there was still a real chance that English-Indian relations would develop harmoniously, despite the troubles of the past. Certainly Christopher Levett found a warm welcome during his travels in Maine in 1623 and 1624; in one encounter near Sagadahoc, a group of sagamores 'after some complements ... told me I must be their cozen, and that Captaine [Robert] Gorges was so, (which you may imagine I was not a little proud of, to be adopted cozen to so many great Kings at one instant, but did willingly accept of it.)' Levett, who not only traded for furs but also took the trouble to develop friendly relationships with his trading partners, eventually left for England from Casco Bay in 1624 with expressions of regret from a further group of sagamores and with invitations to return with his wife and children and 'all my friends.'[25] Among Levett's well-wishers was the sagamore Samoset, the same who, travelling further south, had assisted the Plymouth colonists in their efforts to survive in 1620–1; if a land deed dated 15 July 1625 is to be regarded as genuine, Samoset was also one of two Indians who sold some 200 square miles of territory in the region of Pemaquid to the Englishman John Brown.[26] For men such as Levett and Samoset, there was no quarrel between English and Abenaki.

Within ten years, however, it would become clear that the earlier instances of hostility were the real forerunners of future developments. As the English population increased, so suspicions were reawakened and disputes increased. In part, this change was prompted by influences from outside Maine itself, since general English attitudes towards the Indian were affected by events in other colonies. The treatment of Indian peoples as inferior or conquered races, which had been evident in the Sagadahoc colony and in the various efforts to colonize Virginia, had on many occasions produced violent Indian reactions and had led to the identification of treachery as a major element of English perceptions of the native. The Virginia uprising of 1622, while it did not create this image, confirmed and entrenched it.[27]

Increasingly from that time, the 'inconstant savage' would be seen as a potential danger to colonists. Even Levett remarked in his volume published in 1628 that the Abenaki were 'full of Tracherie amongst themselves' and not to be trusted by any Englishman except by keeping 'a strickt hand over them.'[28] The arrival of the Massachusetts Bay colonists added another element. While Old Testament theology had never been absent from justifications of European conquests in the New World – Spanish theologians had early compared the actions of the conquistadores with those of Joshua in the conquest of Canaan by the Israelites – the explicitly religious purpose of the Massachusetts colony gave particular point to this strain of thought. For John Winthrop and the other early Massachusetts leaders, New England was an actual wilderness and a potential Canaan, and although the Indian was to be converted and treated kindly if possible, treachery or resistance to the godly endeavours of the colonists would bring about severe retribution.[29] Although the English settlements in what was to become the Province of Maine were far away from

Virginia and did not form part of the Massachusetts colony, they could not be uninfluenced by such attitudes.

At the same time, English encroachments on Indian land were emerging as a further source of tension. John Winthrop in 1629 enunciated what was from an English point of view an appropriate theory of Indian land rights: 'As for the Natives in New England, they inclose noe Land, neither have any setled habytation, nor any tame Cattle to improve the Land by, and soe have noe other but a Naturall Right to those Countries, soe as if we leave them sufficient for their use, we may lawfully take the rest, there being more than enough for them and us.'[30] For those settlers who were either more scrupulous of Indian land-ownership, or who could obtain land title in no other way, there was of course the option of making formal deeds of purchase from those they identified as the Indian owners. On 17 April 1629, the promoters of the Massachusetts colony wrote from England to Boston to advocate this course, 'that wee may avoyde the least scruple of intrusion'. Much later, in 1661, Ferdinando Gorges, the grandson of Sir Ferdinando who by that time claimed by inheritance the ownership of the Province of Maine, also stated willingness that his tenants should 'give somewhat to the adjacent Sagamore or Native for their Consent.'[31] On the other hand, such deeds would easily raise rival titles to those depending upon the central colonial authority, as the Massachusetts General Court apparently realized by 4 March 1634 when it tersely ordered 'that no person whatsoever shall buy any land of any Indean without leave from the Court.' In 1661, Gorges likewise ordered that until tenants had first contracted with him, 'they do forbear to make Purchase of the pretended Tytle of any of the Sagamores or Indians which is derogatory to the Grant to me.'[32]

Whatever the status of Indian deeds for European colonial authorities, however, the effect on the Indian was the same: exclusion from traditional lands. Even in selling land to English settlers, the Indian intent would normally reflect not the European notion of sole and permanent occupation of land by a single owner and his heirs, but rather the more flexible Indian concept of landholding as an admission to the same rights to use the land as were already exercised by the native bands through their sachems. Indian sellers did not expect to surrender their land but rather to share its use. When they found themselves excluded, whether by sale or simply by virtue of a European land grant, conflict inevitably arose, with the Indians making efforts to assert their claims through incursions which were seen by the settlers as invasions of newly acquired property.[33] Thus, while Levett in the 1620s had no difficulty, as a single isolated Englishman, in being welcomed as a resident at Casco by 'the consent of them who as I conceive have a naturall right of inheritance,' the growth of the English population was soon to bring about a change.[34]

All of these elements combined after 1630 to set the course of Abenaki-

English relations on a course which would soon prove dangerous and destructive for both sides. A specific example of the growth of hostility can be found at Richmond's Island, the site of the Trelawny plantation. Even before the grant of the island to Trelawny and Goodyear, it had been the scene of the killing of an English trader, Walter Bagnall, in 1631, by Indians whom he had, according to Winthrop, 'much wronged'; although Winthrop considered Bagnall to be 'a wicked fellow,' a Massachusetts expedition had nonetheless assisted in the capture and hanging of one of the Indians held responsible.[35] When John Winter arrived on behalf of Trelawny, he hoped to re-establish the fur trade but found, perhaps not surprisingly, little co-operation: 'the tradinge heare aboutes with the Indians is not worth any thinge,' he reported to Trelawny in 1634.[36] Another of Winter's activities was the building up of both pastoral and arable agriculture on the mainland opposite Richmond's Island, and it was this which brought the settlement, and indeed the whole province of New Somersetshire as it then was, into direct conflict with the native inhabitants. On 28 June 1636 one Narias Hawkins, who had been left in charge of Richmond's Island a year previously when Winter had departed on a visit to England, reported to Trelawny that 'we have sustaynd losse of a great Manie hoggs; 30 fatte hogges gate away when the tyme was come that they should be kild, some the Indians and some the woules, and harsh winter hath brought 150 to nothinge.' Winter, newly returned, wrote that 'theris no Indians Comes neare us that we know since the[y] killed our pigs: the[y] stand in fear we will take hold of them for yt, and so I will yf I Cann meete with them that did yt.'[37]

Measures had already been adopted at the New Somersetshire court in the previous March, when it had appeared that another colonist, Thomas Wise of Saco, had also had swine killed by Indians, for 'Mr. Hawkines [was] to have power and authority to execut any Indians that ar proved to have killed any swyne of the Inglishe.'[38] Four days later, on 29 March 1636, the same court adopted a more general law: 'It is ordered that every planter or Inhabitant shall doe his best indevor to apprehend, execut or kill any Indian that hath binne known to murder any English, kill ther Cattell or any waie spoyle ther goods or doe them violence and will not mack satisfaction.'[39] Even Thomas Gorges, the first deputy governor under the charter of the Province of Maine, saw his early optimism on Indian relations turn by 1642 to dismay at the 'insolencies' offered to English settlers. Gorges initiated attempts to disarm the various branches of the Abenaki, a course of action which was bound to create further tension.[40] Robert Trelawny had been accurate in his assessment five years earlier that 'those Indians that were befor friends and peaceable' were now 'Ennemys to us, and we to them.'[41]

The strained relations with the native inhabitants caused by the early English settlements did not improve with time. As the English population of Maine grew towards perhaps one thousand in 1650 and the major settlements grew into towns, tensions increased. The English, for their part, feared a general Indian conspiracy to destroy them. Thomas Gorges believed in 1642 that 'they have all combined themselves together from Penobscot to the [South?] to cut off the English. These meetings are often, dangerous words have they vented.'[42] Eleven years later, 'some thousands of Indians' at Piscataqua caused 'the great affright of the people in those parts' and resulted in the sending of an armed force from Massachusetts as a precaution.[43] Thus, proof of the existence of 'the inconstant savage' no longer depended upon past events in Virginia. For the English in Maine, the plottings and manœuvring of the native peoples were perceived as an immediate reality.

From the Indian side, the perspective was naturally rather different. It is doubtful whether English fears of a general Penacook, Abenaki, and Penobscot alliance against them were justified in reality (although any definite statements on English-Indian relationships in Maine in the middle part of the century are hindered by lack of direct evidence).[44] Certainly by the 1670s, according to William Hubbard in his *History of the Indian wars in New England*, at least one Indian leader was taking a resigned view of English encroachment. Within the past seven years, wrote Hubbard in 1677, the Piscataqua sagamore Rowles had reproached the men of Kittery that 'he expected some of the English, that had seized upon his Land, should have shown him that Civility, as to have given him a Visit in his aged Infirmityes and Sickness,' He might, continued Rowles, 'challenge all the Plantation for his own, where they dwelt,' but instead he desired only to have a small land grant made to him by the town, which he could then pass on to his children: they would not then be 'turned out, like Vagabonds, as destitute of an Habitation amongst or near the English.'[45]

Yet this acceptance of English land customs represented only one sagamore's view. It seems clear that the English fears must have been accurate at least to the extent that talk of war had taken place and that alliances had been canvassed among the various branches of the Abenaki. Rowles himself had indicated with regret that he felt that 'a War between the Indians and the English all over the Country' was inevitable and would not be long delayed.[46] For the Indian, a war against the English was not to be undertaken lightly, since it would promise enormous damage to both sides. Traditional Indian methods of waging war, based on swift and unexpected raids, would prove later in the century to be devastatingly effective against the Maine towns, where houses were often scattered and could be attacked one by one. Traditional Indian warfare, however, was also not prolonged, and was normally devoted to the avenging of particular wrongs and insults.[47] A war against the English would not be short, especially given military support from Massachusetts, and would pose a serious threat to the hunting and agricultural pursuits on which the Maine

Indians depended, as well as to the supply of trade goods upon which they had come to rely. Thus, although the reasons for war existed in the continuing encroachment of English settlement and in the affronts implied by English attempts at disarming Indian bands, there were also reasons for caution. It would be in the 1670s, as Rowles had predicted, that conflict would finally burst forth.

The achievements of the English in Maine, therefore, had a characteristic which was not uncommon in successful colonies: they had been built at the expense of the alienation of the Indian. In areas of America where the Indian had been conquered, or where 'directed acculturation' had been imposed, this situation presented no danger to the colonist.[48] In the northeastern maritime region, where the European population was sufficient to cause disruption to the Indian but too sparse to conquer, the Indian remained a potent force. Between 1675 and 1678 this would be proved in a bloody war which was ended only by a treaty favourable to the Abenaki. When the English not only ignored the terms of the treaty, but also recommenced their encroachment on Indian land, a further war ensued, which virtually wiped out any semblance of a stable colonial society in Maine.[49] Everything which the European created in America, in the northeastern maritime region as elsewhere, depended upon the recasting and reconceptualization of American territory, so that American reality was brought into conformity with European conception. The English in Maine had achieved some success in this, but the achievement was fragile. The Abenaki wars which took place later in the century would constitute the reverse of the alienation of the Indian, for they would represent the renewed alienation of the European.

Thus, the characteristics of European-Indian relationships in Maine, which had been established in the early stages of colonization, led to conflict, and one in which the European came off worst. In Acadia, matters would develop quite differently. Yet it would be a mistake to portray the difference simply as one determined by contrasting attitudes of English and French. In reality, the initial perceptions of the Indian which had contributed in the early years to the making of conflict between English and Abenaki were not confined to the English. Champlain, for example, thought in terms of pacifying the Indian population of Acadia 'pour en tirer à l'advenir du service.'[50] Following a skirmish on the coast of what was to become New England in which a Frenchman had been killed, Lescarbot wrote in outraged terms of 'l'insolence de ce peuple barbare.'[51] Another instance of armed conflict between French and Indian was the Micmac raid in 1635 on Fort Saint-François, Razilly's outpost at Canso. Although this incident was initiated by a French sea captain and trader, Jean Thomas, its result was a sharp encounter between French and Micmac in which the French commander, Nicolas Le Creux Du Breuil, was seriously wounded.[52] In the following year, a report reached Boston that d'Aulnay's settlement at Pentagouet was the scene of further conflict between French and Indians: 'Here comes natives,' reported Abraham Shurt, an early English inhabitant of Pemaquid, 'from thence and sayes that they will remove to some other parts, they are soe abused by them.' D'Aulnay himself referred in a document of 1643 to Indian hostility, blaming La Tour for deliberately stirring it up.[53]

It was not only the English, therefore, who were capable of antagonizing the Indians of the region. Furthermore, the career of Abraham Shurt provides an illustration that it was not only the French who were capable of coexisting with the native people. Shurt was one of several Englishmen who would continue to trade peacefully with the Kennebecs and Penobscots while residing at Pemaquid, between these two rivers. As late as the eve of the Abenaki-English war in 1675 another such trader, Thomas Gardner, would flatly contradict the assumptions of his compatriots southwest of the Kennebec that the Kennebec Abenaki were enemies of the English: a view which would be justified by the subsequent efforts of the Kennebecs to stay out of the war.[54] Thus, the difference between English-Indian relations and French-Indian relations was not neatly defined. That the colony of Acadia did eventually contrast with Maine in this respect was the result of the growth of a particular pattern of relationships in that colony. In large measure it depended upon an attitude which again was European in origin rather than primarily French, and which had close links with the Spanish example: the view of the Indian as a man to be Christianized and civilized by peaceful means and perhaps even assimilated into colonial society.

Christianity and the Indian

Almost all European colonies in America professed that their chief purpose was the advancement of the Christian faith through the conversion of the native pagans. The glory of spiritual conquest had been one of the principal themes advanced by the propagandists of the northeastern maritime colonies, and had been duly incorporated in the respective royal grants and charters. The charter of the Council for New England, despite its earlier assertion that this territory had been 'deserted' by its native inhabitants, affirmed that 'the principall effect which we can desire or expect of this Action, is the Conversion and Reduction of the People in those Parts unto the true Worship of God and Christian Religion'. Similarly, the New Scotland charter of Sir William Alexander remarked prominently upon the 'infidels whose conversion to the Christian faith most highly concerns the glory of God'. The first motive for the establishment of the Compagnie de la Nouvelle-France in 1627 was to continue efforts 'd'essayer, avec l'assistance divine, d'amener les peuples qui en habitent les terres à la cognoissance de Dieu, les faire policer et instruire à la foy et religion catholique Apostolique et Romaine.'[55] The religious purpose thus ascribed to the colonies could in some cases become a mere ritual observance and lack practical implications. For the early colonists, however, in the northeastern maritime region as elsewhere, the obligation of conversion was often taken seriously; this was particularly true of the French, whose temporal and spiritual activities in the New World were strongly influenced by the religious orders and other agencies of the Roman Catholic Church.[56] The resulting French attitude towards the Indian provided a basis for continuing good relations, and the scattered nature of French population in Acadia prevented the colonists from being perceived as a threat to native land. Thus, although the attitudes of the English in Maine and the French in Acadia towards the Indian, and vice versa, started with important similarities, the relationships developed differently as the century went on.

For the Spanish Scholastic thinkers, who opposed the concept of the fundamental savagery of the Indian, lack of civilization and of Christianity could be remedied by education. Las Casas, while admitting that there might be a category of barbarians who were sufficiently depraved to merit treatment as wild beasts, nevertheless held in practice to the concept of the essential rationality of all mankind and held therefore that the rational attributes of the Indians could be elicited, 'once they are brought under control and persuaded by reason and love and industriousness.' This view was incorporated in the bull issued in June 1537 by Pope Paul III which, as well as asserting Indian rights to personal freedom and personal possessions, enjoined that 'the Preachers of the faith' should 'go to all men, indiscriminately, for all are capable of receiving the teaching of the faith.' Thus, while this strain of thought still regarded the Indian as inferior to the European, it was not the inferiority of a conquered and barbarian race but an inferiority that proceeded from a state of ignorance which was capable of being rectified through evangelization.[57]

The emphasis laid by colonial promoters upon conversion clearly implied an acceptance of this proposition. Sir Ferdinando Gorges, whose interest in America had first been kindled in 1605 by contacts with Indians brought back by the explorer George Waymouth, certainly professed an obligation to free 'those poor distressed creatures' from the bonds of paganism.[58] Gorges' perception of the Indian was of innocence, one which agreed well with that of later Jesuit missionaries in New France. Gorges manifested, moreover, an appreciation rare among European colonizers for the crucial importance of Indian help in establishing a colony: he remarked, for example, on the 'civil respect the natives used' in the early days of the Plymouth colony, 'tending much to their happiness in so great extremity they were in.'[59] Sir Ferdinando's kinsman, Thomas Gorges, though soon disillusioned, showed an initial concern for conversion and a marked respect for the intellect of the native: 'The great Sagamour hath bin with me to welcome me to his country. I find them very ingenious men only Ignorant of the true wisdome. I told him I pittied his case that he was soe Ignorant of God. He answered me that he knew his great God Tanto ... Truly I take great delight to discourse with them.'[60]

These views of Sir Ferdinando and Thomas Gorges show that the colony of Maine, despite the drastic laws passed under the New Somersetshire government in 1636, was not devoid of the impulse to educate and civilize rather than to conquer and alienate the Indian. What was signally lacking, though, was any strong institutional framework for doing this. Provision for religious ministration was considered essential to all European colonies; even the small and abortive New Scotland expedition of 1622 had intended to include a Church of Scotland minister, a Mr John Welsh.[61] The few clergymen who were available, however, had a large enough task in ministering to the English inhabitants, often complicated by local hostility among the colonists; if they had any inclination to act as missionaries also, they had little opportunity to do so systematically.[62] Even the Massachusetts colony made only modest efforts at evangelization. Although conversion of the natives was one of the avowed purposes of that colony as defined in its royal charter, the colony was primarily concerned not with the expansion of Christianity to the heathen but with reform of English Christianity from what was seen as its degenerate condition. Indeed, the predestinarian beliefs which prevailed in Massachusetts implied a different view of conversion from that which had been embodied in the charter and afforded little encouragement to Indian missions in the conventional sense. Although isolated individuals did make converts, it was not until the middle of the century that Thomas Mayhew, John Eliot, and Edward Winslow began to enjoy more widespread success; and even so their evangelical efforts were centred in the 'praying towns' of Massachusetts rather than being extended to outlying districts of Maine.[63]

In Acadia, as in New France as a whole, this need for an institutional framework for evangelization was filled by the Roman Catholic church, both through the religious orders and through the missionary efforts of the Séminaire de Québec. Although a secular priest, Jessé Fléché, had previously administered baptism to a number of Indians, including the chief Membertou and twenty of his family, the introduction of the Jesuit order to Acadia in 1611 in the persons of Biard and Énemond Massé represented not only the beginning of systematic catechism and evangelization but also the entry of the religious orders into the temporal affairs of the colony, in which they were to have considerable influence throughout much of the seventeenth century. The contacts of the Jesuit order at court through Madame de Guercheville and the involvement of Biard in the colonizing attempt at Saint-Sauveur are two examples of this influence. The Recollet mission on the St John river between 1620 and 1624 lent support, albeit probably only moral support, to the Biencourt colony, and the Capuchin missionaries, who had come to Acadia with Razilly in 1632, gave practical support to d'Aulnay against La Tour both in the colony itself and at court.[64] The Séminaire de Québec's interest in Acadian affairs continued through the latter half of the seventeenth century and culminated in the activity of the seminary priest Louis-Pierre Thury on the French side in the war of 1689–97.[65] This temporal influence of the missionaries in Acadia was not uniformly effective and was not always wielded in favour of established secular authority, but it illustrates that the religious function of colonization in Acadia had not only good will, but also real power.

The missionaries also provided a direct link with Spanish views of the Indian. In this respect their position was analogous to that of those in New England with links to Irish colonization; but the effect was the opposite, for the view brought by the religious orders was that of the Scholastic as opposed to that of the conquistador. The Jesuits in particular had a direct link with Las Casas through José de Acosta, a Jesuit who had played a prominent role in further developing benevolent views of the Indian after the death of Las Casas and in applying them in Peru.[66] Just as important in the northeastern maritime region, however, was the question of whether the Indians would take a benevolent view of the missionaries. The Algonkians with whom the European colonists came in contact had a self-confident regard for their own culture and religion, especially as compared with its European equivalents, and were far from being passive participants in the contacts which took place. Although benevolent, the missionaries' view of the Indians still assumed European superiority, an assumption which the Indians did not share.

In practice, however, the missionaries were able to establish close relations with the Indians, which in turn added much stability to the colony. There were, of course, instances of frustration and resentment. Biard was early confronted with the Micmacs' realization that the coming of the French had coincided with the great reduction of their numbers through disease, from which some concluded that the French were deliberately poisoning them.[67] Though there is no direct evidence of it in the northeastern maritime region, Algonkians elsewhere had from time to time specifically suspected the Christian religion to have brought bad luck through the activities of missionary priests as sorcerers. Certainly there was opposition to the missionaries by native shamans who saw their functions being usurped, and cases arose where missionaries and shamans competed in attempts to prove their spiritual powers.[68] More generally, since the priests advocated radical change from traditional Indian religions to Christianity, any success which they might have could easily be perceived as a threat to the security of the Indian way of life.

Nevertheless, the missionaries were not always seen in this way. For those whom they succeeded in converting completely to Christianity, the priests were seen as agents of divine revelation. More important, however, was the potential for perception and treatment of the missionary priests neither as threatening sorcerers nor as exclusive purveyors of truth, but as the representatives of a faith which had aspects – especially mystical aspects – capable of being fused with those of traditional Indian religion. Since the Indian view of the world did not involve an exclusive funnelling of truth through a particular set of beliefs, but was concerned rather with the accumulated power of a large number of spiritual forces, the acceptance of Christianity need not imply the abandonment of other beliefs.[69] The Indians were therefore free to take a selective view of the missionaries. As with the material aspects of European culture, those features of Christianity that seemed most useful in the context of traditional belief would be accepted as such, and Christianity as a whole would be seen as one of a large number of acceptable beliefs.

Although the missionary priests often did not understand these characteristics of Indian religion – Biard, for example, declared that 'toute leur Religion, pour le dire en un mot, n'est autre qu'és sorceleries et charmes des Autmoins' – they were not necessarily unaware of the need to lead the Indian gradually to Christianity rather than to attempt a quick and radical breach with previous beliefs.[70] Some ten centuries previously, in connection with the Roman mission to Anglo-Saxon England, a missionary effort with which Biard was familiar through the *Ecclesiastical history* of Bede, Pope Gregory the Great had enjoined that 'it is doubtless impossible to cut out everything at once from their stubborn minds: just as the man who is attempting to climb to the highest place, rises by steps and degrees and not by leaps'; Gregory had therefore encouraged the temporary retention of non-Christian ceremonies.[71] In the same way, the Recollet missionary Le Clercq remarked of his evangelization among the Micmacs that 'Il est bon de ménager les Sauvages, et de differer quelquefois à les instruire, jusqu'à ce qu'ils aïent levé l'obstacle qui s'oppose à leur conversion.'[72]

In such ways as these, an understanding could be achieved between Indian and missionary which was in all likelihood illusory at a theological level – the Indian acceptance of Christianity not being what it seemed to the missionary – but which promoted mutual respect. This was accentuated by the common ground which lay between missionary and Indian in the concept of religion as a healer and a bringer of luck. For the Indian, such functions formed the principal test of the usefulness of a religious belief. The Micmacs of the Gaspé, reported Le Clercq, 'croïent que dans toutes leurs maladies il y a un Demon, ou un ver dans la partie affligée, que ces Barbares que nous appelons Jongleurs, ont le pouvoir de faire sortir, et de rendre la santé aux malades.'[73]

Thus one possibility for the missionaries was to compete with the native shamans in terms of miracle cures: this branch of religion was not as central to the faith of the missionaries as it was to that of the Indians, but was still a highly accredited part of the traditions of the church. A miraculous intervention was suspected by Biard, for example, when the dying son of Membertou was suddenly cured, the result being that Membertou 'fut fort confirmé en la foy.'[74] According to Le Clercq, moreover, the sign of the cross was early accepted by the Gaspesian Micmacs as having magic power. A woman who belonged to the 'Gaspesiens dits Porte-Croix' testified 'qu'il n'y avoit rien de plus precieux que la Croix, puisqu'elle l'avoit preservée d'une infinité de dangers; qu'elle luy avoit procuré toute sorte de consolation dans ses disgraces; et qu'enfin la vie luy paroîtroit tout-à-fait indifferente, s'il faloit qu'elle vêcût sans la Croix.'[75] A similar manifestation in a collective fashion is indicated by a reference in the Jesuit relation for 1644–5 to the assiduity of Micmac war parties in praying at the Jesuit mission at Nepisiquit.[76] If Christianity, or its symbols, could be established as bringing luck either to an individual or to a people, then it would certainly be regarded as foolishness to ignore its power. Just as an Anglo-Saxon high priest had accepted Christianity because it had proved 'effectual' in bringing earthly success, so the Indians of the northeastern maritime region were prepared to take the same view if appropriately convinced; indeed, the most influential of all missionaries were those who gained acceptance as shamans.[77]

Since this selective and utilitarian conception of conversion was very different from that held by the missionaries, the latter often found themselves confused as to how solid their achievements really were. Le Clercq lamented that 'le nombre est tres-petit, de ceux qui vivent selon les regles du Christianisme, et qui ne retombent dans les déreglemens d'une vie brutale et sauvage ... d'où vient que quoique plusieurs Missionnaires aïent beaucoup travaillé pour la conversion de ces Infideles, on n'y remarque cependant, non plus que chez les autres Nations Sauvages de la Nouvelle France, de Christianisme solidement établi.'[78] The Jesuit Joseph Jouvency also expressed frustration with 'their ready assent to whatever one teaches them; nevertheless they hold tenaciously to their native belief or superstition, and on that account are the more difficult to instruct. For what can one do with those who in word give agreement and assent to everything, but in reality give none?'[79]

Despite this tension, even a superficial understanding between Indian and missionary on spiritual matters was of great assistance in the overall pattern of Indian relationships which developed in the colony of Acadia. One of the aspects of European culture which the Indian found disappointing was the absence of spiritual awareness among colonists, and the accompanying preoccupation with material values.[80] The missionaries were the exceptions: their predominantly religious view of the world, although much more systematized and exclusive than that of the Indian, enabled them to speak to the Indian in terms that were meaningful to both, and consequently to derive respect at a deeper level than the ordinary European colonist. Le Clercq, refusing gifts of furs on taking leave of the Micmacs among whom he had lived, was addressed by a Micmac chief in terms which made this distinction explicit: 'Il est vrai, dit-il, que tu les [furs] as toûjours méprisez; le peu d'état que tu en as fait, pendant que les François les recherchent avec tant d'empressement, nous a bien fait connoître il y a longtems, que tu ne desirois rien au monde, que le salut de nos ames.'[81] The missionaries were able, at least to an extent, to counterbalance the materialism of the French colonists; in the English case such a balance was largely absent.

It is of course true that the ultimate aims of the French for the Indians included not only their conversion to Christianity but also the alteration of their way of life. Champlain had put this in a predominantly secular context in referring to the Indians as those 'lesquels avec le temps on esperoit pacifier, et amortir les guerres qu'ils ont les uns contre les autres, pour en tirer à l'advenir du service: et les reduire à la foy Chrestienne.'[82] Lescarbot further recommended for the northeastern Indians, 'qui sont vagabons et divisés,' that 'il les faut assembler par la culture de la terre, et obliger par ce moyen à demeurer en un lieu,' a process from which he predicted great temporal as well as spiritual profits for France.[83] Biard also favoured inducing Indians to make a sedentary life around a mission centre, and this aim was followed at the Jesuit mission at Miscou, as described in the Jesuit relation for 1645–6: 'Deux familles de Sauvages Chrestiens, composées de seize personnes, estoient dés l'an passé habituées en ce lieu ... une troisiéme plus nombreuse nous est venüe trouver au commencement de Septembre, en dessein de jouïr du mesme bon-heur; quelques autres nous ont promis de la suivre au plustost ...'[84] Le Clercq too remarked that 'la vie errante et vagabonde de ces Peuples ... [est] incontestablement un de principaux obstacles à leur conversion,' and hoped to be able to establish 'une Mission sedentaire' on the land of Richard Denys, son of Nicolas Denys, at Nepisiquit; although this particular plan was abandoned, Denys did in August 1685 make grants of land for sedentary missions at Restigouche, Miramichi, and Cape Breton, of which only that at Miramichi made a temporary beginning in the following year under Abbé Thury, who shortly afterwards moved to Port Royal and then to Pentagouet.[85]

Thus, the French did have objectives in Acadia which involved deliberate alteration of the Indians' traditional way of life. They never had any direct means to enforce such a change, however, and indeed the Jesuit missionaries came increasingly to accept the need to preserve aspects of the traditional Indian economy even in sedentary missions. It was consequently possible for the Indians to regard these missions as yet another element of French culture which could be accepted or rejected in a selective manner. Seen in this way, the mission represented not so much a distortion of Indian customs as an environment in which new adaptations could be made to accommodate the irreversible changes which had already taken place through acculturation.[86] Many did choose to frequent such establishments, the most striking being the Abenaki migrations in the later years of the century to Jesuit missions in Canada – at Sillery and on the Chaudière River.[87] As increasing numbers of Abenaki resorted to the Canadian missions to gain a respite from the pressures induced by war against the English, it became clear that the presence of the English and the French had had, in practical terms, very different results for the Abenaki. For native people who had to find a way in which to retain self-confidence and self-reliance while adjusting to cultural change, English colonization had come to mean the threat of total disruption while French missions offered a framework within which choices could be made.

In Acadia itself, moreover, the effects of European settlement as experienced by Micmac and Malecite were different from those felt by the Abenaki in Maine. The major Acadian settlements – those located in the Port Royal valley, on the Minas Basin, and at the head of the Bay of Fundy – were based upon the cultivation of marshlands which were of little value to the primarily non-agricultural Micmac. Outside these marshland communities, settlements remained small, isolated, and largely devoted to fishing and the fur trade. Nowhere did French settlement of Acadia pose any serious problem of encroachment for the Indian, and French colonization therefore did not threaten the good Indian relations promoted by the missionaries.[88]

These relationships were indeed strengthened by certain ties of kinship between French and Indians. The predominantly male colony at La Hève between 1632 and 1635 left behind a métis settlement after d'Aulnay's removal of his headquarters to Port Royal, and there may well have been others. Certainly, French officials in Acadia in later years were apt to comment at length upon what the governor, François-Marie Perrot, described in 1686 as the 'vie feneante, Libertine et vagabonde' lived by young Acadian males who wintered in the woods to gather furs.[89] By this time also, there is clear evidence in a few cases of formal intermarriage: Acadian censuses up to 1686 afford five examples of Indian wives. An especially prominent intermarriage was that of Jean-Vincent d'Abbadie de Saint-Castin and the daughter of a Penobscot sachem, which was formalized by the Jesuit missionary Jacques Bigot in 1684. Saint-Castin, a French officer and nobleman, spent the rest of his life at Pentagouet with his Penobscot kin.[90]

In Acadia, later years would see the accentuation of the close ties between Indian and Acadian French that had emerged by 1650. These ties strengthened as the Indian became increasingly estranged from the English in Maine, particularly after the failure in 1650 of a French initiative to New England. Originating from Quebec, this proposal was for an alliance of New France, the Abenaki, and New England against the Mohawk nation; despite a friendly reception accorded to the emissary, the Jesuit Gabriel Druillettes, it was not seriously considered by the English. Of the negotiations, a Christian Indian chief wrote in 1651 that 'on m'a envoyé au pais des Abnaquiois et des Anglois, qui leur sont voisins, pour leur demander du secours contre les Iroquois. J'ay obey à ceux qui m'ont envoyé, mais mon voyage a esté inutile, l'Anglois ne répond point, il n'a pas de bonnes pensées pour nous, cela m'attriste fort: nous nous voyons mourir et exterminer tous les jours.'[91] Thus, although there is no evidence of combined military operations by Indians and Acadian French against New England until 1690, the polarization which led to that alliance was apparent by mid century.

Viewed as marking a stage in the worsening relations between the Abenaki and the English in Maine and elsewhere in New England, the Druillettes mission was an ironic turn of events, for one of the strongest of Druillettes's personal impressions of New England was a fellow-feeling for those missionaries whom he met there, although they were Protestants and he a Jesuit. Of the brothers John and Edward Winslow, with whom he professed a particular friendship, he remarked that each had 'un zelle particulier pour la Conversion des Sauvages.' At Roxbury, Massachusetts, he recounted how 'le ministre nomme Maistre heliot [John Eliot] qui enseignoit quelcques sauvages me recust chez lui a cause que la nuict me surprenoit et me traita avec respect et affection me pria de passer liver [l'hiver] avec luy.'[92] The missionary impulse, like the desire to trade for furs, was not confined to either French or English, and both were capable of promoting good European-Indian relations. In practice, though, they did not necessarily do so. Both French and English had relied upon a common European fund of knowledge and opinion, much of it drawn from the Spanish experience, for their preconceptions of the Indian. There were many different conclusions which could be drawn from that Spanish example, however, and while the English had tended to be the more powerfully influenced by the concept of the Indian as fit only for conquest, the French had had direct links through the religious orders with the more benevolent view of the Spanish Scholastics. The practical development of colonization, too, in the respective colonies of Maine and Acadia had made for an alienation of the Indian in the English case and for a framework of good relations in the French case. Thus in this regard the two colonies had diverged significantly even by 1650. How powerful the Indian could be as an enemy and as an ally would be seen in the second half of the seventeenth century.

CHAPTER 4

Relationships with
Other Colonies

Interrelationships within the Northeastern Maritime Region

European claims in the northeastern maritime region gave ample scope for conflict. New Scotland, comprising the modern Maritime provinces and the Gaspé, was wholly within the grant of the Compagnie de la Nouvelle-France, which had been sweepingly defined as extending from the Arctic Circle to Florida. The patent of the Council for New England, which included all lands between the 40th and 48th parallels, overlapped with both. Taking the region as a whole, the area between the Piscataqua and Ste Croix rivers could conceivably be claimed by France and England, and the Gaspé by France and Scotland; the middle territory, north of the Ste Croix and south of the Gaspé, could be claimed by all three countries.[1] Although settlement in the three colonies was initially sparse, these boundary conflicts naturally produced tension and hostility.

Between Scotland and England, the disputes were least virulent. Although Scots and English had by no means finished fighting each other in Europe, in America the peace which befitted the subjects of a single monarch (although of different crowns) was maintained. This did not mean, however, that the ambiguous boundaries went unnoticed, particularly in the context of disputes between the Kirkes and the Alexanders. The quarrels between the two families, which had led in 1629 to the foundation of the English and Scottish Company, had chiefly concerned the St Lawrence region and not New Scotland. None the less, the Kirkes had ranged the coasts of New Scotland, prompting a Scottish observer to note in 1628 that 'the Englische men ar suiten [have requested] of his Majestie a patent to plant and possesse quhatsumever lands thairof quhilk they please, and these to be halden of the Crowne of England.'[2] Later, the

Kirkes held themselves aggrieved by the treaty of Saint-Germain-en-Laye, since they had had no reimbursement for their surrender of Canada, 'whereas Sir William Alexander hath had good content for the surrendering of New Scotland, and Port Roiall to the French.' Thus, after the treaty, renewed conflict broke out over rights to the St Lawrence trade. The Kirkes and certain associates attempted to show not only that the Alexanders' Scottish grant in the St Lawrence region 'cannot debarre us that are English,' but that the English right to New Scotland rested upon the discovery of Cabot and so predated that of Scotland. 'If the French usurped it,' they maintained, 'it was uppon the English and were not ejected by the Scottish: the Scottish patent cannot bee of force against the one nor the other.'[3] The Kirkes received little satisfaction from their claims against the Scots, and the disputes never provoked actual hostilities in America, but the tension certainly existed.

The contradiction between the existence of New Scotland and Acadia was a more active issue. In view of the Scottish claim to that area which had been and still was the site of French settlement, it is not surprising that relations between the two nationalities were largely characterized either by wary avoidance or outright hostility. Indeed, a sporadic form of raiding warfare demonstrated the twin aims of both sides: to make good their territorial claims and to obtain untrammelled access to the natural resources of the region. When, for example, the French sea captain Charles Daniel took by storm Lord Ochiltree's New Scotland settlement on Cape Breton, the writer of a contemporary French account noted that 'on verra dans ce Narré l'exercice de la Pesche assuré pour nos François, l'heresie qui commençoit, arrachee dés sa naissance, la saincte foy de l'Eglise Romaine installée, et un petit tyranneau debusqué aussi honteusement, qu'il avoit injustement usurpé ce nouveau Païs, et traicté iniquement les sujets de nostre France.' Both in the placing of a settlement within Acadia and in an attempt to regulate the fishery by charging French fishermen a licence fee of one-tenth of their catch, Ochiltree had in French eyes offended the legitimate ownership, faith, and commercial patterns of the Acadian colony.[4] Daniel was thus held to be justified in his attack and in the reduction of the Scots fort, even though, as the defeated occupants complained, the two countries were at peace and Daniel had obtained entry to the fort on false pretences. Ochiltree later informed Charles I that 'the king off france ... doeth assume to himself all that pert of America which lyeth by elevatioune from the fortie too the sixty degree [this was in fact an understatement] wherby he doeth include all new ingland and new scotland,' and quoted Daniel as saying 'that the king off france did mynd nothing by the peace with Ingland bot to endur for too yeiris till he secured America ...'[5] In furthering the French aims in this regard, Daniel also created an opportunity for his own intervention in the fishery and the fur trade in Cape Breton; from the spoils of Ochiltree's settlement, he set up a fort at Sainte-Anne, some twenty-five leagues from the Scottish site.[6]

The Scots colony at Port Royal was considered a more difficult target, as might be deduced from the brief flirtation of the elder La Tour with Alexander. Indeed, it was a lieutenant of the La Tours, after their decision to give allegiance to Acadia rather than to New Scotland, who brought news to France in the summer of 1631 'comme les Escossois ne se resoudoient point à quitter le Port Royal, mais qu'ils s'y accommodoient de jour à autre, et y avoient fait venir quelques mesnages et bestiaux pour peupler ce lieu qui ne leur appartient que par l'usurpation qu'ils en ont faite.' The Scots settlement, by the standards of communal colonization, was clearly becoming well established, and the Cent-Associés, well informed as to diplomatic progress towards the treaty of Saint-Germain-en-Laye, made no plans for an assault; instead, they concentrated upon strengthening La Tour's posts at Cap de Sable and on the St John River by the sending of both artisans and Recollet fathers.[7]

No such strategic scruples hindered the Scots themselves, however, for one of the last acts of the Port Royal colonists was to launch a raid on La Tour's fort on the St John River. On 18 September 1632, by which time Razilly had already landed at La Hève unknown to them, twenty-five armed men were led by Andrew Forrester, the Scots commander, across the Bay of Fundy to the mouth of the St John. Entering the fort on false pretences, as the French occupants later complained, the Scots took possession and symbolically pulled down the cross and the arms of the king of France. Beating one of the fort's occupants to force him to divulge the location of its stores in a nearby wood, they thereupon seized several hundred assorted furs, along with munitions and trade goods, and returned to Port Royal with several prisoners. There they embarked the prisoners on an English pinnace bound for the Penobscot, with instructions to maroon them on some suitably deserted island. According to Jean-Daniel Chaline, commander of the St John fort in La Tour's absence and now one of the prisoners, the English captain proved to be 'plus humain' than Forrester, and released them at the mouth of the St John; Chaline thereupon travelled to Cap de Sable to make his report. The release of the prisoners, as well as the fact that neither of the La Tours had themselves been in the fort to share the defeat, meant that little harm had been done beyond the loss of furs and other goods. The raid had shown once again, however, the nature of relations between Acadia and New Scotland, each group of colonists seeking opportunities to dispossess the other of its territorial claim and its wealth in the form of natural resources.[8]

The conflicts between Acadia and New Scotland were, of course, brought to an end in late 1632 by the Scots' surrender of Port Royal to Razilly and their return to Europe. There remained the potential for similar conflict between Acadia and New England. It is necessary here to deal with 'New England' rather than 'Maine,' for two reasons. First, the Province of Maine, as eventually bounded, was not created until 1639. Secondly, the principal location of French-English friction at this time was the area between the Ste Croix and Kennebec rivers, a part of the northeastern maritime region which, though later incorporated into the modern state of Maine, was never a part of the seventeenth-century province of that name. Instead, it had a complex pattern of various ownerships, which reflected the confusion in both French and English minds as to its proper status.

The French position was the simpler of the two. The 1627 grant to the Compagnie de la Nouvelle-France had included the entire east coast of North America, and it was thus not surprising that John Winthrop's first intimation in January 1633 of the Scots surrender of Port Royal should have prompted him to initiate a hurried fortification of the approaches to Boston harbour. By 1636, however, both La Tour and d'Aulnay had declared or at least implied that they would not take any measures against English establishments southwest of Pemaquid and the Kennebec River.[9] With occasional variations, the French contention remained for most of the seventeenth century that the Kennebec should be the boundary between New England and Acadia. For the English, who in Europe were always unwilling to recognize formally the legitimate existence of Acadia but were usually inclined to recognize that of New Scotland, the southern boundary of the latter colony – the Ste Croix River – was naturally assumed to mark the northern extent of New England.

In the division of New England of 1623, the area between the Kennebec and Ste Croix rivers had been severally allocated to six of the councillors of New England.[10] None of these grants, however, produced settlements, and in subsequent years the council granted further patents in the area, notably that conveying fifteen miles of land on either side of the Kennebec River to the Plymouth colony for a trading post; this grant, made in 1630, replaced a more restricted one of 1628.[11] Despite the allocation of the entire Kennebec-Ste Croix territory to the Alexanders in 1635, the Plymouth trading ventures and other independent settlements remained the only representatives of the English presence. The area was granted in 1664 to the Duke of York, along with that territory which was to become the colony of New York, and with the exception of a brief interlude of annexation by Massachusetts in the 1670s, it remained under the duchy of York until 1686. With the Duke of York by then on the English throne as James II, it was integrated into the Dominion of New England and subsequently joined to Massachusetts in the charter of 1691. Thus, as an area of English colonization, the territory between the Kennebec and the Ste

Croix had a chequered history. Most Englishmen could agree, however, that English rule extended at least to the Ste Croix River, and so long as both French and English positions held firm, this was disputed territory.[12]

The Plymouth colony had early discovered the potential of the fur trade northeast of it, Edward Winslow having made a successful voyage to the Kennebec River in 1625 and brought back 700 pounds of beaver skins in exchange for a boat-load of corn. Especially after 1627, when the Plymouth colonists had agreed to buy out their London mercantile supporters for an annual payment of £200, to a total of £1,800, the fur trade assumed a growing importance to the colony as a source of revenue. Accordingly, Isaac Allerton, the colonist who had successfully negotiated the settlement in London, was sent back to England in 1628 to 'conclude the forementioned bargain and purchase' and also to 'procure a patent for a fit trading place in the river of Kennebec.' When Allerton had successfully completed both pieces of business, the permanent trading post was set up at Cushnoc, the site of the modern Augusta, 'in the most convenientest place for trade ... and furnished ... with commodities for that end, both winter and summer.' In the following year, the Plymouth colonists came into possession of a second trading post, on the Penobscot river. The circumstances of this acquisition were rather different, arising from the decision of Allerton and certain of the former London backers to establish the post by virtue of the 'Muscongus patent' obtained from the Council for New England; somewhat disillusioned by recent financial man-œuvrings and mistrustful of Edward Ashley, the 'profane young man' who was designated to manage the enterprise, the Plymouth colonists, 'to prevent a worse mischief, resolved to join in the business.' This expedient, however, did not prevent the widening of the breach with Allerton, who in 1631 (after his associate Ashley had been sent back to England under arrest for 'trading powder and shot with the Indians') moved further east to establish a trading post at Machias, an enterprise in which he was joined by Richard Vines, the close associate of Sir Ferdinando Gorges who had recently been granted land at Saco, Maine, by the Council for New England.[13]

The Plymouth colonists, operating in the fur trade in southeastern as well as northeastern New England, had thus built the framework for a potentially lucrative trade. They had created tempting targets, however, for competing and hostile interests. Not only were they 'kept hoodwinked' by Allerton and his London associates to such an extent that most of the profits were funnelled away from the Plymouth colony, but in 1634 a Plymouth employee on the Kennebec was killed in an encounter with a competing English trader from the Piscataqua River, John Hocking, who was himself killed in the exchange.[14] Not surprisingly, the northeastern trading posts were also subject to French incursions. As early as 1632, in fact, the post at Penobscot was rifled by

Frenchmen, unidentified in surviving records, who arrived in 'a small ... ship' accompanied by 'a false Scot,' presumably a deserter from Port Royal. Using the same tactics as had Daniel at Port aux Baleines and Forrester on the St John, they gained access to the settlement by using 'many ... compliments' and thereupon took command, removing goods 'to the value of £400 or £500,' including three hundredweight of beaver.[15]

This raid was evidently purely for material gain, without any additional function of asserting territorial authority. Weightier in purpose was an attack mounted shortly afterwards by La Tour upon the post at Machias. Returning from France in 1633, armed with his newly granted half share in the Acadian fur trade, La Tour descended upon Machias in or before November of that year and, as Bradford recorded, 'displanted them, slew two of their men and took all their goods to a good value.'[16] Having thus benefited his own fur-trading interests, La Tour in early 1635 also made his territorial assertions clear, when visited by Allerton to procure the release of the remaining prisoners from the Machias episode: 'he had authority from the king of France, who challenged all from Cape Sable to Cape Cod, wishing them to take notice, and to certify the rest of the English, that, if they traded to the east of Pemaquid, he would make prize of them.'[17]

As for the Machias trading house, Bradford concisely remarked, 'this was the end of that project'; the Plymouth colony made no counter-attack, and indeed there was little reason why it should do so, since the post had been set up despite its wishes and since the loss sustained had been 'most if not all Mr. Allerton's.'[18] Less easily ignored was 'another great loss from the French,' when in 1635 the trading post at Penobscot was seized by d'Aulnay, who gained entry using a tactic which again proved effective in a territory of confused ownership at a time of nominal peace: 'having ... got some of the chief that belonged to the house aboard his vessel, by subtlety coming upon them in their shallop he got them to pilot him in; and after getting the rest into his power he took possession of the house in the name of the King of France.' Territorial assertion and future control of the fur trade rather than immediate profit would seem to have been the primary motivation of the expedition, since d'Aulnay promised to reimburse the Englishmen for their confiscated stock. 'For the house and fortification etc. he would not allow nor account anything, saying that they which build on another man's ground do forfeit the same. So thus turning them out of all, with a great deal of compliment and many fine words, he let them have their shallop and some victuals to bring them home.'[19] The Plymouth colony, which clearly could not afford to accept this reverse passively, mounted a counter-offensive with co-operation, though without material support, from the Massachusetts colony. The attempt was, however, easily resisted by d'Aulnay, especially since the attackers used up most of their ammunition at a harmless distance. Such was, Bradford noted, 'the end of this business.' An attempt by Plymouth to attract assistance from Massachusetts for another assault met with encouragement but no offer of monetary contribution, which resulted in the creation of feelings of animosity and aggrievement between the Massachusetts and Plymouth colonies. The Plymouth fur-trading operations in the northeast would henceforth be restricted to the Kennebec.[20]

English-French relationships in the northeastern maritime region, therefore, had resulted by 1635 in a considerable advance for Acadia at the expense of New England. The English retrenchments were not willing ones, since the value of the fur trade was well known not only to the Plymouth colonists but also to those inhabiting the area which was to become the Province of Maine. Thomas Cammock, a patentee of the Council for New England who had interests at Piscataqua and later at Black Point, wrote in July 1632 to Robert Trelawny that it was his intention to 'range all the coast alonge to the Eastwarde allmost to the Scotts plantation, wher I know ther is more store of beaver and better tradinge than is heer with us ...'[21] An English document regarding fisheries, moreover, in the handwriting of the secretary of state, Sir John Coke, had noted in 1633 the importance of the newly discovered fishing grounds off 'Virginia, New England, New Scotland and the rest' and commented upon the necessity to resist both French and Dutch competitors there.[22] What the English settlers of the northeastern maritime region lacked, however, was military strength of any kind. As Edward Trelawny informed his brother in early 1636, 'either wee muste better fortifye [at Richmond's Island], or els expose our selves to the Losse of all, which may bee prevented by a speedy preparation against all Assaultes.'[23] John Winter, writing some five months later, warned that 'the French have made them selves stronge at the place [they] tooke last yeare heare from the English [Penobscot], and do report they will have more of the plantations heare about us, and this for [one]: therfore we shall need to strengthen this plantation, for yt lyes very open as yet for the enymye.'[24]

The sporadic hostility which passed for peace in the northeastern region in the early 1630s was characterized, like medieval warfare, by the attempted capture, whether by storm or stratagem, of strongholds which both symbolized and constituted local power.[25] Since this was so, and since populations were so small, battles or skirmishes were on a small scale but could have radical results. The aim of either side, as well as the securing of natural resources, was to 'displant' the other, and thus to make good the particular European claim which was being upheld, be it English, Scottish, or French. Because this involved the uprooting of colonies, it also implied the deportation of populations and total loss of property. Although much less hardship was caused by these expedients in the early stages of colonization than in the later seventeenth century and afterwards, the stakes of such warfare were by no means as slight as was the fighting itself, and inter-colonial hostility could never be taken lightly.

This being so, the question sooner or later had to be asked in the colonies as to whether the enforcement of European claims was worth the risk of war. In the northeastern maritime region, the period to 1636 saw the Scots eliminated by diplomatic means, the French well established on the Pentagouet River, and the English still in possession on the Kennebec. D'Aulnay, it emerged, was content at least for the moment to allow this position to stand. As Winthrop recorded of the Penobscot raiders, 'it appeared they had commission from Mons. Roselly [Razilly] ... to displant the English as far as Pemaquid, and by it they professed all courtesy to us here'; this attitude of the French was borne out for Winthrop by the kind treatment at La Hève of the crew of a Massachusetts ship which had been wrecked on Sable Island.[26] There remained in Massachusetts, as in Plymouth and in the settlements to the northeast, a profound suspicion of the French. Winthrop noted in the context of the Penobscot raid that 'we saw that their neighborhood would be very dangerous to us', and an English visitor to New England wrote in July 1636 that 'the present face of things here is very tumultuous. The French continually encroach and by venting of Peices, and Powder strengthen the Natives for civill warrs, and gayne all the Trade.'[27] And yet, there was little to be gained for Massachusetts by provoking war simply to safeguard the Plymouth fur-trading interests. On the contrary, as Bradford complained, certain Massachusetts merchants saw and grasped an opportunity to trade on their own account with the French. Bradford also accused the English of Pemaquid of co-operating with the French, and again he was correct, since Abraham Shurt of Pemaquid was trading with both d'Aulnay and La Tour. 'So as in truth,' reflected Bradford, 'the English themselves have been the chiefest supporters of these French ... So as it is no marvel though they still grow and encroach more and more upon the English ...'[28]

The English up and down the New England coast, therefore, were now divided in their feelings towards the French, fear and suspicion competing with the desire for peaceful relations. In the northeastern maritime region, the first phase of frequent conflict arising from contradictory European conceptions had passed, though hostility between French and English had by no means been laid to rest. What had emerged for the moment was a kind of equilibrium. Significantly, it was an equilibrium in which the balance was held not within the region itself, but by the external presence of the Massachusetts colony; without it the English settlements would have been no match for the French after the Scots evacuation and the consequent strengthening of Acadia.

Canada and Massachusetts

None of the northeastern maritime colonies was originally designed to stand in isolation in America; according to the hopes of their European promoters, all were intended to maintain close relations with neighbouring populations of the same, or friendly, nationality. In many respects, however, European concept failed to be justified by American reality, and the respective English, Scots, and French visions of populous settlements existing in peaceful proximity one to another, under the dominion of a single monarch, certainly were never realized. The practicalities of the situation, involving the difficult tasks of developing an economic base, searching for some form of political stability, and competing for survival in both respects against the other nationalities, dictated that the danger of isolation was a cause for profound concern. The colony of New Scotland was particularly isolated, though intended to maintain contacts with the English settlements further south. Maine and Acadia, on the other hand, were conceived as parts of New England and New France; also within these larger entities were the neighbouring colonies of Massachusetts and Canada.

The period during which the New Scotland enterprise subsisted at Port Royal was one in which all European settlements in the northeastern region, as in the St Lawrence valley and further south in New England, were small and isolated. Only the incipient growth of the Massachusetts colony was offering to break the bounds of communal colonization. Nevertheless, efforts were being made to offset this situation and to build commercial links between New Scotland and the English colonies. On 16 May 1631, Charles I wrote to inform the government of Virginia that 'our trustie and weilbeloved William Clayborne, one of our Counsall, and Secretarie of State for our Colonie of Virginia, and some other Adventurers with him, have condescendit with our trustie and weilbeloved Counsellour Sir William Alexander, knyght, principall Secretarie of our kingdome of Scotland, and others of our subjects who have charge of our Coloneis of New Scotland and New England, to keip a course for interchange of trade amongst them as they shall have occasion, as also to mak discovereis for increase of trade in these parts ...' Accordingly, the Virginia colony and all other English colonies in America were instructed to assist Claiborne in any trading activities which did not contravene existing monopolies.[29] Claiborne's opportunities for trade in New Scotland were obviously cut short by the evacuation of 1632, and he pursued his colonial career subsequently in Virginia and Maryland, although recalling his New Scotland privileges to the attention of Charles II some forty-five years later in petitioning for sustenance as a 'Poore Old Servant of your Majesty's ffather and Grandfather.'[30]

Acadia, described in La Tour's commission of 1631 as a province within the greater whole of New France, was bound at least by theoretical links to whatever other French settlements might be made. Although the habitations of Tadoussac and Quebec had in 1629 fallen into the hands of the Kirkes, the English evacuation in the summer of 1632 in fulfilment of the treaty of

Saint-Germain-en-Laye, brought the St Lawrence region back into the fold of New France. The colony of Canada, however, was by no means the powerful centre of French settlement which it was to become in the second half of the century. Although the Compagnie de la Nouvelle-France was quick to recruit colonists and to start granting seigneuries on the St Lawrence, the population of Canada by 1645 had reached only some 600, somewhat more than that of Acadia but far from the 15,000 projected by the Cent-Associés. The more positive achievements included the re-establishment of Quebec and the foundation of new settlements at Trois-Rivières and Montreal, but a shortage of colonists after the first influx in the 1630s and the increasing depredations of the Iroquois had rendered the colony very fragile. In 1645, the trading monopoly, along with responsibility for government, was surrendered by the Cent-Associés into the hands of the Communauté des Habitants. Led by a council of merchants which administered on behalf of the whole community, the inhabitants now took full responsibility for the St Lawrence region, Acadia not being included in the transaction. In the next few years, various regulations were introduced in Canada to govern the administration both of the fur trade and of the colony itself. These changes, although aimed at solving the colony's outstanding problems, could not but have a temporary effect of disruption, and the new organization had hardly had time to become established when Iroquois warfare broke forth, resulting in 1649–50 in the virtual destruction of the French colonists' Huron allies, paralysing the vital fur trade, and threatening Canada itself with devastation.[31]

In the period 1630–50, therefore, the colony of Canada remained small and preoccupied with many internal difficulties. Since this situation applied also to Acadia, it is not surprising that few contacts existed between the two colonies. Even though, for example, Isaac de Razilly came to Acadia with the title of 'lieutenant-général pour le Roi, en la Nouvelle-France,' there is no evidence that he looked outside his tasks in the Acadian region. There were, of course, certain respects in which the common French origin of the colonies of Acadia and Canada made for connections between them. The trading and fishing posts operated at various times by Nicolas Denys in Chaleur Bay and on the gulf coast generally, were part of the economy of the St Lawrence rather than of that of the more southerly areas of Acadia, and the religious orders, notably the Jesuits, continued to maintain missions both in Canada and in Acadia. Nevertheless, even for the Jesuits, communications were uncertain and infrequent. In the Jesuit relations for 1636, for example, Le Jeune noted that he could not write with assurance about Acadia: 'Les Sauvages seulement traversans les terres, ou navigeans dans leurs petites gondoles sur les Fleuves, nous rapportent par fois quelques nouvelles de ces habitations plus esloignées.'[32] The effectiveness with which distance and terrain separated Canada and Acadia was further underscored in 1646, when the defeated La Tour was able to find a secure refuge in Quebec, and the two colonies' divergence in terms of institutions, which had begun with the commission accorded to La Tour in 1631, became a definite and virtually formalized separation in 1647 with the according of new powers to the Communauté des Habitants in Canada and to d'Aulnay in Acadia. The two French colonies, therefore, although never completely losing touch, showed a tendency during the years 1630–50 to drift apart.

Between Maine and the more southerly parts of New England – especially Massachusetts – an opposite tendency was at work. When the Massachusetts colony was bounded, first in a grant of the Council for New England and then in a royal charter of 1629, its northern extent was envisaged as stopping well short of northern New England; the boundary was defined in the charter as 'within the space of three English myles to the northward of the ... river called Monomack, alias Merrymack ... '[33] At the time the charter was issued, the Merrimack river was thought to run practically due west to east, and it was some years later that its true source was found to be far to the north, whence it flowed south-southeast and then curved eastward some forty miles from its mouth. When this was discovered, the potential was created for a claim that the Massachusetts line lay not three miles north of the latitude of the Merrimack at its mouth, but was instead a straight east-west line drawn three miles north of the river's head. A cautiously phrased version of this argument was used by the Massachusetts colony in 1641 in asserting a claim to all the New Hampshire settlements as far as the Piscataqua River, and the argument would be given its fullest form in the 1650s when the Bay colony proceeded to annex the Province of Maine, and thus to originate the major source of political controversy in Maine over the subsequent forty years.[34] Nevertheless, during the period 1630–50 the prevailing view on both sides of the Piscataqua River was, as John Winthrop remarked in 1646, paraphrasing the feelings of the Massachusetts General Court, that the Bay colony had 'no jurisdiction' in Maine.[35] Throughout the period, the two colonies of Maine and Massachusetts were, in formal terms, as separate as Canada and Acadia had become in 1647, both relationships coming under the loose general authority of New England and New France, respectively.

While the relationship between Canada and Acadia was further weakened by an absence of practical contacts, however, Maine and Massachusetts increasingly were linked in several important facets of colonial life. This is not to say that relations were always cordial. In 1633, for example, John Winthrop and Walter Neale, governor at Piscataqua on behalf of the Laconia Company, exchanged discourtesies over Neale's cool reception on a visit to Boston at a time when he was viewed there as the instrument of Gorges and Mason in designs to put Massachusetts under a general government of New England.[36] In general, however, both sides had good reasons for maintaining links. The growing economic power of Boston underlay the whole relationship.[37] But there were other respects in which Massachusetts, by virtue of its large population and its consequent ability to subdue the American environment quickly and thoroughly, had an influence on its northeastern neighbours.

Courts of justice had soon been organized in Massachusetts on a firm basis, and before the establishment of the judicial processes of the province of New Somersetshire in 1636, several cases were dealt with at the Court of Assistants in Boston which concerned inhabitants of the northeastern region. On 3 October 1632, for example, the fisherman Nicholas Frost was sentenced for theft, drunkenness, and fornication committed at Damerill's Cove, near Sagadahoc. In a further appearance at the same court in early 1636, Frost had as surety Henry Jocelyn, a patentee at Black Point and later one of the most prominent magistrates of Maine. Even after the system of courts had been established in New Somersetshire and subsequently in the Province of Maine, the prestige of the Massachusetts courts made them attractive for the arbitration of disputes in exceptional cases, as when the governor and magistrates of Massachusetts were asked in 1646 to hear a jurisdictional dispute involving a possible partitioning of Maine.[38]

As a source of religious ministration, the Massachusetts colony was useful to the Maine settlements. Although the colony of Maine did not share the specifically religious purpose of Massachusetts, the need for ministers was deeply felt, as indeed it was by most seventeenth-century Europeans. Thomas Jenner, for example, was a minister who moved from Massachusetts to Saco in late 1640 or early 1641, probably at the recommendation of John Winthrop. Thomas Gorges wrote to Winthrop on 23 February 1641 that 'Mr. Jenner I hear is like to remain at Sacoe, it is an argument I hope that God intends good unto these parts.' Gorges also mentioned that he hoped shortly to bring another minister from Massachusetts to Maine, a Mr Ward of Newbury.[39] The contemporary quarrels within the Church of England found echoes to some extent in Maine. Richard Vines, an inhabitant of Maine who had first come to New England some twenty-five years previously in the employ of Sir Ferdinando Gorges, informed Winthrop that 'I like Mr. Jenner his life and conversacion, and alsoe his preaching, if he would lett the Church of England alone ... '; Jenner himself reported 'hot discourses, (especially about the ceremonies).' Nevertheless, the thrust of Vines' letter was to thank Winthrop for his help in obtaining a minister, and Jenner found himself sufficiently 'loveingly respected' to remain in Saco for at least four years, during which he was one of the more acute observers of the internal conflicts then prevalent in Maine.[40]

Massachusetts could also assist in defence against any military threats that might arise. Ever since the first establishment of the Massachusetts colony, it had been the habit of those in authority in the English settlements in the northeast to appeal to Boston for help in the case of any such emergency. In

October 1631, for example, a message reached Winthrop from Thomas Wiggin, in the employ of the Laconia Company at Piscataqua, asking for the dispatch of 'twenty men presently to take revenge' for the alleged murder by Indians of Walter Bagnall, on Richmond's Island. Although the Massachusetts colony declined to take immediate action on the matter, it agreed just over a year later to send a similar force northeastward at the request of Walter Neale to attempt to apprehend an English pirate crew which had 'rifled Pemaquid.' Two attempts in fact failed to find the renegades, whose leader was later reported to be 'gone to the French,' though the first expedition did capture and execute an Indian in connection with the killing of Bagnall.[41] The efforts of the Plymouth colonists to enlist Massachusetts' help in their efforts to safeguard their interests in the northeast are a further instance of the perception of the Bay colony as a military resource. The period of equilibrium which followed was one in which potential military threats were less immediate, but Thomas Gorges recognized that Maine and Massachusetts were closely bound together in this respect when he wrote to Winthrop in the summer of 1643 to urge caution in dealing with La Tour: 'I doubt not only these parts [Maine] which are naked, but all New England will finde d'Aulnay a scourge.'[42]

The power of Massachusetts evoked mixed responses in the northeast. By some it was resented. In late 1632, the younger John Winthrop was told of 'a most egregious knave' from the Piscataqua region, who had been in London and had there described the Massachusetts colonists as 'Hereticks, and they would be more holy then all the world.'[43] Again, Thomas Wannerton, a fishing captain who was eventually to be killed assisting La Tour in a raid on d'Aulnay at Pentagouet, was brought into court in Boston in 1635, charged with having 'att the Eastward' spoken abusively to one John Holland of Massachusetts 'and called him roage and knave, and said they were all soe in the Bay, and that he hoped to see all their throates cutt, and that hee could finde it in his heart to begin with him ...'[44] The population of Maine, initially attracted by the fishery and not by any religious purpose, was mixed and in many respects rough and ready. Yet the unruliness of the Maine colonists should not be overestimated. As agriculture developed, stability was increasingly sought, and the original inhabitants were joined by later arrivals – often from Massachusetts – whose values were centred on strong family and community ties. As the sense of community grew in the various settlements, so did the inclination to look to Massachusetts as a model of what an English colony might be. The towns of Massachusetts, though providing no one pattern, offered examples of the successful regulation of those functions essential to a community, including the church, town government, and the allocation of land. Thomas Gorges wrote in 1640 that 'our province which had the report to be a Gardein of vice and a harbour of vicious men is reduced to a marvailous civility,' and the Massachusetts minister Hugh Peter declared that 'they grone for Government and Gospell all over that side on the Country.' The biases of each are apparent in their statements, but both were nearer to the aspirations of the Maine settlements than those who thought and acted as did Wannerton.[45]

Those who governed Maine endeavoured consistently – and wisely – to maintain good relations with Massachusetts. This was the preference of Sir Ferdinando Gorges who, despite (or perhaps because of) his hopes for a general government of New England, professed great respect for Winthrop and his colleagues. In 1637, in fact, Gorges twice requested Winthrop and others to act as his intermediaries in settling the government of New Somersetshire after the departure of William Gorges; the request was declined.[46] Three years later, Gorges again wrote to Winthrop, to introduce Thomas Gorges: 'I haveing given him command to be carefull to doe his best that all fayr corrospondency be maintayned between these two severall Plantations ...' When Thomas Gorges arrived in Boston on his way to Maine, he impressed Winthrop favourably as 'sober and well disposed ... and was very careful to take advice of our magistrates how to manage his affairs etc.'[47] In the following year Gorges and Edward Godfrey, a prominent magistrate and patentee of Maine, wrote to Winthrop to assure him that Maine 'shall be noe refuge for runnaways,' in the context of promising their best efforts to return one Reuben Guppy, a fugitive from Massachusetts justice.[48] A further letter of November 1648, from Godfrey and a fellow magistrate to Winthrop and his deputy governor Richard Bellingham, promised similar efforts in the case of one Anne Cronder, 'who maid an escape and as supposed into this jurisdiction.'[49] Throughout this period, during which the Massachusetts colony had become an even closer neighbour through the annexation of all the New Hampshire settlements by 1643, the authorities of Maine remained anxious to have friendly contacts and to prove themselves desirable neighbours.[50]

For its part the Massachusetts colony, as a corporate body, took a disdainful view of the small and occasionally turbulent settlements of Maine and tried as far as possible to avoid any involvement in the affairs of the northeastern province. Six years after the refusal of the General Court to intervene in New Somersetshire at Gorges' request, Winthrop recorded that Maine was deliberately excluded from the confederation of New England colonies formed in 1643: 'Those of Sir Ferdinando Gorges his province, beyond Pascataquack, were not received nor called into the confederation, because they ran a different course from us both in their ministry and civil administration; for they had lately made Acomenticus (a poor village) a corporation, and had made a taylor their mayor, and had entertained one Hull, an excommunicated person and very contentious, for their minister.'[51] In 1646, although it made an attempt at arbitrating a dispute from Maine, 'for that it was a usual practice in Europe for two states being at odds to make a third judge between them,' the General Court was eventually unwilling to offer any other advice than to refer the matter to England.[52]

Despite reluctance on the part of the General Court to recognize the fact, the links between Maine and Massachusetts were real. The economic dominance of Maine by Massachusetts had created strong merchant interests, especially as the economic and ecological exigencies of the 1640s had forced Massachusetts merchants to look further afield for their natural resources. The timber reserves on the north side of the Piscataqua River were arousing particular interest, and now that the New Hampshire settlements had been annexed, there was an obvious argument for making the Piscataqua wholly a Massachusetts river.[53] If Maine was valuable for such reasons as these, it was equally true that Maine, an area of weak and fragmented authority, was a potential danger, both as a refuge for fugitives from and enemies of Massachusetts and as a possible springboard for French or Indian hostility. Whether those who governed Massachusetts liked it or not, and in many ways they did not, the strong practical links which had grown up between the two colonies by 1650 could not be ignored.

Conflict or Coexistence?

Following his seizure of the Plymouth colony's trading post at Penobscot, great pains were taken by d'Aulnay to assure the colonists of New England that he intended them no further harm. Abraham Shurt, the trader at Pemaquid, reported to Winthrop in June 1636 of 'a Franciscan ffryar insinuatinge unto me that Mr. Comander [Razilly] and Mr. Donye desired nothing but fayre passages betwixt us, and that he was sent purposely to signifie so much unto me.' Later in the year, Winthrop himself recorded that d'Aulnay had in a letter 'professed, that they claimed no further than to Pemaquid, nor would unless he had further order; and that he supposed, that the cause why he had no order, etc., was, that the English ambassador had dealt effectually with the cardinal of France for setting the limits for our peace, etc.' The question which had to be considered in Boston was whether d'Aulnay's professions were merely tactical efforts to buy time during a period of temporary equilibrium, and that, as Shurt felt at the time despite his trading links with d'Aulnay and La Tour, 'we must feare the worst, and strive our best to withstand them,' or whether, despite the conflict of European boundary claims, there was a real likelihood of peaceful, advantageous coexistence between English and French.[54] This question had no conclusive answer in Massachusetts for the time being, though there is strong evidence that such a relationship with Acadia was indeed possible, especially during the short time when d'Aulnay had paramount authority in the French colony. What also emerged, however, was that the Massachusetts colony had acquired an unavoidable interest in the internal affairs of Acadia because of economic links forged by Massachusetts merchants. Relations between the two colonies would henceforth inevitably be seen from Boston in this light.[55]

In the event, New England was not called upon to come into contact with Acadia between 1636 and 1641, the occasion in 1641 being the arrival in Boston of the emissary of La Tour, asking and obtaining 'liberty of free commerce' with Massachusetts. On La Tour's further requests, notably for assistance against d'Aulnay, the Massachusetts colony procrastinated and 'excused any treaty with him.'[56] The first approach by La Tour not only set the tone for future contacts, but also indicated rather clearly the considerations which motivated either side. For La Tour, as for the colonists of Maine, Massachusetts was a resource, one that could supply those needs which had hitherto required recourse to Europe. La Tour's need was a particularly urgent one, since the decision by the French crown in favour of d'Aulnay in early 1641 had put him on the defensive. For Massachusetts, two considerations were predominant. On the one hand was a desire to be left alone to proceed with the task of building the colony; this implied a basic disposition to resist any involvement in Acadia but also led to a fear of provoking hostility through any offensive rejection of French advances. On the other hand, Massachusetts merchants were able and willing to expand their commercial operations north-wards, and in the economic depression which followed the end of large-scale immigration in the early 1640s, the colony could hardly afford to obstruct such enterprises. These two considerations, although not entirely in harmony with one another, did suggest a possible approach by Massachusetts to La Tour: to refuse any political involvement within Acadia, but to give no discouragement to arrangements between La Tour and private merchants.[57] This was the approach adopted in 1641 and when La Tour sent a further mission the following year.

As begun in 1641–2, this approach seemed simple and effective. La Tour, for his part, behaved with ostentatious courtesy, even making concessions to the Protestantism of the English colony: the emissary of 1641 was himself 'a Rocheller and a Protestant,' and those of 1642, 'though they were papists, yet they came to our church meeting ... ' On the Massachusetts side in 1642, 'some of our merchants sent a pinnace to trade with La Tour in St. John's river,' being welcomed 'very kindly.'[58] There were, however, two complications. First, any kind of contact with Acadia implied involvement in the La Tour-d'Aulnay dispute. If it had not been so before, this was made clear in 1642 when the returning merchants 'met with D'Aulnay at Pemaquid, who wrote also to our governor, and sent him a printed copy of the arrest against La Tour, and threatened us, that if any of our vessels came to La Tour, he would make prize of them.'[59] To incur the hostility of d'Aulnay was a grave risk, especially if he should eventually emerge the victor over La Tour. Indeed, even if La Tour should be victorious, there was no guarantee that he would then feel any further need for good relations with Massachusetts, and he might thus become a strong and dangerous enemy. Secondly, rivalries were aroused within Massachusetts itself. The more northerly counties of Essex and Norfolk were not content to see the merchants of Suffolk and Middlesex derive the benefits of trade with La Tour, partly because they in the north were particularly vulnerable to attack by d'Aulnay, and partly because they themselves had designs upon the northern fishing and fur trade and were not anxious to have competition.[60]

Within Massachusetts, this issue came to a head in 1643, when La Tour arrived in Boston with a large ship and a force of 140 men – sufficient, as Winthrop observed, that 'had [he] been ill minded towards us, he had such an opportunity as we hope neither he nor any other shall ever have the like again.'[61] La Tour's request was for no less than military assistance in raising d'Aulnay's blockade of his fort on the St John River. Whether through fright at the armed power of La Tour, or because Winthrop, who had recently returned as governor to replace the more strictly isolationist Richard Bellingham, took a more favourable view of involvement in Acadia, it was decided that although the colony as such would not assist La Tour, the latter would be permitted to recruit volunteers. This La Tour soon did.[62] Although not a fundamental breach of the approach adopted in 1641–2, the decision was clearly based upon a much more liberal interpretation, and it aroused bitter opposition in the northern counties. On 14 July 1643, the day La Tour sailed from Boston with four hired ships and crews, seven influential magistrates and elders of Essex county wrote to 'wash our hands wholly' of the decision to allow La Tour to be aided. Whether admitted or not, they argued, the expedition was a warlike one, undertaken by greedy merchants in the hope of gain. In this view they had much justification, for the aid to La Tour had been provided through the Boston merchants Thomas Hawkins and Edward Gibbons, and in the following year Gibbons and Hawkins became associated with Winthrop's own son, the younger John Winthrop.[63] The results of the expedition of 1643, moreover, turned out to be 'offensive and grievous' to the elder Winthrop and those who supported him; Massachusetts forces were directly involved in a partially successful assault upon d'Aulnay's settlement at Port Royal, which was not only distasteful in itself but the worst kind of provocation to d'Aulnay.[64]

This venture marked the height of Massachusetts' support for La Tour, and it played a major part in the replacement of Winthrop as governor early in 1644 by John Endicott of Salem. La Tour, increasingly at a disadvantage in his struggle with d'Aulnay, continued to request assistance and continued to be permitted to trade with Massachusetts merchants. After the fall of his fort on the St John in April 1645, however, he was clearly a defeated man. For a time he re-established contact with an old acquaintance, visiting Sir David Kirke in Newfoundland and obtaining a ship for a fur-trading voyage on the Atlantic coast of Acadia. He thereupon returned to Boston and persuaded several merchants to relieve his 'present poore distressed Condition' by furnishing him with the necessary trade goods for the venture; he then reneged and fled into exile in Quebec, leaving Winthrop to reflect '(as the scripture saith) that there is no confidence in an unfaithful or carnal man.'[65]

The attitude of d'Aulnay towards the Massachusetts colony was rather more complex. As the legitimate representative of direct royal authority in Acadia, especially after 1641, it was not open to him to take a cavalier attitude towards European restraints, and in communications to France, he and his Capuchin associates took an appropriately hostile view of the usurping heretics of New England. On 10 September 1647, d'Aulnay wrote to the French chancellor to give fulsome thanks for his recent appointment as royal 'Gouverneur et ... Lieutenant Général'; in an obvious reference to New England, he went on to promise strenuous efforts to protect the royal authority in Acadia, 'nonobstant toute La resistance que pourroist fayre les Religionnayres estrangers qui les [the lands of Acadia] ont usurpees sur la france par la negligence ou Impuissance des francois qui y ont este devant moy.'[66] In practical terms, moreover, the help afforded to La Tour in Boston and the involvement of English forces in the attack on Port Royal in 1643 were matters which d'Aulnay could not overlook, and they occasioned a stern admonition to the Boston authorities in an exasperated letter of 1645.

> If you call that satisfaction [referring to the further, though more restricted, help given to La Tour in 1644] unto a Governour for the King, after sending with strength of arms even unto his Port without declaration of warre, nor giving any other reason than by lively force to kill his men, burne one mill, slay cattall, and to carry away a Bark, laden with Peltry and other goods, to say that your English, who have done such acts of hostility, were not sent by you, pardon me, Sir, if you please, if I tell you this is the mocking of a Gentleman to render such answers.

Continuing, he asserted that even had the attack succeeded in capturing Port Royal, 'you have to doe with a king, who would not soe easily have let you digested the Morsell as you might be given to understand.'[67]

None the less, d'Aulnay's correspondence with Massachusetts contrasted with the hostile fashion in which he portrayed the English colonists when writing to France. His first reaction to the attack of 1643 had been to issue instructions for the capture of any Massachusetts ships found in Acadian waters. Then, however, he received a guardedly conciliatory letter from Governor Endicott, asking that 'wee may understand how you are at present disposed, whether to warre or peace' and assuring that none but genuinely private mercantile connections with La Tour now remained.[68] D'Aulnay now reverted to his professedly friendly style of 1636. In a letter of October 1644 from Port Royal, he praised 'the great order which you observe in your Government, and that civility which is naturall unto you, as allso your generousness towards all your Neighbours,' though advising Massachusetts 'for the time to come not soe easily to receive impressions ... and set an high price upon your ffriendship.' Protesting the legitimacy of his claim to Pentagouet and dealing with certain other Massachusetts complaints, d'Aulnay promised to send an emissary to Boston and closed with a remarkable proposal: 'whatever troubles may fall out ... between the two Crowns of ffrance and England (which I heartily pray God not to grant) to keep inviolably with you and those which are under your Authority that peace and intelligence which is requisite in these beginnings ...'[69]

Here, then, was d'Aulnay proposing, as one American colonizer to others, that peace should be maintained in all circumstances to facilitate the vital task of colonial development. There remained distrust of d'Aulnay in Massachusetts for his previous deeds, and his hold on Penobscot had become an especial concern following the buying out of the Plymouth interest there by Hawkins, Gibbons, and the younger Winthrop in August 1644 – La Tour, in a letter of 27 October 1644, was certainly right to emphasize the memory of 'L'Affaire de Penobsquit' in attempting to persuade the Massachusetts colony of d'Aulnay's 'perfidie et sa rage contre la Nation Angloise.'[70] Nevertheless, d'Aulnay's offer was an extremely attractive and realistic one, and negotiations began in Boston with the arrival of d'Aulnay's representative, the Capuchin brother François-Marie de Paris.[71]

The eventual treaty, signed on 18 October, gave both d'Aulnay and the Massachusetts colony much of what they wanted. On the one hand, Massachusetts recognized the existence of 'Acadie, a province of New France,' a recognition which had never been made in England, and d'Aulnay as the 'Governor and Lieutenant General of His Majesty the king of France'; further, all the English settlers were to keep 'a firm peace with Mr. D'Aulnay,' as he would do reciprocally. No boundaries were mentioned, but it was informally assumed that Pentagouet and points northeast would remain to the French and Pemaquid and points southwest to the English. Thus the political disassociation of Massachusetts from Acadia, one of the English colony's two major concerns, was assured. The second major concern, that of trade, was also covered – 'it shall be lawful for all men, both French and English, to trade with one another' – and even private trade with La Tour was safeguarded. Thus the interests of d'Aulnay and the Massachusetts colony, as fellow colonizers, coalesced.[72]

This treaty of 1644 did not mark the end of friction between d'Aulnay and

Massachusetts; private assistance to La Tour brought about another acerbic exchange of letters in 1645, and this renewed mood of hostility persisted for a short time while d'Aulnay hoped to exploit the now-evident desire of Massachusetts, and indeed of the United Colonies of New England, to make a lasting peace. In 1646, however, François-Marie de Paris again went to Boston and a compromise was agreed upon by which both sides were absolved of blame for the misunderstandings of the previous two years.[73] The Indian trade was not included in the treaty, and in 1647 conflict flared briefly when a Massachusetts ship was seized by d'Aulnay for trading with the Indians near Cap de Sable. This action, however, was adjudged in Boston not to be 'any manifest wrong ... [by] D'Aulney, seeing we had told him, that if ours did trade within his liberties, they should do it at their own peril,' it being thought 'not safe nor expedient for us to begin a war with the French.'[74] What the situation would be after d'Aulnay's death was, of course, another question, since the stability of authority in Acadia depended heavily upon his personal power; for the moment, though, it seemed that a working relationship had been established between Acadia and New England.

Two rather different French views of New England have, therefore, been identified: La Tour's view of New England as a useful resource, and d'Aulnay's of New England as a separate colony to be negotiated with. Both contrasted with the radically hostile European conceptions which would have placed New England and New France in fundamental conflict with one another. A third 'American' view of New England also became evident, this time from Canada: a view of New England as a potential partner in an alliance of colonists against the Iroquois. In Canada, a colony which by virtue of its large extent and small population could not hope to metamorphose the American environment as quickly and thoroughly as had Massachusetts, a consciousness had for some time been growing of the European settler as opposed to the Indian, rather than of different nationalities of settlers as opposed to each other. In the Jesuit relation of 1636, for example, Le Jeune had noted that 'Monsieur de Rasilly estoit dans l'estime d'un tres grand Capitaine, non seulement parmy les François et les Anglois; mais encore dans la creance de tous les Peuples de son Païs.'[75] The following year's relation, moreover, had occasion to refer to 'un European de l'Acadie.'[76] Such a bracketing of European nationalities did not necessarily imply cordial relations between them, but the Jesuit father Druillettes, on a mission to the Abenaki in 1647, found considerable good will in the English settlements on the Kennebec: 'il visite sept ou huict habitations d'Anglois, qui le receurent tous, avec une affection plus extraordinaire, qu'elle estoit moins attenduë.'[77]

It was perhaps because of this experience that Druillettes was chosen in 1650 to go to Boston, Plymouth, and New Haven (though this stage of the journey was in the event prevented by bad weather) to propose free trade between New France and New England and a military alliance against the Mohawks. The suggestion of free trade, which in fact derived from a proposal made some time previously by Massachusetts, received a friendly enough reception. The Massachusetts council was unable to give a final reply until the next meeting of the General Court, 'but till then, if any of yours shall come into our Jurisdiction wee shall not Interrupt them but gladly embrace them' – provided, of course, that reciprocal treatment was given. The council also dealt with guarded favour with a proposition which paralleled that made by d'Aulnay in 1644: 'That however it may ffall out that the kingdome of ffraunce and Commonwealth of England maybe at enmitie one with another yett that there might be and Remayne a firme peace betweene you of new ffraunce and us of New England wee Answer wee desier peace with all men as much as in us lieth, (as we are bound) and hope there wilbe no cause demonstrated by you or us to make warre.' On the alliance against the Mohawks, however, the council procrastinated upon the impeccably valid grounds of awaiting the next meeting of the United Colonies in September 1651.[78]

Druillettes, who had continued to Plymouth and there received courteous treatment and some apparent encouragement for the alliance, reported optimistically when he returned to Quebec.[79] Accordingly, the Quebec council wrote on 20 June 1651 to the United Colonies to announce its approval of the freedom of commerce 'et Ensemble l'Union des cœurs et des Esprits entre vos colonies et les nôtres,' provided that 'une ligue offensive et deffensive avec vous contre les iroquois' was at the same time concluded; further, Druillettes and another envoy, Jean Godefroy de Lintot, were empowered to represent the French at the meeting of the United Colonies in September and would be joined by an ambassador with full powers to conclude a treaty.[80] It soon emerged, however, that Druillettes had misread the intentions of the New England colonies, since the alliance, although with pious hopes for the continuation of trade and friendship between New England and New France, was rejected.[81] Certain unnamed individuals in Boston had in early 1651 assured Druillettes 'que le sentiment commun des particuliers du dict boston est que sy le republique ne veult pas se resoudre a ce secours contre l'Irocquois par authorité publique les volontaires particuliers sont preste a ceste expedition avecq la simple permission de la dite requeste comme en faveur de Monsieur Guebins [Gibbons] pour Monsieur latour quelcques troupes allerent contre feu Monsieur daunay.' In the event even this kind of aid was not forthcoming; the United Colonies professed themselves unable to 'permitt volenteers or Auxiliarye forces to bee taken up against the Mohaukes.'[82]

In truth, the only close relationship that New England might desire with New France, either Canada or Acadia, was that exemplified to Druillettes by a ship's captain at Kittery, who 'de son plein mouvement me demande un simple certificat de la paix et bonne intelligence entre la Nouvelle France et la Nouvelle Angleterre pour se rendre a lisle percee environ le mois dApril ou de May avecq trente thonneaux de bled dinde oultre les autres denree.'[83] Increasingly large, vested interests were beginning to be held by Massachusetts merchants in the northeastern maritime region, both in Maine and in Acadia. The Gibbons, Hawkins, and Winthrop interests were cases in point. So too were those of Joshua Scottow and John Leverett, who in 1653 were granted a special licence by the General Court to trade to Acadia.[84] Leverett, who had inherited from his father a half share in the Muscongus patent at Penobscot but apparently never made use of this holding, was to figure prominently in the affairs of both Maine and Acadia in the three decades to follow; Scottow too acquired interests in Maine and indeed took up residence there in 1671.[85] Valentine Hill, who had been delegated by the Plymouth colony in 1644 to receive payment for the sale of its rights at Penobscot, had by 1651 moved to New Hampshire and had already by 1647 been sending employees across the Piscataqua River into Maine to prospect the timber trade.[86]

Such interests as these, and the related growing awareness of the usefulness of the northeastern maritime region both for trade and for exploitation of natural resources, were not necessarily a barrier to the maintenance of a politically isolationist stance by Massachusetts towards its northeastern neighbours, either English or French. They did ensure, however, that these neighbouring colonies would be closely watched by strong interests in Boston which could not afford change in the existing state of affairs there: they could not afford to see political and social chaos which might threaten the safety of their investments; nor could they afford to see the northeastern maritime colonies become more strongly established by support from Europe, since this might lead to competition and possible exclusion. For the moment, the Massachusetts colony was disinclined to have any formal involvement in the northeast, 'having enough to do at home'.[87] But if either or both of these situations should come about in the colonies of Maine and Acadia, as indeed happened in the 1650s, then pressure would begin to mount for intervention from Boston.

During the period 1630–50, therefore, the external relationships of the north-eastern maritime colonies underwent several phases. First European conceptions and assumptions pitted the various nationalities against each other in small but damaging outbreaks of warfare. Gradually, in the northeastern region and in Canada and Massachusetts, the colonists realized that despite nationality they had a common interest in peaceful relationships which would make possible and might even facilitate, in the case of economic links, the consolidation and development of the colonies. In Massachusetts this realization led to a desire for political dissociation from the affairs of the colony's neighbours, combined with an increasing expansion of mercantile activity. This desire was compatible with the wishes of d'Aulnay and those of the rulers of Maine in the 1640s; the more dangerous involvements requested by La Tour and the Quebec council were given much more cautious treatment, especially after the events of 1643. The fact was that the inter-colonial relationships of the northeastern maritime region were by 1650 increasingly being influenced by Massachusetts; the question after 1650 would be whether, and in what way, this influence would be extended to the internal affairs of those colonies.

CHAPTER 5

Internal Relationships

Elements of Stability

The period between 1630 and 1650, one of great uncertainty in the development of European colonies in the northeastern maritime region, was also one of
population growth. From the scattering of English, French, and Scottish
settlements which had existed in 1630, the colonies of Maine and Acadia had
grown twenty years later to have approximate populations of 1,000 and 400
respectively. In neither of the colonies did a numerous tenantry cover the land
as completely as the early colonial promoters had envisaged. Yet gradually, in
certain areas, communities were emerging which were based on extensive
agricultural cultivation and structured according to seigneurial or proprietorial
principles. In Acadia, as for the short-lived colony of New Scotland, the
principal centre of agricultural cultivation was Port Royal. Although the
headquarters of Razilly from 1632 to 1635 were on the opposite side of the
peninsula at La Hève, the colony was moved to Port Royal when d'Aulnay took
command. Razilly, like Gorges before him, had sought to finance colonization
not only through the fur trade but also through the fishery. The expenses of
transporting and equipping agricultural settlers would be offset, he had hoped,
by the profits of marketing fish in southern Europe, a vision which had been
wholeheartedly shared by Nicolas Denys.[1] The disastrous Spanish seizure of
Denys's ship at Oporto in early 1635, however, was followed by the sudden
death of Razilly at La Hève; henceforth the rather different vision of d'Aulnay
would prevail. Port Royal offered extensive marshland, which d'Aulnay
ordered drained for agriculture, and it was also conveniently close to the
lucrative fur-trading areas across the Bay of Fundy. The resources of the sea
were not forgotten by d'Aulnay – he was aware that the marshes could provide

salt for use in the fishery as well as serving as agricultural land, and he also encouraged a seal hunt off the south coast of the peninsula – but the resources of the land would henceforth be paramount.[2]

Over the settlement and organization of Port Royal, d'Aulnay maintained personal control. The preparation of the marshes for agricultural use was carried out under his supervision, no doubt by the same specialized craftsmen, described as 'saulniers et bastisseurs de maraix sallans,' who were hired by the Razilly company in 1636 to begin the production of salt.[3] When the first marshlands were diked and drained, new colonists were brought over in families with a view to offsetting the predominantly male environment of which Razilly had complained at La Hève in 1634; in later years, a number of the oldest inhabitants of Acadia would certify that d'Aulnay had settled several families at Port Royal and had built ships and installations.[4] D'Aulnay himself affirmed that he had at Port Royal '200 hommes, tant soldats laboureurs que autres Artisants sans compter les femmes et enfants, les Peres Capuchins ny les petits enfants sauvages qu'Il fault nourrir dans le Seminaire estably pour cela. Il y en outre 20 mesnages françois qui sont passez avec leurs familles pour commencer a peupler les Païs dans lesquels ledit sieur d'Aulnay en feroit bien passer d'advantage s'il avoit plus de bien.'[5]

In a later document, no earlier than 1685, the Le Borgne heirs, who claimed d'Aulnay's legacy on the grounds of his debt to their merchant ancestor, stated that 'depuis que le sieur de Menou [d'Aulnay] s'est veu seul proprietaire de l'accadie il a faict bastir au port Royal le fort quy supciste, une Eglize, et un Convent, Des moulins, beaucoup de logemens, et fait desfricher un nombre considerable D'arpens de terre quy font trois grosses metairies quy luy coustent plus de cent cinquante mil livres.'[6] It is possible that the term 'métairie' was used literally in this description, implying a form of tenure by which equipment and land were provided by the seigneur in return for rents either in money or in kind, and a sharing between lessor and lessee of the products of the year's farming; such an arrangement would enable d'Aulnay to reap continuing benefits from the lands of Port Royal without being distracted from his efforts to monopolize the fur trade. It is unlikely, though, that there was any one form of land tenure used by d'Aulnay. In 1649, he made a small concession of two *arpents* of already cultivated land to the ship's carpenter, Martin de Chevery, on relatively lenient *cens et rentes* terms, an example of his efforts to attract skilled craftsmen to the colony.[7] The religious needs of the settlement were attended to by Capuchin friars, who used Port Royal as a base for both missionary and pastoral activities throughout Acadia.[8] Thus, working with settlers who were drawn at least in part from his own family lands in France, d'Aulnay had for the moment a tightly organized, though small, seigneurial settlement as his base.[9]

The colony of Maine also developed a small area of settlement based on *féodalité*, in this case a cluster of villages in the southern part of the province, Kittery, Agamenticus, Wells, and Saco, shading off into looser settlements towards Casco Bay.[10] This development was larger and rather more complicated than that of Port Royal, involving not the direct effort of a single seigneur to produce agricultural settlement, but the action of several land-owners holding ultimately from the grants of the Council for New England or of Sir Ferdinando Gorges as lord proprietor. In the early years, particularly in the case of those settlements which derived from the Laconia Company's operations at Piscataqua, this southern area of Maine resembled the settlement of Razilly at La Hève in that it was based on a combination of agriculture and fishing. Several of the early patentees had been involved in the Laconia Company, a prime example being Edward Godfrey, who had charge of the company's fishing operations and became an early settler of Agamenticus. Although Godfrey was not specifically mentioned in earlier land grants at Agamenticus by the Council for New England, a meeting of members of the former council voted on 22 March 1638 that a grant of 1631 should be renewed to Edward Godfrey, among others. In future years, Godfrey's practice would be to sublet land to tenants who would either pay rents or perform services in return.[11]

The proprietary land structure, though, was not uniform. The grants of the Council for New England had ranged widely both in size and in terms of tenure over an active period of some eleven years. Variation was also typical of the Province of Maine under the charter of 1639. Thomas Gorges, for example, received in March 1642 a personal grant of 5,000 acres on the Ogunquit River, a short distance south of Wells, with provision for full manorial rights as well as for the subdivision of land.[12] Although Thomas had little time to organize his own land before his departure from Maine in 1643, he made numerous grants on behalf of Sir Ferdinando Gorges as lord proprietor. Much more limited than Thomas Gorges' own grant in the scope of rights and privileges conferred, these concessions ranged from small grants of marshland, such as the two acres granted to Peter Weare near Agamenticus in July 1643, to large grants of mixed land, such as the 600 acres on the Piscataqua River (including two islands) granted to Thomas Withers in March of the same year.[13] Thus, land tenure in Maine was characterized by complexity and variety. What bound the strands together was the consistency of the various forms with conventional European forms, and the hopes entertained for the settlement of a numerous agricultural tenantry. As John Josselyn remarked during his second visit to Maine in the 1660s, 'the people in the province of Main may be divided into Magistrates, Husbandmen, or Planters, and fishermen.' Magistrates in the period prior to 1650 were, with few exceptions, also large patentees. The fishermen and planters, who might according to Josselyn in many cases be the same individuals, comprised the province's tenantry.[14]

Sir Ferdinando Gorges himself retained considerable direct interest in his province. Although never himself coming to America, he had performed functions similar to those of d'Aulnay in providing equipment, settlers, and supplies. In July 1634, John Winthrop recorded that 'Sir Ferdinando Gorges and Captain [John] Mason sent ... to Pascataquack and Aquamenticus, with two sawmills, to be erected, in each place one.' Again, in late 1636, Winthrop wrote that a ship had arrived in Boston from Bristol; 'but she had delivered most of her cattle and passengers at Pascataquack for Sir Ferdinando Gorge his plantation.'[15] Gorges' continuing interests embraced both dues arising from equipment, and rents, as Thomas Gorges made clear shortly after his arrival as deputy governor in 1640:

> Christopher Rogers [an employee of Gorges] I intend to put into the grist mill as soone as I have it a litle repaired, which mill and the saw mill with a litle cost if they be well mended, as I hope they shall, will bringe in 200 li per annum to Sir Fardinando at the least. As yet he hath but halfe the profit. Likewise the smiths mill will bringe in a good round sum, and in the interim he works it and will be every day comminge. Likewise the rents of the Province will amount to a good round sum in time. Some now pay 10s per annum, some 5s, some more, some lesse. At the next Court we intend to confirm all theyr leases and have exact account of arrears.[16]

Thus in 1640 Gorges was optimistic of the continued working of the proprietorial structure in Maine. Like that of d'Aulnay in Acadia, the achievement was real, even if limited in scale.

Elements of Instability

Yet the achievements of seigneurial and proprietorial colonization were flawed, for the 1640s saw the outbreak of internal disputes which threatened the existence of both Maine and Acadia. In connection with the land dispute between the Trelawny plantation and George Cleeve, John Winter remarked to Trelawny in 1639 that 'for to seeke any right by law, hear is none, but every man is a law to hims selfe. Yt is a bad kind of living to live in a place where is neather law nor goverment amonge people.' Trelawny himself, some two years later and in the context of the same dispute, admonished Thomas Gorges that, although 'in New Plantations, formes and Legalityes are not Exactly to be Expected,' nevertheless 'Just things are, and must be.' Otherwise, he went on, 'I dare saye noe men of quallitye will sett [down amo]ngst you, and how Longe itt wilbe before you Cann expecte perfection to the Countrye without them, you that are such may Judge.'[17] Nicolas Denys, having been dispossessed by d'Aulnay at Miscou, wrote with striking similarity that 'tant qu'il n'y aura point d'ordre et que l'on ne sera point asseuré de la joüissance de ses concessions, le païs ne se peuplera jamais et sera toûjours à l'abandon des Ennemis de la France.'[18] These complainants, Winter, Trelawny, and Denys, were all interested parties. Nevertheless, they expressed a real sense of disorder and lack of generally respected authority.

Sir Ferdinando Gorges, aged seventy years and in uncertain health when he received his proprietorial grant in 1639, had intended as late as January 1640 to go to Maine in person, but he eventually delegated his powers to Thomas Gorges as his deputy, assisted by a council of patentees.[19] Shortly after his arrival in Maine in the summer of 1640, Thomas was optimistic regarding his task ahead: 'at my arrival heer,' he wrote to his father, he had been shown 'all theyr proceedings and I protest I admir'd to see soe excelent way of orderinge all thinges. They doe it with grand and pety Juries and the officers of a court as they do in England and all the fines go to Sir Fardinando.' Gorges' reference here was to 'the first Generall Court' of the Province of Maine, which had been held at Saco by four of the councillors on 25 June.[20] Before this date, however, the history of government in the area of the Province of Maine was less encouraging. Robert Gorges had failed entirely in 1623 to assert the authority of the Council for New England over New England as a whole. The short tenure of William Gorges, nephew of Sir Ferdinando, as governor of New Somersetshire in 1636–7 had been only slightly more successful. Although William had held courts from March 1636 until the summer of 1637, he had been unable to enforce his jurisdiction over recalcitrant land-owners. On 28 March 1636, for example, a case arose involving Thomas Lewis, a patentee at Saco, and his disputed title to an offshore island. On having the trial of his title deferred and being ordered in the interim to allow access to his rival, 'Mr. Thomas Luis did opprobriusly in open Court lascerat and teare an order maid to that purpose ...'[21] That this contempt apparently went unpunished is a striking indication of weakness on the part of the court. Even more destructive to the authority of William Gorges was his involvement in the dispute between Cleeve and Winter, concerning land claimed by both at Spurwink and Casco. After Cleeve had been fined £5 in March 1636 'for rash speches,' he went to England and avenged the affront by successfully advising the recall of William Gorges by his uncle. Sir Ferdinando wrote in August 1637 of Cleeve's 'misreports to mee' of the 'miscarriage in theire places' of his New Somersetshire officers; but although he later regretted having heeded Cleeve's advice, no further courts were held until 1640.[22]

Previous to Thomas Gorges' arrival, therefore, the precedents for effective central authority were not promising. The General Court which was opened at Saco on 8 September 1640 was more successful, with a large number of suits being decided. One notable episode was the successful prosecution of a slander suit against John Bonython of Saco, who over the next forty years was to be a constant opponent of authority in any shape or form in Maine. On this occasion, perhaps somewhat restrained by the presence of the bench of his father, the Saco patentee Richard Bonython, John appeared in court and was ordered to pay damages to the Reverend Richard Gibson, formerly minister at Richmond's Island, 'The defendant,' charged Gibson, 'did unjustly and wrongfully slander the plaintiff for a base preist, a base knave, a base fellow and ... Mary his wife for a base whore, an impudent whore, a base strum-pett ...' This rare censure of John Bonython for wrongfully impugning the moral character of the Gibsons was followed by an exposition of the evidently real sexual misdemeanours of the Reverend George Burdett, after which the hitherto influential Agamenticus minister returned to England in disgrace. Having thus displayed a determination to administer justice effectively in Maine, Gorges and the court made an important recognition of the far-flung nature of the province in prescribing that courts would in future be held annually both at Saco and, 'for the avoydeing of trouble and charge to the Inhabitants of this Province, who many of them live farre remote from this place,' at Agamenticus. Although all major cases, as well as minor cases originating between the Kennebec and Kennebunk rivers, would continue to be heard at Saco, minor cases from between the rivers of Piscataqua and Kenne-bunk could be decided at Agamenticus. Thus, the government of Thomas Gorges, which was apparently chiefly represented by courts which could and did make administrative orders, was at the least a serious attempt to provide sufficiently strong and mobile rule to reduce the Province of Maine to some semblance of order and unity.[23]

The real test, however, would come if and when Gorges entered into conflict with any of the patentees on matters which affected their real interests. The Cleeve-Winter dispute was just such a case, and it was one which the court of September 1640 did indeed take on immediately. Although judgment was deferred in a case of slander in which Winter charged Cleeve with describing his wife as 'the veriest drunkenest whore,' in the town of Plymouth, the land claims at Spurwink and Casco were heard by jury and decided in favour of Cleeve.[24] The question now, predictably enough, was whether Winter would accept the verdict. In October, the marshal of the Maine General Court visited Richmond's Island, as Winter reported, 'to take my body or the goods heare on the Iland by force, for the satisfying of Cleves execution.' On being 'Carried ... out of our house betwixt 3 or 4 [of Winter's men],' the marshal departed and presently returned with '30 men in armes,' who were held off by Winter's fishermen.[25] There the matter rested until Winter was forced by a storm in early 1641 to put in to Agamenticus harbour and was there arrested by '[Gorges'] officer with 5 or 6 men,' and released only after giving bond for a subsequent court appearance at Saco to answer for 'resisting the Provost Marshall (by force of armes.)'[26] At the court, Winter caused a great 'clamor' by impugning the integrity of the original jury; although he was forced to retract his statement, the court was 'somthing pusselled' as to how to proceed, and eventually submitted the whole case to arbitration.[27] Even this did not provide a settlement, for after the arbitrators had decided in favour of Cleeve on all counts, news was brought that Sir Ferdinando Gorges had responded to an appeal by Winter and Trelawny, 'and had given Order that all proceedings should be stopte.'[28] Although Thomas Gorges had little personal sympathy for Cleeve, remarking on one occasion that 'never was there such a factious fellow in a Collony,' Sir Ferdinando's intervention implied a repudiation of Thomas' contention that 'the Councellors [of the Lord Proprietor] are invested with all his power.'[29] it not only produced a stalemate in the dispute but also demonstrated that despite Thomas Gorges' determined efforts his authority rested on two uncertain supports: the backing of Sir Ferdinando Gorges in England, and an armed force which could not be relied upon to prevail against any recalcitrant patentee who chose to fortify himself on his lands.[30]

In Acadia, the problem of governmental authority at this time was even more acute. Although d'Aulnay was by now experienced in such matters, he faced a potentially more dangerous enemy than did Gorges in Winter: La Tour totally rejected his authority and was willing to fight to a finish to maintain his own position. La Tour and d'Aulnay from the start drew their mercantile support and their governmental authority from rather different sources. La Tour had been named royal lieutenant general in Acadia in 1631, and had henceforward maintained close relations with the Compagnie de la Nouvelle-France; d'Aulnay's position, on the other hand, had had its origins in the separation of the Razilly company from the Cent-Associés, had been strengthened by his assumption of command after the death of Isaac de Razilly in 1635, and had first been offically recognized in his royal nomination as lieutenant general of half of Acadia in 1638. Although La Tour and the Razilly company were able to maintain friendly and co-operative relations during the earlier years of their coexistence, the potential for conflict both in government and in trade was quite clear and was exacerbated by the attempted royal division of Acadia of 1638.[31] Denys remarked of d'Aulnay that 'son humeur et celle de son conseil estoit de regner'; it would seem also that the Razilly company was in much poorer financial condition that La Tour's profitable fur-trading interests in the area surrounding his post on the St John River.[32] Whether or not d'Aulnay, for these reasons, was the precipitator of hostilities is not clear from direct evidence, but whoever struck the first blow, warfare was the result.

D'Aulnay, of course, blamed La Tour, whom he accused of stirring up trouble and dissension in 1639 during visits to La Hève and Port Royal.[33] In the following year, still according to d'Aulnay's account, La Tour seized nine of d'Aulnay's employees who were on their way to supply the fort at Pentagouet in two small vessels. This incident was followed by a hasty visit to Pentagouet by d'Aulnay to secure his position, and then by an armed encounter with La Tour at Port Royal on his return. In this combat La Tour was worsted and captured, but was shortly released when the two rivals decided to take their grievances to France.[34] As a result of the visit to France projected at this time, d'Aulnay was able to obtain the support of the crown and thus to have justification henceforth for regarding La Tour as an outlaw rebelling against legally constituted authority. There followed several years of intermittent raiding warfare, similar in nature to that which had until 1636 prevailed among the various colonies of the region. D'Aulnay, having razed La Tour's settlement at Cap de Sable in 1641, was by 1643 blockading his rival's last stronghold, on the St John River. La Tour, however, had succeeded in obtaining a ship and crew in France which, with the reinforcements obtained in Boston, was able both to break the blockade and, later in 1643, to make a partially successful attack on Port Royal. Because of the reaction which this event produced in Massachusetts, however, La Tour was soon again short of resources and was decisively defeated when his St John fort was overwhelmed in April 1645.

This war in itself, like the warfare between 1630 and 1636, was sporadic and small in scale. Again, however, its results could be major for those involved. This was particularly true for Madame La Tour and the garrison of the St John river fort in 1645: although certain of the defenders were spared, 'la reste des plus seditieux [by d'Aulnay's definition] fut pendu, et Etranglé pour servir de memoire et d'exemple a la posterité.' Madame La Tour herself was imprisoned and died some three weeks later.[35] For La Tour himself, although his absence in Boston precluded his capture or death, little was left but exile. La Tour's loss appeared to be d'Aulnay's gain, particularly after the issuance of the latter's far-reaching commission of 1647 and his subsequent dispossession of Nicolas Denys at Miscou and the representatives of the merchant Gilles Guignard at fort Saint-Pierre on Cape Breton. These depredations were certainly sufficient to alarm the Compagnie de la Nouvelle-France and, along with the whole question of the obvious contradiction between the company's grant and d'Aulnay's commission of 1647, to prompt the Cent-Associés to initiate legal proceedings against d'Aulnay.[36] The conquest and unification of Acadia by d'Aulnay, however, was in reality neither a lasting nor a profound achievement. Without the financial means to repair the damage caused by the pillage of several of the colony's settlements, let alone to promote further development, all d'Aulnay had done was to establish his position as the most powerful individual. On his death in 1650, Acadia once again threatened to fall apart, with Madame d'Aulnay, the creditor Le Borgne, La Tour, Nicolas Denys, and other lesser interests, competing furiously among themselves.

The Province of Maine too fell into a situation of conflicting local powers during the 1640s, as a direct result of the failure in 1641 to settle the dispute between Cleeve and Winter. Casting around for ways in which to reopen the question, Cleeve's attention was drawn towards the Plough patent, a grant of the Council for New England dated 26 June 1630 to 'the company called the Husbandmen,' as Winthrop described them. 'They came,' Winthrop had recorded, 'with a patent to Sagadahock, but, not liking the place, they came hither.'[37] The territory to which this group had title was a massive one, taking in most of the Province of Maine from Cape Porpoise to the Kennebec, to a total of 1,600 square miles. Since this grant included all the land disputed between Cleeve and Winter, indeed predating the Trelawny patent, and had never been settled as such, Cleeve now planned to have the old patent purchased, by whatever wealthy ally he could find, with a view to setting up a separate province from that of Maine. Accordingly, he sailed for England in June 1642 and eventually arranged for the purchase of the Plough patent from its surviving owners by Colonel Alexander Rigby, a Lancashire member of parliament. The new province was named 'Lygonia,' apparently, though surprisingly, after Cicely Lygon, the mother of Sir Ferdinando Gorges, and Cleeve returned to America with a commission as 'Deputy President.'[38]

Cleeve had now elevated a relatively minor land dispute into a conflict of colonial jurisdictions, on a scale parallel to that of d'Aulnay and La Tour, and it is not surprising that he encountered the total opposition of all those who held office in the Province of Maine. Even in 1640–1, several of the patentees had sided with Winter, rather than with Cleeve and the Maine General Court. Edward Godfrey had considered Cleeve in 1640 as a 'Turbulent fellow,' while Richard Vines, a long-time servant of Sir Ferdinando Gorges' American interests, had similarly regarded him as 'a ffire brand of dissention.' No doubt they had agreed that Cleeve's departure for England had been, as Godfrey put it, 'a fayre riddance.'[39] Now Cleeve was much more dangerous and had, moreover, chosen his time well. Thomas Gorges had returned to England, probably to fight in the civil war, in the summer of 1643, shortly before Cleeve's reappearance in Maine.[40] Sir Ferdinando Gorges was similarly occupied by the war and unable to give attention to Maine, to such an extent that the Maine General Court on 21 October 1645 appointed Vines as deputy governor, 'whereas wee have not heard of late from the Honoured Sir Ferdinando Gorges ...' Even Vines quickly became discouraged and left for Barbados, and in the following year the deputy governor's position passed to Henry Jocelyn, patentee at Black Point and brother of John Josselyn.[41] Cleeve, therefore, was facing the Province of Maine at a time when it lacked strength; although the outcome of the English civil war was by no means predictable in 1643, he had made a useful parliamentary connection in Rigby, and had taken the precaution of petitioning parliament against the 'unlawful and arbitrary power and jurisdiction' of the Maine magistrates. To this petition he had 'avowed' some thirty names apart from his own; although ten of those named subsequently disavowed their support, the House of Commons had appointed a commission of New England residents to look into the matter.[42]

The parliamentary commission included among its members John Winthrop and Edward Gibbons of Massachusetts, as well as two Maine residents, Arthur Mackworth and Henry Boade. The commission did not immediately become active, despite the urgings of Cleeve – the Massachusetts General Court voted on 1 September 1643, in accordance with its disinclination to involve itself in such disputes, that it was 'not meete to write to the eastward about Mr. Cleaves, according to his desire' – but the inclusion of the members from Massachusetts was significant in underscoring the power and prestige of that colony throughout New England.[43] Indeed, the entire quarrel between the respective proponents of Maine and Lygonia was conducted over the next four years in two fashions: by repeated, though unsuccessful, appeals by both sides to Massachusetts for support, and by the threat of violent conflict in Maine itself. The tone was set in letters to Winthrop as governor in early 1644. On 9 January, Vines wrote to complain of the 'exorbitant practices' of Cleeve and his associate Richard Tucker, after they had 'perswaded Mr. Rigby, (a worthy gent. by report) to buy the Plough patent, which I esteeme no better than a broken tytle'; Vines hoped that 'if wee be forced to take such courses with Cleives as the necessity and the equity of our cause requires, you will not thinke wee have don amisse in it ...' Cleeve, on the other hand, wrote on 27 January to accuse Vines and his associates – especially Robert Jordan, an Anglican priest who had recently become the son-in-law of John Winter and had taken over Winter's vehement opposition to Cleeve – of blasphemy as well as tyranny, 'which inforseth mee,' he went on, 'once more to joyne with the inhabitants of Ligonia and humbly to desire your assistance against there unlawfull practisses ...'[44]

While paper warfare continued in this vein, threats and counter-threats went back and forth between the rival groups in Maine. By late March 1646, Thomas Jenner reported from Saco that the proponents of the Gorges claim were 'resolutely bent ... forthwith to apprehend Cleaves and Tuckar, and to subdue the rest unto their obedience, and to that end have fitted them selves with bilbowes, and ordained Captain [Richard] Bonython, Colonell General: and will not by all good counsell be diverted; I think counsell, to the contrary, doth rather (like oyle on the fire) enflame them.'[45] This threat had certainly been sufficient to alarm Cleeve, who with three colleagues had written to Winthrop on 18 February regarding 'their wicked plotts against us,' which would involve an armed disruption of a Lygonia court called for 31 March at Casco. 'And further,' continued Cleeve, 'we are truely informed that they intend to make this the beginning of a sivill warre, which they intend to blowe abroade into all parts of this land ...'[46] The civil war, however, proved in the event to be a damp squib. Although 'Mr. Jocelyne and his company came armed with gunes and swords, or both,' their determination wavered when Cleeve and his followers showed no inclination to make a fight of the occasion. Instead, a conference was held at which it was eventually decided to seek arbitration in Boston. 'Thus,' reported Jenner, 'after two or three daies agitation, each man departed very peaceably to his owne home.'[47]

This end to the armed phase of the dispute was in accordance with the urging of Winthrop and his colleagues in the Massachusetts government, who had noted 'that the differences between you are growne to a great height of contention, which we are very sorrye for, and would not be wantinge to doe what lyes in us for composinge the same,' although they had advised awaiting a decision from England rather than a hearing in Boston.[48] The real key to the outcome, however, had been the realization by Jocelyn and his colleagues of their weakness. A forcible solution to the dispute was in fact no solution if Cleeve had sufficient support in the Casco region, as he evidently did, to organize and operate his jurisdiction; the Maine patentees, with their own power locally circumscribed and with, as Jenner observed, 'their manifold debts to people in the Bay and else wher,' were in no position to attempt a conquest at Casco, and were well aware of this fact.[49] Once their bluff had been called, they were forced to acknowledge their powerlessness to prevent the fragmentation of Gorges' province.

The agreed hearing in Boston, referred by the governor and magistrates to a somewhat reluctant Court of Assistants, ended indeterminately: 'both parties,' it was decided, 'failed in their proof.' The court therefore 'persuaded the parties to live in peace, etc., till the matter might be determined by authority out of England.'[50] On 27 March 1647 such a determination was indeed made by the parliamentary commissioners for foreign plantations, who were by now picking up the threads of colonial administration after the defeat of Charles I in the first civil war. The decision was in favour of Rigby's proprietorship of Lygonia, 'and all the Inhabitants thereof were then commanded to Submit [to Rigby] ... which all or most of the Inhabitants in Anno 1645 had done ...'[51] Since all the fight had gone out of the Maine patentees after the abortive confrontation at Casco, this ruling effectively confirmed the partition of the Province of Maine. Indeed, by May 1648 Jocelyn and Jordan, whose lands now fell within the limits of the Province of Lygonia, were sitting as magistrates together with Cleeve.[52]

The Maine patentees in the remaining southern corner of the province now saw their jurisdiction restricted to the three settlements of Wells, Agamenticus, and Kittery. Indeed, it seems that Wells had withdrawn its allegiance in all practical terms by 1649 and stood temporarily as a town in its own right – a Maine court record of December 1651 referred to 'the inhabitants of Wells, who formerly deserted this goverment' – so that the Province of Maine was then reduced to two small towns.[53] News of the death of Sir Ferdinando Gorges, which had taken place in 1647, reached Maine also in 1649, and the result was the formation in July that year, under the governorship of Edward Godfrey, of a 'boddy politick and Combination to see thes partes of the Cuntery and province regulated according to such lawes as formerly have bine exersised and such other as may be thought meet not repugnant to the Fundamentall lawes of our Nation and Cuntery ...' This government persisted for three years, explicitly characterized by Godfrey and his fellow magistrates as a government of patentees.[54] The result in Maine of the interaction of local power and legitimate authority had been partition into three small jurisdictions.

Marginal Colonies

On 11 March 1651, Margery Rendell, the bigamous wife of a Cape Porpoise fisherman, was presented at a court session in Kittery for 'abusing the Government in sayeing heare is none.'[55] Her sharp tongue, as well as her other faults of lying, threatening behaviour, and sexual incontinence, cost her a fine of twenty shillings. Her observation, though, had been accurate. The truth that Maine had no effective government was an insulting and damaging one to Godfrey and his colleagues, who claimed to rule on the basis of legitimate authority derived from Europe. The same claim could also be made by La Tour in Acadia, since his rival d'Aulnay had perished in a boating accident in 1650, and on 27 February 1651 he had succeeded in obtaining a royal commission as lieutenant general of Acadia.[56] But La Tour had no prospect of unopposed authority, any more than did Godfrey. Somewhere the splendid visions of 1630 had gone astray. The failure of Alexander's concept for New Scotland was easy enough to explain: in all practical terms the colony had simply ceased to exist. The cases of Maine and Acadia were more complex. Both of these colonies had breached the bounds of communal colonization and had accommodated more extensive agricultural settlements structured on proprietorial or seigneurial lines. Yet Razilly's vision of a 'terre de benédiction' had proved as elusive as the 'Province both fruitful and pleasant' for which Ferdinando Gorges, grandson and heir of Sir Ferdinando, was still hoping in 1658.[57] Instead of well-regulated colonial societies, in which landlord and tenant lived out their mutually beneficial lives under the paternalistic rule of their legitimately appointed governors, the two provinces had been torn by factional strife. What had gone wrong? Though not apparent to contemporaries in 1650, the answer lay in both environmental and social problems.

The areas of successful European settlement in the northeastern maritime region were simply too small to offset the dangers of geographical fragmentation within the large areas claimed as the colonies of Acadia and Maine. Although Port Royal and the southern corner of Maine contained the largest populations, they were not dominant social influences. Nor did either one form the core of any coherent colonial economy. Especially in the case of Acadia, the shape and configuration of the colony made for fragmentation. The ports of the Atlantic coast of the peninsula and Cape Breton, relatively near to Europe and offering easy access to the best fishing grounds, tended to be centres not of colonial settlement but of the seasonal fishery. The St John, Ste Croix, and Pentagouet rivers, on the other hand, offered rich resources not so much for agricultural settlement as for the fur trade. The coasts of the Gulf of St Lawrence offered opportunities for both fishery and fur trade. Thus, the small settlement of Port Royal was surrounded by vast areas which were exploited only by essentially commercial enterprises that depended for their subsistence not upon the land of Acadia, but upon exportable natural resources and predominantly European marketing. Hence the colony inevitably lacked economic coherence. Outside of massively subsidized emigration of colonists, or the kind of unusual circumstances that had brought the outpouring of English colonists to Massachusetts Bay, there were few prospects of the large-scale agricultural settlement which alone could rectify this situation.

The force of environmental pressures in dividing the colony of Acadia becomes more apparent when it is considered that the situation was not the result of deliberation by those individuals involved. 'Bien qu'on ait crû,' wrote Nicolas Denys, 'que mon principal bût dans toutes mes entreprises en ces pays-là à toujours esté le negoce des pelleteries avec les Sauvages; je n'ay jamais compté là-dessus que comme sur un accessoire qui pouvoit servir en quelque façon au capital de ce qui peut faire dans le païs qui est la pesche sedentaire et la culture de la terre ...'[58] Denys had hoped to stimulate settlements which, like those in southern Maine, would combine agriculture with a sedentary fishery, but his fishing, fur-trading, and lumbering enterprises on the Atlantic and gulf coasts never developed in this way, much to his chagrin. La Tour, the principal exponent until 1645 of the St John River fur trade, also protested in 1644 that, although he had been accused 'que je n'ay rien fait dans le Pays ...,' d'Aulnay was to blame for this falsehood. 'Car j'ay batty deux Forts et luy m'en a bruslé un,' he wrote in reference to his establishment at Cap de Sable, 'et si rien a basty aucun ny defrichée que sept ou huit Arpens de Terre il a aussi bruslé l'Eglise le Monastere contre la teneur de l'arrest qui luy ordonnoit de mettre dans les places hommes qui en puissont repondre et par consequent de les conserver.'[59] The differences between d'Aulnay, La Tour, and Denys as colonizers arose not so much from different ambitions – La Tour and Denys were no more indifferent to the prestige to be derived from founding extensive settlements than was d'Aulnay to the profits of the fur trade – but from the differing practicalities and potentialities with which each was faced in his principal sphere of activity. D'Aulnay's solution to the problem of fragmentation was to extend his control over all, but this was only a superficial, personal unification. Seigneurial colonization had taken hold at Port Royal, but it did not characterize the colony as a whole.

In Maine, a similar problem existed. The Isles of Shoals, some fifteen miles southeast of the mouth of the Piscataqua River, formed in the early years a counterpart to the Atlantic coast of Acadia as a centre of the migratory fishery. The most lucrative areas for the fur trade, on the other hand, were in the northeastern parts of the province, and beyond the province's boundaries in the area disputed between English and French. This situation of proprietorial settlements between centres of the fishery and the fur trade would have been less socially and politically divisive than in the case of Port Royal, because of the greater compactness of Maine as compared to Acadia, had it not been for one other factor: the particularism of certain Maine patentees, and especially those in the more isolated northeastern areas. The patents granted by the Council for New England predated the formal inauguration of the Province of Maine, and those patentees who had settled on their lands had become accustomed by 1639 to a large measure of local autonomy. As an anonymous observer noted during the 1630s, 'there are but few of those, who have Patents granted unto them that doe observe the Lawes, and orders of Plantation appointed unto them in their Patents.' In the case of disputes between settlers of different patents, 'those quarrells are seldome, or never ended because there is none in the countrie that hath authoritie to decide them; every mans power beinge limitted, with his owne Patent.' What was lacking, the author concluded, was 'a generall unitie, in things that concerne the publique good of the Countrie.'[60] This was not only an accurate description of the prevailing situation, which Thomas Gorges consciously laboured to correct, but also a foreshadowing of the Cleeve-Trelawny disputes with all their disastrous consequences for the Province of Maine.

The deep internal conflicts in Acadia and Maine could be resolved only by armed conquest or partition, for the large areas of both colonies which lay outside of Port Royal or the towns of southern Maine gave ample scope for the creation of private strongholds. D'Aulnay and La Tour had each operated a series of such fortifications. Winter had fortified Richmond's Island in 1640. In 1645, Richard Vines and thirty supporters had written to Massachusetts on behalf of the General Court of the Province of Maine to appeal for support, and complained that John Bonython had gone over to the side of Cleeve. The signatories, who included Bonython's father, confessed that it was beyond their power to arrest him, 'he threatening to kill any man, that shall either touch his person or cattell.'[61] Outside the main settlements, local power and armed force ruled. It is tempting to characterize these conflicts as 'feudal,' involving as they did a fundamental fragmentation of authority and the building up of particular ties of loyalty in small and isolated settlements.[62] However, as when discussing *féodalité* as a principle of land tenure, precision demands that such terminology be used cautiously. It certainly cannot be argued that the whole paraphernalia of medieval feudalism, particularly as it has been elaborated by British historians, existed among the tiny populations of the northeastern maritime colonies. Recent scholarship, moreover, has introduced strictures upon the promiscuous use of the word feudalism, and if it is true that this term has often produced confusion rather than illumination in the study of medieval Europe, it could hardly be expected to give better service when transplanted to the historiography of North America.[63] This is especially true in view of the absence of the military fief; the few examples of land tenure by knight service bore no practical relation to military action.

What the northeastern maritime colonies did have in common with medieval Europe was the over-mighty subject. Both the French and the English crowns recognized that they could not rule their American colonies exactly as they would their European realms, and the granting of sweeping powers to d'Aulnay and Gorges respectively exemplified this recognition. But this only delegated the problem. In Port Royal, d'Aulnay ruled. In Kittery, Agamenticus, Wells, and Saco, Thomas Gorges could enforce the rule of his courts. Outside those areas, their authority was open to challenge. Medieval problems demanded medieval remedies. D'Aulnay's seigneuries at La Hève, Port Royal, and Ste Croix, for example, amounted to a complex of demesne lands, though still hardly large enough to provide solid support for his authority. Mobile government was another necessity. D'Aulnay as lieutenant general was frequently on the move on the Bay of Fundy and beyond, and Thomas Gorges made his more modest, though more orderly, effort in this direction by providing for courts to be held both at Agamenticus and Saco. Such expedients, however, could not long disguise the truth that the Province of Maine from Piscataqua to Kennebec, like the colony of Acadia from Pentagouet to the gulf, simply could not effectively be ruled by governors whose base of power was restricted to the seigneurial or proprietorial areas. The geographical extent and fragmentation of the colonies had defeated European concepts unless the population could be increased. Furthermore, the resulting conflicts threatened to disrupt even those communities which had been established on a stable basis. Lastly, the fact that the colonists of Acadia and Maine could not resolve their own internal conflicts, except by partition or by armed might, illustrated the essential weakness of the European hold upon the region.

Thus, environmental factors operated against the fulfilment of the great European visions for Maine and Acadia: Port Royal and the villages of southern Maine were too small to be dominant influences upon the colonies as a whole. But even within those settled areas, there were social tensions which threatened disruption. Both the proprietorial structure in Maine and the seigneurial structure in Acadia had much more obvious advantages for landlords than for tenants, and social relationships were beginning to develop independently of these formal structures. By 1650, the communities of colonists were no longer mere aggregations of transplanted Europeans. They were composed of individuals and families who had adapted their way of life to the realities found in America, and they contained a large and increasing proportion of American-born members. They were, in short, Euramerican rather than European communities. The residents of these communities, like the promoters who had first envisaged colonization, aspired to stability and prosperity. Their aspirations, however, were not necessarily wedded to the forms under which settlement had begun, and they were apt to evaluate these forms according to practical considerations. *Féodalité* had its advantages. It provided a legitimization of land titles by accommodating American lands into the ancient national patterns of landholding which stemmed from the respective crowns. On a practical level, *féodalité* had played a vital role in bringing settlement to both Acadia and Maine and in laying the foundations of communities. Yet the foundations were now laid, and the sway of the existing landlords was not necessarily helpful in the work of development and consolidation, especially since the landlords were endangering the stability of the colonies by furiously contending among themselves. How far, therefore, was the prevailing state of affairs justifiable?[64]

Nicolas Denys described the Port Royal inhabitants as 'toûjours [les] esclaves' of d'Aulnay, who never allowed them, he went on, to make any profit from their lands.[65] Denys, of course, had his own reasons for wishing to discredit d'Aulnay, and it is doubtful whether the Acadians themselves ever shared his definition of slavery. A new society, though, was emerging on the marshlands of Port Royal – one which owed its establishment in large measure to d'Aulnay, but which might in due course find his domination restrictive. Acadian agriculture, based on the diking of Fundy marshes for arable and pastoral fields, was beginning to flourish, and at the same time the Acadian community was emerging as a coherent entity. During the 1640s, much of the Acadians' resentment was directed against La Tour, understandably in view of his armed attempts to destroy their settlement.[66] But the difficulties encountered by the Le Borgnes in maintaining any workable seigneurial system after d'Aulnay's death in 1650 show the Acadians increasingly independent of the initial structure.[67] The marshlands of the Bay of Fundy were far larger than the 'trois metairies' of d'Aulnay, and as the Acadian people grew in numbers and confidence they were unlikely to accept restrictions easily, especially once the personal prestige of d'Aulnay had disappeared with his death.

The social tensions inherent in the proprietorial structure of Maine are better documented than those of Port Royal and more complex, involving a number of patentees who acted and thought in a variety of ways. Francis Champernowne, patentee at Kittery and a member of a prominent gentry family of Devon, for example, was among the highest in terms of social origins, but was chronically in debt since his operations as a fish merchant failed to yield adequate profit to support him.[68] Edward Godfrey had been a London merchant and had come to Maine as an employee of the Laconia Company. According to his own later statements, however, he had soon become dependent upon the rents and services of his tenants to supplement his mercantile income and maintain his 'very good howes' at Agamenticus.[69] Thomas Withers, on the other hand, who had also come to Maine with the Laconia Company, had received an extensive land grant in Kittery from Thomas Gorges in 1643 and sat with Godfrey as a magistrate in 1651, was still describing himself in 1681 as a 'yeoman.'[70] That the patentees were socially and economically diverse would not necessarily have caused discontent – so too were the seigneurs of Canada.[71] That they could not maintain governmental stability was more damaging. That they were suspected, with some justification, of self-seeking motives was worse still. Of Vines and his fellow magistrates in 1646, the minister Thomas Jenner suggested that they were desperate to maintain control of the province to avoid paying off 'their manifold debts.'[72] Like d'Aulnay in the fur trade, the Maine patentees were finding out that the fishery afforded insufficient profit to offset the expenses of colonization, and their efforts to remain solvent all too often made them appear not so much as founding fathers but as leeches on the community.

For the communities of Maine, there was an alternative model close at hand. The Massachusetts system of land distribution by towns was not fundamentally an exception to *féodalité*, since it depended ultimately upon the colony's royal charter. To individual settlers, though, the land could be distributed free of encumbrance and according to the wishes of the town's inhabitants as expressed in a town meeting. Land, in a Massachusetts town, could thus be distributed most generously to those whose status derived from their standing within the community and their public services, rather than to patentees whose status depended on their earlier European origins. Furthermore, at least during the early years, before a town's land was fully allocated, an adequate land grant could be guaranteed to each adult male and his family.[73]

The advantages of such a system were obvious, and by 1643 they had already played a part in the successful annexation of the New Hampshire settlements by Massachusetts, completed in that year. Not all of the New

Hampshire communities had been inclined at first to welcome the intrusion of Massachusetts into their local affairs, but all were eventually swayed by the stability offered, by the opportunity to structure the distribution of land according to the real needs of the towns, and not least by the implied freedom from the demands of the heirs of John Mason. Mason, the former partner of Gorges, and proprietor of New Hampshire by virtue of grants from the Council for New England, had died in late 1635, and with him ended the active life of proprietorial rule in New Hampshire. For many decades thereafter, however, members of the Mason family sought to reimpose their control of the province's land with a view to deriving profits from rents. For the communities, becoming part of Massachusetts was a safeguard against these demands.[74]

Thus, opponents of the proprietorial system in Maine had only to look across the Piscataqua River for their precedent. Even within Maine, there was one community which was founded along lines which resembled the Massachusetts model. At the time of the Antinomian controversy in Massachusetts in 1636–7, the Reverend John Wheelwright had become a close supporter of Anne Hutchinson, his sister-in-law, and had consequently been expelled to New Hampshire where he and a number of supporters founded the settlement of Exeter. In 1641, with the Massachusetts expansion into New Hampshire now in progress, Wheelwright and some of his followers again fled northwards and settled at Wells.[75] By the later part of that year, the new settlers in their need for land were looking as far as the lands of Thomas Gorges at Ogunquit where, as Gorges reported to Sir Ferdinando Gorges, 'ther is good marsh on which theyr eys are.'[76] Eventually, the land structure of Wells was decided by a grant given by Thomas Gorges himself on 14 July 1643 to Wheelwright and two associates, Edward Rishworth and Henry Boade, as trustees of the town. The trustees were empowered to grant out lands within the town, on condition that all grantees paid a rent of five shillings per hundred acres annually to Sir Ferdinando Gorges as lord proprietor. This grant, unique in Maine, suggests a compromise between proprietorial and town authority: the rights of the proprietor were reserved, but the town itself could organize its lands as it deemed best.[77]

Wells was unique in Maine in another sense. Alone of the Maine communities, its beginnings were directly influenced by the religious persuasions of the settlers. The other settlements had originated as unplanned agglomerations of exploiters of natural resources, and religious belief had not played a direct role in attracting colonists. The resulting religious diversity, however, did not induce strife within the communities to any uncontrollable extent. Thomas Jenner, the Massachusetts divine who arrived in Saco as minister in 1640 or 1641, found the inhabitants 'very ignorant, supersititious, and vitious,' and his personal disputes with such individuals as Richard Vines smouldered on through the six years of his stay. Vines particularly objected to Jenner's attacks on the sacraments of the Chruch of England, but even he undertook to 'love, honour and cherish Mr. Jenner in his calling.' As Vines professed in a letter to Winthrop, the Maine inhabitants were 'beleiving Christians, although greate sinners,' and this common Christianity made it possible for even the more orthodox of Maine churchmen to approve of the bringing of ministers from Massachusetts.[78] If Massachusetts itself could afford a gracious welcome to the Jesuit Gabriel Druillettes, not merely as a diplomatic emissary but as a man of religion, then the differences in Maine did not need to be destructive.[79] Thomas Gorges, personally sympathetic to Massachusetts in religious matters, was aware that Maine was 'in church discipline not altogeather adhaering to the [Massachusetts] bay,' but warned that Sir Ferdinando would be foolish to impose rigorously 'the goverment of the Church of England.' What was required, he believed, was 'liberty of conscience in many particulars.'[80] Thus, the Maine communities did not share the homogeneity of values that initially characterized those of Massachusetts, but religious diversity did not prevent the inhabitants from perceiving their common interests or from looking to Massachusetts for a model.

Some of the Maine patentees early recognized that the proprietorial system was in danger of becoming untenable in the face of growing community pressure. As early as 1641, Thomas Gorges had noted with disquiet that some patentees at Agamenticus had abdicated their position and were allowing settlers 'to sit down if they please.' By 1643 even Gorges, his final departure for England imminent, conveyed extensive areas of marshland to the town of Agamenticus, as well as a neck of land by the harbour and certain nearby islands. He did, however, reserve timber rights and the right of the proprietor to set up houses for fishermen on the shore.[81] More wholehearted was the patentee Nicholas Shapleigh of Kittery. Kittery, with its position on the Piscataqua River, its beginning in sedentary fishery projects in the 1620s, and its prominence as one of the centres of the Laconia Company, was the most developed of all the Maine towns. By 1647, at least two shipyards were in operation there, and trading links were being forged with the West Indies. By 1648, Kittery had quietly begun to operate along the lines of the towns further south, and among the first officers to be elected was Nicholas Shapleigh as one of three 'Townsmen and rate makers,' with powers to allocate land subject to confirmation by the town meeting.[82] By May 1652, Thomas Withers had followed Shapleigh into this position and had also taken the precaution of having his large proprietorial land grant confirmed by the town.[83] Both continued as magistrates of the Province of Maine, but their local activities were no longer entirely within the proprietorial system. But Shapleigh and Withers were not typical of all their colleagues. Robert Jordan, who was closely associated with the Trelawny patent as the son-in-law of John Winter and who eventually took over the patent after the deaths of both Trelawny and Winter, had complained in 1642 that 'in thees parts ... actions are passed according to the conceipts of unknowing Planters.'[84] Edward Godfrey had also warned Trelawny in 1640 that 'heere planters would have all Common,' fearing at that time that this feeling would lead to popular support for George Cleeve. By 1647, his feelings were still defensive. In a letter to Winthrop in the summer of that year, he complained of 'the rud multitud in waie of pretence of common priviledg ...' and confessed that the more turbulent elements 'ar hard to bee suppressed by our weake power.'[85] Godfrey was fully prepared to fight a rearguard action, but the fact remained that the proprietorial structure was deeply flawed.

Thus, in the three colonies of the northeastern maritime region, European concept and American reality had not been successfully reconciled. The colony of New Scotland had for the moment been entirely submerged. The remaining two colonies reached 1650 with relatively substantial permanent populations, but with outstanding problems. Certainly the bounds of communal colonization had been breached in two principal locations: the seigneury of Launay-Rasilly (from 1642 that of d'Aulnay) at Port Royal, and the southern part of the Province of Maine, comprising the settlements of Kittery, Agamenticus, Wells, and Saco. In these areas, a seigneurial or proprietorial structure of land tenure was created and operated, along with governmental authority stemming from the chief land-owner. Yet these areas were small by comparison with the full geographical extent of the colonies, and even in these areas it was doubtful that the existing land structure could hold out for long against pressures from within the communities themselves. In 1650, the Europeans in the region were still weak. Geographically dispersed, politically unstable, and economically dependent, first upon Europe and then increasingly upon Massachusetts, the northeastern maritime colonies were crucially lacking in social homogeneity and internal coherence. They had become marginal colonies, existing only on the fringes of other societies. They continued to depend on their European mother countries as the ultimate fount of all legitimacy in matters of law, authority, and formal structure. They depended economically and for other forms of support on the larger Euramerican colony of Massachusetts. They existed too on the margins of native society, since the Indians – not the Europeans – were still by 1650 the predominant peoples of the region.

The tenuousness of the northeastern maritime colonies had been exemplified in 1632 by the dislodgement by directive from Europe of the New Scotland colony, which in 1630 had seemed to be the best established of the three. Although Maine and Acadia were still in existence by 1650, their position was far from secure. The Province of Maine, effectively cut off from its European roots by the English civil war, was partitioned into three small jurisdictions. Scattered and disunited, the inhabitants of Maine had provoked potentially serious Indian enmity by their appropriations of land, and thus stood in danger of an attack which they would be hard pressed to withstand. One factor that mitigated this vulnerability was the close proximity of the Massachusetts colony. It was questionable, however, how long the Massachusetts colony would tolerate the presence of the chronically weak and divided Province of Maine on its northeastern boundary, and the dependence of Maine upon Massachusetts had raised the possibility that the latter might become not only a support but a paramount political force.

The colony of Acadia enjoyed much more harmonious Indian relationships than did Maine. The activities of the missionaries, though not usually productive of the firm conversions for which they hoped, provided a useful framework for good relations; the agricultural population of Port Royal, moreover, had been established largely upon marshland, which was not of any great value to the primarily non-agricultural Micmac, and so the embitterment which sprang up in Maine had no significant counterpart in Acadia. For all this, however, the colony of Acadia shared the characteristics of economic, social, and political fragmentation. Cut off by distance from any worthwhile contacts with Canada, which was in any case itself a tiny and economically insecure colony, Acadia fell increasingly into the economic, and even at times the political, orbit of Massachusetts. As in the case of Maine, the possibility therefore existed that the Massachusetts colony, though by preference isolationist in outlook, might at some stage consider political intervention in Acadia if it deemed its interests to be threatened by the internal condition of the French colony. As long as the supremacy of d'Aulnay continued, such intervention was hardly likely, but it remained a possibility, especially after d'Aulnay's death in 1650. The younger John Winthrop's remark in 1644, that 'the English Colonies heere would be gret to have their brethren of Scotland to be their neighbours in enjoying that antient right is conceived they had of Nova Scotia,' was a mere straw in the wind; but it was one which deserved to be remembered.[86]

All three of the northeastern maritime colonies had at one time or another been regarded as colonial projects of great importance by their European progenitors. The New Scotland colony had been founded as a counterpart to New England, New France, New Netherland, and New Spain; the intended primacy of Acadia within New France had been shown by sending Razilly there as lieutenant general of New France; Gorges' Province of Maine had been seen as a powerful proprietary colony which would counterbalance the influence of Massachusetts. By 1650, however, New Scotland no longer existed in any practical form, and Maine and Acadia were only marginal colonies. In some respects progress had been made toward realizing the ideals of the original European promoters, but it had been slow and limited. The truth was that the northeastern maritime colonies for the moment had little power to influence their own destinies. In order to promote some modicum of internal stability, they desperately needed larger European populations and more complex economic structures, but these were available only from outside. The future of the region and of the colonies within it would ultimately depend upon the interplay of three forces which all, in different ways, retained a potentially effective power of intervention: the Massachusetts colony, the European crowns, and the Indians.

Part III
The Interplay of Forces, 1650–1690

CHAPTER 6

Euramerican Adjustment
1650-1660

Chaos in the Northeastern Maritime Region

The years immediately following 1650 were years of social and political disruption in the northeastern maritime colonies. The colony of Maine, splintered into three smaller jurisdictions, had become virtually ungovernable. Acadia, superficially unified under d'Aulnay, fell into extreme disorder on his death in 1650, since conflicting claims to his authority combined with the reassertion of the pretensions of La Tour and Denys. At this time, as the British Isles struggled to cope with the aftermath of the English revolution, and France became increasingly preoccupied with the disorders associated with the Fronde, there was little effective recourse to Europe. In this situation, the attitude of the Massachusetts colony assumed immense importance and came to be of prime concern to the participants in the various disputes.

The death of d'Aulnay, as the result of a boating accident near Port Royal, created the conditions for a renewal of the factional conflicts which his ascendancy had temporarily halted.[1] Not only was the validity of the d'Aulnay claim to rule Acadia contested, but so was the inheritance of the d'Aulnay claim itself. The principal surviving members of the family were d'Aulnay's widow and father, but the massive debt owed by his estate to Emmanuel Le Borgne gave the latter a strong interest. Initially all three co-operated – Charnisay, d'Aulnay's father, provided the legitimate authority, and Le Borgne sent out a strong commercial expedition under his son Alexandre Le Borgne, while Madame d'Aulnay remained at Port Royal – and made a joint approach to the Massachusetts colony in June 1651 to promise goodwill and good neighbourhood. They received a cautiously favourable response from Boston.[2]

In the meantime, however, Charles de Saint-Étienne de La Tour had seen his opportunity and had travelled to France. Although thrown into jail on his arrival, he shortly procured his release and obtained on 27 February a royal commission as 'gouverneur et notre Lieutenant general au pays de Coste de l'Acadie.' Powers of government were thus conferred upon La Tour, together with the confirmation of all his previous holdings of land, and exclusive rights to trade.[3] This commission amply displayed the tenuous nature of the royal authority in Acadia. Although a show was made of reopening enquiries into the La Tour-d'Aulnay dispute and finding reason to exonerate La Tour, the truth was that the crown at this point had no effective power in Acadia, nor any great interest in it, beyond the extension of official recognition retroactively to any individual who convincingly purported to hold a position of strength in the colony; although the royal authority had always been weak in Acadia, the minority of Louis XIV and the faction-ridden state of the court made it all the more so in 1651. La Tour now sailed for his old base on the St John River and took it over from Madame d'Aulnay. The latter, through an agent in France, turned for help to the Duc de Vendôme, an illegitimate son of Henri IV and a powerful figure as superintendent of navigation and commerce of France. According to an agreement concluded between the two on 18 February 1652, Vendôme agreed to give his assistance in reversing 'l'usurpation faite par Charles de Turgis dit St Estienne de la Tour ... du fort et habitation de la rivière S. Jean,' and also in resisting the encroachments of Nicolas Denys on Cape Breton and the gulf coast. In return, Vendôme was to rule Acadia jointly with Madame d'Aulnay and to share the profits of the fur trade.[4]

This agreement, however, was short-lived, since Le Borgne responded quickly by personally assuming a claim to be 'Seigneur de tous ces pays-là, comme créancier du sieur d'Aunay.' Le Borgne had, according to Nicolas Denys, the support of an 'Arrest du Parlement de Paris,' and thus in 1652 took possession of Port Royal by means of a strong and forceful expedition.[5] Madame d'Aulnay, having again received a disastrous blow, and now quickly abandoned by Vendôme, turned elsewhere. On this occasion, she chose a marriage alliance with La Tour: a contract was drawn up on 24 February 1653 and the marriage took place shortly after. After settling the question of the division of property among the heirs of both partners, the contract expressed the 'principal dessein de leur pretendu mariage, qui est la paix et tranquillité du pays et la concorde et union entre les deux familles ...'[6]

Also still in existence was the interest of Nicolas Denys and his family. As Madame d'Aulnay had complained in 1652, Denys had taken advantage of d'Aulnay's death to return to his old haunts and activities: an attack on him in Cape Breton by Madame d'Aulnay in 1651 had not been an effective deterrent.[7] In October 1653, Denys was successful in obtaining extensive rights of land

and government on the gulf coast from Canso to the Gaspé from the Compagnie de la Nouvelle-France, which were confirmed by royal letters patent on 30 January 1654. Dispossessed and captured by Le Borgne in 1654 by military force, Denys subsequently won a decree in his favour from the royal council and again resumed his commercial projects.[8]

In Acadia, therefore, there existed three separate factions. Each opposed the others, and each enjoyed some form of official countenance from France. Clearly destructive for Acadia itself, this situation was also perplexing for the Massachusetts colony. In the context of the events of the previous decade, the Boston authorities were only too uncomfortably aware of the dangers posed by a faction-ridden and unpredictable Acadia. On the other hand, any active effort to influence events there would involve certain dangers. In the event, a cautious and essentially passive attitude was taken, and was clearly evidenced as early as June 1651 in the Massachusetts reply to the approach made by the Charnisay-Le Borgne-d'Aulnay alliance. In a letter to Madame d'Aulnay on 12 June, for example, the Massachusetts council assured her that they did not 'Intend any thinge but all neighborly loving and freindly Compliance with you unlesse ought shall proceed from yourselves towards us Contrary thereto.'[9] Further evidence of caution may be found in powers taken by the Massachusetts General Court in 1652 and 1653 to license any traders going from Massachusetts to Acadia: only in selected instances was such trade permitted and then only by merchants of known probity who had long had a previous interest in the trade.[10] For the moment, therefore, Massachusetts preferred to take a passive attitude towards Acadia. This corresponded with the attitude which it had long taken towards Maine. The closest the Massachusetts colony had ever come to an intervention in Maine had been its reluctant and indecisive arbitration in 1646. Nevertheless, strong unofficial links had been forged between Maine and Massachusetts by 1650, and the chaotic situation which had grown up in Maine could not but be of concern to the Boston authorities; in this case, a particular series of events did indeed lead to a more active approach. On 31 October 1651, the General Court decided to act upon an interpretation of the bounds of its patent which would bring Maine within its jurisdiction.[11]

The considerations prompting this step, according to the General Court, included, first, 'the comodiousnes of the River Piscataque, and how prejudiciall it would be to this government if the aforesaid place and river should be possessed by such as are no freinds to us.' This was a genuine fear, and thus a genuine reason; nevertheless, it does not explain the sudden change of approach by Boston. A clue can be found elsewhere in the General Court's explanation: 'there hath binn a late endeavor of severall persons thereabouts,' it was stated, 'to drawe the inhabitants of Kettery &c. who governe now by combination, to petition the Parliament of England for a graunt of the said place.' In fact just such a petition was sent from Maine to the English Council of State later in the year.[12] Should it be successful, the fragmentation of Maine would be further entrenched, which would hardly be in the strategic interests of Massachusetts. More urgent, however, was a further consideration: a concurrent movement in New Hampshire, ruled by Massachusetts since 1643, to follow the example of Maine. On 6 September 1651, the Massachusetts council had received a letter 'informing of some serious labouring in the easterne parts with some that are subjected to us to withdrawe their subjection from this Government.'[13] The centre of this 'Sedition' was said to be Portsmouth, directly across the Piscataqua River from Kittery, and the Massachusetts authorities clearly felt that their access to the Piscataqua was in jeopardy unless they took action quickly.

Once the General Court had overcome its disinclination to involve itself in Maine, there were further potential advantages to be gained thereby. The strategic motivation itself had wide ramifications, as the Piscataqua region was potentially dangerous not only in unfriendly English hands, but even more so in non-English ones. The chaos in Acadia had necessarily to be regarded as a potential threat, jeopardizing the working arrangement which had been reached with d'Aulnay. Furthermore, tension between English and Dutch had followed the passage of the Navigation Act of 1651, by which Dutch vessels were impeded in the profitable carrying trade in the English colonies, and this issue was to lead to the outbreak in early 1652 of the first Dutch war.[14] Conflict between English and Indian was yet another possibility, as reports from Piscataqua would show in the summer of 1653, when 'some thousands of Indians' were said to have gathered and to have menaced the English settlements.[15]

The strategic motive, then, was an important and complex one. Obviously also of great importance was the economic motive. With Maine already under the economic domination of Boston, political annexation had clear advantages of convenience. In addition, the natural resources of Maine were powerful inducements, both to the General Court and to interested private individuals. The fur trade in Maine offered tempting possibilities at a time when stocks of fur-bearing animals were running low in Massachusetts.[16] The timber trade, moreover, was growing in importance in the forests north of the Piscataqua River; a recent study has noted that almost all of the Massachusetts commissioners who acted on behalf of the General Court in Maine during the controversies which accompanied and followed the annexation were merchants with an involvement in the timber trade.[17] A specific example is the partnership of the merchants Thomas Clarke and Thomas Lake, which established a post in 1654 at Arrowsick, on the extreme northeastern boundary of the Province of Maine. By the time of its destruction by the Abenaki in 1676, this complex included a fort, sawmills, a shipyard, a foundry, and a trading post.[18] Finally, for potential land speculators, the availability of large expanses of land in Maine was a further attraction and would lead in due course to extensive engrossments by Massachusetts residents, though not to intensive settlement in the seventeenth century.[19]

Thus, in the case of Maine, events in 1651 prompted the Massachusetts colony to abandon its previous aloofness and to project a direct intervention. The existence of chaos and fragmentation in the northeastern maritime region, whether in Maine or in Acadia, was uncomfortable for Massachusetts at any time. What had been proved in 1651, though, was that the authorities in Boston were not irrevocably opposed to direct connections with that region if circumstances should point in that direction. This did not imply that an intervention was likely in Acadia, towards which a passive attitude was for the moment maintained. It did, however, show that a passive attitude was not immutable.

Massachusetts and Maine

It was the hope of the Massachusetts authorities that the annexation of Maine could be carried out with a minimum of conflict and upheaval. The first step ordered by the General Court was the sending of 'a loving letter and friendly' to inform the Maine inhabitants that they were within the northern line of the Massachusetts patent and that a committee had been appointed 'to treat with them.'[20] When Edward Godfrey wrote back in protest, Secretary Edward Rawson of the General Court assured him that there was no intention 'to bereave you of any of your just rights, imunitys or priviledges, which you say you have soe dearly bought.'[21] In the event, the annexation did not go unchallenged, with Godfrey being one of the chief opponents; but the opposition was largely ineffective, and Maine was slowly but steadily taken over. Indeed, the Massachusetts authorities enjoyed considerable popular approval in Maine, stemming not so much from a strong positive desire for Massachusetts government as from the practical advantages it would bring: more effective defence, and the wider distribution of land that would result from the further application of the principles of the New England town. The rule of Maine by Massachusetts, while infringing on certain vested interests, was a logical step both for the new rulers and, for rather different reasons, for most of Maine's inhabitants.

The first foray of Massachusetts commissioners into Maine in the summer of 1652, however, ended in stalemate. The three commissioners – including John Leverett, who had long had an interest in trade not only in Maine but also in Acadia – were met by Godfrey and four of his magistrate colleagues, who affirmed the separate status of Maine. Resting their case firmly upon property rights, they rehearsed the great sacrifices which had been made by the Maine patentees and their immense expenditures over a twenty-year period.[22] Discomfited by this opposition, the Massachusetts commissioners returned south, and once again Godfrey wrote to Rawson. Against the 'pretended Jurisdiction over our persons and lands' claimed by Massachusetts, he again defended existing rights of property: 'they are appropriated to us, and must not soe easily be parted with.'[23] Nevertheless, in November a further group of Massachusetts commissioners arrived in Maine, this time fully prepared to hold public court in the Maine towns. On the 16th, they held court at Kittery, and took the submission of the town.[24] On the 22nd, they took the submission of Agamenticus – 'onely mr Godfrey did forbeare untill the vote was past by the Rest and then Immediately he did by word and vote expresse his Consent also' – and renamed it York, the whole Province of Maine being redesignated the county of Yorkshire.[25]

In May the following year, two prominent inhabitants of Wells sent petitions, one in the name of the town as a whole, to the General Court at Boston, asking that Massachusetts jurisdiction be extended to that town.[26] Accordingly, commissioners took the submission of the town in July 1653, along with those of Cape Porpoise and Saco.[27] In the statement of the General Court ratifying the return of these commissioners, George Cleeve was specifically marked out as a man of discredited authority. This indication that the Massachusetts authorities regarded him as a formidable opponent is borne out by the delay which preceded the annexation of the remaining Lygonia settlements. Although the General Court informed Cleeve by letter in 1653 that it intended to assume jurisdiction throughout Lygonia, it was not until 1658 that this was successfully done. In July 1658, Massachusetts commissioners received the submissions of Black Point and Blue Point, henceforth to be known as Scarborough, and those of Spurwink and Casco, henceforth to be known as Falmouth; among those submitting was George Cleeve.[28] This completed the annexation of the entire settled area of Sir Ferdinando Gorges' Province of Maine.

With each submission, further evidence can be found of the desire of the Massachusetts authorities to avoid controversy. At York, for example, the Massachusetts commissioners 'thought meet to expres our desires that neither mr Godfrey nor any other may be injuried nor suffer any damag by reason of his Change of Goverement'; this indeed was embodied in the grants of liberties to the various towns established by Massachusetts in the newly created county of Yorkshire, in that property rights were to be firmly upheld unless otherwise determined by due course of law.[29] Moreover, goodwill was further shown in the appointment of Godfrey, along with two other former Maine magistrates, to serve on the bench of the county of Yorkshire. Furthermore, Henry Jocelyn and Robert Jordan, former officials of the Province of Lygonia, both officiated at courts in 1659 and 1661; George Cleeve was also appointed a magistrate, though he is not known to have been active in that capacity.[30]

On the surface, then, the transition from Province of Maine to county of Yorkshire was accomplished smoothly and with surprisingly little rancour. Subsequent events were to show, however, that the matter was not so simple. In reality, a very fundamental change had taken place, in the form of an adjustment of basic institutions away from the initial European concept towards conformity to American reality and the convenience of Euramerican settlers. Throughout the controversies leading to the annexation of Maine, the Maine magistrates had consistently taken pains to defend the *status quo* of landed property, in such a sustained way as to suggest that they feared losing their estates. This fear was by no means a frivolous one, for when the towns of the county of Yorkshire were granted 'the priviledges of a Towne as others of the Jurisdiccon have and doe enjoy,' this implied power to allocate the land within the town's boundaries (both to individuals and for common purposes) either directly through town meetings, or through selectmen elected by the town.[31] No matter how much it might be protested that no man was to be deprived of his property, the fact was that there now existed two land systems in Maine: that of proprietorial patents, and that of the town governments. The two did not necessarily conflict in every particular, but it was inevitable that in some places there should be confusion and dispute. The town system was a potential vehicle for the growth of a real sense of community, with all the benefits which that could bring in terms of security and stability. Thus, in any settlement where a patentee was seen to stand in the way of this desirable end, conflict was likely.[32]

The clearest case of such conflict occurred at York and involved a dispute between Edward Godfrey and the town inhabitants. After the change of jurisdiction, the town of York had not delayed to exercise its powers: on 8 December 1652 a town meeting made nine grants of ten-acre house lots, and these were followed by regular disposals of land throughout the following year and thereafter.[33] That these grants infringed upon Godfrey's property is made clear by a petition from him which was considered by the Massachusetts General Court on 30 October 1654. 'The Inhabitance have binne soe Bould,' he complained, 'as amongst them selves to share and devid these lottes and pportions of land as ware soe long time sence alotted being not proportionable and Considerable to our great Charge.'[34] The General Court ordered the appointment of a commission to look into the matter, and its report on 20 April 1655 favoured Godfrey, even to the extent of ordering his costs reimbursed at the town's expense. The York inhabitants, however, refused to accept this verdict and succeeded in having the case reopened later in 1655.[35] The nature of the final decision has not survived on record, but it clearly went against Godfrey, who returned to England in 1655 and some four years later complained of his 'extreame poverty.' Appealing to parliament, he stated that he had been 'forced to leave' New England by the deprivation of 'the greatest part of my lands Marshes and all priviledges'; his whole family, he affirmed, was 'utterly ruinated,' a charge which is given substance by his death in debtors' prison in early 1664.[36]

Godfrey's personal disaster was an extreme example of the fate which a patentee could suffer under the new regime: as Godfrey had been in previous years an exceptionally uncompromising upholder of the proprietary system, so now he was the victim of an exceptionally uncompromising interpretation of the rights of the town. Elsewhere in Maine, there was less overt conflict than in York. In Kittery, for example, the two largest patentee land-owners, Nicholas Shapleigh and Francis Champernowne, were little affected by the change, partly because of the availability of land elsewhere in Kittery but also because of their own close relations with the town organization. Shapleigh had already served as selectman, and both he and Champernowne were to receive land grants from the town over the ensuing years.[37] Even in Kittery, however, a dispute briefly flared between the inhabitants and Richard Leader, an associate of Godfrey, who was alleged by several petitioners from the town to have 'intruded himself among us by such as had no Just power to dispose of our lands,' and to have 'deprived some of the inhabitants of theire just rights and posetions.'[38] In the more northeasterly settlements which were absorbed by Massachusetts in 1658, matters were complicated by a revival of the old dispute between rival land-owners George Cleeve and Robert Jordan, and no immediate effort was made to allocate town lands. Even here, though, a petition from a group of Cleeve's supporters in Falmouth to the Massachusetts General Court in 1660 looked forward to the time when 'we shall injoy our preveleges and towne a fares with the rest of the townes in the Dueredicon.'[39]

Local factors, therefore, were crucial in determining the exact consequences in the various parts of Maine of the Massachusetts annexation. In a community such as York, the results were immediate and dramatic; elsewhere there was more continuity. What was clear was that the six towns of the county of Yorkshire – Kittery, York, Wells, Saco, Scarborough, and Falmouth – were being shaped according to the interests and aspirations of the communities which had grown up there. Although this was not necessarily achieved at the expense of the patentees, the case of Edward Godfrey was an indication of the social forces that could be set in motion, much more powerfully than had been anticipated by the Massachusetts authorities. Massachusetts had been somewhat reluctant to involve itself in Maine and had done so only because the dangers inherent in refusal had begun to appear greater than those of commitment. The annexation had been carried out as far as possible without upheaval. The Maine inhabitants, however, had proved fully capable of using the annexation to bring about real change. It is doubtful whether the Massachusetts government in itself commanded widespread allegiance at this time – indeed in 1656 great difficulty was experienced in finding signatories for a petition to Oliver Cromwell in favour of the annexation – but the new town structures unquestionably did.[40]

Acadia or Nova Scotia?

The extension of the power of Massachusetts into Maine was an act of convenience on the part of Euramericans: both for Massachusetts itself and for the greater proportion of the Maine inhabitants. The same may be said of the relationship which emerged concurrently between Massachusetts and Acadia/ Nova Scotia, though in this case the change was not directly initiated by the Massachusetts colony. An English conquest of the principal settlements of Acadia in 1654 led to the revival, in somewhat dubious circumstances, of the concept of 'Nova Scotia' and its establishment as an English colony. The new Nova Scotia was soon espoused by the Massachusetts colony as providing, as did the county of Yorkshire, a useful framework for its strategic and economic interests. As in Yorkshire, the arrangement had certain advantages for the Acadian inhabitants and thus became yet another instrument of Euramerican convenience. In this case, continued resistance was put up by those dispossessed, but never to such a degree as to pose a lethal threat.

On 1 June 1654, Robert Sedgwick, a Massachusetts merchant and militia officer, returned to Boston from a visit to England at the head of a military expedition commissioned by Oliver Cromwell, and with John Leverett, his son-in-law, as second in command. The purpose was to attack New Netherland, in pursuance of the Anglo-Dutch war then in progress. By the time of Sedgwick's arrival in Boston, however, that war was virtually over, and news of the peace was received before the expedition had time to move on. Sedgwick was thus left unemployed and, as he reported to Cromwell on 1 July, he 'thought best ... to spend a lyttle tyme in rangeing the coast against the French, who use tradinge and fishinge hereaboute.'[41] Leaving Leverett in Boston to arrange a return cargo of timber, Sedgwick sailed for Acadia; according to Mark Harrison, the captain of one of his vessels, the intention was 'onely to spend that time we are forced to stay for our masts.'[42]

Once on the Acadian coast, Sedgwick enjoyed great success. His force arrived at the St John River on 14 July, one day after Le Borgne had abandoned an attack on La Tour, and on the 17th it took La Tour's fort, which was already depleted of food and supplies. On 8 August, 'the fforte Commonly Called Fort Riall' fell; despite the presence of a relatively strong garrison, Port Royal was surrendered after only a short skirmish. Then on 2 September, the fleet took

Pentagouet, where the French had had, reported Harrison, 'a small forte yett in ther possestion.' Garrisons were left at all three locations under the general supervision of Leverett, and the fleet took on a cargo of masts at the Piscataqua River and returned to England.[43]

That this was a conquest was indisputable. The question of what kind of conquest it was, however, was more complex. Certainly there was no effort to remove the entire French population from Acadia. An uncertain number of French were returned to France from the St John and Pentagouet, but the terms of the capitulation of Port Royal gave that community's inhabitants the freedom to return to France or to stay, as they preferred.[44] Protection was afforded to the d'Aulnay family on its estates. Even the Capuchin missionaries – presumably included in Leverett's hostile designation of 'the locusts, as were crept in among the blind Indians, to deceive them [in religion]' – were allowed to stay in Port Royal, 'moyennant qu'ils soyent eloignés de deux à trois lieues de la forteresse.'[45] Nor, at this point, was there any thought of restoring the colony of New Scotland: even when the episode was discussed in London, reference was at first invariably made to some such designation as 'the fforts taken from the French in America.'[46] Nor, indeed, did the French themselves take the conquest very seriously. On 31 December 1654, Antoine de Bordeaux, ambassador in London, reported to Mazarin the arrival in London of the captured La Tour, whom he perhaps over generously described as 'le Gouverneur des forts que les Anglois ont pris,' and ventured the opinion that 'la restitution de ces places ne se pourait contester.'[47]

Bordeaux, however, was quite wrong. By 18 February 1655, he was reporting that the English had started to make difficulties over the restitution, and might not be easily budged: 'la prise a passé pour une Conqueste tres importante.'[48] A week later, Bordeaux was threatening to withdraw his mission from England over this issue, and a sharp diplomatic quarrel was in full career.[49] Cromwell himself was involved in the question, attempting at one point in late March to link the restitution of the Acadian forts with discontinuance of French support for Charles II.[50] In reality, however, Cromwell was not averse to the retention of Sedgwick's conquest; it was an achievement which fitted his attitude towards empire and which also had possible strategic value in opening up a source of timber and naval stores.[51] Furthermore, Mazarin on the French side was anxious to stabilize Anglo-French relations with a view to an alliance against Spain, and was unwilling to allow colonial matters to obstruct this aim. Hence, by 5 April a decision had been taken in France to defer the question of the Acadian forts to be settled subsequently by special commissioners, and this was duly agreed.[52]

La Tour, for his part, was making no great haste to return to France, and his reasons became apparent in early 1656 in a petition he presented to the English

Council of State. In the petition, La Tour recalled his father's agreement with Sir William Alexander in 1629 and claimed powers of government and trade in the region of 'Nova Scotia' on the basis of the baronetcy conferred upon him at that time; his claim received guarded approval from the Council of State on 29 May 1656, on condition that La Tour share his rights in a joint patent with two Englishmen, Thomas Temple and William Crowne.[53] La Tour, by reviving the near forgotten concept of 'Nova Scotia,' did a useful service in providing some clothing of legitimacy for the retention of Sedgwick's conquests; obviously he hoped also to benefit himself. La Tour, Temple, and Crowne were jointly granted 'the Country and Territories called Lacadie and that parte of the Country called Nova Scotia' in a patent dated 9 August 1656.[54] La Tour himself derived little positive benefit from his new status; on 20 September 1656, some six weeks after the issuance of the Nova Scotia patent, he sold his share to Crowne and Temple, in return for a small stake in the anticipated Nova Scotia fur trade.[55] He had, in fact, been used as a tool both by Cromwell and by his own partners. Once his legal title had served its purpose, he was cast aside; he retired to Nova Scotia where he died in 1663.[56]

Temple and Crowne were left as partners. Temple had obtained his share of the Nova Scotia grant largely through being an indigent kinsman of Lord Saye and Sele, a member of the Council of State and a long-standing influence upon English attitudes towards America. Crowne, a merchant, provided financing. Accordingly, it was Temple who was named governor of Nova Scotia, while Crowne retained his essentially financial interest.[57] The terms in which the patent of 1656 was couched, however, were such as to give rise to a century of confusion over the precise definition of Nova Scotia. The definition given in the patent extended from Mirliquesh around Cape Sable and the Bay of Fundy as far south as Muscongus, on the coast of the modern state of Maine. It was based on two erroneous assumptions: first, that Sir William Alexander had granted La Tour the whole colony of New Scotland; and secondly, that the bounds of Alexander's grant to La Tour were as stated. In reality, Alexander's grant of 1629 had covered only a relatively small section of territory between Mirliquesh and Cap Fourchu, or the Cloven Cape, including Cape Sable.[58] Thus, the myth was created at this point that 'Acadia' (from Mirliquesh to the gulf coast) and 'Nova Scotia' (from Mirliquesh around the Bay of Fundy and thus southward) were two separate parts of a region bounded by New England and the St Lawrence, although in actual practice both France, and intermittently England, would continue to claim ownership of the entire territory.[59]

The Massachusetts colony had regarded this whole process with mixed feelings: the seizure of the Acadian forts had certainly put an end to the colony's careful efforts to maintain diplomatic harmony with Acadia. Thus the General Court's first reaction in 1654 was an angry questioning of Sedgwick's authority for his conquests.[60] On the other hand, as with Maine, there were obvious advantages, and advantages of a similar nature, to a close political control of the Acadian region. By late 1655, this was clearly appreciated in Boston and was reflected in instructions given to John Leverett on 23 November, on his departure for England as agent of the colony. Leverett was instructed not only to answer any complaints arising from the annexation of Maine, but also to request the 'obtayning' of the 'French fortes' by Massachusetts, 'provided they be free from charges and other ingagements.'[61] Thus, while neither of the two interventions in the northeastern maritime region can be characterized as the result of deliberate expansionism by Massachusetts, both had by late 1655 become closely identified with the interests and actions of that colony.

The revival of the concept of Nova Scotia had not, of course, been foreseen by the Massachusetts authorities, and its granting to La Tour, Temple, and Crowne was not what the colony would have wished. Nevertheless, even this grant was turned to good account on the arrival of Thomas Temple in Boston in 1657. Welcomed with all the honour and ceremony due to his official position, Temple soon became assimilated into the society of Boston.[62] Never, in fact, did he take up residence in Nova Scotia, nor did he make any serious efforts to promote English settlement there; an anonymous French memoir in 1667 commented upon 'le peu de soin qu'ont eu les Anglois de s'habituer en ces lieux' and noted 'qu'ils n'y ont mis du monde que par forme sans y avoir faict la moindre amélioration.'[63] Instead, Temple was content to leave the management of Nova Scotia to others and, in practice, to leave the field open for Massachusetts traders, such as the associates Thomas Lake and Richard Walker, both in the fur trade and in trading with the Acadian population. Even in the extent to which he himself partook in the trade, he became a prime target for hard-headed merchants. 'The merchants advance upon their goods 50 per cent,' he wrote in late 1658, 'and after prise my furs and peltry themselves, and ... I came hither before I knew eyther how to mannage the Trade or what goods were fitt for it.'[64]

Even when Temple gained in experience and expertise, his financial difficulties were simply too deep seated to permit success, despite his hopes 'to carry on all my Designs and settle this Country.'[65] From the outset, he had lacked financial resources, especially when presented by Leverett with bills amounting to over £3,000 for the garrisoning and supplying of the Acadian forts from 1654.[66] In view of these large liabilities, as well as the need for further capital expenditure in Nova Scotia, Temple received stern financial advice from Thomas Lake on his arrival in Boston in 1657. 'My selfe and some other ffreinds have spoaken seriously to him,' wrote Lake to the creditor Leverett, 'for a frugall management of the same [Nova Scotia], he Accepts of advice and sayth he will by degrees clear himselfe of the unnecessary charges which he is at ...'[67] As a trading venture, Nova Scotia was successful, but Temple's financial predicament was not easily alleviated. His were the expenses of rebuilding the Nova Scotia forts, especially that at the mouth of the St John River; the greater his expenditures, the more his trading profits flowed to creditors in Boston and London, and the less able he was to finance any English settlement of his colony. Temple continued for several years to be deeply in debt and may have been on the verge of attaining solvency when the Anglo-French war of 1666–7 brought about his final ruin.[68]

To add to his difficulties, Temple was plagued throughout his term of office in Nova Scotia by litigation with partners, employees, and rivals. Captain Thomas Breedon, a Boston merchant, did Temple good service in helping him to survive the early years in Boston, but subsequently he not only involved Temple in litigation with his partner William Crowne but also for a time identified himself with a rival claim to Nova Scotia through Thomas Elliott, a royal courtier at the time of the Restoration.[69] Elliott, in fact, was only one of a number of rival claimants who hoped to take advantage of the uncertainties of the Restoration to dispossess Temple; the Kirke family, which had been associated with the Alexanders long previously, and descendants of the Alexanders themselves were others.[70] Thus, although Temple eventually emerged in 1662 confirmed in his command of Nova Scotia and with the additional title of knight-baronet, he did not do so without severe financial strain, including the cost of an extended visit to England.[71] He also gathered the burden of an annual payment to Elliott of £600, 'his rent as he tearmed it,' which he paid regularly until disabled from doing so during the Anglo-French war.[72]

Temple also faced a dangerous enemy in Le Borgne, who made intermittent efforts to win back control of Acadia. In early 1658, Le Borgne's son, Emmanuel Le Borgne Du Coudray, recruited military officers in La Rochelle in preparation for an armed descent upon La Hève, led by another son Alexandre Le Borgne. A pitched battle in May was won by Temple's forces, but the victory only underscored the need for defensive vigilance.[73] Le Borgne, under pressure in France from litigation against the d'Aulnay family – which he was seeking to displace even from its possessions in France itself – briefly proposed a compromise by which Temple would continue to hold the forts of Pentagouet and the St John, but conflict resumed when this was refused. A further attack by Le Borgne was beaten back by Temple in 1659 and, as Nicolas Denys succinctly put it, there followed 'plusieurs guerres entr'eux.'[74] It was with good justification that Temple worried in a letter of December 1659 that 'I want men and money to defend my self if the french should with any considerable strength assault mee ...'[75]

In short, Temple's 'Nova Scotia' was an ideal stalking-horse for the economic interests of Massachusetts. At the same time as Temple was prevented by lack of resources from having any dangerous pretensions, he retained the responsibility for all the administrative and defensive complications that might arise. As an anonymous contemporary confided to Sir Joseph Williamson, English secretary of state, 'T. Temple dwells idly at Boston and is fooled by them.'[76] In these conditions, and with the county of Yorkshire providing similarly favourable conditions in the former Province of Maine, merchant interests in the whole northeastern maritime region now expanded and solidified. Thomas Lake was one Boston merchant who operated in both Yorkshire and Nova Scotia. Another was Edward Tyng, who was one of a partnership which in 1661 bought out the Plymouth colony's interests at Kennebec and bought an island in Casco Bay in 1663; at the same time he was deeply involved in the rapidly growing New England fishery off the coasts of Cape Sable and other areas of peninsular Nova Scotia. In 1666, Tyng attempted, albeit unsuccessfully, to institute a commercial seal hunt on Sable Island.[77] With these commercial developments increasing their contributions to the economy of Massachusetts, the General Court might well throw its support behind Temple's trade concessions in 1658, 1663, and 1666.[78] In addition, the Massachusetts colony might well protest several years later, in 1669, when the question again arose in England of a restitution of Nova Scotia to France. Through Secretary Rawson, the General Court represented that New England's defensive position would be weakened, and that a restitution 'would not only obstruct the present trade of Peltry, but of ffishing, which is most Considerable.'[79] As it stood from 1657, Temple's Nova Scotia was a comfortable and convenient arrangement for Massachusetts.

It had real advantages too for the Acadian population. One of these was the regular availability of supplies and provisions from Massachusetts traders. Moreover, as in Maine, the intervention of an alien force had had the effect of drastically weakening the seigneurial system, with the concomitant loosening of its restraints. The parallel with Maine is not exact in every detail: in Nova Scotia, for example, there was no effort to impose a system of New England towns. Moreover, the continuing military presence of the Le Borgnes gave a focus to any discontent with the new government; Temple in 1659, listing his many troubles in a petition presented through Thomas Breedon to Richard Cromwell, asserted that 'diverse hundreds of the ffrench nation which by Articles doe remaine there, are apt and have attempted to mutinie against your Highness Government therein.'[80] Many Acadians, however, took a more pragmatic attitude. A recent study of Acadian trade with Massachusetts in the second half of the seventeenth century has succinctly summed up the choices facing Acadian entrepreneurs as 'l'indépendance, le patriotisme [français], l'assimilation [à Massachusetts] et l'accommodation.' Of the four, the last was by far the most attractive, since it permitted Acadian merchants to trade freely as Acadian needs dictated.[81] More generally, accommodation and adaptability offered the greatest prospect, indeed the only prospect, of retaining the way of life which had been established on the marshlands of the Port Royal valley; and Temple's Nova Scotia provided an excellent framework for such an accommodation. After the Sedgwick conquest, a substantial migration took place in the valley. As recorded by Nicolas Denys, 'les habitants qui s'estoient logez proche le Fort, ont la pluspart abandonné leur logemens, et se sont allez establir au haut de la riviere.'[82] While this movement was no doubt partly motivated by the desire to remove from the English presence at Port Royal, it also had the effect of shifting the Acadians to extensive marshland where Le Borgne had no practical authority even though it was still technically within his seigneury. When Alexandre Le Borgne took up residence in Port Royal after the restitution of Acadia to France in 1670, he would attempt to reimpose seigneurial authority, but would succeed only in stirring up conflict and division in a community where the seigneurial system had become an annoyance rather than a social institution. It was this experience which would prompt the Le Borgnes in later years to reflect darkly on the existence of a 'party ... anglois' among the Acadians.[83]

The complex series of changes which had taken place in Nova Scotia / Acadia during the decade of the 1650s had resulted, as in Maine, in the establishment of a state of affairs more closely shaped to the practical convenience of Euramericans. Though there had been no deliberate intervention by the Massachusetts colony as such, the result was the establishment of a new colony of Nova Scotia, connected only by the most tenuous of links to the old colony of New Scotland, under the effective tutelage of New England commercial interests. The population of Nova Scotia remained predominantly French, but as in Maine, it was a population of Euramerican settlers who were well capable of turning the new situation to their best advantage.

Stability Established?

There is no doubt that the decade between 1650 and 1660 saw far-reaching changes in the northeastern maritime region. The decade had opened with the two colonies of Acadia and Maine in similar conditions of chaos and fragmentation. Over the ensuing years, however, the power and influence of Massachusetts expanded into both and established itself. In neither case was this the result of long deliberation – there was considerable reluctance in Massachusetts to become involved in either Acadia or Maine – and both interventions were responses to circumstance. Once reluctance had been overcome, however, the new arrangements had clear advantages both for the rulers and the ruled. The new forms which had emerged by 1660 were the products of convenience, the outcome of a series of expedients and adaptations. Most of all, they had the advantage of preserving the agricultural and trading economies which had been established in Acadia and Maine, while mitigating the more restrictive aspects of the original European projects, notably the seigneurial and proprietorial structures. The result, in terms of the new pattern of the region, was very much a Euramerican answer to the problems which had arisen in the formative period.

Nevertheless, by no means all the problems that had emerged during those formative years had been solved. In particular, no solution whatsoever had been found to the most basic problem of all: how to reconcile American reality with European concept. For Euramerican convenience in the seventeenth century was by no means the only or even the most vital consideration in the regulation of colonial affairs. The power of European concept, and ultimate legality and authority, retained immense importance, especially in regard to the legitimacy of governmental authority; and there could be no doubt that the adjustments made in the northeastern maritime region had treated European concept in an extremely rough fashion. Indeed, these changes amounted to nothing less than a total reconceptualization of the region, with Maine and Acadia simply ceasing to exist, to be replaced by the county of Yorkshire and the new version of Nova Scotia. The process had been one of metamorphosis; as a perceptive French observer pointed out shortly afterwards, an effort had been made to 'metamorphozer la nouvelle france en nouvelle Ecosse.'[84] The question was, however, whether the metamorphosis would turn out to be real or illusory.

One factor which was bound to work against the new pattern was the continued opposition from those representatives of the old order whose interests had been infringed. The military power which the Le Borgnes periodically wielded on the Atlantic coast, although never enough to destroy Temple's Nova Scotia, was a persuasive reminder that the concept of Acadia had not entirely succumbed. In London, Edward Godfrey and a handful of aggrieved colleagues kept alive the concept of Maine through constant efforts to have their dispossession reversed by the English government. Furthermore, the changes in the northeastern region had been made at a time of exceptional preoccupation with internal affairs both in France and in the British Isles. The French government, thrown into confusion by the Fronde and struggling to sustain the Spanish war, had been in no position to play an active role in Acadia, even to the limited extent it had been involved during the formative years. England was in the throes of consolidating a recent revolution, of which the results were still in doubt and would remain so up to and beyond the Restoration in 1660. Once these circumstances changed, a reckoning would inevitably come. Whether Yorkshire and Nova Scotia would survive would then be an open question.

There was also a further aspect which rendered the stability of 1660 more apparent than real in the northeastern region. Even for Massachusetts, the entities of Yorkshire and Nova Scotia, while useful, were essentially labels of convenience. Massachusetts still remained what it had been in the formative period: a powerful, but none the less an outside force, seeing the region as a quarrying-ground for economic resources and as a bulwark of defence. If these characteristics could be maintained by other means, the Boston authorities would be no more anxious to retain their new-found tutelage than they had been actively concerned to establish it in the first place. Even in Euramerican terms, the arrangement lacked stability. The colonies of the northeastern maritime region, therefore, continued to lack identity and integrity. The adjustments made after 1650 had given apparent solutions to long-standing problems. That the adjustments were matters of convenience was their strength, but that they were solely matters of convenience was their greatest weakness.

CHAPTER 7

European Reassertion
1660-1675

Renewed Negotiation

The Restoration of Charles II in England and the beginning of Louis XIV's personal rule in France saw the elaboration of economic and political approaches to North American colonization. Following the precedent set during the interregnum, the English Navigation Act of 1660 expanded and systematized the principles laid down in the 1651 act, prohibiting foreigners from trading to English colonies. To this was added the concept of 'enumerated goods,' to be exported from English colonies only to England, Ireland, or some other English colony. Under Jean-Baptiste Colbert, the regulation of the French colonies proceeded from 1663 on the assumption that colonies should be so developed as to afford the maximum economic benefit both to the mother country and to the imperial system as a whole. Although French measures tended to be paternalistic and English measures more immediately responsive to the demands of private interests, the aims were not significantly different. Politically too, both crowns developed a heightened awareness of colonial affairs, albeit for rather different reasons. The French crown was virtually forced in 1663 to reorganize the rapidly disintegrating colony of Canada; the English crown came to see proprietorial grants in the colonies as cheap and convenient rewards for its many political creditors: the Carolina grant, again in 1663, is a prime example.

In the case of the northeastern maritime colonies, however, it was not broad considerations of policy that initially dictated royal approaches. Indeed, the Navigation Act of 1660 bore little upon Maine, since its major export commodities of timber and fish were not enumerated and were specifically exempted by an order of 1661.[1] Acadia, moreover, was necessarily excluded from the early planning of Colbert, since it remained largely in English hands until 1670.[2] Nor did overall political factors play a major part; it was rather the complaints of aggrieved subjects which brought these colonies within the royal purview. In the case of the French, this began soon after the treaty of 1655, when it quickly became apparent that the provision for settlement of the Acadian question by further negotiation was an empty one. Accordingly, Le Borgne was commissioned in late 1657 as royal 'Gouverneur et ... Lieutenant General en ladite province de l'Acadie,'[3] and sent on a mission to England in early 1658, as Louis XIV himself informed Bordeaux, to demand a start to negotiations. The failure of this mission led in turn to the military attempt at La Hève in May, led by Le Borgne's son. In October, Louis wrote again to Bordeaux enjoining a strong protest and instructing the ambassador to 'poursuivre Incessamen' the release of the younger Le Borgne from captivity in London and the restitution of the occupied forts.[4] Now again the elder Le Borgne returned to London and discussed plans for a division of the lands of Nova Scotia/Acadia, but without satisfaction to either side. In early 1659 Le Borgne was reported to be planning further forcible measures, and in the summer of that year yet another attempt at La Hève was beaten off by Temple's forces.[5] Not surprisingly, Temple wrote to London shortly afterwards to implore 'if possible a peaceable settlement with the French.'[6]

Temple's wish was never fully realized, and violence smouldered on in Nova Scotia throughout his ascendancy there. By March 1662, Temple was complaining to the Massachusetts authorities 'of monsieur laborne his acting in a way of piracy against himselfe and severall of the English in these partes [Nova Scotia] taking of severall vessells and taking away severall Goods to value of two thousand pounds and upwards.' The English there, he asserted, had been 'cruilly handled.'[7] Shortly afterwards, the tables were turned when Alexandre Le Borgne was ambushed in Nova Scotia and once again taken captive, this time to Boston. Although acquitted of piracy, the younger Le Borgne was held responsible for the seizure of a fishing vessel and kept imprisoned for debt until he escaped in 1665.[8] Later in 1665, one of his brothers, Le Borgne Du Coudray, complained to the French government of Temple's renewed aggression. Not only had the English begun to extract a levy of 10 per cent from the catch of all French fishing vessels in Acadian waters, he stated, but they had also made violent raids upon French fishing settlements on the Atlantic coast of the peninsula at Mirliquesh and Port Rossignol. Le Borgne intended now 'de faire la guerre aux anglois et les Incommoder sur touttes la Coste de L'accadye ...' and had accordingly established a small garrisoned habitation near La Hève.[9] Thus, Nova Scotia was never entirely at peace before war broke out between England and France in 1666. Temple was then ordered 'to Annoy, Dammage, and Destroy the French ... in those parts.'[10] As Temple was to reflect bitterly and expressively in 1669, 'I have supported our Pigmy war with the french and preserved the kings Country at my own proper charge ...'[11]

Meanwhile, however, the question of Nova Scotia/Acadia had become prominent in Anglo-French diplomacy. Upon the Restoration, the French had naturally renewed their efforts for the restitution of the 'forts in America ... with the countries and habitations thereupon depending.' Again naturally, they had made much of the connections between Temple and the discredited Cromwell, and argued that Charles II 'cannot in Justice refuse to Command a present restitution ...' 'Here the principall point is,' continued the submission by the French ambassador, 'to re-establish the King [of France] in his rights not disputed usurped upon him and his subjects in full peace.' At first, Charles II seemed ready to yield on the question: in August 1661 a French envoy had described him as prepared to give 'toute la satisfaction quy dependroit de luy.'[12] However, the king and his councils were also under pressure to retain Nova Scotia, largely from the various claimants to the colony. Breedon and Elliott, for example, submitted a draft response to the French ambassador, dated 7 February 1662, which described Nova Scotia as 'of great importance and weight to his Majesty,' and protested bitterly the incursions of Le Borgne. Invoking a strategic argument, the authors contended that 'it would not bee Honourable or safe to give up Nova Scotia bordering so upon New England to the ffrench which may enable them to invade and infest New England at their pleasure ...'[13] Temple, Crowne, and La Tour also responded to the arguments of the French ambassador, with a memorandum to Charles II, in which they tactfully minimized the role of Cromwell and took pains to derive their title from the original New Scotland grant: 'the said fforts lye in New Scotland and the Sovereignty thereof doth as properly belong to your now Royall Majesty as old Scotland doth ...' After enumerating their own personal sacrifices, they concluded that 'there is not a person that holds any part of the Land there under the great seale of ffrance or ever did that ever was heard of but under Scotland.'[14]

One result of these conflicting pressures, and of the clashes between rival claimants to Nova Scotia, was an investigation of the details of the case. Accordingly, on 7 March 1662, the Privy Council ordered enquiries to be made in Scotland for any surviving documentation.[15] Shortly afterwards, in early April, machinery was set on foot to confirm Thomas Temple in the possession and governorship of 'the Countries and territories called Liccadie [sic] otherwise Accadia and part of the Country called Nova Scotia,' though still with bounds as defined in 1656. With the conferral upon Temple of the title of knight-baronet and the passage of his patent as governor, both in July 1662, the royal espousal of Temple's claims seemed complete.[16] For the French, this situation was a frustating one, though certainly not sufficiently to prompt abandonment of the Acadian question. Indeed, in 1663 a French fleet bound for Newfoundland was given royal orders to carry out a reconnaissance of Acadia, clearly with a view to a subsequent assault. A shallop was to be sent to Port Royal, 'pour y apprendre des nouvelles du sieur de la Tour qu'on presupose y estre encore. Et s'informer de l'Estat des forces et de L'Establissement que Luy et les Anglois peuvent avoir non seulement audit port Royal, mais encore en la rivierre de St. Jean et au lieu appellé Pentagouet.'[17]

The strength of the English crown's commitment to Temple, however, may be questioned, especially in view of the use of Nova Scotia, throughout 1663 and 1664, as a bargaining counter in negotiations directed towards a new Anglo-French treaty. When Louis xiv on 17 July 1663 empowered his ambassador, the Comte de Commenges, to enter into negotiations, one of his conditions was that Charles ii 'fera restituer sans aucun delay ... les forts de Pentacoet, St. Jean et Port Royal, occupez dans l'Amerique par les Anglois.' A further instruction in October asserted flatly that 'c'est une notorieté ... publique que les François ont possedé toute l'Acadie, le Canada, et tous les autres pays circonvoisins plus de quatre Vingts ans ... et que les Anglois en ont chassé par force et par Violence.'[18] The English answer to this contention was by no means categorical, and in October Commenges confessed his complete uncertainty as to their real intentions. As negotiations were prolonged inconclusively throughout 1664, the English constantly procrastinated on the point, though seeming occasionally to be ready to agree to the French terms.[19] The French opposition to the entire concept of Nova Scotia was absolute; so much was clear. The English commitment to it was firm in public. In private, however, the negotiations of 1663–4, though never concluded would have brought little comfort to Sir Thomas Temple had he known of them. They foreshadowed the rather easy decision to exchange Nova Scotia for the English half of the West Indian island of St Christopher in the treaty of Breda in 1667.

The royal attitude towards the county of Yorkshire had by this time shown greater definition. It too had been the subject of complex enquiry and argument in London since the Restoration. Edward Godfrey had lost little time in writing to the secretary of state, Sir Edward Nicholas, to emphasize the damage done to the king's interests by the continued rule of Massachusetts over Maine. Massachusetts he had described as 'in practice ... a free state,' while also stressing his own poverty-stricken state, 'for all my services for my Cuntery like to perish for want.'[20] In his efforts, Godfrey had the support of others with grievances of various kinds against the Massachusetts colony, and in early 1661 a joint petition was presented to the newly formed Council for Foreign Plantations of 'divers persons who have been sufferers in New England.'[21] Thus, the case of the Maine patentees was quickly brought to the fore.

Ferdinando Gorges, now the inheritor of his grandfather's interests in Maine and elsewhere, was also active. Petitioning the king in early 1661, he recalled his family's long involvement in the discovery and settlement of New England, and in particular the role of his grandfather. Now that the Massachusetts colony was attempting to usurp his province, and with Maine inhabitants 'who at most were tenants' claiming land-ownership, he maintained that only royal intervention could ensure his legitimate enjoyment of his property.[22] Gorges' petition was considered by the Council for Foreign Plantations (as were the separate complaints of Godrey and his associates); it reported to the king in May 1661 that the Massachusetts colony had indeed 'in these late times of general disorder strayed into many enormities, and hath invaded the rights of their neighbours.' In the absence of any communication from Massachusetts itself – a deliberate absence – the council felt unable to recommend any course of action, and the issue was referred to a special committee of the Privy Council.[23]

Nevertheless, for Gorges the report of the Council for Foreign Plantations was good enough, and he accordingly issued in the same month a commission for the government of his province of Maine. The result was a meeting held at Wells on 27 December by Gorges' four 'trustees,' all former magistrates of the Province of Maine and large land-owners under the proprietary system. An order was first adopted to proclaim Charles II 'throughout the Province of Maine.' Secondly, the meeting resolved 'that our diligence and care shall be exercised in searching and enquiring after all such Arrears of Rent as shall be found due from any of the Inhabitants or others within this province according to Charter.'[24] With such an aim as this, it is hardly surprising that Gorges' trustees met with considerable popular resistance in Maine, and by late 1662 it had become clear, as one contemporary observed, that 'those that doe sticke close to the [Massachusetts] bay ... is almost all ...' But Gorges' commission had created much fear and confusion. In the words of the same contemporary report, it 'puts the pepell into such a feere that they know not what to doe ...'[25] Legitimate authority was known to flow from Europe, and the wealth and security of the Maine inhabitants could only be adequately safeguarded by legitimate authority. Thus arose the confusion which prompted, for example, one Jonas Balie to describe himself in his will as 'of blew poynt alias Scarborrough In the province of Mayne alias the Countie of yorke ...'[26] More seriously, it showed that the county of Yorkshire was by no means unshakeably established when confronted by European-based authority.

In London, deliberation continued. Godfrey continued to press his case until his death in 1664.[27] On a broader front, the crown attempted with little success to negotiate with the Massachusetts colony on the series of complaints against it.[28] In June 1664, however, Gorges' petitions at last bore real fruit, when his complaints of usurpation by Massachusetts were comprehensively vindicated in a report to the king by the attorney general, Sir Geoffrey Palmer.[29] Accordingly, on 11 June, similar letters were sent by the crown to both the governor of Massachusetts and the inhabitants of Maine to require 'that you forthwith make restitution of the said province unto him [Gorges] or his commissioners, and deliver him or them the quiet and peaceable possession thereof ...' Ten days later a new commission was issued from Gorges to his supporters in Maine to take possession of the province.[30]

Thus, both Temple's Nova Scotia and the county of Yorkshire had decisively fallen foul of European authorities – the crown of France and the crown of England respectively. Nova Scotia was temporarily in a less dangerous position because of the support given to it by the English crown on grounds of its theoretical links with the previous Scottish colony, but this royal support was far from unflinching and was abandoned altogether in 1667. European concept had been vindicated in Europe; it remained to be seen whether this concept could now be made an adequate basis for the northeastern maritime colonies themselves.

Maine and the Royal Commission

At the time of the attorney general's report on Maine, a royal commission was already on its way to New England on a different mission. Consisting of four members and led by Colonel Richard Nichols, an officer in the service of the Duke of York, the commission had two major roles to play in America. First, as agents of the Duke of York, they were to take possession of the large area recently granted to the duke, both in the Hudson River region and between the Kennebec and Ste Croix rivers. This would, of course, entail the conquest of the colony of New Netherland and also the possession of disputed land in the northeastern maritime region. Secondly, as royal commissioners, they were to regulate the various governments of New England along lines acceptable to the crown, paying especial attention to that of Massachusetts. Sailing for America in the early summer of 1664, the commissioners made their first landfall at Piscataqua on 20 July.[31]

Nowhere did the royal commissioners' instructions contain any specific mention of Maine. Nevertheless, in early June 1665, three of the four commissioners set off from Boston for the northeast, having decided that the prevailing conflicts in Maine came within their instructions by implication. The commissioners, in truth, were somewhat short of success. Although the conquest of New Netherland had been carried out with expedition in the late summer and autumn of 1664, and had been followed by satisfactory receptions in Plymouth, Rhode Island, and Connecticut in early 1665, the commissioners had proved impotent in the face of Massachusetts' refusal to allow its government to be regulated according to royal wishes. Thus, the settlement of Maine provided a possibility for the commissioners to relieve their frustration.

On their arrival in Maine, they found an extremely confused situation. The commission issued a year before by Ferdinando Gorges had in some respects been a conciliatory one: about half of the magistrates named, for example, had had no close connection with the proprietary system, either as patentees or as close associates of the Gorges family. Moreover, Gorges had ordered an oblivion on all previous activities in favour of Massachusetts rule, 'which I am more ready to look upon as the Influence of the Disorders of the late Tymes than any Disaffection to me ... '[32] Despite these and other concessions, Gorges' instructions to his magistrates enjoined the Maine inhabitants 'to remember that I am singly the Lord Proprietor of that Province, whereas in other adjacent Governments the Property is in the Commonalty of Inhabitants,' and laid down detailed instructions for the transition back to the payment of rents and the control of land tenure on the proprietary pattern.[33] That these instructions had a practical effect on Maine is evident from the cessation of land grants by the towns: in the York town book, for example, nothing was recorded from October 1663 until October 1665. Furthermore, the series of Yorkshire county courts was broken off after 5 July 1664, not to resume for some four years.[34]

Thus, Gorges' commission had had real effects in Maine. They were, however, essentially negative ones, not necessarily indicating the effective resumption of government in Gorges' name. The Massachusetts colony certainly did not renounce its claim to the county of Yorkshire and had said so in forceful terms.[35] The assessment of George Cartwright, one of the royal commissioners, prior to his departure for Maine, was that the Maine inhabitants 'now ... stand out, and will not submitt to their peculiar patent, but will adhear to the government of this jurisdiction [Massachusetts].'[36] In short, confusion and stalemate prevailed. The dilemma of the inhabitants was acute: on the one hand they were asked to give up the stability of land tenure and the defensive strength that came from Massachusetts, while on the other they risked the accusation of rebellion. However biased in its other opinions on the matter, the Massachusetts General Court was no doubt accurate when it referred on 25 May 1665 to 'the distracted condition of the people of the county of Yorkshire.'[37]

For the royal commissioners, too, the situation was a delicate one. In view of the royal letter of 11 June 1664 in favour of Ferdinando Gorges, they clearly could not leave the county of Yorkshire intact. Nor, in view of their recent unsuccessful skirmishes with the Massachusetts authorities on other matters, would this be a palatable course of action even if it were possible. If, however, they supervised the withdrawal of Maine from the jurisdiction of Massachusetts in favour of Gorges, they would be espousing the proprietary system, a cause which had foundered in the past in the face of strong popular opposition. If they were seen to favour that system, their whole status as impartial commissioners would inevitably be jeopardized; already the warrant summoning the inhabitants of York to attend the commissioners on 22 June had been signed by two of Gorges' magistrates 'in the Kinges name and by Authority from him to ffardinando Gorge Esq.'[38]

In the event, the royal commissioners favoured the claims of neither Gorges nor Massachusetts. The Maine inhabitants, they reported to London, were 'weary of the unjust and partiall actings of the Massachusetts and fearefull of the proceedings of the other ... ' They had therefore taken the province 'into his Majesties more immediate Government,' and named eleven royal justices of the peace to exercise authority in Maine 'until his Majesty will please to Appoint another government.' The justices themselves were a well-balanced group: geographically evenly distributed, they included both old patentees and others who had been closely associated with the town organizations. All the justices, moreover, accepted their positions and were to serve actively during the next three years. As for the land question, the commissioners ordered a moratorium, providing that 'all who lay claime tó any land in this Province by Patents [are] to have them forthcoming by this time twelve month.' With this, the commissioners departed, leaving a stern prohibition of any effort by 'as well the Commissioners of mr Gorges, as the Caporation of the Massachusetts Bay, to molest any of the Inhabitants of this Province with their pretences, or to execute any Authority within this Province untill his Majesties pleasure be further known.'[39]

Thus, the commissioners had taken a bold step: they had taken the question of Maine beyond the mere accommodation of private interests, and had made it the subject of direct royal intervention. This in itself was entirely new among the northeastern maritime colonies. In making such a settlement, moreover, they had made a major commitment on behalf of the crown – to take up the issue and settle it. The land question in particular would require further attention once the moratorium on claims had expired. More fundamental was the question of whether any means could be found to give a real identity to the re-established colony of Maine. If the contradictions which had emerged during the formative years were to be resolved, both political and economic organization would be required to give Maine roots in America as well as in Europe. The commissioners themselves had found solutions to virtually none of the fundamental problems, but they had certainly thrown down a challenge to the English government to do so.

The result, however, was not as the royal commissioners had hoped. For the moment, the signs were favourable: regular courts were held under the authority of the royal justices; the connection with Massachusetts was broken by the discontinuation of the practice of sending Yorkshire deputies to the General

Court in Boston; and the proprietary and town land systems apparently coexisted, with town lands being allocated in certain localities at the same time as rents were being collected on Gorges' behalf elsewhere. The English government, however, failed to respond. A royal letter of 10 April 1666 directed the Massachusetts colony to respect the commissioners' settlement in Maine, and the Earl of Clarendon wrote to assure Nichols shortly afterwards that 'his Majesty will not sit down by the affronts which he hath received.'[40] This was, however, a difficult time for the English government. The fall of Clarendon as chief minister in 1667 brought about a reorganization of the patterns of power, which now rested largely with the 'Cabal.' Arlington, the member of the Cabal who had been most closely involved with New England affairs in the past, was now bound up with the much more pressing matter of foreign policy as it affected France and the Netherlands: the policies which had produced the Triple Alliance of 1668 against France gradually gave way to the pro-French policy which was to bring about the secret treaty of Dover in 1670. Thus, not only did Whitehall have little time to attend to the settlement of Maine, but there also existed an almost total lack of surveillance over the actions of Massachusetts.

It was in this context in 1668 that the county of Yorkshire was successfully re-established. The royal commissioners' settlement had been purely a temporary one, and in early 1668 a petition was addressed to the king from 'the inhabitants of Maine,' regarding the 'general disturbance' arising from 'clandestine applications ... to the Massachusetts.' Initiated by the royal justices, and signed by six of them, this petition gathered only fifteen other signatures; it was hardly a sign of strength.[41] On the other hand, petitions went to Boston from Wells and Cape Porpoise to ask for the resumption of Massachusetts government, and it was on this basis that the General Court empowered four commissioners, led by John Leverett, to go to York and hold a county court. With the aid of all civil and military officers, the four were ordered to bring to trial any persons 'under the pretence of any other authority that shall swerve from the due obedience they owe unto this jurisdiction ... ' Leniency was to be used where possible, though the inhabitants of Yorkshire were rebuked for 'their late causeless revolt.' The land situation was to be returned as far as possible to what it had been 'before the revolt'; but in the appointment of new civil and military officers, the commissioners were 'not altogether obleiged to strict forme of lawe.' This suspension of law was symptomatic of the General Court's determination this time to make a lasting settlement.[42] The re-establishment of Massachusetts rule was not achieved without opposition, which in some individuals and in some areas persisted for as much as two years. However, in general, the process went smoothly. When the Massachusetts commissioners met the royal justices in York in early July, for example, even the justices were forced to concede that 'the motions of these Gentlemen had more countenance from our people than our selves ... ,' and the justices eventually left to vent their frustration in a protest to the crown, while the Massachusetts commissioners 'proceeded to the worke of the Court.'[43]

The existence of the county of Yorkshire continued with relative stability for a number of years. Indeed, in 1672, the Massachusetts colony began to investigate the possibility of extending its rule even further, beyond the Kennebec River. This move would take the Massachusetts authority beyond the bounds of the Province of Maine (which, unlike the modern state of Maine, extended only from the Piscataqua to the Kennebec) and into an area which was the subject of several conflicting European claims. The whole area between the Kennebec and Ste Croix rivers was claimed by the French as part of Acadia, and to symbolize this claim in 1670 Hector d'Andigné de Grandfontaine was instructed to establish his stronghold at Pentagouet when he took command of Acadia. None of the area had been included in the New Scotland grant of Sir William Alexander, but all of it had been granted to him in 1635 as part of New England, to be known as the county of Canada. Thomas Temple's Nova Scotia patent of 1662 included all of the area as far as Muscongus, southwest of Penobscot Bay. Most recently, in 1664, the entire territory had been granted to the Duke of York, and for all practical purposes his and the French were the two major competing European claims by 1672.[44] To complicate matters further, the Plymouth colony had held land on both sides of the Kennebec from the Council for New England and had continued to be active there until selling out to a Boston-based partnership in 1661.[45] It was partly through this Plymouth operation, and partly through direct immigration connected with the fishery, that a substantial English population had been gathered on the Kennebec and northeast at Pemaquid, Sheepscott, and on Penobscot Bay.[46] Samuel Maverick, who would become one of the royal commissioners to New England, wrote in 1660 of 'many families.'[47]

The royal commissioners did not visit the area beyond the Kennebec, although three of the Maine justices had taken tenuous possession of it in the name of the Duke of York. The commissioners advised the justices 'to keepe the business of Mayn distinct from the more easterly parts' and little else was done.[48] The commissioners' report, probably written by Cartwright, stressed that the settlements in the northeastern area were tiny and disorganized, but Cartwright had never been there. Maverick in 1660 had given a different impression, describing the raising of cattle as well as fishing and trading; John Josselyn, who revisited Maine between 1667 and 1671, also wrote of 'Cattle and Cornlands' in this vicinity.[49] What was certain was that these English inhabitants lived in debatable land, and showed on several occasions a desire for stability and security, which paralleled that of the settlers of the Province of Maine.

In the late 1650s, enquiries had been made to Boston about the possibility of extending Massachusetts government beyond the Kennebec, but at that stage the General Court had suggested that Temple might more appropriately assume this responsibility.[50] When Temple's Nova Scotia offered little beyond the operation of a trading-post at Penobscot, and when the Duke of York's rule appeared to lapse after 1665, there were strong inclinations to affiliate with Acadia. Grandfontaine in 1671 reported that a promise of liberty of religion would secure the allegiance of the English settlements of 'Kennebequy et Paincouit,' while Jean Talon, the intendant of New France, enthusiastically passed on a similar report which he had received in the same year from Simon-François Daumont de Saint-Lusson, an envoy he had sent to explore the Kennebec-Pentagouet region for possible river routes from Quebec to the Atlantic. Talon was not sure whether the desire of the English settlements for French rule was 'un effect de la crainte qu'ils ont du voisinage des Francois ou d'une veritable passion de passer sous la domination de Sa Majesté'; but he believed the feelings to be real in either case.[51]

Grandfontaine, less cautious than the intendant, went so far as to suggest in 1671 that the English inhabitants of the disputed land 'ne veullent point reconnoistre baston.'[52] In stating the case this strongly, he exaggerated. In the following year a petition, bearing ninety-six signatures from the various settlements of this area, requested that the General Court authorize the extension of Massachusetts government northeastwards. After some hesitation, a court was ordered to be held in Pemaquid in 1674; the result was the creation of the county of Devon, in which no township privileges were granted but officers were appointed and submissions received from eighty-one inhabitants.[53] What this whole episode had again shown was the willingness of Euramerican inhabitants to adapt to the changes in European authority; the English here had been prepared to consider relating to Grandfontaine in the same manner as had the Acadians to Temple.

Even when the extension of Massachusetts jurisdiction offered stability in an English context, relations with the French were not necessarily cut off. Two of the leaders of the movement for political affiliation with Massachusetts, Thomas Gardner and Silvanus Davis, maintained cordial relationships with Henri Brunet, a French merchant who frequently travelled at this time in Newfoundland, Acadia, and northern New England, trading a variety of manufactured goods and clothing for fish, furs, and timber. Brunet's venture was short-lived – his travels occurred between 1673 and 1678, though little is known of his movements after 1675 – but it showed that northern New Englanders were potentially as willing to trade with merchants of France as were Acadians to trade with those of Massachusetts, depending upon where the most practical advantage lay.[54] Whether Brunet and his French principals could ever seriously challenge the economic domination of Massachusetts merchants in northern

New England, as Brunet confidently hoped in 1674, was another matter entirely, especially after the Massachusetts expansion. One of the Massachusetts commissioners, for example, was Thomas Clarke, joint owner of the trading, lumbering, and industrial operation at Arrowsick on the Kennebec; the other partner, Thomas Lake, was named by the General Court to be one of the magistrates of the Devon County Court in both 1675 and 1676.[55] More generally, that the power of Boston should have taken a further step northeastwards is striking testimony to the security of the Massachusetts colony's hold upon Yorkshire and to its self-confidence.

While this went on, however, European interests were not entirely forgotten. Again at the behest of Ferdinando Gorges, the question of Maine was gradually reopened in London during the early 1670s, at which time a number of expedients were considered for its solution. Prominent among these was the suggestion that the crown should purchase Gorges' title to Maine; this course of action was strongly recommended by the royal Council of Foreign Plantations in June 1671, with a view to enabling 'the King to curb Boston.'[56] Apparently no progress was made on this matter, since almost three years later, in early 1674, Gorges joined with Robert Mason, proprietorial inheritor of New Hampshire, and the Earl of Stirling, claimant to the Alexander patent of New Scotland, to offer 'for the service of your Majestie and the good of this Kingdome to surrender up ... our Patents,' in return of course for suitable compensation.[57] The proposal was taken seriously by the crown as regards Maine and New Hampshire but, in view of the treaty of Breda, not with regard to New Scotland; and it certainly remained a possibility well into 1675, when Charles II was inclined to make of the two colonies a fief for his illegitimate son, the Duke of Monmouth. No conclusion was arrived at, however, perhaps because Gorges and his associates were holding out for too high a price, as was reported at the time to John Leverett, now governor of Massachusetts.[58] No effort had been made by the royal government to take up the challenge posed by the royal commissioners' settlement of 1665, and still Gorges' private claims were being discussed and negotiated in London. The direct influence of European concepts of Maine, therefore, remained at this point dormant despite all the efforts of the royal commissioners; it was not, however, by any means dead.

Acadia Re-emergent

While the English crown had been suddenly confronted with responsibility for the rehabilitation of Maine in 1665, the French crown found itself in a similar position with regard to Acadia following the treaty of Breda in 1667. After some hesitation, and considerable procrastination on the part of Sir Thomas

Temple, Acadia was restored to France in 1670 under royal command. High hopes were entertained at that time for the future of the colony, and the French crown certainly did not display a comparable inactivity to that which characterized English dealings with Maine. The Acadian colony's deep-seated weaknesses, however, those that had emerged during the formative years, remained to be corrected. Initial optimism thus gradually disappeared in the face of a difficult dilemma for the Acadian inhabitants and their governors: how far to allow the realities of American colonization to compromise European concepts of legitimacy and authority.

The Anglo-French war of 1666-7 had temporarily thrust Temple's Nova Scotia into a position of strategic significance. Instructed on 22 February 1666 to co-operate with the New England colonies in attacks upon the centres of French settlement, 'more specially that of ... Canada,' Temple was ordered to join in the sending of 'some Fit number of Forces' to the relief of the English West Indies. Although the prudent reluctance of the New England colonies prevented the prescribed attack on Canada, Temple himself, as he reported with pride to Arlington on 24 May 1667, sent a shipload of provisions to the relief of Barbados.[59] Writing a further letter to London on 10 December, he again cited this self-sacrifice, adding that the ship had been taken by a Dutch vessel within sight of the island. As for Nova Scotia, Temple reported that he had successfully defended it 'from divers small attempts made by the French,' and claimed considerable success in driving the French completely out of peninsular Nova Scotia, with the aid of a new fort at Port La Tour, near Cap de Sable. Although certainly expensive for Temple, as he had complained in his letter of 24 May, the war was proceeding satisfactorily. The tone of his correspondence, however, changed abruptly in the course of his letter of 10 December; while writing this letter, Temple received the first news of the treaty of Breda. Naturally, his reaction was one of bewilderment and bitter protest. Citing his hereditary title to Nova Scotia and his expenditures in defending it, Temple expressed incredulity that the crown should relinquish 'this great kingdome.' If Nova Scotia should be surrendered, moreover, without his receiving 'some real satisfaction,' he would personally be 'utterly ruined,' being 'now much in yeares and broaken with Cares, toyles, and misfortunes.'[60]

Temple's fears were well justified. The English crown, never entirely solid in its commitment to Nova Scotia, had found the colony to be a useful bargaining counter in regaining the more valuable English half of the divided West Indian island of St Christopher, which had been seized by the French during the war. The treaty was accompanied by much confusion as to the exact extent and bounds of 'the said Country called Lacadie lying in North America, which the said king [of France] did formerly enjoy,' and a letter to Temple was drafted in London in November 1667 which instructed him 'that it is only the

Country of Acadie which you are to restore, not any part of Nova Scotia, or of any other Country or Province adjoyning.'⁶¹ This letter, however, was never dispatched, and subsequently the English government apparently became convinced that Nova Scotia and Acadia were indeed one and the same. The secretary, Williamson, noted, 'Nova Scotia or L'Acadie ... consists chiefly of the forts, places and habitations of Cape Sable, the river St. John, the Port Royal, Le Have, and all that has been in the possession of the French,' giving the bounds simply as the St Lawrence and the northern extent of New England.⁶² Accordingly, an order sent to Temple on 31 December specified that the restitution of Acadia was to include 'nommement les fortes et habitations de Pentagouet St Jean Port Royal la Heve et le Cap de Sable.'⁶³

Temple continued to protest. In a letter of 24 November 1668, for example, he maintained to the Privy Council that 'Acadia Is but a Small part of the country of Nova Scotia,' and beseeched the council furthermore to have regard to his own 'Sad Condition.'⁶⁴ When the representative of the French crown, Morillon Du Bourg, arrived in 1668 to take possession, Temple raised what were reported to Colbert de Terron, the French ambassador in London, as 'des difficultez et des ambiguitez sans suitte et sans fondement pour me faire perdre du temps.' Moreover, justification was briefly given to Temple's procrastination when 'certain new overtures' by Colbert de Terron regarding St Christopher prompted the English crown to order a delay in the restitution. Further justification was alleged by Temple on grounds of harassment by the Le Borgnes, now naturally scenting victory, and they were roundly rebuked by Du Bourg for their behaviour.⁶⁵ Despite all of this temporary confusion, however, the restitution was eventually made. The English crown's order for delay was withdrawn in March of 1669, and a sharp reminder sent to Temple in August, in accordance with the king's opinion of Temple (as Colbert de Terron reported) that he was 'un coquin ... et qu'il le feroit bien obeïr.'⁶⁶ On 7 July 1670, Temple finally relinquished control of Nova Scotia to Grandfontaine, who had been commissioned by the French crown to take command.⁶⁷ Temple, for his part, continued to complain that he must 'miserably perish (for well doeing) in the lowest poverty,' flirted briefly with the idea of accepting the French citizenship that was offered to him by Intendant Talon, but then returned to London where he died in 1674.⁶⁸ Thus began the renewed existence of the colony of Acadia, and a further period of dormancy for that of Nova Scotia.

The colony regained by France in 1670 had changed remarkably little in its sixteen years of English domination. The anonymous French memoir of 1667, which remarked upon 'le peu de soin qu'ont eu les Anglois de s'habituer en ces lieux,' made particular mention of the lack of exploitation of the area's agricultural potential.⁶⁹ Further detailed comment upn the agricultural possibilities of a large number of Acadian sites was made in another anonymous memorandum of this period, and the upshot was clearly a renewal of the earlier French determination to cover Acadia with agricultural tenants.[70] Now, however, the crown was taking a more active role than previously, and an official dispatch in 1669 even speculated upon the possibility 's'il ne seroit pas plus avantageux de revoquer et annuller toutes les donations et concessions qui ont esté faites en ce Pays la, et d'y envoyer en mesme temps quelqu'un qui fût capable de faire un bon fort sur la rivière qui fait la separation des Anglois pour ensuitte y envoyer tous les ans un nombre d'hommes, et travailler a le peupler insensiblement.'[71] In the event, no formal revocation of grants was made; Grandfontaine, however, was instructed to set up his base at Pentagouet – not the Kennebec, claimed by the French to be the border with New England, but close thereto – and to encourage trade, fishing, and settlement there. It was even hoped, as Colbert wrote to Talon in early 1671, that Acadia would prove 'non seulement en estat de se soustenir par elle mesme, mais aussy de fournir aux isles françoises de l'Amerique quelque partie de ce qui leur est necessaire, pour la subsistance de ceux qui les habitent, et pour leurs autres besoins.'[72]

Thus, high hopes were entertained for Acadia on its restitution to France. The optimistic mood was continued in Talon's reply to Colbert in November 1671. Acadia, he reported, had a population of some 389, together with large stocks of cattle; it should soon be possible for Acadia to be 'en estat de fournir aux antilles les chaires sallées.'[73] But it would be necessary – and here Talon introduced a crucial point – 'interrompre sans violence le commerce que font les anglois avec les subjects du Roy habitans du Port Royal, desquels ils tirent tous les ans quantité de viande en eschange de quelques droquets et autres estoffes de la fabrique de Baston, ce qui se peut à mon sentiment assez naturellement faisant passer de france ou d'icy au Port Royal quelque peu d'estoffe pour fournir aux besoins plus pressants.'[74] Here once again the marginal status of Acadia, as a colony dependent upon outside assistance, is evident, and once again the question of relations with Massachusetts was paramount. When Talon stressed the need to break the colony's dependence upon Massachusetts, he was, of course, quite right: such a break was indeed necessary if Acadia was to become a well-established French colony with its own internal complexity and integrity. To effect the break, however, was a difficult matter, and to effect it 'sans violence' might well prove impossible, as indeed it eventually did. Furthermore, Acadia was in no fit state to withstand violence. Unless, therefore, a speedy and thorough re-establishment of the colony could be achieved, the contradictions which had arisen during the formative years would go unresolved.

What was needed above all in Acadia was population: what was less obvious was the means of attracting it. As in the formative years, the Port Royal valley and neighbouring areas were the major populated regions of the colony. The population of Port Royal itself was growing only slowly at this time, but settlement was steadily being expanded up the valley to Les Mines and Pigiguit and then to Beaubassin.[75] Thus, in this sense, the second half of the seventeenth century was a period of expansion. The area of the colony affected by this, however, comprised only a limited part of the peninsula and the isthmus of Chignecto; the old disconnection between the Atlantic coast, the area of marshland agriculture, and the commercial ventures of the region comprising modern New Brunswick was in no way solved thereby. Grandfontaine's base at Pentagouet, envisaged as a centre of growing population, proved able to attract soldiers, but only in small numbers. Nicolas Denys continued with his projects in the north, largely now through his son Richard, but in essentially the same way as in past decades; few traces of Denys's efforts remained after his death in 1688.[76] At the other geographical extreme, near Cap de Sable, Philippe Mius d'Entremont lived on the seigneurial estate which had been granted to him in 1653 by his personal friend La Tour. Here again the inhabitants were few and, as the later Acadian governor François-Marie Perrot complained in 1686, more solid pursuits were neglected in favour of the fur trade.[77]

Jean Talon was well aware of the difficulties arising from the size of Acadia in the early 1670s and realized that it was essential to establish substantial French populations in all the various parts of the colony. Pentagouet and the St John River attracted his attention particularly, and he felt that the latter might serve as an 'exemple à tous autres.' But Talon's attempts to stimulate settlement through revitalization of the seigneurial system and the granting of vast seigneuries on the St John encountered an old problem: seigneurs in this region were pleased to hold their lands as areas of fur-trading activity but showed little interest in colonization as such.[78]

The fact was that local, piecemeal developments could not afford greater integrity to the Acadian colony, either by binding its various localities together, or by rendering it significantly less dependent upon Massachusetts. If there were to be any possibility of a real re-establishment of Acadia along the lines conceived in Europe, much more thorough innovation would be necessary; as in Maine, only the crown could hope to attempt this. As Nicolas Denys assured Louis xiv in the dedication of his *Description géographique*, 'ce Pays tel et meilleur encore que je ne le represente, a besoin pour devenir utile au nostre de ses bien-heureuses influences dont il a plû à Vostre Majesté de regarder ses voisins.'[79] Even assuming, however, that Acadia could have been redeemed by attentions such as those given to Canada in the previous decade, there was now little possibility that such continuing assistance could be afforded by a French crown increasingly preoccupied with European warfare. Any suggestion of direct royal subsidy soon came to be unfavourably regarded by Colbert. As Bishop Laval of Quebec was informed in 1677 by Father Jean Dudouyt, the representative of the Séminaire de Québec in France, Colbert's curt replies to such approaches were 'qu'il n'y a rien a faire pour le présent,' and as regards support for missionary priests, 'tout va pour la guerre.'[80]

In this situation, Acadia remained weak and fragmented. Among the Acadian people, deep divisions paralleled those in Maine and were symptomatic of a similar dilemma. First of all, the restoration of French authority meant the return of the Le Borgne family to Port Royal and the neighbouring marshland settlements, just as the restoration of the Province of Maine had meant the renewal of the authority of Gorges, with all its implications for the structure of landholding. Alexandre Le Borgne de Belle-Isle arrived in Port Royal in 1670, as the representative of his father, and, after the latter's death in 1675, as seigneur in his own right. Within a year of his arrival, Le Borgne had caused such chaos that Grandfontaine sent word that he was not to be recognized as any other than 'comme simple habitant' pending the hearing of charges against him; according to the reports reaching the governor, Le Borgne had already banished three Acadians from their lands.[81] Undeterred by Grandfontaine, Le Borgne continued to live in Port Royal and to style himself seigneur, though not in circumstances which suggest that he was a genuine leader of the community. Perrot in 1686 described him as 'extremement debauché au vin,' and described his drunken habit of signing over leases indiscriminately, giving 'souvant la mesme terre a plusieurs.'[82] Three years later, the governor, Louis-Alexandre Des Friches de Meneval, described Le Borgne as living in poverty, despite receiving some rents from Port Royal inhabitants.[83] In petitions to the French crown for reimbursement of their expenses in fighting Temple, the Le Borgne family consistently and accurately disclaimed any significant profit from seigneurial payments.[84] Such payments were being made on a small scale by inhabitants who felt that security in their land titles was thereby ensured; conversely, in 1673, an assembly of the parishioners of Port Royal resolved to try to derive some benefit from Le Borgne by seeking a subsidy towards the building of a parish church from him in his capacity as 'seigneur et propriétaire de partie de Lacadie.'[85] But the seigneurial system was moribund. The only real power left to the seigneur in Port Royal was the power to create confusion and conflict by throwing doubts on the validity of land titles.

The Acadians also faced a dilemma in their relationship with Massachusetts, which had developed as one of the more attractive aspects of rule by Temple. Sometime later, in 1679, Governor Frontenac of New France reported to France that the Acadians had been slow to obey orders given them, either because they had been without a governor for some time, 'soit par les divisions qu'il y avoit entre eux, soit enfin par quelque Inclination Angloise et Parlementaire, que leur inspire la frequentation et le Commerce qu'ils ont avec ceux de Baston ...' Here Frontenac was overstating the case, since there is no evidence that the Acadian community was favourably impressed by the political ideologies of its Massachusetts trading partners, any more than that of Maine was attracted by Massachusetts government *per se*; but the real conveniences and advantages of close association with Massachusetts were undeniable in either case. Equally undeniable in either case was the perceived necessity of legitimate government and the desire to avoid any accusation of rebellion. As Frontenac went on to record in 1679, the Acadians were easily induced to 'faire des rejoüissances publiques, pour les glorieuses conquestes que Votre Majesté fit l'annee dernière.'[86] The dilemma of the Acadians was by no means simple, and it posed a grave threat to the integrity of the colony.

For royal governors of Acadia, a similar dilemma existed. On the one hand, a governor was expected to foster the development of Acadia away from dependence upon Massachusetts. On the other, he was expected to maintain 'sur toutes choses une bonne correspondance avec les Anglois de Baston,' and even at his discretion 'en tirer tous vos besoins.'[87] Any tolerance of the activities of Massachusetts merchants could lead to the kind of abuse of which Grandfontaine complained to the Massachusetts governor in January 1672: Daniel Dennison, a merchant, had not only engaged illegally in the Acadian fur trade, but had 'traitté mesme aux sauvages une piece de canon quy apartient au roy.' Grandfontaine was quite correct in his accusation, and Dennison was not by any means the only one involved.[88] But any abstinence from the ministrations of Massachusetts traders could lead to what Frontenac reported in November 1672 as 'l'estat miserable ou Mr le chevalier de grand fontaines … a mandé a Mr. Talon qu'il se trouvoit avec sa garnison,' for the relief of which Frontenac had hurriedly sent a shipload of provisions.[89] Grandfontaine had other problems (he had disputes, for example, not only with the Le Borgnes, but also with his own lieutenant, the Sieur de Marson[90]), but it was this difficulty over Massachusetts which led to his eventual recall in 1673. The large debts that Grandfontaine had contracted in Boston gave rise to the suspicion that he had traded more than necessary, possibly to his own personal profit; 'il sera bon de faire ententre,' read the letter of recall, 'que Sa Majesté n'a pas approuvé que l'on se soit ainsy engagé envers des Estrangers, qui nous sont supérieurs en force leurs habitations estant plus enciennes et mieux fournies que les nostres.'[91]

Grandfontaine was replaced in his command by Jacques de Chambly, who began his tour of duty by reporting unfavourably to Frontenac on the resentment aroused in the colony by his predecessor.[92] Chambly, however, soon had personal experience, in a different way, of the trials of commanding a marginal colony. The weakness of Acadia was graphically revealed in the summer of 1674 when the rivers of Pentagouet and St John were both invaded and captured by a small Dutch sea force. Both Chambly and Marson were carried to Boston, where the Dutch leader, Jurriaen Aernoutsz, left John Rhoades, a Boston merchant, in nominal charge of Acadia, now renamed the colony of New Holland.[93]

This episode eventually proved to be of limited duration for Acadia, since the pretensions of Rhoades, and his harassment of Massachusetts merchants in the Acadian region, soon led to his arrest and conviction in Boston on charges of piracy and thus to the end of the short Dutch interlude.[94] What was striking, though, was the total inability of Acadia to withstand the attack even of a small force. As in the formative years, little help could be expected from Canada. In November 1674, Frontenac lamented to Colbert: 'Jestois dans l'impuissance de pouvoir envoyer a l'acadie du secours, quand mesme j'aurois eu les choses necessaires pour cela, je me suis contenté d'envoyer quelques gens avec des Canots pour essaier d'avoir des nouvelles de l'estat, ou ils auront laissé le fort, et s'ils n'auront rien entrepris contre le Port Royal.'[95] Colbert wrote back to Frontenac in the following March, to give word that 'Sa Majesté a esté surprise d'apprendre' the news of the Dutch raid and 'ne peut se persuader qu'il n'y ayt un peu de la négligence du Sieur de Chambly.'[96] In reality, there was little cause for surprise. Acadia was still in the condition where, as d'Aulnay and the Massachusetts colony had agreed long before, a state of peace was 'requisite in these beginnings'; the marginal status of Acadia thirty years later, despite French efforts, was conclusively demonstrated by the Dutch episode.

Limitations

If the decade of the 1650s had seen a process by which the pattern of the northeastern maritime region was adjusted to fit the convenience of Euramerican settlers and societies, the ensuing period to 1675 saw the revival and reassertion of the colonial projects which had originally been conceived in Europe. These projects did not necessarily appear in forms identical to the original ones. The individuals concerned changed: the grandson of Sir Ferdinando Gorges and the sons of Emmanuel Le Borgne were now among the chief European participants. Another change lay in the more direct role played by European governments, with both English and French crowns moving away from mere support of private interests. Nevertheless, the aim of both governments continued to be the re-establishment of old colonies in the name of legitimacy and at the expense of the arrangements that had evolved between 1650 and 1660.

In certain respects, this aim had been achieved. The English crown had early identified itself with the re-establishment of the Province of Maine, and had attained, through its commissioners, an opportunity to attempt this. Although the opportunity was lost for the moment, the later reopening in London of the question of Maine showed that at least the concept of the colony of that name had not been submerged. The French crown, in its efforts to revive the colony of Acadia, had proceeded in a rather more practical fashion. At the expense of the colony of Nova Scotia, Acadia was again extant in 1670 and measures taken to provide government and to facilitate development. To that limited extent, direct European influence had been restored in the northeastern maritime region.

These achievements, however, were essentially negative, consisting of little more than the disruption of the immediately previous state of affairs. The European governments showed no sign of any capacity to solve the major practical difficulties which had arisen during the formative years. Nova Scotia, as in 1632, had felt only the negative capability of royal influence, which had again in 1667 put the colony out of existence. By its failure to respond to the temporary settlement established by the royal commissioners, the English crown had also, for the time being at least, disqualified itself from finding any effective means of stimulating the development of Maine or of extending government there. The vacuum had again been filled by the Massachusetts colony. The French crown in Acadia had certainly attempted to give government and, to a limited degree, had planned the development of the colony. No way had been found, however, of binding together the colony's far-flung regions, of giving it an economic base, or of solving the basic problem of defence.

More generally, there had again been a failure to reconcile European concept with American reality. Nova Scotia no longer had any legitimate existence; but in America its memory survived, and the English-French fishery disputes of the 1680s were often referred to in New England as concerning 'the Coast of Nova Scotia.'[97] Regarding Maine and Acadia, the European influence had been exercised largely in favour of the colonies' revival and continued existence. What had not been solved in either case, however, was the question of how to give the respective colonies a real identity to match, and indeed to coalesce with, their existence in European minds. Hence the continuing confusion of loyalties among the colonies' respective populations: there was no good Euramerican reason why Maine and Acadia should exist as entities, and no good European reason why they should not. What had emerged by 1675 was an uneasy compromise. It was one which left the northeastern maritime colonies still desperately weak and vulnerable, and the region as a whole in a state of potentially violent turmoil.

CHAPTER 8

Violent Dissolution
1675-1690

Indian Influences

The background of relations between Indians and Euramericans in the north-eastern maritime region in the later seventeenth century, as in comparable periods elsewhere in America, was the steady weakening of traditional Indian culture in the face of alien values and ways of life. Although the introduction of European material culture, weaponry, and economic practices was as real in Acadia as in Maine, the embitterment of relations between English and Abenaki and the engrossment of Indian lands in the Maine towns had made the destructive effects of English colonization more obvious. Relations between French and Indian had developed more harmoniously, and this difference began to assume increasing importance from the European point of view in the years following 1675. The Indian peoples of the region, despite acculturation, remained a strong and independent force. Because of acculturation, and the other pressures imposed by the English presence in Maine, the Abenaki felt increasingly constrained to oppose the English threat with violence. Thus, although formal military co-operation between Indians and French did not occur until 1690, Indian friendship emerged as a major source of strength for Acadia just as Indian hostility was a crucial weakness for Maine.

The French missionary effort, one of the chief vehicles of French-Indian communication, had been severely retarded by the Sedgwick conquest and the subsequent establishment of Nova Scotia. Although the Capuchin missionaries were not expelled from Port Royal in 1654, they left the following year and one of their number, Ignace de Paris, submitted a report to his superiors calling fervently to have Acadia restored to France, to save both French and Indians there from 'the powers of darkness.'[1] The fears of Ignace were not entirely realized, since Catholic Christianity did not die out in Acadia, but missionary activity was interrupted. In the northern part of Acadia, three Jesuits continued at first to be active, but the establishment was shortly reduced to one and then abandoned, 'voyant,' as Nicolas Denys recorded, 'qu'il n'y avoit plus rien à faire avec des gens que la frequentation des navires entretenoit dans une perpetuelle yvrognerie.'[2]

Following these setbacks, missionary efforts gathered momentum once again, though with a slowness which religious leaders were inclined to blame upon the government of France for its lack of financial support and for its tolerance of the liquor trade.[3] In 1676, the Séminaire de Québec finally dispatched a priest, Louis Petit, to Port Royal to serve as vicar-general for all of Acadia. Petit experienced grave difficulties in carrying sole responsibility throughout the colony for both Indian missions and pastoral care of the French population and several years later Abbé Louis-Pierre Thury took charge of a mission on the Miramichi River.[4] Meanwhile, the Recollet order had also become active. In addition to Chrestien Le Clercq, who spent most of the years 1675–86 among the Micmac of the Gaspé, a mission was intermittently maintained by the Recollets at Beaubassin and on the St John River, despite the unwillingness of Bishop Laval to recognize their activities.[5] With the aim of inducing greater organization and co-ordination, the Sulpician order was introduced as a result of the visit to Acadia in 1685 of Jean-Baptiste de La Croix de Chevrières de Saint-Vallier, then vicar-general at Quebec and soon to become bishop. Furthermore, Jesuit missionaries had returned to Acadia, though they now eschewed fixed missions in the colony in favour of their remarkably successful establishment at Sillery, near Quebec.[6]

The success of the Sillery mission is indicative of the profundity of the attraction which French friendship by this time exercised upon the Indian peoples of the northeastern maritime region. Although the Sillery experiment had failed to attract the Montagnais, it was revived in the winter of 1675–6 when a small number of Abenaki fled to Canada to escape the newly begun Abenaki-English war in Maine. As the war continued, increasing numbers of Abenaki reached Sillery on either a temporary or a permanent basis, and this trend was perpetuated even after the war ended in 1678; in 1683, the exclusively Abenaki mission of Saint-François-de-Sales was instituted on the Chaudière River, and within six years it had a population of some 600. For a people who found their traditional way of life already indirectly disrupted by acculturation and now directly by warfare, the secure and humane environment of the missions was attractive. Even more important, however, the Canadian missions offered a model for adaptation to the changed situation brought about by European colonization. Here, cultural change could take place in a framework which preserved important aspects of the traditional order: the hunting economy, religious symbolism, and the absence of the liquor trade. As one historian has remarked, 'these communities served as retreats and models for adaptation for the many Abenaki bands which chose to remain on their lands in Maine.'[7]

Thus, the framework of French missions was reconstructed within, and outside, Acadia. On a secular level, harmonious relationships between French and Indian were promoted and symbolized by the residence with the Penobscots at Pentagouet of Jean-Vincent d'Abbadie de Saint-Castin, who had first come to Acadia with Grandfontaine as a French regular officer. At the time of the Dutch attack in 1674, Saint-Castin had fled to the interior and from that time 'threw himself among the Savages,' as was later recorded by a French traveller, 'whose Language he had learn'd.'[8] Saint-Castin was in no sense a typical European settler and was often regarded with disapproval by French authorities based at Port Royal; in 1686, he was described by Governor François-Marie Perrot, as 'un gentilhomme ... qui n'a defriché ny rien fait.'[9] Nevertheless, Saint-Castin was a Frenchman who forged a deep and long-lasting relationship with the Penobscot, based on kinship. In this way, he promoted trust and friendship between French and Indian. He was able, moreover, to serve as a direct link between the two, especially since he had a close relationship with Abbé Petit at Port Royal, with whom he had served in the Régiment de Carignan-Salières.[10]

The framework of French-Indian contacts in the later seventeenth century, therefore, was sufficient to prevent any rupture of the relationships that had existed in the formative years. This is not to say that there did not still exist ambitions among the French to destroy the Indian way of life. A memorandum presented to the minister of Marine in 1686, for example, recommended that all Indians in Acadia should either be Europeanized 'c'est a dire d'Estre catholiques, prendre des terres et travailler comme les françois,' or expelled.[11] However, the means for imposing such a change were totally lacking and in practice even the inclination was lacking among the French missionaries. Thus, French-Indian relations were able to proceed on a basis of mutual respect and co-operation.

The case of English-Indian relations in Maine, while originally stemming from attitudes on either side which were not basically dissimilar to those prevailing between Indian and French, was by now entirely different. It was true that in the area northeast of the Kennebec there were English traders, such as Thomas Gardner at Pemaquid, whose close relationship with the Kennebecs and Penobscots was based on trade. Significantly the pragmatic Gardner had also been among those who had welcomed the visit of the French merchant Henri Brunet in 1674. Within the bounds of the old Province of Maine, however, the days when such Englishmen as Christopher Levett and Thomas Gorges had been able to meet with native leaders on a basis of mutual friendship and respect were now long gone. In the virtually total absence too of any contact between English and Indian on a religious basis, a growing sense of mutual grievance and hostility had little potential outlet other than violence. Open warfare broke forth in September 1675.

The Abenaki war was no mere northern extension of King Philip's War, which had begun some three months earlier in southern New England. In Maine, or Yorkshire, there were particular reasons for warfare, arising from the deteriorating relations between English and Abenaki. But as news of the conflict further south spread northeastwards, it acted as a catalyst. There were also certain immediate causes of Indian resentment, notably a food shortage caused by the Massachusetts authorities' efforts in 1674 to prevent the trading of powder and shot to the Abenaki for use in hunting. This was aggravated by hasty English attempts in the late summer of 1675 to disarm completely the various branches of the Abenaki. At the same time, further tension was caused when English sailors drowned the infant son of the Saco sachem, Squando, and it was the Sacos along with the Androscoggins who were the first Abenaki groups to fight. As Gardner pointed out on 22 September writing from Pemaquid, 'the Reason of our Troubles hear may be occationed not only by som southern Indianes which may Com this way But by our owne Acctings.' Gardner's view, however, was not widely shared among the English, and shortly afterwards he was arrested and brought to Boston to explain his continuing trade with the Indians.[12] With resentment and mistrust kindled on the Indian side by such actions and fuelled on the English side by suspicions of a general Abenaki conspiracy, the war continued until 1678.[13]

For both sides, it was a damaging conflict. Contrary to English allegations, not all the Abenaki took part; the Kennebecs attempted throughout to remain neutral, as did the Penobscots further north. All, however, shared the stresses of the war to some extent. Food shortages arose from the disruption of Indian agriculture, hunting, and trading; and it was this situation that influenced several unsuccessful Abenaki efforts to find a peaceful settlement to the war in 1676 and 1677 and prompted the first Abenaki migrations to the Sillery mission.[14] The war, which lasted almost three years, had initially been fought by the Abenaki by means of swift raids, a traditional form of warfare made more effective by European weaponry. The length of the war, however, had been far from traditional, and its protracted pressures upon Indian society could only intensify the already profound effects of acculturation.

The English had been severely damaged also, since the raiding warfare of the Indians had proved devastatingly effective against the Yorkshire towns. The number of English lives lost has been estimated at 260 out of a population of perhaps 3,500, a proportion significantly higher than that of casualties in southern New England as a result of King Philip's War.[15] In addition, many colonists abandoned their homes. On 6 October 1675, Richard Waldron, commanding the Yorkshire militia, ordered that 'all persons are hereby prohibited from goinge outt of there owne towne to anye other place to inhabitt in.' The context of the order was the departure of refugees from Falmouth, to the detriment of the town's defences; by 9 December, the Massachusetts council felt constrained to issue a similar order specifically for the town of Wells.[16] By this time, troops had been dispatched from Massachusetts, but only in small numbers; the Massachusetts authorities were already hard pressed by the war further south, and took the opportunity to point out that the Yorkshire towns in the past had paid little or nothing to Boston in taxes and so could not expect favoured treatment.[17] By late 1676, Waldron's major concern had become the encroachment of Indian raiding parties into the southernmost communities of Yorkshire and even into New Hampshire and towards Massachusetts, and he advocated the abandonment of all territory northeast of Wells.[18] In the event, English military expeditions to the Kennebec and the Penobscot were able to stave off this drastic move but not to protect the towns from further raids. In May 1677, a petition of York inhabitants complained to the Massachusetts General Court of 'the daly Molestations and Massacers which wee have mett with all from our cruell and sculkeing adversarys,' while later in the year the inhabitants of Scarborough complained similarly of 'the trecherous Enimy.'[19]

Thus, one result of the Abenaki war was to heighten the English perception of 'the inconstant savage.' The fury of the Yorkshire colonists was reflected elsewhere in New England: at Marblehead in the summer of 1677, two Abenaki prisoners, captured at sea after they had attacked a Salem fishing vessel, were torn limb from limb by an assembled crowd of women.[20] Yet the bitterness of the colonists' feelings could only obscure the real significance of the Abenaki war, which was to demonstrate that great power in the northeastern maritime region still lay with the Indian. King Philip's War in southern New England had broken the power of the Indian in that area and had destroyed the remnants of the traditional Indian way of life.[21] Further north, this was not true. Certainly, the Abenaki suffered severely through the rigours of an exhausting war. The peace settlement of 1678, however, depended upon Indian sufferance, which was clearly symbolized by the provision of an annual tribute of corn to be paid by the English.[22] From the beginning of settlement, the northeastern maritime colonies had existed only as long as they were tolerated by the native inhabitants. For Acadia, and indeed for the tiny and short-lived settlement of New Scotland, this had presented little difficulty. In Maine, as the growth of towns had given an apparent solidity to English colonization, the Indian had come to be seen as an alien. The war between 1675 and 1678 was a warning, though one not taken to heart by the colonists, of how fragile the English achievement could be.

The reality was stated by a group of Kennebec sachems in 1677. Writing to the Massachusetts governor to affirm their desire for peace, the Kennebecs nevertheless warned that they were the 'owners of the country and it is wide and full of enjons [Indians] and we can drive you out.'[23] Indian power remained a potent and independent force; that it was not recognized as such in Maine was a grave weakness in a colony already subservient to the whims of external forces.

Euramerican Interludes

Nevertheless, the Indian war in Maine was followed by a period when, in Euramerican terms at least, it seemed that a workable solution might have been found to the problems which had assailed the colony since the formative period. In 1678, the Massachusetts colony succeeded in buying the Maine patent from Ferdinando Gorges, thus apparently extinguishing his interest in Maine and establishing its own on a legitimate basis. Thus, Maine became a separate but subordinate adjunct to Massachusetts. By quite different means, Acadia had at this time arrived at a similar relationship with Canada, governed by a Canadian agent of Governor Frontenac in the person of Michel Leneuf de La Vallière. For a short time, these arrangements not only functioned but also coexisted with relatively little friction. Their weakness, however, was lack of specific approval from the respective European governments.

The years during which the Abenaki war was in progress saw the controversy over the Gorges claim to Maine being examined with unprecedented thoroughness in London. The Privy Council's Committee for Trade and Plantations had been reconstituted and revitalized in early 1675 and this, along with the increasingly close personal involvement of the king and the Duke of York in colonial affairs, had led to a considerably harder scrutiny of the claims and actions of the Massachusetts colony.[24] By early 1678, two agents of the colony, William Stoughton and Peter Bulkeley, were fighting a rearguard action before the committee, both over the Gorges claim and over that of Robert Mason to New Hampshire. On 9 January that year, Gorges and Mason offered yet again to surrender their titles to the crown to facilitate the formation of a royal government.[25] It was therefore a surprise when, on 25 March, the committee was informed by Mason 'that Mr. Gorges either out of a distrust of his Majesties justice of doing him right, or else overcome by the Sollicitations of the Boston Agents or some imployed by them, He hath sould the Province of Maine and the Government therof to them.'[26]

For Mason, this turn of events was clearly embarrassing. Yet Gorges' action was understandable: nearly seven years had passed since the possibility of transferring Maine to the crown had first been raised. Especially with the value of his property reduced by the damage done during the Abenaki war, the thought of yet further efforts in support of his New England claim must have been unwelcome. For the Massachusetts agents, his willingness to sell had brought about the chance of a genuine consolidation of the Massachusetts position in northern New England. Accordingly, Gorges deeded the Province of Maine to an intermediary, John Usher, on 13 March 1678, for the sum of £1,250. Two days later, Usher in turn deeded the province to the governor and company of Massachusetts Bay.[27]

Despite strong but temporary objections in the General Court, chiefly from the ranks of the magistrates, the purchase of Maine was confirmed; from 1680 to 1684, Maine was governed by the Massachusetts colony as lord proprietor. Accordingly, at York on 17 March 1680, a new government was established in Maine under the presidency of Thomas Danforth, one of the magistrates of the General Court.[28] Thus, rather than relying upon the forms of the county of Yorkshire, the paraphernalia of proprietorship was instituted. This had the advantage of adhering to the obligations of the Maine charter of 1639, on which the Massachusetts authority was now based. More important was the way in which the new arrangement would allow Massachusetts to rid itself of the previously burdensome aspects of ruling Maine, by forcing the province to be financially self-sufficient. Through a new provincial assembly, 'all publique charges' were to be defrayed.[29] An attempt was made also to levy rates outstanding since 1675, though the assembly admitted in 1682 that little success had been achieved in this.[30]

Much more controversial was the reimposition of quitrents, at a minimum rate of twelve pence annually from each family, and scaled upwards according to the family's wealth. In this provision lies further proof that the relationship between Maine and Massachusetts had all along been one of convenience: the free distribution of land through the towns was revealed as a mere by-product of the original annexation, a privilege and not a right. Not surprisingly, great difficulty was encountered in collection, and in 1684 Danforth himself wrote of 'the great Neglect in gathering up the quitt Rents.'[31] Nevertheless, despite these annoyances and despite the self-aggrandizement of Danforth and a number of associates through large personal land grants in Maine, this new settlement had much to commend it, even to the Maine inhabitants.[32] It was preferable to be the object of quitrent claims from Massachusetts, which was at least prepared to guarantee the existing land structure of the towns (as was manifested by the transfer in 1684 of all vacant lands within towns to the town authorities), than from a proprietor who might attempt to upset the entire structure by such expedients as claiming the ownership of common lands.[33] Such was the concurrent experience, for example, of New Hampshire. Under the Danforth government, too, power rested in the familiar hands of those who had been magistrates and town selectmen for many years. This again was an agreeable contrast to the sway of men such as Robert Mason and the royal agent

Edward Randolph in New Hampshire. Although divisions of opinion persisted in Maine, and were reflected in contradictory petitions for and against the Danforth government in 1680, the settlement certainly commanded enough support to survive.[34]

Maine was thus apparently put in a situation where Euramerican government was accompanied by a due observance of the forms of European concept. At the same time, Acadia reached a similar postion by different means. Following the Dutch raid of 1674, the Acadian commander, Jacques de Chambly, had been carried to Boston and subsequently returned to France. In 1676, Chambly was re-commissioned to his post in Acadia but was rumoured in Paris to be unwilling to return there. In the event, he received another command in the West Indies, thus leaving Acadia still without government.[35] Since overall responsibility for Acadia still rested with the governor of New France, it was Frontenac who took the initiative, working at first through Pierre de Joybert de Soulanges et de Marson, Chambly's lieutenant, who had returned to Jemseg on the St John River after being released from captivity. With Marson's death in 1678, however, no official representative of the crown remained in Acadia.[36] Accordingly, Frontenac proceeded to make other arrangements. 'J'eus l'honneur de mander a Votre Majesté,' he reported in November 1679, 'que j'avois l'année dernière envoié le Sieur de la Valliere commander dans l'Acadie, apres la mort du Sieur de Marson et en attendant ce qu'elle ordonneroit du Sieur de Chambly, auquel j'apprens qu'elle a donné un autre commandement dans les Isles.'[37]

La Vallière, born in Canada in 1640, already had strong connections with Acadia. Connected by marriage since 1655 to the family of Nicolas Denys, he had strengthened this link by marrying Denys's daughter while in Cape Breton in 1665 or 1666. After returning to Canada to pursue his military career, he had attracted the favour of Frontenac for his activities with Richard Denys, in cruising the Acadian coasts in search of Dutch vessels. It was for this that he was granted a seigneury at Beaubassin on the isthmus of Chignecto in 1676; originally made by Frontenac and the Intendant Jacques Duchesneau, the grant was confirmed by the crown in 1680.[38] Thus, in La Vallière, Acadia obtained a commander who had a strong personal interest in the colony. He was also one who, through Frontenac, had a realistic claim to wield legitimate European authority. What was new, however, was the combination of these characteristics with La Vallière's strong link with Canada, both through his own family and through his close relationship with Frontenac. Acadia could now, for the first time, operate with the support of a relatively strong and well-developed French colony in America; here, as in Maine, the forms of European concept were given flesh by Euramerican rule.

As commander in Acadia, La Vallière certainly could not avoid the difficulties which had assailed the colony in the past. Frontenac reported in 1679 on the reluctance of the Port Royal inhabitants to obey orders, though they were shortly brought to profess their fidelity to the French crown's authority vested in La Vallière. La Vallière clashed with the Le Borgne family over its claims to seigneurial rights, but the results of this quarrel were indecisive: an order in favour of Le Borgne in 1683 by the new governor of New France, Le Febvre de La Barre, was ruled by the crown the following year to be beyond the governor's powers.[39] Ironically, La Vallière himself aroused resentment among Acadian settlers on the outskirts of his seigneury by demanding seigneurial rights and dues. It would certainly seem that his seigneury was less than successful; he attempted to populate it by importing tenants from Canada, but the majority remained only a short time.[40]

Despite these difficulties, La Vallière's term of command in Acadia was a time of relative stability. La Barre's first impression was that 'le Sieur de La Valiere est un fort honneste gentilhomme qui y agit fort bien.'[41] A major aspect of his exercise of authority in Acadia was a frank recognition of the need for coexistence with the English colonists further south. Although committed in the long term to weaning Acadia from the economic domination of Massachusetts, both La Vallière and Frontenac envisaged this as a task to be achieved by positive support from France, rather than by any drastic measures against New Englanders. In the meantime, La Vallière was willing to allow English colonists to trade in Acadia within certain limits and even to fish on the Acadian coast on payment of a licence fee.[42] The practices which grew up were summarized in La Barre's instructions to La Vallière in late 1683, and justified on the grounds that 'sans le secours Des anglois qui y ont Tousjours porte le Necessaire Ce pays savoit abandonné ... ' Trading with Indians, however, was prohibited, and the taking of coal and other minerals was permitted only on due payment to the owner of the land concerned.[43]

For their part, the Massachusetts authorities and individual traders were largely content to respond to La Vallière's permissions and requirements. The chief merchant involved in the trade was John Nelson, nephew and inheritor of Sir Thomas Temple and his claims in Nova Scotia. That Nelson remained conscious of his claim to Nova Scotia is demonstrated by his citation before the Committee for Trade and Plantations in 1679 as 'concerned in the busines of Nova Scotia as Administrator to Mr. Thomas Temple'; but for the moment Nelson was able to achieve his mercantile aims by close co-operation with the French in Acadia.[44] He was able to forge strong links with Saint-Castin and on 22 October 1682 was made La Vallière's agent in the sale of fishing licences for Acadian waters.[45] This connection between Nelson and La Vallière was symbolic of a more general accord which had recently been reached in Boston. In late 1681, Frontenac had complained to the Massachusetts council 'that they continue to come from your Quarters to fish to trade with the Indians and to take coale upon our coast without leave.' An attempt to allay the complaint, by sending Nelson personally to Quebec, failed because of 'my [Frontenac's] absence from Quebeck, when he arrived, and that he did not resolve to find me in a canou at Monreall.' Frontenac renewed his complaints, but indicated that La Vallière was empowered to negotiate 'the Conditions upon which shall be accorded ... the said permission' to obtain licences for fishing and trading in Acadia. This was agreed in October, and the General Court in return voted its condemnation of any 'irregularityes' which might occur in the future, 'and that all persons soe offending are liable to the penaltyes and forfeitures by the Courts of those Governments where there offences are committed provided against them.'[46]

This latter part of the agreement was largely a polite fiction, since both sides were aware of the limited practical powers of enforcement available to the Acadian authorities. Nevertheless, a framework had now been established within which the fishery dispute could be shelved, and, more broadly, within which Acadian commercial entrepreneurs could trade freely with their Massachusetts counterparts.[47] Indeed, within this framework the existence of Acadia and Nova Scotia was not mutually exclusive. Since 1657, Nova Scotia had been essentially a mercantile concept, and so it could now remain. Acadia was able to continue to function as a political and strategic outpost of Canada, just as Maine functioned in a similar fashion with regard to Massachusetts. In each case, the forms of past European claims and concepts were catered to, at least in a formal sense. Apparently, therefore, a genuine reconciliation had been reached between European concept and American reality, one which would permit peaceful development and coexistence for the Euramericans of the northeastern maritime region.

The apparent reconciliation was, however, deeply flawed. One basic weakness was that it depended upon the maintenance of peace between English and Indian, at best an uncertain prospect. A second weakness was that it depended also upon European satisfaction with the somewhat minimal recognition afforded to forms and proprieties in a European sense. Certainly, there had been no recognition by European governments of the new arrangements in either Acadia or Maine, In the latter case, the purchase of Maine had been one of a number of New England questions which had brought the Committee for Trade and Plantations to resolve in April 1678 that 'this whole matter [of New England] ought seriously to bee considered from the Very Root.'[48] In the case of Acadia, the crown had instructed La Barre in May 1682 that 'comme il n'y a point eu de gouverneur depuis longtemps en cet endroit, et que le Sieur de la Valiere en a fait les fonctions sans commission depuis deux ans, Sa Majesté veut qu'il examine si le dit la Valiere en est capable ...' Although the result was the announcement in 1683 of royal intent to name La Vallière as governor, no commission was issued.[49] Thus neither the English nor the French government had endorsed the existing situation in the northeastern region, and events were to prove that no such endorsements would be forthcoming.

European Concept Refurbished

European concepts of American colonies in the seventeenth century were never static. From the vague hopes and promises which had characterized the plans of the earliest colonial promoters, who had envisaged great kingdoms on the European model, peopled by a prosperous and numerous tenantry, a considerable distance had been travelled by the later decades of the century. In particular, the more practical, utilitarian view of colonies, which had been inchoate in 1660, had undergone definition and refinement. In both France and England, a determination had grown up to maximize the benefits derived from each colony, in economic and strategic terms. The northeastern colonies were included in this desire, all the more so because they were situated in a region which contained an ill-defined international frontier, at a time when frontiers were assuming unprecedented significance. In Europe the development of concepts of sovereignty was leading nations to define their boundaries, and in North America the proximity of English, French, and Spanish settlement was tending in the same direction.[50] Thus, the northeastern maritime colonies, still subservient to outside forces, were caught up in imperial designs which had no commitment to their welfare or survival as colonies.

Signs of a change in European requirements and expectations were apparent in the early years of the 1680s, though the potential was not fully realized until the middle of the decade. An early indicator was the revival of the Duke of York's interest in his territory northeast of the Kennebec, which he began to exercise through the governor of New York, Sir Edmund Andros. In the later stages of the Indian war, on 9 June 1677, it had been resolved by the New York council that 'it would be advisable to send to take Possession and assert the Dukes Interest at Pemaquid, and parts adjacent Eastward.'[51] A fleet was accordingly sent, peace made with the Indians in this region, and a fort erected at Pemaquid; from this time forward, the Duke of York's representatives at Pemaquid took an agressive attitude towards all of their neighbours, especially in regard to any alleged intrusions into trade and the fishery. Indian relations were brusquely defined in September 1677: 'No man to trust any Indyans.'[52] In the following year, John Alden, a Boston merchant whose involvement in the eastern trade was to extend over two decades, was seized for trading in the St George River and brought to Pemaquid, though he was subsequently released.[53]

In the same year of 1678, a claim was asserted by the New York authorities to rule 'as farre westward as Blacke Point,' and in the summer of 1680 this was at least partially implemented in the practical form of the deposition of certain town officers of Falmouth on the orders of Andros: the General Court of Massachusetts noted on 16 August that Andros' men had 'so farr threattened the Inhabitants as that they are affraid to abide under' the Masssachusetts authority.[54] Furthermore, the interests and security of Saint-Castin, whose residence at Pentagouet put him within the limits of the Duke of York's grant, were regarded as 'of noe Importe ... Knowing the Extent of his Royal Highnesses Limitts which must be Maintained'; by 1687, the pressures exerted on Saint-Castin had brought him to request military support from Port Royal in resisting encroachments from Pemaquid.[55] A similar attitude was taken towards his associate John Nelson, and was exemplified by a decree of the New York council in late 1683; 'no one whatsoever as he will answer it at his perill shall take a permitt or lycense to trade there [between the Kennebec and Ste Croix] from John Nellson at Boston or any other person whatsoever, except such as are appointed and Commissionated by the Governor of New York.'[56]

This was a wedge driven into the state of coexistence between Maine and Acadia, and was all the more considerable because of the influence wielded by Andros in London. Called in by the Committee for Trade and Plantations to give information on both New York and New England in April 1678, Andros subsequently entered into a correspondence with William Blathwayt of the plantations office, in which he continued to comment on New England affairs. The correspondence was regarded by Blathwayt as 'not only a particular kindness to me, but a service to the King.'[57] Also influential in London was Edward Randolph, a cousin of Robert Mason who had first gone to New England as a royal agent in 1676, and subsequently served there frequently in similar capacities.[58] Randolph, like Andros, held a prickly regard for English royal interests and was particularly outspoken against the control of Maine by Massachusetts. On his first visit in 1676 he had noted that from the Piscataqua River 'is brought all the Masts and plancks that come for England,' and subsequent visits confirmed his high estimate of Maine's potential economic importance.[59] Randolph, in his capacity as a customs officer, also complained repeatedly during the early 1680s of the practice of concealment of 'prohibited goods and Vessels' on the Maine side of the Piscataqua River, and he met with little success in prosecutions through the courts of Maine.[60] For these reasons, as well as possibly for the prospect of personal gain, Randolph favoured the extension of direct royal government to Maine, and pursued this end even to the extent of charging 'articles of high misdemeanour' against Danforth personally in 1681.[61]

If the English crown was receiving strong advice against the existing situation in the northeastern maritime region at this time, so also was that of France. In an effort to further the economic development of Acadia, the French crown in 1682 gave permission to a group headed by Clerbaud Bergier, a Huguenot merchant of La Rochelle, to establish a sedentary fishery in Acadia. Despite furious protests from the church, Bergier arrived shortly afterwards to found a base at Chedabouctou.[62] The grip held upon the Acadian fishery by New England vessels, however, was clearly a threat to the new project, and the protests of Bergier's company at this state of affairs soon focused on La Vallière's system of licences and on La Vallière himself. In 1682, for example, it was alleged to the minister of Marine 'que la coste [d'Acadie] etoit entiere-ment ruinée par les Anglois sy l'on n'y apportoit un promt remede, et que cela etoit causé par l'entrée que le nommé La Valière de Quebecq leur donne en nos ports pour de l'argent, de son autorité, et sans avoir aucuns ordres de Sa Majesté ...'[63] Bergier demanded an aggressive effort to expel the English fishermen from Acadian waters and was rewarded in April 1684 with a commission as royal lieutenant in Acadia. La Vallière was prohibited from exercising governing functions, and a former governor of Montreal, François-Marie Perrot, was appointed governor with instructions to supervise the expul-sion of English interests from Acadia.[64]

Bergier hereupon began a serious offensive against New England vessels, and a letter from Boston in September 1684 informed the English government that he, 'without ever publishing his pretensions or power, or giving any time or opportunity for the vessels to depart and carry away their ffish, hath surprized and carried away eight or nine of our Ketches.' Perrot later denied the charge that no warning had been given; but the result – retaliation by New England vessels – was predictable in any case. As the sedentary fishery company gloomily reported to France in the following year, numerous of the company's ships had been harassed, and a twenty-five ton barque had been taken.[65] So thorough was the reaction that Perrot doubted that the trend could be reversed. Although, in a memorandum of August 1686, he admitted the desirability of 'un establissement fort et considerable a la coste' to forestall the English, he also suggested possible schemes by which the English might be induced to continue fishing but to sell their catch in Acadia in return for French merchan-dise. Perrot also had kind words for John Nelson, 'qui a tousjours commercé a cette coste et qui a fait beaucoup de bien aux habitans par les grandes prests qu'il leur a fait dans leur plus grande necessité,' and was by now suspected by Bergier's company of trading on his own account with both Indians and Eng-lish.[66] Whatever Perrot's faults, the company itself was in grave difficulty. One of its employees, Robert Challes, later commented that 'si Bergier ne nous avait pas brouillés avec les Anglais, Chedabouctou aurait pu se soutenir'; certainly it was clear that Acadia must bear the consequences of Bergier's efforts.[67]

The company, blaming Perrot for their problems, emphasized to the French crown the urgent need for '[un] homme de probité et de Courage et d'un desinterressement connu' as governor. They recommended Louis-Alexandre Des Friches, Sieur de Meneval, a professional soldier, and agreed to contribute to his salary and establishment.[68] It was on this basis that the French crown decided to put in hand a thorough fortification and reform of the Acadian colony. In his instructions dated 5 April 1687, Meneval's tasks included the prohibition of the English trade and fishery, with the aid of a frigate dispatched from France. His area of government was defined simply as extending from the Gaspé to 'la riviere de Quinibiqui'; within this territory, Meneval was to establish his control and was informed of the royal intent 'de faire rêtablis le fort du Port Royal, ou d'en construire un nouveau a l'androit qui sera trouvé le plus avantageux.' Within the colony, it was his task to heal all divisions among the colonists and to provide for the efficient administration of justice, as well as to prohibit 'la course dans les bois' and to ensure that every colonist was put to 'des employs utils.' Encouragement was to be given to the commercial activities of the sedentary fishery company, and every effort to be extended to attract 'dans ce pays des Negotiants francais.'[69]

In short, Meneval was expected to supervise a radical effort to re-establish Acadia as a colony under the French crown; the scheme was similar in scale and implications to the re-establishment of Canada which had been projected in 1663 and successfully carried through. In view of the wider concurrent responsibilities and difficulties of the ministry of Marine, however, it was unlikely that solid support could be afforded to Acadia at this time. Although French support certainly increased in 1687, it was not sufficient to persuade Acadian commercial entrepreneurs to cut their ties with Massachusetts.[70] Given this difficulty and given the forces unleashed by the activities of Bergier, Meneval's task was perhaps an impossible one, and by late 1689 his reports to France had a tone of frustration and even despair.[71] What was certain was that the arrangements which had prevailed under La Vallière were irrevocably destroyed.

Destroyed also by now was the Danforth government of Maine. After long consideration and negotiation, the Committee for Trade and Plantations had finally decided on a frontal attack upon the charter of the Massachusetts colony: the charter had been vacated by writ of *scire facias* on 13 October 1684. In the following month the attorney general, Sir Robert Sawyer, gave his opinion as to the status of Maine following the dissolution of the Massachusetts Bay Company: government was devolved to the crown, as was the control of all unappropriated land.[72] For Maine, this opinion opened the way for the full integration into the new royal colony of New England. Accordingly, a temporary government was commissioned in October 1685 for Massachusetts, Maine, New Hampshire, and the King's Province, to be headed by Joseph

Dudley as president of an eighteen-member council. In December 1686, Sir Edmund Andros arrived in Boston as governor and captain-general of a more centralized dominion which included Plymouth colony; Rhode Island soon joined the dominion, closely followed by Connecticut and the territory of the duchy of York north of Maine; in the spring of 1688 a new commission included both New York and the Jerseys under Andros' authority.[73]

For Maine as a colony, integration into the Dominion of New England meant the abandonment of Gorges' original project and the submergence of its identity. For Maine as a community, the changes involved were not great. Lists of magistrates showed considerable continuity.[74] It is true that members of the Dudley council made large engrossments of unoccupied Maine lands, though after the Danforth government this was hardly a new phenomenon.[75] An issue which caused much controversy elsewhere in New England but little or none in Maine was the imposition of quitrents by the Andros government. Quitrents were not new, and the prospect of security and rationalization of land titles was an attractive one. In this respect, the Andros government presented the Maine inhabitants with all the advantages offered by the Massachusetts authority, with the added security of assured royal support.[76]

There was, however, one further aspect to Maine's integration into the Dominion of New England, which concerned its position within the northeastern maritime region. Acadia was by now committed to the assertion of French rights both in coastal waters and on land as far southwest as the Kennebec. The Dominion of New England was equally committed to the assertion of English rights, both in the fishery and on land at least as far as the Ste Croix. Both Maine and Acadia had thus been subsumed into imperial strategy, and into a situation quite different both from the working arrangements which had from time to time been arrived at between Euramerican colonists and from the weak and over-idealistic plans which had previously constituted European concepts. More than ever, the northeastern maritime region was an area of marginal settlements, in which events depended ultimately upon outside forces, and in which the threat of violence was now immediate.

Dissolution

There remained, in the years from 1686, one major safeguard against an outbreak of violence on a catastrophic scale: the refortified Acadia and the Dominion of New England were not intended as aggressive weapons by the respective crowns of France and England. Indeed, the two crowns had been joined in exceptionally close relations since the treaty of Dover in 1670, and this had been accentuated by the accession of the Catholic and pro-French Duke of York as James II in 1685.[77] Thus an effort was made to reconcile the divergence of interest between the two crowns in the treaty of Whitehall of 1686. Although this treaty had only a limited practical bearing on the situation in the northeastern maritime region, it did provide a minimal framework within which to contain potential conflicts. With the English revolution of 1688–9, which brought about the accession of William of Orange, an inveterate enemy of France, however, all such restraints were lost. The outcome for the northeastern colonies was violent conflict which left all three barely in existence.

The concept of neutrality in American colonies, when the European parent countries went to war, was by no means a new one in the northeastern maritime region. It had, for example, been an important part of the accommodation between the Massachusetts colony and d'Aulnay in the 1640s. Some forty years later, however, it was Europe that enunciated the aim, embodied in the treaty of Whitehall, or the treaty of Neutrality. The treaty had its origins in the wider desire of James II and Louis XIV to maintain the peace between their realms at a time of growing international tension in Europe.[78] In January 1686 in a conversation in London between Usson de Bonrepaux, an agent of the French ministry of Marine, and the Earl of Rochester, lord high treasurer of England, the two agreed that it would be 'très utile pour l'avantage du commerce des deux nations qu'il fust envoyé de nouveaux ordres de part et d'autre aux gouverneurs de l'Acadie, et de la nouvelle Angleterre pour l'entière execution du traité de Breda.'[79] Later in the month, the French proposed a treaty of neutrality along the same lines as had been negotiated in 1681 with respect to the West Indies. Although an enthusiastic response from James II was followed by slow and uncertain negotiations, the treaty was concluded in November.[80] In accordance with the original intent, the treaty confirmed the provisions of the treaty of Breda in full force; it affirmed the permanence of the two crowns' American possessions as they presently existed; furthermore, no trading was to be permitted 'dans tous les lieux dont l'on est ou l'on sera en possession de part et d'autre dans l'Amérique,' nor fishing in the immediate vicinity of the other's coastline.[81] In the case of a European war, it provided, 'il y aura toujours une véritable et ferme paix et neutralité entre les dits peuples de France et de la Grande Bretagne, tout de même que si la dite rupture n'étoit point arrivée en Europe.'[82] The statement of this principle was a recognition that the respective European crowns had an interest in ensuring the survival of their American colonies, in the northeastern region as elsewhere.

The treaty of Whitehall, which also sought to define the complex disputes over Hudson Bay by referring them to subsequent negotiation, was vague and unsatisfactory in a number of respects.[83] Nevertheless, it did signify a shared desire to mitigate tensions between English and French in North America. It was based on the practical belief, which was further expressed by Barillon and his colleague Usson de Bonrepaux in 1687, that there was no other way to preserve colonies 'que de regler les Limites des Terres que chacune des deux nations doit posseder,' and then to hold the home governments entirely responsible for any violations; 'l'experience a fait voir que ceux qui commandent agissent plus souvent par le motif de leur Interest particulier que pour le bien General et l'advantage des Colonies.'[84] Put another way, the treaty aimed at forcing colonial governors to recognize that, no matter what the exigencies of any particular situation, the overall intent of the two crowns was to have peace, and that the actions of governors would invariably be scrutinized in that light. By virtue of the treaty, 'les Intentions de nos Maistres' became an unprecedentedly prominent force in any colonial negotiations.[85] On a practical level, the provisions of the treaty were used by Captain Francis Nicholson, an envoy of Andros to Acadia in 1687, to win an assurance from the commander of the French frigate in Acadian waters that 'he had positive Orders from the King his Master strictly to Observe the Treaty, and to assist any English Shipp or Vessell that desired his helpe.' No further seizures of New England vessels were recorded until after the outbreak of war in 1689.[86]

Nevertheless, the results of the treaty of Whitehall were not as intended. The treaty failed to prevent conflict on Hudson Bay and on the New York-Canada border. In the northeastern region, its crucial flaw was its failure to define boundaries except by reference to the vague and imprecise treaty of Breda. In particular, the area between the Kennebec and the Ste Croix was left entirely without agreed status. Thus, the long-standing friction between Andros and Saint-Castin continued, with all its accompanying threats to peace. Edward Randolph had already commented in 1686 that 'there will be I fear an eruption betwixt the French of Nova Scotia and our people of Mayne and New Hampshire,' occasioned by raids upon Saint-Castin from Pemaquid.[87] His metaphor became even more threateningly appropriate as Andros continued to apply pressure upon Saint-Castin to recognize his authority. The spring and summer of 1688 found Andros in Pemaquid in person, whence he conducted a raid upon Saint-Castin's house and, as Randolph noted, 'tooke away all his armes, powder, shott, iron kettles and some trucking cloath and his chaires,' stating that 'he should have all his goods restored if he would demand them at Pemaquid and come under obedience to the King.' Randolph betrayed a hint of disapproval of this action, in observing 'how resented we were'; Andros, however, reported to Blathwayt on 4 June that he had 'left all well in those parts.' Back in Boston on 9 July, Andros reported confidently that his investigations had confirmed that the boundary of New England 'hath always been and Deemed and knowne to be the River St Croix and a right Lyne from the head of that River to the River Canada.'[88]

Andros was too sanguine. Further tension was caused shortly afterwards when English pirates not only made a devastating raid upon the sedentary fishery at Chedabouctou, but also seized at Canso a trading vessel belonging to Saint-Castin, 'comeing from Quebecke, loaded with provisions, and merchandise, to the value of five hundred pounds.'[89] In August, Nicholson took note of 'a reporte among the ffishermen that St Casteen was come to Penopscott with a ffrigatt, to build a fort there.' The French, he went on, 'stand mightily upon Penopscott's being in their precincts.' Furthermore, despite an assertion by Andros in July that he had found the Indian sachems of the northeast 'very orderly,' Saint-Castin's enmity also implied the enmity of his Indian kin.[90]

The outbreak of a further Abenaki-English war, however, was not directly connected with the tension between English and French, though the two conflicts soon coalesced. Persistent remours of Abenaki hostility in 1684 had led to an English attempt at appeasement. But English-Indian relations were soon strained once again by disputes over land, with related disputes over river fishing rights, and over damage done to Indian crops by English cattle. Furthermore, Indian resentment was aroused by English neglect to pay the annual tribute agreed in the peace treaty of 1678. The final incident came at Saco in the autumn of 1688 when twenty Indians were gratuitously seized 'on Suspition' and sent captive to Boston. A reciprocal seizure of hostages by the Indians was followed by misunderstanding over arrangements for an exchange, which led to a battle at Falmouth. Andros, confronted by this news, resolved in October 'to send three or four vessells and forces suitable to secure and settle the Easterne parts ... '; thus was begun a full-scale military campaign.[91] Even at this stage, the conflict thus ignited need not have involved the whole northeastern maritime region. Although it must have been clear to Saint-Castin that French and Abenaki might profitably unite against the English, no such alliance existed. The French-English dispute was in fact circumscribed and effectively quarantined by the general provisions of the treaty of Whitehall.

In March 1689, however, Andros received word of the invasion of England by William of Orange, and he himself was overthrown in Boston in the next month. For the northeastern colonies, the English revolution had two major implications: one specific, one more general. In specific terms, the sudden withdrawal of Andros and the military support of the Dominion of New England for the English in Maine meant that the war turned in favour of their Indian opponents. Mutinies in the English ranks, according to the account given by Edward Randolph on 29 May, led to a partial collapse of English resistance, and a letter of 10 July, possibly also written by Randolph, said of the Maine inhabitants that 'they draw of apace and I am jealous they will leave all to the Eastward of Piscataqua River to the Indians and french.' Randolph, imprisoned by the new Massachusetts regime, was a biased observer, but his verdict was borne out in August by the fall of Pemaquid and the consequent abandonment of the English settlements on the Kennebec.[92] Early in the following year, the English military leader and strategist Benjamin Church accused the Boston government of inaction with regard to Maine: 'If nothing be performed on the said account (The best way under Correction) is to Demolish the Garrison [i.e. the garrison-house], and draw off the Inhabitants.' By the summer of 1690, his pessimism had been justified by the loss of Casco Bay and the abandonment of all settlements northeast of Wells.[93] With the exception of the three towns of Wells, York, and Kittery, which continued to be subject to Indian attack well into the eighteenth century, the English settlement of Maine was destroyed.

The more general effect of the revolution was the abandonment of the provisions of the treaty of Whitehall and the formal outbreak of war between France and England. On the French side, this led to a military alliance with the Abenaki. Particularly impressed by Indian successes in 1689 at Pemaquid and elsewhere, the French authorities permitted official participation in Indian operations in 1690 and thereafter. On the English side, directives were sent from London which enjoined the use of all possible hostile measures against the French in America as elsewhere. It was in this spirit, as well as to protect the economic interests of Massachusetts merchants from the reciprocal violence of the French, that in early 1690 an expedition was mounted from Boston to attack and seize Port Royal.

John Nelson had suggested the expedition in the hope of reasserting the Temple claim to Nova Scotia, but it was adopted by the Massachusetts council and the newly reinstated General Court for broader economic and strategic reasons. Popular support for the venture was stimulated by news of increasingly successful French and Indian raids on both New York and New England and was channelled with religious fervour by Cotton Mather.[94] The eventual expedition in May, under the command of William Phips, was remarkable more for plunder and pillage than positive achievements. Certainly oaths of allegiance to the English crown were extracted from all French and Indians encountered, under Phips' orders 'upon refusal hereof, to burn, kill and destroy them'; and a local government of Nova Scotia was set up at Port Royal under an Acadian president and magistrates.[95] With injunctions to these appointees to maintain contacts with Massachusetts, 'in order to your Receiving further instructions,' however, the English expedition departed without leaving a garrison.[96] Cotton Mather had written in April to a Scottish minister, James Brown, that 'wee have newly made an Expedition against Nova Scotia, and Old Scotland will not complain of it, that wee have brought that country under the English Government,'[97] As a resurrection of the colony of New Scotland, however, Phips' creation was the emptiest of shells.

For Acadia, the negative achievements of Phips were, of course, of crucial significance. As Meneval reported gloomily to France from his captivity, 'Ce que j'ay eu sujet d'appréhender tous les jours, depuys que je suis icy, est enfin arrivé, Monseigneur.'[98] The pillage of Port Royal and Chedabouctou at the hands of the Phips expedition, moreover, was followed by a further raid on Port Royal a month later by two pirate vessels, which, according to a report soon afterwards, 'commirent mille violences sur les peuples.'[99] In the meantime, Meneval's lieutenant, Joseph Robinau de Villebon, had returned from a visit to France and now took control. Rather than stay at Port Royal, he decided to transport all the supplies he had brought with him to the St John River, and to make his headquarters there.[100] First from Jemseg and then from further upriver at Fort Naxouat, Villebon for the next seven years kept the colony of Acadia alive by waging guerrilla warfare upon northern New England, though solely through the support of Indian allies, and with only limited contact with the Acadian population on the peninsula and the isthmus.[101]

In the years 1689 and 1690, therefore, all Euramerican settlement in the northeastern maritime region had been drastically disrupted and curtailed by violent conflict. Even where settlement remained, in southern Maine and peninsular Acadia, the isolated colonists were vulnerable to hostile incursions. The three northeastern colonies, as entities, each had only a tenuous existence: the status of Maine was uncertain since the fall of the Dominion of New England; Acadia survived as a military camp on the St John River; Nova Scotia had been proclaimed in Massachusetts but had little reality elsewhere. The original European conceptions of these colonies were scarcely fulfilled in these fragile remnants. The Euramerican colonists, those who were left, could derive but an uncertain subsistence in the region. The Indian native inhabitants, now the most powerful military force in the region, suffered from acculturation and from the effects of sustained warfare. Whatever the achievements of European colonization elsewhere in America, they had come here to low ebb by 1690.

Conclusion

The northeastern maritime region provides an example of European failure in America. Despite the high hopes of the earliest colonists and despite the adaptations made by the promoters of seigneurial colonization, the seventeenth-century colonies of the region never provided for the transplanting of populous European societies to extensive areas of the New World. Instead, they emerged only as marginal colonies, existing on the fringes of other societies – European, Euramerican, and Indian – and developing no intrinsic strength or integrity. By 1650, this state had become clear. Although communities on the seigneurial or proprietorial pattern had been established successfully in Acadia, at Port Royal, and in the towns of southern Maine, these achievements were on too small a scale to offset the centrifugal forces created by external pressures and internal tensions. In 1650, it was the internal tensions which were causing disruption: the Province of Maine had disintegrated into three smaller jurisdictions, and the unity of Acadia was barely preserved by the military ascendancy of d'Aulnay. These internal problems in themselves rendered the northeastern colonies chronically vulnerable to external forces.

Thus the second half ot the century saw these colonies subjected to outside influences. Their marginal status remained essentially unchanged, but it was complicated by changes in America itself, arising from the development of Euramerican communities, and by changes in European concepts and expectations, arising from the increasingly direct and aggressive involvement of European governments in colonial affairs. A variety of governmental regimes – each with social as well as political implications – succeeded one another in the region, and each of the three colonies was intermittently eclipsed by a different entity. The colony of Maine, for example, was temporarily metamorphosed into the county of Yorkshire; those of Acadia and Nova Scotia alternated with each other on the same territory. None of the patterns that emerged, however, succeeded in reconciling European concept with American reality. The American fact was that the marginal colonies could function satisfactorily only when subsumed into a larger Euramerican entity; the European fact was that such coalescences threatened both private rights and the interests of national governments.

This state of affairs was not only unsatisfactory but also dangerous to the small communities in the northeastern colonies. Sparsely settled in isolated locations, these groups of colonists were intensely vulnerable to violent assault throughout the seventeenth century. The very changes and metamorphoses which were taking place carried threats of violence: although conflicts of this kind never reached catastrophic proportions, new rulers seldom came unarmed to any of the three colonies. More threatening was the increasing international friction between French and English. One of the real, though precarious, achievements of the formative years had been the minimizing of such tensions by the agreement between d'Aulnay and Massachusetts, and the pragmatic attitudes of the respective inhabitants of the northeastern colonies had perpetuated this situation. As European governments became aware, however, of the economic and strategic value of colonies in a general sense, they became more aggressive in defending national claims in particular locations, especially where those claims adjoined and overlapped. In the northeastern maritime region, European claims were offensive not only to one another, but potentially to the Massachusetts colony also. The result, once the fragile safeguards of the treaty of Whitehall had been thrust aside in 1689, was violence on a disastrous scale.

Furthermore, the Europeans in this region were also potentially endangered by Indian warfare. Both Indians and Europeans had made the grave error of underestimating each other. The Indians, justifiably contemptuous of the early travails of the Europeans in their tiny communal colonies, underestimated the strength of European technological resources and adaptability, and paid the penalty in terms of acculturation and exclusion from traditional lands. The Europeans, whether benevolent or hostile, regarded the Indian as a savage – either innocent of civilization or incapable of it – and neglected to realize that the northeastern colonies in their marginal state could not exist unless tolerated by the native inhabitants. For the French in Acadia, whose settlement offered little threat to Indian lands and who developed close contacts with the native peoples as the century went on, this neglect was unlikely to be dangerous. For the English in Maine it was crucial, as the devastation of two Indian wars was to prove by 1690. Despite cultural disruptions arising from European colonization, it was the Indian peoples of the northeastern maritime region who held sway in 1690, and not the European colonies.

Here, then, is a major exception to the seemingly ineluctable progress of European colonization of America. Successful colonization required both physical strength, in terms of numbers, organization, and economic prosperity, and a reconceptualization of American land to give it a European identity. The corollary of successful colonization was the destruction of the native way of life; this had been shown in the aftermath of King Philip's War in southern New England. Further north, the native way of life was by no means fully intact, but the failure of the Europeans to reconcile conception and reality had, for the time being, left the field open for the Indian peoples in their modified cultural form. The impact of the Europeans was undeniable, but throughout most of the northeastern maritime region it had taken negative rather than positive forms.

For the historian, the European failure is one major conclusion to be drawn from the study of the marginal colonies in the seventeenth century. The second, however, concerns the real similarities which may be discerned between the various European nationalities in their approaches to the theory and practice of colonization. At a governmental level, parallels can be observed between the attitudes and actions of France and England, as with those of Scotland during that country's brief involvement with North America. During the sixteenth century, both France and England shared an admiration of Spanish achievement, a brief royal interest in discovery, and a general preoccupation with internal affairs which precluded practical support of colonization. Both crowns, however, were susceptible to the possibilities of profits from colonial endeavours in the early seventeenth century, and all three were receptive to the promoters of seigneurial schemes between 1620 and 1630. Both French and English crowns, under the respective influences of Richelieu and Laud, flirted briefly thereafter with efforts to bring North American colonies into the ambit of more direct royal influence, even at the expense of financial disbursement, but neither succeeded in doing so before internal concerns again began to claim exclusive attention.

Mazarin and Cromwell concerned themselves with colonial affairs in a fitful way, but it was following the peace of the Pyrenees between France and Spain in 1659, and the Restoration in England in 1660, that both France and England were able to give attention to colonial affairs in a more stable fashion. After 1660, the intent to derive economic profit and strategic advantage from American colonies was made clear in both countries. The French re-establishment of Canada in 1663 had no direct parallel until the later establishment of the Dominion of New England, but the English Navigation Acts envisaged a similar role for the English colonies as that prescribed by Colbert for the French. The northeastern maritime colonies, however, for the moment commanded lesser royal attention. The failure of the English crown to respond to the royal commissioners' settlement of 1665 in Maine and its disposal of Nova

Scotia in 1667, as well as the French crown's lack of subsidy to shore up its efforts in Acadia from 1670, all bespoke a lack of effectiveness. Nevertheless, led by the Duke of York's aggressive regard for his territory between the Kennebec and the Ste Croix, the respective European crowns rediscovered a more urgent interest in the northeastern region after 1680. The treaty of Whitehall, in its effort to safeguard the colonies against an outbreak of actual warfare, is perhaps ironic evidence of this renewed interest; the devastating war which began in 1689 was a more direct result.

Further similarities between European nationalities may be found in the concepts of colonial promoters. The influence of the Spanish example, reinforced in the cases of England and Scotland by experience in the colonization of Celtic lands, was combined in the early seventeenth century with the knowledge and expertise which had been built up through commercial voyages to North America for the fishery and the fur trade. Failures at Sagadahoc and Port Royal, however, enforced refinement of colonial plans, and the result after 1620 was the production of analogous seigneurial or proprietorial schemes by Sir Ferdinando Gorges in England, Sir William Alexander in Scotland, and Isaac de Razilly in France. None of the three lived to see his plan fulfilled, and indeed that of Alexander was effectively disabled in 1632; however, the heirs and associates of Gorges and Razilly continued for several decades to attempt to give practical expression to this form of colonization in their respective colonies.

In so doing, neither group was fully successful, and the resultant vacuum was in both cases somewhat reluctantly filled by the colony of Massachusetts, acting in the one case through the annexation of Maine under the guise of the county of Yorkshire, and in the other by transforming the old Scottish concept of New Scotland into the convenient form of Temple's Nova Scotia. From this point, although by no means ready to concede defeat, the heirs of the original promoters of the northeastern colonies had only limited influence. In the persons of Ferdinando Gorges, as grandson of Sir Ferdinando, and the family of Emmanuel Le Borgne, as creditor of d'Aulnay, they were reduced to importuning for the restoration of their private rights. Both were able to obtain countenance from the respective crowns, and both were able to cause confusion in their colonies by harassing the inhabitants for payment of rents and seigneurial obligations. Neither, however, was able to realize his pretensions in any full or positive way, and the onus of European interest in Maine and Acadia effectively devolved upon the crowns.

If the roles of the European crowns and those of the European colonial promoters are analogous in regard to the northeastern maritime colonies, then so too are the practical results of colonizing attempts. The intitial tendency to small communal colonies was found in Acadia, Maine, and New Scotland. In

Acadia and Maine, this was followed by the gradual growth of small seigneurial or proprietorial communities, but these communities were prevented from
becoming effective core areas by fragmentation, which arose in both colonies
from the geographical separation of these communities from the principal
centres of the fishery and the fur trade. Along with the failure of the colonial
promoters to provide a solid basis for political stability and social order, this
fragmentation facilitated in both colonies the ascendancy of local power over
legitimate authority, and thus led to disorders that may be compared to those
loosely designated 'feudal' in medieval Europe and elsewhere.

In turn, this state of affairs led to the Euramerican adjustments of the decade
between 1650 and 1660. Albeit reluctantly, the Massachusetts colony assumed
effective control of the northeastern maritime colonies at this time, aided by a
sense among the respective inhabitants of the advantages and conveniences
which were offered by such an arrangement. The Euramerican populations of
Maine and Acadia/Nova Scotia remained deeply divided between 1650 and
1690; this was natural since they faced a choice which involved, in its most
extreme terms, on the one hand isolation from effective defence and the supply
of essential provisions, and on the other rebellion against legitimate authority.
The result in both colonies was the growth of a basic pragmatism.

In all of these respects, comparisons may be made among the northeastern
maritime colonies, despite variety of European nationality. Certainly, there
were differences too. One important distinction is that between Indian-French
cordiality in Acadia and Indian-English hostility in Maine. Even this, however,
arose not from fundamentally different European national attitudes and characteristics, but rather from the different patterns of relationships. These patterns
evolved not only from initial attitudes but also from the influence of such
factors as the extensive nature of English land use in Maine and the lack of
effective religious contact between English and Indian. Other important distinctions arose primarily from American circumstance: the more scattered
coastlines of Acadia made for greater geographical fragmentation than in
Maine, and the geographical proximity of Maine to Massachusetts led to an
earlier and more extensive assertion there of the economic and political power
of the Bay colony. Contrasts between any of the three northeastern colonies
purely on grounds of European nationality are remarkable only by their absence.

Perhaps the outstanding parallel between the three colonies, at least from the
point of view of the subsequent development of the northeastern maritime
region, lies in the condition of all three colonies in 1690. Following the
revolution of 1689, the territory which Gorges had owned as the Province of
Maine was without fixed legal status and lacked any location which was free
from the likelihood of violent assault. The area which Alexander had bounded

as the 'National Patent' of Scotland was still regarded as 'Nova Scotia' in Massachusetts and had a proprietary claimant in the person of John Nelson, but it again lacked any agreed legal status, and entirely lacked a population of its own. The same area, as the colony of Acadia, had both a governor and a population – the former a virtual guerrilla leader, the latter chronically subject to hostile incursion, and with only tenous contacts between the two. All three colonies, in short, existed as shells.

Although the reduction of the original colonies of the region to this condition was the logical culmination of the formative process, the year 1690 also marked a great discontinuity. It represented the final crushing of the European concepts which had originated the colonies. Furthermore, the external forces which continued to have an effect upon the remaining colonists of the region had changed their nature by the time the ensuing twenty-three years of almost continuous warfare came to an end. The native inhabitants, weakened by the continuing process of acculturation and by years of warfare, exercised a diminishing influence. The European governments' interest in the region now had an overtly military and strategic aspect, manifested in the establishment of garrisons of regular troops by both French and British, and especially in the proliferation of military installations which preceded the outbreak of the decisive imperial war in the 1750s. The interest of the Massachusetts colony changed also. Faced with increasing pressure of population on the existing lands occupied in the colony itself, northeastward movement began to assume a more deliberate and a more popular form than had been true of the seventeenth-century mercantile and fishing activities. Massachusetts traders and fishermen continued to frequent the coasts of Maine, Nova Scotia, and Cape Breton, but increasingly important was the penetration of the region by organized military forces from Massachusetts, the activity of Massachusetts-based land companies, and the foundation of new towns by groups of migrants, first in Maine and then in Nova Scotia.[1]

As for the names of the three seventeenth-century colonies, these remained in existence and indeed came in due course to represent real entities. A colony of Nova Scotia was brought into existence in 1713, reversing a previous integration with Massachusetts under the charter of 1691. After refusing to take part in the American revolution in 1775–6, the province of Nova Scotia took on its more limited modern form with the foundation of the province of New Brunswick in 1784. Maine, along with the territory between the Kennebec and the Ste Croix, was also included in the Massachusetts charter of 1691, with more lasting results than in the case of Nova Scotia. During the eighteenth century, the district of Maine developed as a distinctive area within Massachusetts; in 1820 it emerged as a state of the union, with an area much larger than that of Gorges' province, despite the competing claims of the province of

New Brunswick. Acadia did not reappear as a political unit, and the remaining French territories in the region – Île Royale (Cape Breton) and the Île Saint-Jean – were finally captured by the British in 1758. This conquest followed by three years the British expulsion of a substantial part of the Acadian population from peninsular Nova Scotia. As a people, however, the Acadians survived and evolved, retaining a conscious distinctiveness which by 1976 had led the Société des Acadiens du Nouveau-Brunswick to envisage the creation of 'une province acadienne autonome' within the Canadian confederation.[2] Thus, the names of the colonies have continued; so also have the descendants of many of the inhabitants of the early communities of the Port Royal valley and southern Maine: Boudreau, LeBlanc, and Melanson are matched by Bragdon, Littlefield, and Weare. In that sense, continuity prevails. The original European concepts, however, and the marginal colonies that resulted, were terminated by the great discontinuity of 1690. The analogous condition of the three seventeenth-century colonies was thus carried to the point of destruction, and the European failure in the region made clear.

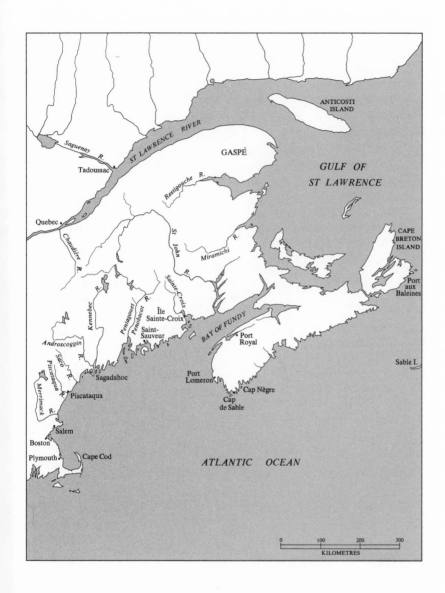

MAP I The northeastern maritime region and surrounds. Showing principal rivers and sites of European settlement attempts to 1630.

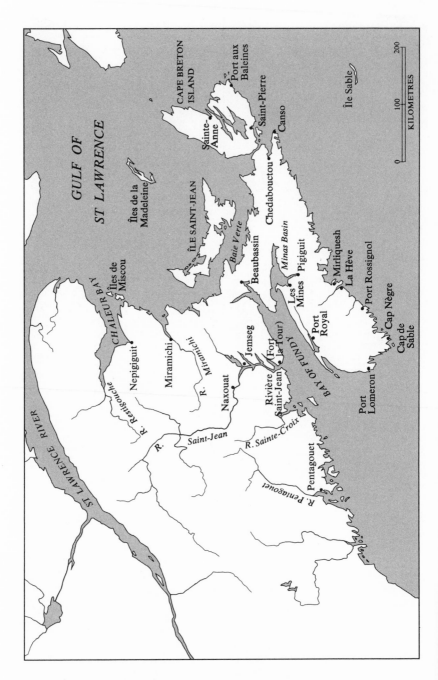

MAP 2 Acadia in the seventeenth century. Showing principal posts and settlements.

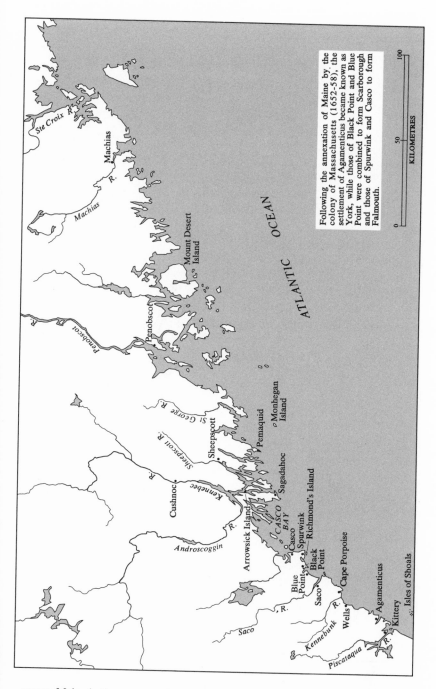

Following the annexation of Maine by the colony of Massachusetts (1652–58), the settlement of Agamenticus became known as York, while those of Black Point and Blue Point were combined to form Scarborough and those of Spurwink and Casco to form Falmouth.

ATLANTIC OCEAN

KILOMETRES

0   50   100

Ste Croix R.

Machias

Machias R.

Machias

Mount Desert Island

Penobscot R.

Penobscot

St George R.

Sheepscot R.

Sheepscot

Pemaquid

Monhegan Island

Cushnoc

Kennebec R.

Sagadahoc

Arrowsick Island

CASCO BAY

Casco

Richmond's Island

Spurwink

Androscoggin

Blue Point

Black Point

Saco

Cape Porpoise

Saco R.

Wells

Kennebunk R.

Agamenticus

Kittery

Piscataqua R.

Isles of Shoals

MAP 3 Maine in the seventeenth century. Showing principal posts and settlements. Showing also the disputed territory between Kennebec and Ste Croix rivers.

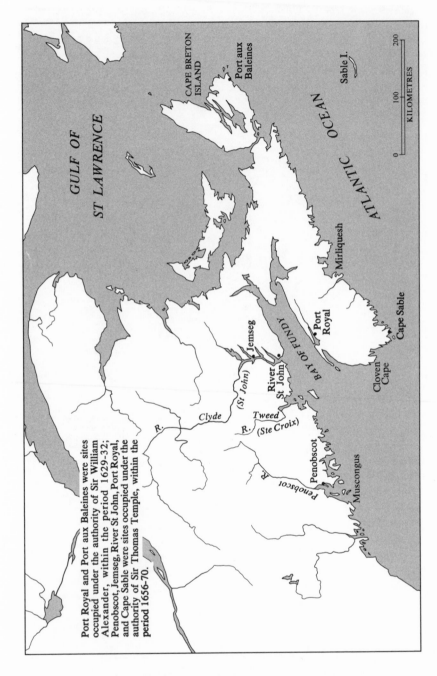

Port Royal and Port aux Baleines were sites occupied under the authority of Sir William Alexander, within the period 1629-32; Penobscot, Jemseg, River St John, Port Royal, and Cape Sable were sites occupied under the authority of Sir Thomas Temple, within the period 1656-70.

GULF OF
ST LAWRENCE

ATLANTIC OCEAN

CAPE BRETON ISLAND

Port aux Baleines

Sable I.

Mirliquesh

Cape Sable

Port Royal

Cloven Cape

BAY OF FUNDY

Jemseg

(St John)

River St John

Clyde

Tweed
(Ste Croix)

R.

R.

Penobscot

Muscongus

Penobscot R.

0   100   200
KILOMETRES

MAP 4 New Scotland in the seventeenth century. Showing principal posts and settlements.

Notes

Abbreviations

AAÉ   Archives du ministère des Affaires étrangères

AC   Archives nationales, archives des Colonies

ACM   Archives départementales de la Charente-Maritime

BL   British Library

BN   Bibliothèque nationale

CÉA   Université de Moncton, Centre d'études acadiennes

DCB   Dictionary of Canadian Biography

HMC   Great Britain, Historical Manuscripts Commission

HNAI   Bruce G. Trigger, ed., *Handbook of North American Indians* 15

MA   Massachusetts Archives

MCR   Massachusetts, *Records of the governor and company of the Massachusetts Bay in New England*

PAC   Public Archives of Canada

PANS   Public Archives of Nova Scotia

PCR   *Province and court records of Maine*, ed. Charles Thornton Libby *et al.*

PRO   Public Record Office

SRO   Scottish Record Office

PREFACE

1 John H. Parry, *The age of reconnaissance* (London, 1963); Immanuel Wallerstein, *The modern world-system: capitalist agriculture and the origins of the European world-economy in the sixteenth century* (New York 1974).

2 Edmundo O'Gorman, *The invention of America* (Bloomington, Ind. 1961).

3 Charles Gibson, *Spain in America* (New York 1966); Clarence L. Ver Steeg, *The formative years, 1607–1763* (New York 1964); W.J. Eccles, *France in America* (New York 1972); Thomas J. Condon, *New York beginnings: the commercial origins of New Netherland* (New York 1968).

4 Richard Colebrook Harris, *The seigneurial system in early Canada: a geographical study* (Madison, Wis. 1966); James T. Lemon, *The best poor man's country: a geographical study of early southeastern Pennsylvania* (Baltimore 1972); Andrew Hill Clark, *Acadia: the geography of early Nova Scotia to 1760* (Madison, Wis. 1968); Douglas R. McManis, *Colonial New England: a historical geography* (New York 1975).

5 See Sumner Chilton Powell, *Puritan village: the formation of a New England town* (Middletown, Conn. 1963); Darrett B. Rutman, *Winthrop's Boston: a portrait of a Puritan town, 1630–1649* (Chapel Hill, N.C. 1965); Kenneth Alan Lockridge, 'Land, population, and the evolution of New England society, 1630–1790,' *Past and Present* 39 (1968); 62–80; Lockridge, *A New England town, the first hundred years: Dedham, Massachusetts, 1636–1736* (New York 1970); John Demos, *A little commonwealth: family life in Plymouth Colony* (New York 1970); Philip J. Greven Jr, *Four generations: population, land, and family in colonial Andover, Massachusetts* (Ithaca, N.Y. 1970). Comparable studies for the colonies of Acadia, Maine, and New Scotland in the seventeenth century have been slower to appear, an exception being Gisa I. Hynes, 'Some aspects of the demography of Port Royal, 1650–1755,' *Acadiensis* 3 (autumn 1973): 3–17.

6 Marcel Trudel, *Les débuts du régime seigneurial au Canada* (Montreal 1974) is one example of the more specialized works among Trudel's extensive writings; Robert-Lionel Séquin, *La civilisation traditionelle de l' 'habitant' aux 17e et 18e siècles: fonds matériel* (Montreal 1967). Sigmund Diamond, 'From organization to society: Virginia in the seventeenth century,' *American Journal of Sociology* 63 (1957–8): 457–75; Diamond, 'An experiment in "feudalism": French Canada in the seventeenth century,' *William and Mary Quarterly* 3rd ser., 18 (1961): 3–34.

7 Alfred G. Bailey, *The conflict of European and eastern Algonkian cultures, 1504–1700: a study in Canadian civilization* (2nd ed., Toronto 1969); Cornelius J. Jaenen, 'Amerindian views of French culture in the seventeenth century,' *Canadian Historical Review* 55 (1974): 261–91; Jaenen, *Friend and foe: aspects of French-Amerindian culture contact in the sixteenth and seventeenth centuries* (Toronto 1976); Calvin Martin, *Keepers of the game: Indian-animal relationships and the fur trade* (Berkeley 1978). A general approach to Canadian Indian history, stressing that the history of colonization can equally well be written with the Indian at the centre and the European on the periphery as *vice versa*, can be found in E. Palmer Patterson II, *The Canadian Indian: a history since 1500* (Don Mills, Ont. 1972).

8 Wilcomb E. Washburn, *The Indian in America* (New York 1975); Francis Jennings, *The imvasion of America: Indians, colonialism, and the cant of conquest* (Chapel Hill, N.C. 1975), esp. 327–35; see also Bruce G. Trigger, 'Cultural unity and diversity,' in Trigger, ed., *Handbook of North American Indians, Volume 15, Northeast* (Washington 1978; hereafter *HNAI* 15), 798–804. One might also illustrate the insights offered by ethnohistory by citing other major recent works such as Gary B. Nash, *Red, White, and Black: the peoples of early America* (Englewood Cliffs, N.J. 1974); or Bruce G. Trigger, *The children of Aataentsic: a history of the Huron people to 1660* (2 vols., Montreal 1976). For a fuller discussion, see James Axtell, 'The ethnohistory of early America: a review essay,' *William and Mary Quarterly* 3rd ser., 35 (1978): 110–44.

9 See, for example, Herbert Eugene Bolton, 'The epic of greater America,' *American Historical Review* 38 (1932–3): 448–74; also H.E. Bolton and Thomas Maitland Marshall, *The colonization of North America, 1492–1783* (New York 1920). For comment on the implications of recent historical trends for the reassertion of the 'Bolton thesis,' see Jaenen, *Friend and foe*, 9; and for a general discussion of the potentialities of comparative analysis, see Thomas J. Condon, 'Early America: old views and present possibilities,' Canadian Association for American Studies, *Bulletin* 1 (1966): 3–14.

10 Silvio Zavala, *The colonial period in the history of the New World*, abridged in English by Max Savelle (Mexico City 1962); Kenneth Gordon Davies, *The North Atlantic world in the seventeenth century* (Minneapolis 1974); David B. Quinn, *North America from earliest discovery to first settlements: the Norse voyages to 1612* (New York 1977); Max Savelle, *Empires to nations: expansion in America, 1713–1824* (Minneapolis 1974).

CHAPTER 1

1 To find satisfactory designations for the native peoples of the region in the seventeenth century, especially the Malecite, is no easy task. It is generally agreed that the modern Malecite people of the St John river valley, and the closely related Passamaquoddy of the Ste Croix, are the descendants of the people described by early French observers as 'Etchemin.' Those observers, however, clearly believed that the territory of the Etchemin included the Penobscot River, and early French usage of the term 'Malecite' may have carried this same wide meaning. Yet native inhabitants of the Penobscot area in later centuries have been classified linguistically with Abenaki, rather than Malecite. The answer may lie in the possibility of an eastward migration of the original Penobscot inhabitants in the early eighteenth century, and their replacement by groups of Abenaki, though conclusive evidence is lacking. For further discussion, see Alvin Hamblen Morrison, 'Penobscot

country: disagreement over who lived there in the seventeenth century needs resolving – if possible,' in William Cowan, ed., *Papers of the ninth Algonquian conference* (Ottawa 1978), 47–54; see also Vincent O. Erickson, 'Maliseet-Passamaquoddy,' *HNAI* 15: 123. There is doubt also as to the precise cultural characteristics prevailing in the southernmost corner of Maine, where eastern Abenaki lands bordered with those of western Abenaki and Penacook; the Penacook lands probably extended approximately as far north as the site of the early English settlement of Agamenticus, and possibly further. See Gordon M. Day, 'Western Abenaki,' *HNAI* 15: 148–9; Bert Salwen, 'Indians of southern New England and Long Island: early period,' Ibid., 161, 169; Dean R. Snow, 'Late prehistory of the east coast,' Ibid., 67. In any case, the significance of the points at issue is limited by certain other considerations. All designations for Indian peoples in the seventeenth century are questionable in the sense that they reflected the predispositions and the incomplete knowledge of European writers. See P.-André Sévigny, *Les Abénaquis: habitat et migrations (17ᵉ et 18ᵉ siècles)* (Montreal 1976), 212; and James Dennis Wherry, 'Abnaki, Etchemin, and Malecite,' in William Cowan, ed., *Papers of the tenth Algonquian conference* (Ottawa 1979), 181–90. Furthermore, all the Indian peoples of the region had important cultural similarities, and rigid distinctions are often misleading. Thus, in this study, the terms Micmac, Malecite, and Abenaki will be used as general terms, while the native inhabitants of the Penobscot valley and those of the southermost part of Maine will be identified primarily by river location. Further useful discussions of the identity of the Indian peoples of the region include the following: Bailey, *Conflict of cultures*, 2–3; Andrea Jeanne Bear, 'The concept of unity among Indian tribes of Maine, New Hampshire, and New Brunswick: an ethnohistory' (Senior scholar's paper, Colby College 1966), 18–46; Alvin Hamblen Morrison, 'Dawnland decisions: seventeenth century Wabanaki leaders and their responses to the differential contact stimuli in the overlap area of New France and New England' (PH D thesis, State University of New York at Buffalo 1974), 13–14, 17–23; Kenneth Myron Morrison, 'The People of the Dawn: the Abnaki and their relations with New England and New France, 1600–1727' (PH D thesis, University of Maine 1975), 11–14; and Dean Richard Snow, 'Wabanaki "family hunting territories",' *American Anthropologist* 70 (1968): 1147.

2 See David Sanger, *Cow Point: an archaic cemetery in New Brunswick* (Ottawa 1973), 125; Sanger, 'Passamaquoddy Bay prehistory: a summary,' Maine Archaeological Society, *Bulletin* 11 (1971): 14–19; and Gordon M. Day, 'The Indian as an ecological factor in the northeastern forest,' *Ecology* 34 (1953): 340.

3 This affinity has led many anthropologists to group these peoples together under the general term 'Wabanaki.' See Morrison, 'Dawnland decisions,' 1; Morrison, 'People of the Dawn,' 11–12; Snow, 'Hunting territories,' 1147. Specific linkages are discussed in Clark, *Acadia*, 56–7; John M. Cooper, 'The culture of the

northeastern Indian hunters: a reconstructive interpretation,' in Frederick Johnson, ed., *Man in northeastern North America* (Andover, Mass. 1946), 279; Regina Flannery, 'The culture of the northeastern Indian hunters: a descriptive survey,' Ibid., 270; Harold Franklin McGee Jr, 'The Micmac Indians: the earliest migrants,' in Douglas F. Campbell, ed., *Banked fires: the ethnics of Nova Scotia* (Port Credit, Ont. 1978), 21.

4 See Clark, *Acadia*, 59–61; Day, 'Indian as Ecological Factor,' 341; and Bernard Gilbert Hoffman, 'Historical ethnography of the Micmac of the sixteenth and seventeenth centuries' (PH D thesis; University of California 1955), 151–86. On agricultural cultivation, see also Morrison, 'People of the Dawn,' 2; and Snow, 'Eastern Abenaki,' *HNAI* 15: 138. Hoffman, 238–41, also raises the possibility that the Micmac had once cultivated both tobacco and corn, though this cannot be shown conclusively. See also Martin, *Keepers of the game*, 29.

5 Cooper, 'Culture of the northeastern hunters,' 286–7; Day, 'Indian as ecological factor,' 341; Martin, *Keepers of the game*, 28–39; Morrison, 'Dawnland decisions,' 73–4; Morrison, 'People of the Dawn,' 25–7; L.F.S. Upton, *Micmacs and colonists: Indian-white relations in the Maritimes, 1713–1867* (Vancouver 1979), 2–4. Archaeological evidence suggests that the beginnings of the European fur trade had a profound effect upon migratory cycles, leading to a greater emphasis upon hunting and to a greater emphasis upon summer occupation of coastal sites to facilitate the trade. See Bruce J. Bourque, 'Aboriginal settlement and subsistence on the Maine coast,' *Man in the northeast* 6 (1973): 3–20.

6 For further discussion of aboriginal social organization, see Philip K. Bock, 'Micmac,' *HNAI* 15: 110–16; Erickson, 'Maliseet-Passamaquoddy,' *HNAI* 15: 130–2; Eleanor Leacock, 'The Montagnais-Naskapi band,' in Bruce Cox, ed., *Cultural ecology* (Toronto 1973), 88–93; Diamond Jenness, *Indians of Canada* (Ottawa 1932), 119–20; McGee, 'Micmac Indians,' 19–21; Morrison, 'People of the Dawn,' 24–5; Snow, 'Eastern Abenaki' *HNAI* 15: 138–41. The question of the allocation of hunting lands by eastern Algonkian peoples for many years caused controversy among historians and anthropologists. Were the hunting lands controlled by the collective authority of the band, or were they owned by individuals or families in severalty? Proponents of the former view, now accepted by the majority of scholars, include Bailey, *Conflict of cultures*, 84–91, and Eleanor Leacock, 'The Montagnais "hunting territory" and the fur trade' (PH D thesis, Columbia University 1952). The opposite view, emphasizing land holding in severalty, was put forward amongst others by John M. Cooper, 'Is the Algonkian family hunting ground system pre-Columbian?' *American Anthropologist* new ser. 41 (1939): 66–90; Frank Gouldsmith Speck, *Penobscot man: the life history of a forest tribe in Maine* (Philadelphia 1940), 206; Speck and Loren C. Eiseley, 'Significance of hunting territory systems of the Algonkian in social theory,' *American Anthropologist* new ser. 41 (1939): 269–80. For further discussion of this whole question,

see Bailey, *Conflict of cultures*, xviii–xxiii; A. Irving Hallowell, 'The size of Algonkian hunting territories: a function of ecological adjustment,' *American Anthropologist* new ser. 51 (1949): 35–6; Snow, 'Hunting territories,' 1143–51; and Washburn, *Indian in America*, 73–6.

7 Pierre Biard, *Relation de la Nouvelle France de ses terres, naturel du pais, et de ses habitations* (Lyons 1616), 66–7. 'They are astonished and often complain that, since the French mingle with and carry on trade with them, they are dying fast, and the population is thinning out' (*The Jesuit relations and allied documents: travels and explorations of the Jesuit missionaries in New France, 1610–1791*, ed. Reuben Gold Thwaites (73 vols, Cleveland 1896–1901), III: 105).

8 Thomas Dermer to Thomas Purchas, 27 Dec. 1619, in Henry Sweetser Burrage, ed., *Gorges and the grant of the Province of Maine* (Portland, Me. 1923), 129. 'The decadence of the Gaspesian nation, formerly one of the most numerous and most flourishing of Canada,' (Chrestien Le Clercq, *New relation of Gaspesia, with the customs and religion of the Gaspesian Indians*, ed. William F. Ganong (Toronto 1910; first published 1691), 402; translation, 234). See also Hoffman, 'Ethnography of the Micmac,' 230–1; Martin, *Keepers of the game*, 43–55; Speck, *Penobscot man*, 13; and the more general discussions in Jennings, *Invasion of America*, 15–31, and Washburn, *Indian in America*, 103–7.

9 See Bailey, *Conflict of cultures*, 87–95. A detailed interpretation of the breakdown of traditional Indian values and restraints is contained in Martin, *Keepers of the game*, 113–56. On the bases of authority within the band before European contact, see Lucien Campeau, ed., *Monumenta Novae Franciae, vol. I, La première mission d'Acadie, 1602–1616* (Quebec and Rome 1967), intro., 129–30; McGee, 'Micmac Indians,' 18–22; Morrison, 'People of the Dawn,' 34–5; Upton, *Micmacs and colonists*, 7–8.

10 'They think they are better, more valiant and more ingenious than the French; and what is difficult to believe, richer than we are' (*Jesuit relations* I: 172; translation, 173). 'They are so infatuated with their manner of dressing, and with their own way of living, that they disdain ours ...' (Le Clercq, *New relation*, 343; translation, 99). For a full discussion of this subject, see Jaenen, 'Amerindian views of French culture,' 261–91.

11 'Their lives are not vexed by a thousand annoyances as are ours' (Le Clercq, *New relation*, 347; translation, 106). See also Biard, *Relation*, 97–8. That there were other Europeans who thought likewise is shown by the number of English captives who became 'white Indians' in both the seventeenth and eighteenth centuries. See James Axtell, 'The white Indians of colonial America,' *William and Mary Quarterly* 3rd ser., 32 (1975): 55–88. See also Jaenen, *Friend and foe*, chap. 1.

12 John Josselyn, *An account of two voyages to New England* (Massachusetts Historical Society *Collections* 3rd ser., III, Boston 1833), 306.

13 G.E. Nichols, 'The Hemlock-White Pine-northern hardwood region of eastern America,' *Ecology* 16 (1935): 403–22. For more detailed discussion of the

subdivisions of forestation within the northeastern Maritime region, see Charles F. Carroll, *The timber economy of Puritan New England* (Providence, R.I. 1973), 30–3; Clark, *Acadia*, 38–45; and P.A. Bentley and E.C. Smith, 'The forests of Cape Breton in the seventeenth and eighteenth centuries,' Nova Scotia Institute of Science, *Proceedings* 24 (1954–5): 1–15.

14 Henry Percival Biggar, ed., *The works of Samuel de Champlain* (6 vols., Toronto 1922–36), I: 321, 327–8. See also Douglas S. Byers, 'The environment of the northeast,' in Johnson, *Man in the northeast*, 16–17, 23–5; Cooper, 'Culture of northeastern hunters,' 286–7; Clarence Albert Day, *A history of Maine agriculture, 1604–1860* (Orono, Me. 1954), 16–24.

15 Biggar, *Works of Champlain* I: 246; John Brereton, 'A brief and true relation of the discovery of the north part of Virginia,' in Charles Herbert Levermore, ed., *Forerunners and competitors of the Pilgrims and Puritans* (New York 1912), 39.

16 'The covetousness of men has caused no country to be thought good unless it has mines of gold ...' (Marc Lescarbot, *The history of New France*, ed. W.L. Grant (3 vols, Toronto 1907–14; first published 1618), III: 442; translation, 259).

17 See Verrazzano's account in George Parker Winship, ed., *Sailors' narratives of voyages along the New England coast, 1524–1624* (Boston 1905), 21–2; and Henry Percival Biggar, ed., *The voyages of Jacques Cartier* (Ottawa, 1924), 53. See also Harold Adams Innis, *The fur trade in Canada: an introduction to Canadian economic history* (rev. ed., Toronto 1970), 9–12: Samuel Eliot Morison, *The European discovery of America: the northern voyages, A.D. 500–1600* (New York 1971), 308–9; and Marcel Trudel, *Les vaines tentatives, 1524–1603* (Montreal 1963), 79.

18 'For in the time of Jacques Cartier, beavers were held in no esteem; the hats made thereof are in use only since that time ...' (Lescarbot, *New France* III: 365–6; translation, 117).

19 John Smith, 'Description of New England,' in Burrage, *Gorges*, 117; Sir William Alexander, *An encouragement to colonies* (London 1624), 39.

20 Smith, 'Description,' in Burrage, *Gorges*, 117. See also the remarks of Lescarbot, in Lescarbot, *New France* III: 441.

21 See Carroll, *Timber economy*, 3–21; Charles Woolsey Cole, *Colbert and a century of French mercantilism* (2 vols.; New York 1939), I: 311, and II: 83–103; T.M. Devine and S.G.E. Lythe, 'The economy of Scotland under James VI: a revision article,' *Scottish Historical Review* 50 (1971): 102; Gordon Donaldson, *Scotland: James V to James VII* (Edinburgh 1965), 243, 248; S.G.E. Lythe, *The economy of Scotland in its European setting, 1550–1625* (Edinburgh 1960), 142–3; and Wallerstein, *The modern world-system*, 44–5.

22 'Some gardens ... wherein many kinds of grain were sown which came up very well ...' (Biggar, *Works of Champlain* I: 277–8). For the incident at Port Mouton, see Lescarbot, *New France* II: 500.

23 John Winter to Robert Trelawny, 9 Oct. 1634, in *Documentary history of the State*

of Maine, ed. William Willis *et al*. (Maine Historical Society Collections, ser. 2, 24 vols., Portland and Cambridge, Mass. 1869–1916), III: 53.

24 See Byers, 'Environment of the northeast,' 9–12; Carroll, *Timber economy*, 29–30; Clark, *Acadia*, 31–6, 51–4; and Arthur Butler Hulbert, *Soil: its influence on the history of the United States* (New Haven 1930), 83–92.

25 Douglas Wilson Johnson, *The New England-Acadian shoreline* (New York 1925), 517–87. See also William Francis Ganong, 'The vegetation of the Bay of Fundy salt and diked marshes: an ecological study,' *Botanical Gazette* 36 (1903): 161–86, 280–302, 349–67, 429–55; and David Pearce Penhallow, 'A contribution to our knowledge of the origin and development of certain marsh lands on the coast of New England,' Royal Society of Canada, *Proceedings and Transactions* 3rd ser., I (1907): section 4, 13–55.

26 See Ganong, 'Vegetation,' 175–6; and Penhallow, 'Certain marsh lands,' 14–15.

27 See Quinn, *North America from earliest discovery*, 60–4.

28 Selma Barkham, 'The Basques: filling a gap in our history between Jacques Cartier and Champlain,' *Canadian Geographical Journal* 96 (1978): 8–19.

29 Harold Adams Innis, *The cod fisheries: the history of an international economy* (rev. ed., Toronto 1954), chaps. 2 and 3, esp. 49–51; Charles de La Morandière, *Histoire de la pêche française de la morue dans l'Amérique septentrionale (des origines à 1789)* (2 vols., Paris 1962), I, chap. 2.

30 On the geological formation of the fishing grounds, see Johnson, *New England-Acadian shoreline*, 260–313.

31 Lescarbot, *New France* II: 580; III: 435. 'By way of pastime on the coasts of New France, I will take in one day in the places where there is abundance of cod, for that kind of fish is there most frequent, fish enough to serve as food for more than six weeks; and he that has the industry to catch mackerel at sea, will catch so many that he will not know what to do with them ...' (Ibid. III: 244–5).

32 Martin Pring, 'A voyage set out from the citie of Bristoll,' in Levermore, *Forerunners and competitors*, 61. It should be noted in the interests of precision that in the seventeenth century Penobscot Bay, referred to as 'Pentagouet,' may be regarded as much as a part of Acadia as a part of New England. The terms 'Penobscot' and 'Pentagouet' were Indian names for particular riverside areas and were adopted by English and French respectively. See Fannie Hardy Eckstorm, *Indian place names of the Penobscot valley and the Maine coast* (Orono, Me. 1941), 1–3, 191–3.

33 James Rosier, 'A true relation of the most prosperous voyage made this present year 1605, by Captaine George Waymouth,' in Burrage, *Gorges*, 61, 66.

34 See Charles E. Clark, *The eastern frontier: the settlement of northern New England, 1610–1763* (New York 1970), 14–15. No comparison is here possible with Scottish views of the American fishery, since the Scots fishery was at this time

confined almost entirely to fishing grounds off Scotland itself, see Donaldson, *Scotland*, 247.

35 [Sir Ferdinando Gorges], 'A brief relation of the discovery and plantation of New England,' in Burrage, *Gorges*, 156. The 'brief relation' was published anonymously by the Council for New England, but historians have generally accepted Gorges as the author; see Richard Arthur Preston, *Gorges of Plymouth Fort* (Toronto 1954), 346. '[Acadia is] difficult to hold because of the infinite number of its harbours which could only be guarded by large forces' (Biggar, *Works of Champlain* IV: 28). See also Johnson, *New England-Acadian Shoreline*, 3–16, and Clark, *Acadia*, 21–2.

36 Byers, 'Environment of the northeast,' 25–6; Nicolas Denys, *The description and natural history of the coasts of North America (Acadia)*, ed. William F. Ganong (Toronto 1908; first published 1672), 599; Hoffman, 'Ethnography of the Micmac,' 129–30, 170–1, 178–9; and Josselyn, *Two voyages*, 305–6.

37 'We see also that all your people live, as a rule, only upon cod which you catch among us. It is everlastingly nothing but cod – cod in the morning, cod at midday, cod at evening, and always cod, until things come to such a pass that if you wish some good morsels, it is at our expense ...' (Le Clercq, *New relation*, 346; translation, 105).

38 Edward Johnson, *Wonder-working providence of Sion's saviour in New England*, ed. J. Franklin Jameson (New York 1910), 113. See also Peter N. Carroll, *Puritanism and the wilderness: the intellectual significance of the New England frontier, 1629–1700* (New York 1969), 45–59.

39 'A wilderness ... Nothing before my eyes but Streams and Forests, Huts of mud and Cottages ...' (Sieur de Dièreville, *Relation of the voyage to Port Royal in Acadia or New France*, ed. John Clarence Webster (Toronto 1933; first published 1708), 250; translation, 82). Sir Robert Gordon of Lochinvar, *Encouragements for such as shall have intention to be under-takers in the new plantation of Cape Briton, now New Galloway in America* (Edinburgh 1625), motive 1, n.p. The perception of the wilderness as a threat, rather than as a challenge, is one which has survived strongly in Canadian literature. See Northrop Frye, *The bush garden* (Toronto 1971), 142, 225; and Margaret Atwood, *Survival: a thematic guide to Canadian literature* (Toronto 1972), 47–67.

40 Smith, 'Description,' in Burrage, *Gorges*, 107. Major studies of the Portuguese and Spanish empires include C.R. Boxer, *The Portuguese seaborne empire, 1415–1825* (London 1969); Gibson, *Spain in America*; Lewis Hanke, *The Spanish struggle for justice in the conquest of America* (Philadelphia 1949); and J.H. Parry, *The Spanish seaborne empire* (London 1966).

41 On the early French attempts of Cartier and Roberval in the 1540s, the Huguenot efforts in mid-century, and those of the Englishmen Gilbert and Raleigh in the

1580s, see Morison, *Northern voyages*, chaps. 13, 17, and 19; Quinn, *North America from earliest discovery*, chaps. 8, 10, 13, 14; William Robert Scott, *The constitution and finance of English, Scottish, and Irish joint-stock companies to 1720* (3 vols, Cambridge 1912), II: 241–5; and Trudel, *Vaines tentatives*, chaps 3 and 4.

42 Henry Percival Biggar, *The early trading companies of New France: a contribution to the history of commerce and discovery in North America* (Toronto 1901), 32; Gillian T. Cell, *English enterprise in Newfoundland, 1577–1660* (Toronto 1969), chaps. 1 and 2; Davies, *The North Atlantic world in the seventeenth century*, 11–16; Innis, *Cod fisheries*, chaps. 2 and 3; Trudel, *Vaines tentatives*, 218–21. This discussion of the importance of the English and French fisheries does not extend to Scotland, since the Scots fishery did not reach Newfoundland until much later. This partly explains the dependence of the New Scotland promoters upon their English counterparts (notably the Newfoundland colonizer John Mason) for much of the expertise which they required. See Gillian T. Cell, 'John Mason,' in *Dictionary of Canadian biography* (hereafter *DCB*), ed. George Brown *et al.* (6 vols. to date, Toronto 1966–), I: 496–7; Lythe, *Economy of Scotland*, 74; and Thomas H. McGrail, *Sir William Alexander, first Earl of Stirling* (Edinburgh 1940), 78–9. In later years, although direct connections between Newfoundland and the northeastern maritime colonies were sparse, the same mercantile interests continued often to be interested in both. Sir David Kirke, who with his brothers was briefly involved in New Scotland in the late 1620s and early 1630s, later became governor of Newfoundland. The Shapleighs, merchants of Dartmouth, were engaged in the Newfoundland fishery in the early seventeenth century and also participated in the colonization of Maine, especially through the longstanding resident of Kittery, Nicholas Shapleigh. The Shapleighs' agent, John Treworgie, also resided in Kittery from 1635 to about 1650, and then moved to Newfoundland. Emmanuel Le Borgne, merchant of La Rochelle and investor in Acadia, also financed voyage, to the Newfoundland fishery. John S. Moir, 'Sir David Kirke,' *DCB* I: 404–7; Thomas Gorges to Sir Ferdinando Gorges, [c. September 1641], in Robert Earle Moody, ed., *The letters of Thomas Gorges, deputy governor of the Province of Maine, 1640–1643* (Portland 1978), no. 37; Gillian T. Cell, 'John Treworgie,' *DCB* I: 652–3; Charter-Party, Lamber-Le Borgne, [1644], Archives départementales de la Charente-Maritime (hereafter ACM), E, Minutes Teuleron, 1643–4, ff.266–7.

43 William Cook Mackenzie, *History of the Outer Hebrides* (Paisley 1903), 174; David Beers Quinn, *The Elizabethans and the Irish* (Ithaca, N.Y. 1966), 106–22.

44 Gordon Donaldson, *The Scots overseas* (London 1966), 28–30; Donaldson, *Scotland*, 252; George Hill, *An historical account of the plantation of Ulster at the commencement of the seventeenth century, 1608–1630* (Belfast 1877); Lythe, *Economy of Scotland*, 66–70.

45 Nicholas P. Canny, 'The ideology of English colonization: from Ireland to America,' *William and Mary Quarterly* 3rd ser., 30 (1973): 577; Quinn, *Elizabethans and Irish*, 111–15.

46 Hill, *Ulster*, 140, 546–8; George Pratt Insh, *Scottish colonial schemes, 1620–1686* (Glasgow 1922), 104–6. The transference was aimed at keeping the title in Scotland.

47 Hill, *Ulster*, 497.

48 This view of America was especially clear in England, where the propagandist Richard Hakluyt was expounding the usefulness of colonization as a means of expanding the Protestant religion, increasing trade, and competing successfully with other nations. See, for example, Richard Hakluyt, *A discourse on western planting*, ed. Charles Deane (Cambridge, Mass. 1877), 7–12, 60–3, 95–7; also Morison, *Northern voyages*, 555–61.

49 Scotland took no interest in American colonization at this time, the first indication of such interest being the involvement of Scottish merchants in a colonial scheme in Newfoundland in 1620–1. Petition of the Treasurer and Company, with the Scottish Undertakers of the Plantations in Newfoundland, to the King, [March 1621]. Great Britain, Public Record Office (hereafter PRO), CO1/1, no. 54; Insh, *Scottish colonial schemes*, 27–39; Ralph Greenlee Lounsbury, *The British fishery at Newfoundland, 1634–1763* (New Haven 1934), 44–5.

50 Royal letter, and articles and remonstrances of de Monts, 1603. France, Archives nationales, Archives des Colonies (hereafter AC), C^{11D}, 1, ff. 17–26; Lescarbot, *New France* II: 490–2.

51 Charter printed in Alexander Brown, *Genesis of the United States* (2 vols; New York 1890), I: 52–63; see also Preston, *Gorges*, 141–2.

52 Preston, *Gorges*, 137–8; Marcel Trudel, *Le comptoir, 1604–1627* (Ottawa 1966), 14, 449.

53 'Many other beautiful things lie hidden in these countries, knowledge of which has not yet been given to us, but which will be discovered as the province grows in population' (Lescarbot, *New France* II: 505; translation, 238). Sir Ferdinando Gorges to Sir Robert Cecil, 1 Dec. 1607, in Henry O. Thayer, ed., *The Sagadahoc colony* (Portland 1892), 132.

54 George Popham to James I, 13 Dec. 1607, in Thayer, *Sagadahoc*, 119.

55 William Inglis Morse, ed., *Pierre du Gua, Sieur de Monts: records, colonial and 'Saintongeois'* (London 1939), 11. See also Biggar, *Trading companies*, 42–3, 51–3; and Trudel, *Vaines tentatives*, 235–44.

56 Virginia Company to Corporation of Plymouth, 17 Feb. 1609, in Thayer, *Sagadahoc*, 131. Preston, *Gorges*, 140–5; Scott, *Joint-stock companies* II: 299.

57 'Having found no place more suitable than this island, we began to erect a barricade on a small islet a little removed from it, and this served as a platform for mounting our cannon' (Biggar, *Works of Champlain* I: 274, 373).

58 Anonymous relation, in Thayer, *Sagadahoc*, 66–7 and passim.

59 Lescarbot, *New France* II: 514. The employees, furthermore, often consisted of forced labour from prisons rather than voluntary colonists. See Biggar, *Trading companies*, 49. For a detailed exploration of the concept of the communal colony in relation to the south Virginian settlement at Jamestown, see Diamond, 'From organization to society,' 457–75; though see also the distinctions introduced in Quinn, *North America from earliest discovery*, 536–44.

60 William Strachey, 'History of travaile into Virginia,' in Thayer, *Sagadahoc*, 85.

61 Ibid., 77–80, 85.

62 Gorges to Cecil, 7 Feb. 1608, in Thayer, *Sagadahoc*, 137.

63 Biggar, *Trading companies*, 60.

64 'Behold the effects of envy, which not only stole into the hearts of the Dutch to ruin so holy an enterprise, but also into those of our own countrymen, so great and insatiable has the avarice proved of the merchants who had no part in the association of M. de Monts' (Lescarbot, *New France* II; 574; translation, 351–2).

65 'But in truth, M. de Monts and his partners were losing money, and receiving no help from the King, and could not without much difficulty support a colony overseas' (Lescarbot, *New France* II: 574; translation, 351). See also Biggar, *Trading companies*, 63–4; Biggar, *Works of Champlain* I: 450; Robert Le Blant, 'Le commerce compliqué des fourrures canadiennes au début du xviie siècle,' *Revue d'histoire de l'Amérique française* 26 (1972–3): 56–7; Trudel, *Le comptoir*, 67.

66 [Gorges], 'Brief relation,' in Burrage, *Gorges*, 142.

67 See Sir Ferdinando Gorges, 'A brief narration of the original undertakings for the advancement of plantations in America,' in Maine Historical Society *Collections* ser. 1, II (Portland 1847), 22–4.

68 Trudel, *Le comptoir*, 15.

69 These events are more fully discussed in Trudel, *Le comptoir*, chaps 3 and 4. On the relationship between the Jesuits and Biencourt, see Biard, *Relation*, 193–8, and the opposing account in 'Factum du proces entre Jean de Biencourt et les PP. Biard et Massé,' in Campeau, ed., *Première mission*, 324–406; see also the discussion in Ibid., Introduction, 223–55. On the Argall raid, see Biard, *Relation*, 237–300; also the official French protest, 28 Oct. 1613, PRO, SP78/61, f.284.

70 See Robert Le Blant, 'L'avitaillement du Port-Royal d'Acadie par Charles de Biencourt et les marchands rochelais, 1615–1618,' *Revue d'histoire des colonies* 44 (1958): 138–52; Robert Le Blant and René Baudry, eds, *Nouveaux documents sur Champlain et son époque*, I (Ottawa 1967), 292–4; Morse, *De Monts*, 11–13. Liaison between Biencourt and his merchant associates was in the hands of David Lomeron, nephew of Georges and Macain. Lomeron made frequent visits to Acadia and had his own establishment at Port Lomeron, near the present site of Yarmouth, N.S. See 'David Lomeron,' *DCB* I: 476; Trudel, *Le comptoir*, 416–19.

On Biencourt's removal from Port Royal, see Le Blant, 'Avitaillement du Port-Royal,' 151–2.

71 Biencourt's letter of 1 Sept. 1618 is printed in *Collection de manuscrits contenant lettres, mémoires, et autres documents historiques relatifs à la Nouvelle-France recueillis aux Archives de la province de Québec ou copiés à l'étranger* (4 vols, Quebec 1883–5), I: 57–9. 'If this country has been undervalued up until now, it has been through ignorance and through the malice of merchants' (author's translation).

72 Biard, *Relation*, avant-propos, n.p.

73 'He who has corn in his barn, wine in his cellar, cattle in his meadows, and finally cod and beaver, is more assured of having gold and silver, than is he who has mines to find victuals' (Lescarbot, *New France* III: 443, translation, 260).

74 John Smith, 'History of New England,' in Levermore, *Forerunners and competitors*, 733.

75 See Quinn, *North America from earliest discovery*, 97; and Trudel, *Le comptoir*, 248–50.

76 Biard, *Relation*, 90–100, 209, 304.

77 Ibid., 29. '[That] we Frenchmen are so willing to go there with our eyes shut and our heads down ...' (*Jesuit relations* III: 65).

78 Biard, *Relation*, 101, 30. 'There are several private houses in Paris, and elsewhere which have the means necessary for such an undertaking'; 'To choose a place where all desirable qualities are united ... [is] the purpose and idea of a wise investigator' (*Jesuit relations* III: 139, 67).

79 It was, of course, no accident that Biard's concept closely resembled the pattern which had been so briefly essayed at Saint-Sauveur; it foreshadowed the scheme of later missionary settlements by Jesuits and other religious orders in Acadia and elsewhere in North America.

80 [Gorges], 'Brief relation,' in Burrage, *Gorges*, 139–64; see especially 139, 142–3, 157, 159.

81 Ibid., 140, 143. The existence of New Scotland was also intended to be seen as an evident denial of the proposition that the Council for New England sought to monopolize entirely the northern reaches of North America, as had been alleged by the Virginia Company and English fishing interests. See Preston, *Gorges*, 166–82.

82 Alexander, *Encouragement*, 32, 38, 39. See also Donaldson, *Scotland*, 252–5. For discussion of the complexities of the relationship between Scottish economy and population at this time, see Devine and Lythe, 'Scottish economy,' 97; Michael Flinn *et al.*, *Scottish population history* (Cambridge 1977), 109–26; and Lythe, *Economy of Scotland*, 28–32.

83 Draft of royal letter, 17 Oct. 1629, in Charles Rogers, ed., *The Earl of Stirling's register of royal letters relative to the affairs of Scotland and Nova Scotia from 1615 to 1635* (2 vols, Edinburgh 1885), I: 386.

84 'Whoever would endeavour to plant a colony in that country would need to restrict

the English as closely as possible.' 'It would have been possible to have more than four thousand people there by this time, and yet no more than twenty-five actually live there.' (Author's translations.) Léon Deschamps, *Un colonisateur du temps de Richelieu, Isaac de Razilly, biographie, mémoire inédit* (Paris 1887; extract from Revue de géographie), 15–16, 25, 31–2. Razilly's approach also shows the influence of the Dutch example, in the form of the Dutch West India Company of 1621. For full discussion of Dutch activities, which also raised the same tensions between commerce and colonization as existed in the northeastern Maritime region, see Condon, *New York beginnings*, passim.

85 Petition of the Council for the second colony, and others, 3 Mar. 1620, PRO, CO I/I, no. 47; Great patent of New England, 3 Nov. 1620, in *Documentary history of Maine* VII: 25.

86 *Documentary history of Maine* VII: 34–9; Preston, *Gorges*, 170–1.

87 *Documentary history of Maine* VII: 25–7; [Gorges], 'Brief relation,' in Burrage, *Gorges*, 160; Preston, *Gorges*, 170–6.

88 Preston, *Gorges*, 186–96; Scott, *Joint stock companies* II: 302–3.

89 Minutes of the Council for New England, 18 Feb. 1623, PRO, CO I/2, no. 6, pp. 32–5; Draft of royal letter, 8 Dec. 1623, PRO, CO I/2, no. 52.

90 William Bradford, *Of Plymouth plantation*, ed. Samuel Eliot Morison (New York 1952), 133–8; Preston, *Gorges*, 225–32.

91 Alexander, *Encouragement*, 32. One question which was raised by this grant was whether the lands granted were still considered to be within the patent of the Council for New England, since they lay south of the latitude of 48°. Sir Ferdinando Gorges later wrote that the territory had been 'assigned' by him to Alexander (Gorges, 'Brief narration,' 48). However, the letter of James VI to the Scots Privy Council of 5 Aug. 1621, in which the Privy Council was instructed to prepare for the inauguration of the new colony, made it clear that the lands granted were 'to be holden of us from our kingdome of Scotland, as a part thereof ...' (Scotland, Privy Council, *The register of the Privy Council of Scotland*, ed. John Hill Burton et al., (38 vols, Edinburgh 1877–1970; hereafter *P.C. register*), ser. 1, XII: 774. The origins of New Scotland were closely connected with New England; but the colony had no formal connection with the kingdom of England.

92 Charter in favour of Sir William Alexander, knight, of the lordship and barony of New Scotland in America, 10 Sept. 1621, in John G. Bourinot, 'Builders of Nova Scotia,' Royal Society of Canada, *Proceedings and Transactions*, 2nd ser., V (1899): section 2, 104–21.

93 Ibid., 110–11; Alexander, *Encouragement*, 33–4; Scott, *Joint stock companies* II: 318.

94 James VI to Privy Council of Scotland, 18 Oct. 1624, *P.C. register*, ser. 1, XIII: 616.

95 Proclamation, 30 Nov. 1624, *P.C. register*, ser. 1, XIII: 649–51; on the involve-

ment of the knights-baronets in government, see the patent of 1630 in favour of Sir James Skene of Curriehill, in William Forbes Skene, ed., *Memorials of the family of Skene of Skene* (Aberdeen 1887), 209.

96 *Documentary history of Maine* VII: 76–80.

97 See Scotland, *The acts of the parliament of Scotland,* ed. Cosmo Innes *et al.* (12 vols, Edinburgh 1844–75), V: 184; also Charles I to Privy Council of Scotland, 12 Feb. 1626, in Rogers, *Stirling's register* I: 18–19.

98 Draft for a commission for completing the arrangements for the Nova Scotia plantation, [1626], *P.C. register,* ser. 2, I: 365. Charles I to the Lard [Laird] of Wemyss, 24 Mar. 1626, in Rogers, *Stirling's register* I: 30; Charles I to Privy Council of Scotland, 28 July 1626, Ibid., 68–9; Charles I [to the Exchequer], 17 Jan. 1627, Ibid., 118–19. A privy seal register records only ninety knights-baronetcies conferred up until 1638, though some twenty others may be added from other sources. Scottish Record Office (hereafter SRO), Privy Seal register, PS5/1; David Laing, ed., *Royal letters, charters, and tracts, relating to the colonization of New Scotland and the institution of the order of knights baronets of Nova Scotia, 1621 to 1638* (Edinburgh 1867), 120–3. Discussion of these early efforts on behalf of the New Scotland colony will also be found in John G. Reid, 'The Scots crown and the restitution of Port Royal, 1629–1632,' *Acadiensis* VI (spring 1977): 41–4. It should be pointed out that footnote 4 on p. 41 of this article contains a partially inaccurate statement on the calendar style in force in Scotland during the seventeenth century: Scottish dates in the article are in fact rendered in accordance with the statement made on p. xvi of the present volume. For a full discussion of calendar variations, see John J. Bond, *Handy-book of rules and tables for verifying dates of historical events and of public and private documents; giving tables of regnal years of English sovereigns, with leading dates, from the conquest to the present time, 1066–1866* (London 1866), ix–xiii, 1–5, 17–28.

99 The Jesuit role is heavily emphasized in Lucien Campeau, *Les finances publiques de la Nouvelle France sous les Cent-Associés, 1632–1665* (Montreal 1975), 9–10. On the general aspects of Richelieu's reorganization, see G. Dagnaud, *L'administration centrale de la Marine sous l'ancien régime* (Nancy 1912), 5–10, and Albert Duchêne, *La politique coloniale de la France: le ministère des Colonies depuis Richelieu* (Paris 1928), 5–12.

100 'All the ... country of New France, called Canada, along its entire coastline from Florida ... to the Arctic Circle'; 'In complete ownership, with judicial and seigneurial functions' (author's translations). Articles granted by the King to the company of New France, 29 Apr. 1627, AC, C^{11A}, 1, f.81. See also Gustave Lanctot, *L'administration de la Nouvelle-France: l'administration générale* (Paris 1929), 16–17; and André Vachon, 'The administration of New France,' in *DCB* II: xv.

101 Articles granted to the company, AC, C^{11A}, 1, ff.80–4; Articles and conventions, 7 May 1627, Ibid., ff.84–8; Edict, May 1628, Ibid., ff.91–8. Campeau, *Finances*

publiques, 10–14; Marcel Trudel, *The beginnings of New France, 1524–1663* (Toronto 1973), 168–72. The proposed capital of 300,000 *livres* amounted to approximately £26,000 sterling and was thus comparable to the £22,500 projected for New Scotland. See John J. McCusker, *Money and exchange in Europe and America, 1600–1775: a handbook* (Chapel Hill, N.C. 1978), 88.

102 On the Kirkes, see John S. Moir's articles in *DCB* I: 404–8.

103 Articles granted to the company, AC, C^{11A}, I, f.80; see also Razilly's comments on the religious functions of colonization, in Deschamps, *Colonisateur du temps de Richelieu*, 15–16, 22. Razilly's concerns clearly complemented those of the Jesuits. See also Campeau, *Finances publiques*, 13.

104 *Documentary history of Maine* VII: 43; Bourinot, 'Nova Scotia,' 116–17; Articles granted to the company, AC, C^{11A}, I, f.83.

105 The term *féodalité* has been adopted here to indicate the use of the device of enfeoffment as a means of land transference and tenure. As discussed later in this chapter and in chapter 5, it does not imply (and did not imply in the seventeenth century) any attempt to recreate in America the feudal society of medieval Europe. In many instances, the term seigneurial colonization is just as satisfactory as *féodalité*, since it is more precise and informative about the relationship between landlord and tenant. The seigneurial system in New France, the plans of Sir Ferdinando Gorges for 'manors and lordships' in New England, and the projected baronial structure of New Scotland can all satisfactorily be described as seigneurial. However, the proprietary system which was gradually emerging out of the Council for New England, and which would be explicitly recognised in proprietary charters such as that accorded to Gorges for Maine in 1639, was somewhat different. Under this arrangement, the power of dispensing justice was usually reserved entirely to the proprietor, rather than being delegated to land patentees as a seigneurial right. The difference, in practice, was not absolute; in an exceptional case, that of his kinsman and lieutenant governor Thomas Gorges, Gorges did grant manorial privileges. Furthermore, in other respects, patentees did preserve practices that were at least emblematic of seigneurial authority, such as the exaction of quitrents or services from tenants. Conversely, the Compagnie de la Nouvelle-France often withheld in practice the power of 'haute justice' from its seigneurs. Nevertheless, the theoretical difference makes the general term *féodalité* more satisfactory as a means of comprehending both the seigneurial and the proprietary forms. See Charles M. Andrews, introduction to Beverley W. Bond, *The quit-rent system in the American colonies* (New Haven 1919), 11–22; Davies, *North Atlantic world*, 203–10; Harris, *Seigneurial system in early Canada*, 3–5; Preston, *Gorges*, 220–3; Trudel, *Débuts du régime seigneurial*, 1–8; and Grant of Sir Ferdinando Gorges to Thomas Gorges, 4 Mar. 1642, Maine Historical Society, *York deeds* (18 vols, Portland and Bethel 1887–1910), I, part 2, ff.5–6.

106 [Gorges], 'Brief relation,' in Burrage, *Gorges*, 159–61.

107 *Documentary history of Maine* VII: 64–71; on this and other aspects of the Council for New England's activities at this time, see Preston, *Gorges*, 218–32.

108 Alexander, *Encouragement*, map facing p. 1. The status of Cape Breton Island in this scheme is not entirely clear: Cape Breton had on 8 Nov. 1621 been confirmed by charter to Sir Robert Gordon of Lochinvar as the Province of New Galloway, along the lines of an agreement between Gordon and Alexander. Scotland, *The register of the great seal of Scotland*, [Vol. VIII], *A.D. 1620–1633*, ed. John Maitland Thomson (Edinburgh 1894), no. 233. Although the New Galloway project was still alive in 1625, as is indicated by Gordon's *Encouragements*, official sources refer only to the two provinces of Alexandria and Caledonia.

109 Privy Council of Scotland to James VI, 23 Nov. 1624, *P.C. register*, ser. 1, XIII: 633–4.

110 'To those who will populate the said country, and to others, in whatever quantity and in whatever manner they shall consider appropriate' (author's translation). Articles granted to the company, 29 Apr. 1627, AC, C^{11A}, 1, f.81.

111 Concession to commander de Razilly, 19 May 1632, AC, C^{11D}, 1, ff.52–3. See also Trudel, *Débuts du régime seigneurial*, 1–8. The Council for New England had also made grants to be held of itself rather than the crown, but these were of doubtful legality in view of the statute of *Quia emptores*. See Preston, *Gorges*, 222, 274.

112 See Trudel, *Débuts du régime seigneurial*, 2–6.

113 La Tour to Louis XIII, 25 July 1627, Université de Moncton, Centre d'études acadiennes (hereafter CÉA), Fonds René Baudry, 20.6–17. See also Trudel, *Le comptoir*, 418–21.

114 'Both against the Sieur de Poutrincourt, a resident of that country, and against other Frenchmen who make voyages there'; '[To] urge them to stay within their limits, so as not to oblige the two sides to resort to the excesses of a minor war' (author's translations). Count de Tillières, French ambassador, to English government, [1624], PRO, CO1/3, no. 13. The reference to 'le sieur de Poutrincourt' presumably refers either to Charles de Biencourt or to his heir, Jacques de Biencourt, both of whom carried the additional title of Sieur de Poutrincourt. The British subjects complained of were apparently the Scots of the Alexander expedition of 1622–3, who had coasted down as far as Cap Nègre during the summer of 1623.

115 'As from the Crown of Scotland, so that his [the king's] subjects of that nation shall similarly have the opportunity of establishing a plantation in these regions.' 'For the better establishment of civil relations between them [the French] and ourselves in the future.' (Author's translations.) Answer to Tillières, [1624], PRO, CO1/3, no. 14.

116 'I have been forced, by the bad treatment which we have received from the English, to live in the same way as the native people of the country and clothed like them, to hunt and fish in order to live ...' 'For the care of the coast of Acadia, with all others forbidden to disturb me.' '[A] small band of Frenchmen, with three medium-sized

boats.' (Author's translations.) La Tour to Louis XIII, 25 July 1627, CÉA, Fonds René Baudry, 20.6–17; La Tour to Richelieu, 25 July 1627, France, Bibliothèque nationale (hereafter BN), Nouvelles acquisitions françaises, 5131, ff. 102–3. Firm evidence is lacking as to the identity of the 'Anglois' by whom La Tour expected to be attacked, although his mention of the Kennebec river in the letter to Richelieu suggests a connection with Plymouth. It is possible also that those involved were English fishermen, contesting the fur trade in Acadia just as English fishermen were coming into conflict with the Plymouth colonists themselves over trade on the Kennebec at this time. See Bradford, *Plymouth*, 193. La Tour also claimed to have been harassed by the French of the St Lawrence, possibly in an attempted enforcement of the trade monopoly of Guillaume de Caën, though this monopoly did not in theory extend to Acadia. See also Robert Le Blant, 'La compagnie de la Nouvelle-France et la restitution de l'Acadie, 1627–1636,' *Revue d'histoire des colonies* 42 (1955): 72; Trudel, *Le comptoir*, 421–4.

117 Bradford, *Plymouth*, 138.

118 Christopher Levett, 'A voyage into New England,' in Levermore, *Forerunners and competitors*, 608–42; see also Henry Sweetser Burrage, *The beginnings of colonial Maine, 1602–1658* (Portland 1914), 167–75. Levett subsequently made repeated appeals for patronage to Sir John Coke, the future secretary of state, and was in 1628 designated governor of New England; there is no evidence that he acted in that capacity in America, though he was in New England briefly in 1630. See Great Britain, Historical Manuscripts Commission, *Twelfth report, appendix: the manuscripts of the Earl Cowper, K.G., preserved at Melbourne Hall, Derbyshire* (3 vols, London 1888–9; hereafter HMC, *Cowper MSS*), I: 178, 287; Great Britain, PRO, *Calendar of State Papers, Colonial Series, America and West Indies, 1574–1660*, ed. W. Noel Sainsbury (London 1860) 87; Burrage, *Beginnings*, 195–6; and James Phinney Baxter, *Christopher Levett of York* (Portland 1893), 63–75.

119 Contract for the transportation of David Thomson and seven other colonists to America, 14 Dec. 1622, in Levermore, *Forerunners and competitors*, 826–31; see also Charles Knowles Bolton, *The real founders of New England* (Boston 1929), 163.

120 See Richard Arthur Preston, 'The Laconia Company of 1629: an English attempt to intercept the fur trade,' *Canadian Historical Review* 31 (1950): 125–44.

121 Order of the Privy Council of Scotland, 23 April 1628, *P.C. register*, ser. 2, II: 313–14; McGrail, *Alexander*, 106–9.

122 See Insh, *Scottish colonial schemes*, chap. 3.

123 For discussion of the basis for selecting 1629 as the correct date, see Reid, 'The Scots crown,' 44.

124 Sir William Alexander to Earl of Menteith, 18 Nov. [1628], in William Fraser, *The red book of Menteith* (2 vols, Edinburgh 1880), II: 98; Sir William Alexander's

information touching his plantation at Cape Breton and Port Reall, [c. 1630], British Library (hereafter BL), Egerton MSS, 2395, f.23; Insh, *Scottish colonial schemes*, 224–6.

125 William Maxwell to Sir John Maxwell of Pollok, 23 Nov. 1628, in William Fraser, *Memoirs of the Maxwells of Pollok* (2 vols, Edinburgh 1863), II: 200.

126 Sir William Alexander had taken the precaution in early 1628 of acquiring a grant of extensive tracts of land in the St Lawrence region under the great seal of Scotland, to be known as the lordship of Canada, and was thus in a position to counter-attack the Kirkes' claims. Grant to Sir William Alexander, 2 Feb. 1628, in Scotland, *Register of the great seal*, VIII, no. 1202; Propositions of accommodation for the settling of the trade and plantation in Canada or New France, 1628, HMC, *Cowper MSS* I: 376–7; and Privy Council of Scotland to Charles I, 18 Nov. 1628, *P.C. register*, ser. 2, II: 489. See also McGrail, *Alexander*, 108–12; Trudel, *Beginnings*, 174–5. It is possible that it was the Kirkes who were responsible for the English attack on the French post at Port Lomeron, 'du temps de la guerre de la rochelle,' mentioned by Nicolas Denys. See Denys, *Description*, 476. Corroborating evidence for this is apparently available in a report dated 14 Aug. 1632 contained in a publication of 17 September, concerning the voyage of Isaac de Razilly to reclaim Acadia for France in that year. Razilly, according to the report, had recovered the fort of 'Thiebée' from the 'Anglois.' Théophraste Renaudot, *Recueil des gazettes, nouvelles, relations, et autres choses memorables de toute l'année 1632* (Paris 1633; hereafter *Gazette Renaudot*), 365. Candide de Nant, more cautiously Robert Le Blant, and most recently Clarence d'Entremont have suggested that 'Thiebée' may be the name rendered 'Chebogue' in modern usage and would, in that case, refer to Port Lomeron. The report is suspect, however, in that it also asserts that Razilly had already received the surrender of Port Royal by the Scots, an event which did not take place until later in the year. See Report of Jean-Daniel Chaline, 1 Nov. 1632, ACM, B, La Rochelle, B.5654, no.21; *Gazette Renaudot*, 1633, 37. Yet even if the 14 August report was based on rumour rather than fact, the English presence in New Scotland deserves further study. Candide de Nant, *Pages glorieuses de l'épopée canadienne: une mission capucine en Acadie* (Montreal 1927), 119; Clarence d'Entremont, 'Nicolas Denys, historien veridique,' Société historique acadienne, *Cahiers* 10 (1979): 152–4; Le Blant, 'Compagnie de la Nouvelle-France et la restitution,' 84.

127 Memorial of Lord Ochiltree to Charles I, [1630], PRO, CO1/5, no. 46; see also Petition of Captain Constance Ferrar [9 Dec. 1629], Ibid., no. 41, and the reports given by Daniel, in André Malapart, *La prise d'un seigneur escossois et de ses gens qui pilloient les navires pescheurs de France. Ensemble le razement de leur fort, et l'establissement d'un autre pour le service du roy, et l'asseurance des pescheurs françois en la Nouvelle France* (Rouen 1630).

128 'It would not have been possible to force him from his fortress, for he had provisions enough for more than two years ... with all kinds of commodities, tools, implements, and workmen,' (author's translation). Malapart, *Prise d'un seigneur escossois*, 20–1.

129 'Out of seventy Scotchmen wintering there, thirty had died of hardship' (Biggar, *Works of Champlain* VI: 176).

130 Fraser, *Menteith* II: 110, 111–12, 113, 118.

131 'New Scotland,' National Library of Scotland, MS 2061 (Hawthornden MSS, IX), ff.148–50.

132 Reverend Joseph Mead to Sir Martin Stuteville, 12 Feb. 1630, quoted in Edmund E. Slafter, ed., *Sir William Alexander and American colonization* (Boston 1873), 66; D.C. Harvey, 'Segipt,' *DCB* I: 605; on Scottish-Micmac relations, see also Hoffman, 'Ethnography of the Micmac,' 59–60.

133 Laing, *Royal letters, charters, and tracts*, 122; for a commentary on the uncertainties of the evidence, see Le Blant, 'Compagnie de la Nouvelle-France et la restitution,' 74.

134 '[To be] good and faithful subjects and vassals of the said king [of Scotland], to render all obedience to him, and to assist him among the peoples of Acadia for the reduction of that country and coastline' (author's translation). Articles of agreement, 6 Oct. 1629, BL, Egerton MSS, 2395, f.17. The provenance and dating of this document are suspect, but the authenticity of the agreement described is confirmed in letters patent granted to the La Tours by Alexander in the following year. See Azarie Couillard-Després, *Charles de Saint-Estienne de La Tour, gouverneur, lieutenant-général en Acadie, et son temps, 1593–1666* (Arthabaska, Que. 1930), 165–9. Specific reference to the agreement was made in later diplomatic documents, as in Articles concluded between the two kings of France and England, [1631], France, Archives du ministère des Affaires Étrangères [hereafter AAÉ], Correspondance politique, Angleterre, 44, f.239; see also Le Blant, 'Compagnie de la Nouvelle-France et la restitution,' 74.

135 Biggar, *Works of Champlain* VI: 172–5; Denys, *Description*, 477–9. Denys's more detailed and dramatic account of a battle at Cap de Sable between father and son may be exaggerated, but its general authenticity is probable. See also George MacBeath, 'Claude de Saint-Étienne de La Tour,' *DCB* I: 596–8.

CHAPTER 2

1 Charles I to Sir William Alexander, 13 May 1630, Rogers, *Stirling's register* II: 439.

2 Memorandum on the restitution of Canada and Acadia by the English, [1629], France, AAÉ, Correspondance politique, Angleterre, 43, ff.290–1.

3 Dorchester to Sir Isaac Wake, 15 Apr. 1630, PRO, SP78/86, f.253. Dorchester was,

of course, quite literally correct in asserting that 'no French' inhabited Port Royal in 1629, since the remaining French, and notably the La Tours, had long been residing in the southernmost area of the Acadian peninsula. The diplomatic negotiations over Port Royal at this time are more fully explored in Reid, 'The Scots crown,' 49–63.

4 Charles I to Privy Council of Scotland, 3 July 1630, Rogers, *Stirling's register* II: 463; Declaration of the convention of estates, 31 June 1630, Scotland, *Acts of the Parliament of Scotland* V: 223–4; Privy Council of Scotland to Charles I, 9 Sept. 1630, *P.C. register*, ser. 2, IV: 46–7; Reasons alleaged by the Scottish adventurers for the holding of Port Royal, [1630], PRO, CO1/5, no. 102 (i).

5 'That the matter of the said Port Royal was inseparable from the rest,' (author's translation). De Vic and Augier to Dorchester, 7 Dec. 1630, PRO, SP78/87, ff.459–60.

6 De Vic and Augier to Dorchester, 28 Jan. 1631, PRO, SP78/88, ff. 50–1.

7 Reported in Dorchester to De Vic and Augier, 2 Mar. 1631, Ibid., f.196.

8 De Vic and Augier to Dorchester, 28 Jan. 1631, Ibid., ff.50–1.

9 Schedule agreed at Dijon, 1 Apr. 1631, Ibid., f.344. Rogers, *Stirling's register* II: 544, 547–8. The patent creating Alexander Viscount of Stirling had been prepared in 1630, but was delivered in July 1631. For further discussion of this whole episode, see Reid, 'The Scots crown,' 53–5.

10 Charles I to the exchequer, 19 Feb. 1632, Rogers, *Stirling's register* II: 575–6. The grant was never in fact paid.

11 Charles I to the knights-baronets, 15 Aug. 1632, Rogers, *Stirling's register* II: 619 Ratification in favour of the Viscount of Sterling, 28 June 1633, Scotland, *Acts of the Parliament of Scotland* V: 43.

12 On the dropping of the Scots colonists on the south coast of England by a French vessel on its way to Le Havre, see *Gazette Renaudot*, 1633, 70–1.

13 See Reid, 'The Scots crown; 56–8.

14 Minute of some points considerable for the king's service, [16 June 1632], PRO, CO 1/6, no. 56.

15 Convention with the Sieur de Razilly, 27 Mar. 1632, AC, C^{11D}, 1, ff. 47–8; *Gazette Renaudot*, 1632, 24, 282–3.

16 'To receive in our name, from the hands of the English or the Scots, the said Port Royal,' (author's translation). Commission to the Sieur de Razilly, 10 May 1632, AC, C^{11D}, 1, ff.50–1; Concession to commander de Razilly, 19 May 1632, AC, C^{11D}, 1, ff.52–3. See also Trudel, *Beginnings*, 192–3; and Le Blant 'Compagnie de la Nouvelle-France et la restitution,' 82–3.

17 For further discussion, see Trudel, *Beginnings*, 192–3; and Le Blant, 'Compagnie de la Nouvelle-France et la restitution,' 83–93.

18 Documents printed in Couillard-Després, *La Tour*, 191–3.

19 Act of association, 16 Jan. 1635, BN, Fonds français, 28927, ff.21–5; Le Blant,

'Compagnie de la Nouvelle-France et la restitution,' 86–7. Razilly himself discussed his financial difficulties in letters to Richelieu and to Marc Lescarbot, and in an unsuccessful appeal for support to the grand master of the Order of Knights of Malta, of which he was a member. Razilly to Richelieu, 25 July 1634, AAÉ, Amérique, 4, f.130; Razilly to Lescarbot, 16 Aug. 1634, reported in *Memorandum*, 1634, BN, Fonds français, 13423, ff.349–50; Grand Master de Paulo to Razilly, 20 Feb. 1636, BN, Nouvelles acquisitions françaises, 9281, f.66.

20 See René Baudry, 'Charles d'Aulnay et la compagnie de la Nouvelle-France,' *Revue d'histoire de l'Amérique française* 11 (1957–8): 226–8.

21 Ibid., 235; see also Clark, *Acadia*, 100–1. Many of the colonists came from d'Aulnay's own seigneury in France. See Geneviève Massignon, 'La seigneurie de Charles de Menou d'Aulnay, gouverneur de l'Acadie, 1635–1650,' *Revue d'histoire de l'Amérique française* 16 (1962–3): 470–1.

22 See Preston, *Gorges*, 308. The resignation of the patent of the Council for New England had been made to facilitate new royal plans for the government of the region, discussed later in this chapter.

23 *Documentary history of Maine* VII: 223–4.

24 Sir Ferdinando Gorges to Sir Francis Windebank, 21 Mar. 1635, PRO, COI/8, no. 52; Royal manifesto, 23 July 1637, PRO, COI/9, no. 60.

25 Gorges, 'Brief narration,' 49.

26 See Preston, *Gorges*, 311.

27 Great Britain, Privy Council, *Acts of the Privy Council of England: colonial series*, ed. W.L. Grant and James Munro (6 vols, London 1908–12), I: 199–201; Preston, *Gorges*, 295–313.

28 G.B., Privy Council, *Acts of the Privy Council* I: 227–30.

29 Petition of Sir Ferdinando Gorges, [c.1640], PRO, COI/10, no. 56.

30 Le Blant, 'Compagnie de la Nouvelle-France et la restitution,' 92; 'David Lomeron,' *DCB* I: 476.

31 Arbitration, 26 Nov. 1636, ACM, E, Minutes Teuleron, pièces extraites des liasses, 1636–79, pièce 1. See also Le Blant, 'Commerce des fourrures,' 63, 65.

32 See Denys, *Description*, 499; also Robert Le Blant, 'La première compagnie de Miscou, 1635–1645,' *Revue d'histoire de l'Amérique française* 17 (1963–4): 367–70; also Bernard Pothier, 'Nicolas Denys: the chronology and historiography of an Acadian hero,' *Acadiensis* I (autumn 1971): 56–9.

33 Baudry, 'Charles d'Aulnay,' 222–33.

34 Obligation of Charles d'Aulnay to Emmanuel Le Borgne and Geoffroy Dusseau, I Apr. 1634. ACM, E, Minutes Juppin, 1632–4, f.325. See also Roger Comeau, 'Pêche et traite en Acadie jusqu'en 1713' (PH D thesis, Université d'Ottawa 1949), 158; and M. Delafosse, 'La Rochelle et le Canada au XVIIᵉ siècle,' *Revue d'histoire de l'Amérique française* 4 (1950–1): 471–2.

35 Comeau, 'Pêche et traite en Acadie,' 159–60; Trudel, *Beginnings*, 199, 200,

203–4; see also the petiton of *c.* 1664 from d'Aulnay's children to Colbert, in CÉA, Fonds René Baudry, 20.8–11.

36 Preston, 'Laconia Company,' 131–2, 138–41.

37 *Documentary history of Maine* III: passim; see also Clark, *Eastern frontier*, 21–6. The Council for New England's grant to Trelawny and Goodyear did not convey outright ownership of Richmond's Island but only the right to operate a fishing establishment. However, the actual grantee of the island, Walter Bagnall, was dead when the grant was made (though the news had not yet reached the Council for New England), and it is likely that from then on the island was simply regarded as an adjunct to the adjoining coastal land which was specifically held by Trelawny and Goodyear. See *Documentary history of Maine* VII: 162–3.

38 Denys, *Description*, 480–2. John Winter to Robert Trelawny, 11 June 1635, *Documentary history of Maine* III: 55.

39 Winter to Trelawny, 26 June 1635, *Documentory history of Maine* III: 60. For some of Winter's comments on the fur trade, see Winter to Trelawny, 18 June 1634, Ibid., 27–9.

40 See Le Blant, 'Commerce des fourrures,' 62–5.

41 Le Blant, 'Compagnie de la Nouvelle-France et la restitution,' 85; Winter to Trelawny, 10 July 1639, *Documentary history of Maine* III: 163.

42 Winter to Trelawny, 29 July 1637, *Documentary history of Maine* III: 119; Denys, *Description*, 480–2; see also Pothier, 'Denys,' 56–7.

43 The Laconia Company eventually operated more in the fishery than in the fur trade – by 1632 it was operating a substantial fishing fleet from its base on the Piscataqua River – but it was originally intended as a fur-trading enterprise. See Preston, 'Laconia Company,' 137–40.

44 *Documentary history of Maine* III: 336–42. Presumably these were among the last indentures made for the Richmond's Island plant. Identures there were made both on a wage basis and on a basis of shares of the catch of fish. See Robert Earle Moody, 'The Maine frontier, 1607–1763' (PH D thesis, Yale University 1933), 21.

45 ACM, E, Minutes Teuleron, Régistres, 1636, ff.23–8. See also Gabriel Debien, 'Engagés pour le Canada au XVIIe siècle vus de la Rochelle,' *Revue d'histoire de l'Amérique française* 6(1952–3): 186.

46 G.B., Privy Council, *Acts of the Privy Council*, 232, 250, 266–7; see also Petition of Sidrack Miller, [c.1631], PRO, CO1/6, no. 35; for an instance of the same problem in Acadia, see Baudry, 'Charles d'Aulnay,' 226.

47 Winter to Trelawny, 28 June 1636, *Documentary history of Maine* III: 92–3. Thus, although short-term labourers received no promise of American land nor any other prospect of an extended stay, a minor augmentation of the permanent European population was a by-product of their importation.

48 Winter to Trelawny, 18 June 1634, Ibid., 33.

49 Alexander to Menteith, 9 Feb [1630], Fraser, *Menteith*, II: 111, Alexander to

Menteith, 23 March [1630], Ibid., 113. Supplication of Sir George Home of Eckills, 11 Mar. 1630, *P.C. register*, ser. 2, III: 488. Home, a notorious debtor, departed for New Scotland much to the chagrin of his creditors: see Supplication of William Watts, 26 May 1630, Ibid., 543.

50 G.B., Privy Council, *Acts of the Privy Council* I: 160.

51 Winter to Trelawny, 10 July 1639, *Documentary history of Maine* III: 162–9; Edward Trelawny to Robert Trelawny, 10 Jan. 1636, Ibid., 80; Winter to Trelawny, 30 July 1638, Ibid., 141. For further discussion of the dependence of the Trelawny plantation upon imported goods, see Moody, 'Maine frontier,' 18–19.

52 'Otherwise they would have been obliged to return empty to France' (Denys, *Description*, 482–3; translation, 150).

53 Declaration, 23 Sept. 1642, ACM, E, Minutes Teuleron, pièces extraites des liasses, 1636–79, pièce 6. See also Comeau, 'Pêche et traite,' 158.

54 'The expense of shipments ... for the subsistence, wages and food of the men who are there [in Acadia] at present ... and those whom it will be necessary to send there for the carrying on of trade' (author's translation). Quoted in Massignon, 'Seigneurie de Menou d'Aulnay,' 480.

55 Comeau, 'Pêche et traite,' 21–2.

56 CÉA, Collection Émile Lauvrière, 3.14–14.

57 John Winthrop, *Winthrop's journal*, ed. James Kendall Hosmer (2 vols, New York 1908), II: 43, 85, 88.

58 Ibid., 105–16, 127–30. For a detailed discussion of this conflict, see Robert Emmet Wall, Jr, *Massachusetts Bay: the crucial decade, 1640–1650* (New Haven 1972), 65–73.

59 Account of Edward Gibbons, 1654, Massachusetts Archives (hereafter MA), 2, f.501; Deeds and indentures, *Suffolk deeds*, I (Boston 1880): 7–11; see also Bernard Bailyn, *The New England merchants in the seventeenth century* (Cambridge, Mass. 1955), 84, 101; and Arthur Howland Buffinton, 'The policy of the northern colonies towards the French to the peace of Utrecht' (PH D thesis, Harvard University 1925), 59–62.

60 *Winthrop's journal* II: 275; for a fuller account of these events and their implications for English-French relations, see chap. 4 below.

61 Winter to Trelawny, 28 June 1636, *Documentary history of Maine* III: 92.

62 Winter to Trelawny, 30 July 1638, Ibid., 141–2.

63 See Bailyn, *New England merchants*, 55–7, 76–9; and Francis X. Moloney, *The fur trade in New England, 1620–1676* (Cambridge, Mass. 1931), 111.

64 Winter to Trelawny, 29 July 1641, *Documentary history of Maine* III: 284.

65 On the growing economic dependence of Maine and its settlers upon Massachusetts, and on the situation in Acadia, see Bailyn, *New England merchants*, 94–5; Jean Daigle, 'Nos amis les ennemis: relations commerciales de l'Acadie avec le Massachusetts, 1670–1711' (PH D thesis, University of Maine 1975),

112–13; Josselyn, *Two voyages*, 348–51; and John G. Reid, *Maine, Charles II, and Massachusetts: governmental relationships in early northern New England* (Portland 1977), 15.

66 Memorandum of d'Aulnay, [c. 1643], BN, Fonds français, 18593, f.392. This situation, with different traders competing for furs, was shrewdly exploited by the Indians. As the deputy governor of Maine, Thomas Gorges, remarked in 1642, 'the Indians [were] understanding the valew of things as well as the Inglish.' Thomas Gorges to his cousin Lutrell, 19 May 1642, in Moody, ed., *Gorges letters*, no. 50. See also Harold F. McGee, Jr, 'Ethnic boundaries and strategies of ethnic interaction: a history of Micmac-white relations in Nova Scotia' (PH D thesis, Southern Illinois University 1974), 51–2.

67 Sybil Noyes *et al.*, *Genealogical dictionary of Maine and New Hampshire* (Portland 1928–39), 9; MA, 3, ff.194–205, 246–7.

68 Thomas Jenner to John Winthrop, [28 Mar. 1646]. *Winthrop papers* (Massachusetts Historical Society *Collections*, 4th ser., VI-VII, 5th ser., I, Boston 1863–71), VII: 358. The actual date on this letter is 28 March 1645; that this is an error, easily made just after the start of the new year according to the English calendar, is established both by the contents and by the fact that the letter was endorsed by Winthrop as having been received on 10 Apr. 1646.

69 Charles I to Sir Ferdinando Gorges, 5 Jan. 1635, Rogers, *Stirling's register* II: 818.

70 Minutes of the Council for New England, 29 Jan. and 3 Feb. 1635, PRO, CO1/6, no. 29, pp.18–22.

71 Charles I to Sir James Balfour, 28 Jan. 1635, Rogers, *Stirling's register* II: 829–30; Sir Ferdinando Gorges to Sir Francis Windebank, 21 Mar. 1635, PRO, CO1/8, no. 52; Grant of the Council for New England, 22 Apr. 1635, PRO, CO1/8, no. 56.

72 Procuratory of resignation by William Earl of Stirling, 31 Dec. 1636, SRO, GD17/501. The closest approximation to a commision for Gorges as governor was a royal manifesto of 22 July 1637, which confirmed the intention of establishing Gorges in office, but did not detail the territory involved. PRO, CO1/9, no. 60.

73 Minutes of the Council for New England, 26 Nov. 1635 and 1 Nov. 1638, PRO, CO1/6, no. 29, pp.37–9; Stirling to Sir Francis Windebank 1 Apr. 1639, PRO, SP16/418, no. 72. Stirling also came to an agreement in 1637 with George Cleeve, an inhabitant of Maine who was later to be deeply involved in the political history of that province, for Cleeve to plant a colony on Long Island, which had formed part of Stirling's grant of 1635 from the Council for New England. Nothing apparently came of this. Grant of the Council for New England, 22 Apr. 1635, PRO, CO1/8, no. 56; *Winthrop's journal* I: 224–5.

74 John Winthrop, Jr, to Lord Forbes, 23 Dec. 1644, *Winthrop papers* VI: 518–19. This sudden interest in New Scotland may well have been stimulated by La Tour in his efforts to gain Massachusetts support in his struggle with d'Aulnay. Certainly in the following year La Tour was representing himself as 'lord of La Tour in fraunce

and Knight Barronet of Scotland' in a deed mortgaging his lands to Edward Gibbons. Indenture LaTour-Gibbons, 13 May 1645, *Suffolk deeds* I: 10. On the younger Winthrop's association with Gibbons and Hawkins, see Edward Winslow to William Bradford and others, 31 Aug. 1644. Massachusetts Historical Society *Proceedings*, ser. I, XVI (1878): 111.

75 'Lieutenant-general in the country of Acadia, Fort Louis, Port de la Tour, and all places thereupon depending in New France.' 'In the said territory of New France are several countries and provinces in which it is necessary to have a commander and lieutenant-general on his Majesty's behalf; as, among others, in the case of the coast of Acadia and its dependent places.' (Author's translations.) Couillard-Després, *La Tour*, 191–3. An original copy of the commission is in the archival collections of the Massachusetts Historical Society.

76 De Vic and Augier to Dorchester, 30 Mar. 1631, PRO, SP78/88, ff.248–50.

77 Concession to commander de Razilly, 19 May 1632, AC, C^{IID}, I, f.52. No actual commission for this appointment is extant. See also Le Blant, 'Compagnie de la Nouvelle-France et la restitution,' 82–3.

78 See Ibid., 86, 91–3. Early copies of La Tour's grants from the company are filed in ACM, B, La Rochelle, B5598 and B5654.

79 'That there will be a good understanding between yourself and the Sieur de la Tour.' 'You shall be my lieutenant-general on the coast of the Etchemins, from the mid-point of the mainland of the Baie françoise around towards the Virginias, and governor of Pentagouet.' 'My lieutenant-general on the coast of Acadia ... from the mid-point of the mainland of the Baie françoise to the strait of Canso.' (Author's translations.) Louis XIII to d'Aulnay, 10 Feb. 1638, AC, C^{IID}, I, f.63.

80 Decree of the Conseil privé, I Feb. 1641, CÉA, Fonds René Baudry, 20.8–12. 'You will make use of all the means and all the forces at your command, and will put the forts which are in his [La Tour's] hands into those of loyal persons" (author's translation); Louis XIII to d'Aulnay, 13 Feb. 1641, AC, C^{IID}, I, f.67. Provisions for the charge and command of Fort Louis, 24 Feb. 1641, quoted in Massignon, 'Seigneurie de Menou d'Aulnay,' 475–6.

81 See Preston, *Gorges*, 291–3.

82 Commission of William Laud *et al.*, 28 Apr. 1634, PRO, CO1/8, no. 12. For further discussion of this measure, see Preston, *Gorges*, 295–7; and Charles McLean Andrews, *British committees, commissions, and councils of trade and plantations, 1622–1675* (Baltimore 1908), 16–17.

83 Declaration of the Council for New England, 25 Apr. 1635, PRO, CO1/8, no. 58.

84 Royal manifesto, 23 July 1637, PRO, CO1/9, no. 60.

85 See the Maine charter, in *Documentary history of Maine* VII: 223–43.

86 Ibid., 225–6; see also Preston, *Gorges*, 321–7.

87 See Gaillard Thomas Lapsley, *The county palatine of Durham: a study in constitutional history* (New York 1900), 12–13, 259–63; also Geoffrey Barraclough, *The earldom and county palatine of Chester* (Oxford 1953), 8, 25–6.

88 The nature of the La Tour-d'Aulnay conflict is discussed in greater detail in chapter 4.

89 Anne of Austria to d'Aulnay, 27 Sept. 1645, AC, C^{11D}, 1, f.76; Louis XIV to d'Aulnay, 28 Sept. 1645, Ibid., f.77.

90 'Our governor and lieutenant general, representing our person, in the entire country, territory, coast and confines of Acadia' (AC, E, dossier 12, author's translation). See also Baudry, 'Charles d'Aulnay,' 230–2; and Trudel, *Beginnings*, 201–3

91 See Robert Le Blant, 'Les compagnies du Cap-Breton, 1629–1647,' *Revue d'histoire de l'Amérique française* 16 (1962–3): 92–3; also Baudry, 'Charles d'Aulnay,' 232–3.

92 See Gorges, 'Brief narration,' 54–7.

93 The internal conflicts in Maine are discussed in chapter 4.

94 Confirmation of the government of Acadia to La Tour, 27 Feb. 1651, AC, C^{11D}, 1, ff.82–3.

CHAPTER 3

1 Brereton, 'A brief and true relation,' in Levermore, *Forerunners and competitors*, 37–8.

2 'Who was bartering for furs with the savages, contrary to the King's inhibition' (Lescarbot, *New France* II: 500–1; translation, 229).

3 Anonymous relation, in Thayer, *Sagadahoc*, 57–8.

4 Levett, 'A voyage into New England,' in Levermore, *Forerunners and competitors*, 623.

5 'New Scotland,' National Library of Scotland, MS 2061, f.149.

6 'We shot off over their heads two small cannon ... [and then] shot off two fire-lances which scattered among them and frightened them so much that they began to paddle off in very great haste, and did not follow us any more,' (Biggar, *Voyages of Cartier*, 50–1).

7 'One must be on one's guard against these people and mistrust them, yet without allowing them to perceive it' (Biggar, *Works of Champlain* I: 353–7; translation, 357). William Strachey, 'History of travaile into Virginia,' in Thayer, *Sagadahoc*, 77–80.

8 Lescarbot, *New France* II: 557; see also Jaenen, 'Amerindian views of French culture,' 265–6; and Jennings, *Invasion of America*, 87–8.

9 This summary of the effects of disease and acculturation is largely based on Bailey, *Conflict of cultures*, chaps 5–8; T.J. Brasser, 'Early Indian-European contacts,' *HNAI* 15: 78–88; Robert Conkling, 'Legitimacy and conversion in social change: the case of French missionaries and the northeastern Algonkian, '*Ethnohistory* 21 (1974) 12–14; Jaenen, *Friend and foe*, chap. 3; Jennings, *Invasion of America*,

87–8; Martin, *Keepers of the game*, chap. 2; Virginia Miller, 'Aboriginal Micmac population: a review of the evidence,' *Ethnohistory* 23 (1976): 117–27; Upton, *Micmacs and colonists*, 20.

10 Jaenen, 'Amerindian views of French culture,' 267; Edwin Ernest Rich, 'Trade habits and economic motivation among the Indians of North America,' *Canadian Journal of Economics and Political Science* 26 (1960): 45–7.

11 On early European concepts of the Indian, see Robert F. Berkhofer, Jr, *The white man's Indian: images of the American Indian from Columbus to the present* (New York 1978), 3–22, 115–20; Olive P. Dickason, 'The concept of *l'homme sauvage* and early French colonialism in the Americas,' *Revue française d' histoire d' outre-mer* 64 (1977): 5–30; Cornelius J. Jaenen, 'Concepts of America, Amerindians, and acculturation,' in Cowan, *Papers of the ninth Algonquian conference*, 81–95; Jaenen, *Friend and foe*, chap. 1; Nash, *Red, white, and black*, chap. 2; H.C. Porter, *The inconstant savage: England and the North American Indian, 1500–1660* (London 1979), part 1.

12 See Silvio Zavala, *The defence of human rights in Latin America (sixteenth to eighteenth centuries)* (Paris 1964), 25–33; also Zavala, *New viewpoints on the Spanish colonization of America* (New York 1943), 59–68; and Hanke, *Spanish struggle for justice*, 83–91.

13 Quoted in Zavala, *Human rights in Latin America*, 41. See also Hanke, *Spanish struggle for justice*, passim.

14 'There is no Indian who does not consider himself infinitely more happy and more powerful than the French' (Le Clercq, *New relation*, 347, translation, 106).

15 Hakluyt, *Discourse on western planting*, 71–82. See also Porter, *Inconstant savage*, 153–80; and Gary B. Nash, 'The image of the Indian in the southern colonial mind,' *William and Mary Quarterly* 3rd ser., 29 (1972): 202–3.

16 Quoted in Porter, *Inconstant savage*, 27.

17 Ibid., 25–7; Canny, 'Ideology of English colonization,' 593–5; Nash, 'Image of the Indian,' 203.

18 'The English, under another captain, changed their tactics. They drove the Savages away without ceremony; they beat, maltreated and misused them outrageously and without restraint.' (*Jesuit relations* II: 44–6; translation, 45.) The Indian account erroneously attributes these events to the years 1608–9, rather than to 1607–8, but the events are clearly the same. For further discussion of the influence of the Spanish example on English colonization, see Edmund S. Morgan, 'The labor problem at Jamestown, 1607–18,' *American Historical Review* 76 (1971): 597–600.

19 Biard, *Relation*, 179–80. '[They] recounted the outrages that they had experienced from these English; and they flattered us, saying that they loved us very much ...' (*Jesuit relations* III: 223).

20 [Gorges], 'Brief relation,' in Burrage, *Gorges*, 144; see also Alden T. Vaughan, *The New England frontier: Puritans and Indians, 1620–1675* (Boston 1965),

15–16. On Hudson's visit, see Samuel Purchas, *Hakluytus posthumus, or Purchas his pilgrimes* (20 vols, Glasgow 1905–7), XIII: 347–8.

21 Gorges, 'Brief narration,' 62.

22 See Thomas Dermer to Thomas Purchas, 27 Dec. 1619, Burrage, *Gorges*, 129.

23 Gorges, 'Brief narration,' 62; *Documentary history of Maine* VII: 23–4.

24 The term 'organized' is here used to signify social organization, rather than to imply any political confederation. The existence of such a political organization has been postulated but remains unproven. See the opposite treatments in Morrison, 'Dawnland decisions,' 10–11, 23–7; and Morrison, 'People of the Dawn,' 40–3. On population size, it is virtually impossible to arrive at precise figures for the Abenaki, or for Micmac and Malecite, for either aboriginal times or the early seventeenth century. Estimates have varied widely. Lucien Campeau has suggested 7,300 as a total pre-contact figure for the area from southern Maine to the Gaspé, which contrasts with a recent estimate of 35,000 for the Micmac alone. Campeau, *Première mission*, introduction, 111; Miller, 'Aboriginal Micmac population,' 117–27. For the Abenaki immediately before the epidemic of 1616–20, Kenneth Morrison cites Biard's estimate of a population of 3,000. Morrison, 'People of the Dawn,' 3; Biard, *Relation*, 73. Biard further estimated a population of 3,000 to 3,500 for the Micmac at the time of his visit, and 2,500 for 'les Etéminquois jusques à Pentégoet.'

25 Levett, 'A voyage to New England,' Levermore, *Forerunners and competitors*, 618, 624; see also Morrison, 'People of the Dawn,' 77–8.

26 Bradford, *Plymouth*, 79–80; Deed, 15 July 1625, Maine Historical Society *Collections* V (1857): 191–2. Though see also the questions raised regarding this deed in Jennings, *Invasion of America*, 134n, and in Edwin A. Churchill, introduction to Helen B. Camp, *Archaeological excavations at Pemaquid, Maine, 1965–1974* (Augusta, Me. 1975), ix.

27 See Karen Ordahl Kupperman, 'English perceptions of treachery, 1583–1640: the case of the American "savages",' *Historical Journal*, 20 (1977): 263–87; Jennings, *Invasion of America*, 76–81; Nash, 'Image of the Indian,' 217–20; Porter, *Inconstant savage*, 459–83.

28 Levett, 'A voyage to New England,' in Levermore, *Forerunners and competitors*, 627.

29 See Carroll, *Puritanism and the wilderness*, 8–16, 137–9; Jennings, *Invasion of America*, 82–3; Porter, *Inconstant savage*, 91–115.

30 Quoted in Vaughan, *New England frontier*, 110–111.

31 Massachusetts, *Records of the governor and company of the Massachusetts Bay in New England*, ed. Nathaniel Bradstreet Shurtleff (6 vols, Boston 1853–4; hereafter *MCR*), I: 394; *Province and court records of Maine*, ed. Charles Thornton Libby *et al.* (6 vols, Portland 1928–75; hereafter *PCR*), I: 205.

32 *MCR* I: 112; *PCR* I: 205.

33 For further discussion of this point, see Morrison, 'Dawnland decisions,' 105–7;

see also the general treatments in Jennings, *Invasion of America*, 128–45; Wilcomb E. Washburn, 'The moral and legal justifications for dispossessing the Indians,' in James Morton Smith, ed., *Seventeenth century America: essays in colonial history* (Chapel Hill, N.C. 1959), 15–32; and Washburn, 'Seventeenth-century Indian wars,' *HNAI* 15: 94–5, 98–9.

34 Levett, 'A voyage to New England,' in Levermore, *Forerunners and competitors*, 619. See also the general comments on the implications of colonists' land hunger in Berkhofer, *White man's Indian*, 129, and Nash, 'Image of the Indian,' 220–1.

35 *Winthrop's journal* I: 69, 98.

36 Winter to Trelawny, 18 June 1634, *Documentary history of Maine* III: 28.

37 Hawkins to Trelawny, 28 June 1636, Ibid., 96; Winter to Trelawny, 28 June 1636, Ibid., 90.

38 *PCR* I: 2; on Thomas Wise, see *Documentary history of Maine* III: 209 n3.

39 *PCR* I: 3.

40 Thomas Gorges to Sir Ferdinando Gorges, 19 Sept. 1642, Moody, *Gorges letters*, no. 64.

41 Robert Trelawny to Sir Ferdinando Gorges, 1637, *Documentary history of Maine* III: 102. Trelawny also accused George Cleeve, a rival colonist, of encouraging the Indians in their hostility, though this charge seems to have rested on uncertain evidence. Ibid., 122 n5.

42 Thomas Gorges to Sir Ferdinando Gorges, 19 Sept. 1642, Moody, *Gorges letters*, no. 64.

43 *MCR* IV (i): 165.

44 The existence of an overall military alliance among the Abenaki to resist the English has been debated, as has the existence of a political confederation, but without conclusive results; see n24 above. For more general discussion of English fears of a conspiracy, Washburn, 'Seventeenth-century Indian wars,' *HNAI* 15: 93. On the lack of evidence on English-Abenaki relations at this period, see also Morrison, 'People of the Dawn,' 121–2. Because of lack of evidence, no confident statement can be made on the role of the small number of Penacooks who comprised the bands on the Agamenticus and Piscataqua rivers. It is clear that the Penacook were particularly hard hit by epidemics of European disease, and this may help to explain the more active role of the Abenaki in Indian-English relations in southern Maine. See Salwen, 'Indians of southern New England and Long Island,' *HNAI* 15: 168–70.

45 William Hubbard, *The history of the Indian wars in New England from the first settlement to the termination of the war with King Philip, in 1677*, ed. Samuel G. Drake (2 vols, Roxbury, Mass. 1865), II: 263–4.

46 Ibid.

47 On pre-contact Abenaki warfare, see Morrison, 'People of the Dawn,' 42–3; on the Micmac, see Hoffman, 'Ethnography of the Micmac,' 608–67, and Upton, *Micmacs and colonists*, 9–10.

48 The concepts of 'non-directed' and 'directed' acculturation, developed by Ralph Linton and more recently elaborated by Edward M. Larrabee, have often been used to distinguish between culture change which was unconsciously produced by interactions between Europeans and native peoples, and that which was deliberately induced by colonizers. See Ralph Linton, ed., *Acculturation in seven American Indian tribes* (Gloucester, Mass. 1963, first published 1940), 501–20; Edward M. Larrabee, 'Recurrent themes and sequences in North American Indian-European contact,' *American Philosophical Society, Transactions* new ser., 66, pt 7 (1976): 3–52. Useful as these concepts are, I have not explicitly made use of them in this study on the simple ground that in the northeastern maritime region in the seventeenth century the relationship of 'dominance and submission,' which is a prerequisite for directed acculturation, did not exist. The acculturation which undoubtedly did take place was non-directed.

49 On these later English-Abenaki wars, see chap. 8 below. The issue of land is especially stressed as a cause of war in a contemporary account quoted by Cotton Mather, *Magnalia Christi Americana, or the ecclesiastical history of New England* ... (London 1702; 2 vols, New York 1852), II: 584.

50 Biggar, *Works of Champlain* I: 272; for an extended treatment of Champlain's perceptions of native people, see Bruce G. Trigger, 'Champlain judged by his Indian policy: a different view of early Canadian history,' *Anthropologica* 13 (1971): 85–114.

51 Lescarbot, *New France* II: 564.

52 Documentation of this incident is in ACM, B5654, nos. 147–70; see especially no. 150. See also René Baudry, 'Nicolas Le Creux Du Breuil,' *DCB* I: 442; and George MacBeath, 'Jean Thomas,' *DCB* I: 642.

53 Abraham Shurt to John Winthrop, 28 June 1636, *Winthrop papers* VI: 570–1; Memorandum of d'Aulnay, [c. 1643], BN, Fonds français, 18593, f.377.

54 Thomas Gardner to John Leverett, 22 Sept. 1675, in *Documentary history of Maine* VI: 91–3; see also chap. 8 below. On Shurt and fur-trading activities at and near Pemaquid, see Burrage, *Beginnings*, 179–80; Moloney *Fur trade in New England*, 32–40; Noyes *et al.*, *Genealogical dictionary*, 632–3.

55 *Documentary history of Maine* VII: 43; Bourinot, 'Builders of Nova Scotia,' 104–5; Articles granted to the company, 29 Apr. 1627, AC, C^{11A}, 1, f.79. 'To endeavour, with God's help, to bring the peoples who inhabit these lands to a knowledge of God, to establish order among them, and to have them instructed in the Catholic, Apostolic, and Roman faith and religion' (author's translation).

56 The religious function of French colonization was stressed even in an account of Razilly's departure which was written largely for secular readers: 'l'embarquement de force noblesse y a rendu illustre ce commencement de Colonie qui va faire ce passage si facile à tous les François zelateurs de leur Religion, de l'honneur de leur nation et de leur repos, qu'il leur fera desormais aisé de seconder les sainctes intentions du Roy, que les grandes affaires de son Royaume n'empeschent pas de

porter au de là des mers les pensées qu'il a de servir à l'augmentation de la foy Catholique.' *Gazette Renaudot*, 1632, 282–3. 'The embarkation there of such a noble company made illustrious this commencement of a colony which will make the crossing so easy for all Frenchmen who are zealous for their religion, the honour of their nation and their own [spiritual] repose, in that it will make it easy for them in the future to support the sacred intentions of the King that the great affairs of his realm should not prevent the spreading beyond the seas of his desire to assist in the growth of the Catholic faith' (author's translation). On the religious responsibilities of the company, see also Campeau, *Finances publiques*, 9–10; and Jaenen, *Friend and foe*, 155–6.

57 See Zavala, *Human rights in Latin America*, 37–42; see also Hanke, *Spanish struggle for justice*, 111–32.

58 Gorges, 'Brief narration,' 17; [Gorges], 'Brief relation,' in Burrage, *Gorges*, 139–40.

59 Gorges, 'Brief narration,' 42.

60 Thomas Gorges to Henry Gorges, 19 July 1640, Moody, *Gorges letters*, no. 1.

61 Robert Blair to Robert Boyd, 27 May 1622, in Robert Wodrow, ed., *Collections upon the lives of the reformers and most eminent ministers of the Church of Scotland* (2 vols, Glasgow 1834–45), II: 170. Welsh apparently died before he could embark.

62 See, for example, Richard Gibson to Robert Trelawny, 8 July 1639, *Documentary history of Maine* III: 159–61.

63 See Vaughan, *New England frontier*, chap. 9. The English colonists' assertion that the Jesuit missionaries claimed 'to convert the red man merely by sprinkling him with water and gaining his permission to raise a cross in the native village,' in contrast to the more 'rigorous intellectual and moral challenge' and 'conversion experience' required by the Puritan, thus explaining the lesser rate of conversions in New England, is certainly not borne out by the writings of Biard. See Biard, *Relation*, chap 10. Furthermore, it has recently been suggested that any interest in Indian conversion in Massachusetts was largely stimulated and governed by pragmatic political considerations. Jennings, *Invasion of America*, chap. 14.

64 Statement of the Capuchins, 20 Oct. 1643, AC, C^{11D}, I, f.70; Letter of Father Ignace de Paris, 1656, in PAC *Report for the year 1904* (Ottawa 1905), 333–41; Trudel, *Beginnings*, 196, 199–201.

65 See Henri-Raymond Casgrain, *Les Sulpiciens et les prêtres des Missions-Étrangères en Acadie (1676–1762)* (Quebec 1897), 135–8; and Noel Baillargeon, *Le Séminaire de Québec sous l'épiscopat de Monseigneur de Laval* (Quebec 1972), 229–39.

66 See Zavala, *Human rights in Latin America*, 43–4; Hanke, *Spanish struggle for justice*, 167.

67 Biard, *Relation*, 66–7.

68 See Bailey, *Conflict of cultures*, 132, 145–6; Conkling, 'Legitimacy and conversion,' 12–16; Jaenen, 'Amerindian views of French culture,' 273–6; and Jaenen, *Friend and foe*, 60–6.

69 Bailey, *Conflict of cultures*, 131–6; Jaenen, *Friend and foe*, 70; Upton, *Micmacs and colonists*, 20–3. See also the observations in Washburn, *Indian in America*, 125.

70 Biard, *Relation*, 93 'All their religion, to speak briefly, is nothing else than the tricks and charms of the Autmoins ... ' *Jesuit relations* III: 131).

71 Biard, *Relation*, 335; Bede, *Ecclesiastical history of the English people*, ed. Bertram Colgrave and R.A.B. Mynors (Oxford 1969), 106–9.

72 'It is well to treat the Indians with consideration, and sometimes to delay instructing them until they have removed the obstacle which is opposed to their conversion' (Le Clercq, *New relation*, 396; translation, 221).

73 '[They] believe that in all their maladies there is, in the part afflicted, a Devil, or germ, which these barbarians, whom we call jugglers, have the power to make come out, and they believe that these jugglers can restore health to the sick' (Ibid., 393; translation, 216).

74 *Jesuit relations* II: 18; see also Biard, *Relation*, 312–20.

75 'That there was nothing more precious than the Cross, since it had preserved her from an infinity of dangers, had procured her all kinds of consolations in her misfortunes, and that, in a word, life would appear to her altogether without interest if she had to live without the Cross' (Le Clercq, *New relation*, 366; translation, 151).

76 *Jesuit relations* XXVIII: 34.

77 Bede, *Ecclesiastical history*, 183. See Conkling, 'Legitimacy and conversion,' 13–16; and Morrison, 'People of the Dawn' 97, 411–12; on the shaman-missionary relationship and the 'amalgam' of belief systems which resulted, see Bailey, *Conflict of cultures*, 145–7; and Martin, *Keepers of the game*, 57–60.

78 'The number is very small of those who live according to the rules of Christianity, and who do not fall back into the irregularities of a brutal and wild life ... Hence it comes about that although several missionaries have laboured greatly for the conversion of these pagans, nevertheless one never observes there, any more than among the other Indian nations of New France, any solidly established Christianity' (Le Clercq' *New relation*, 383; translation, 193).

79 *Jesuit relations* I: 274–5.

80 See Jaenen, 'Amerindian views of French culture,' 267.

81 'It is true [he said] that thou hast always scorned them. The little value thou hast placed upon them, whilst the French seek them with so much eagerness, has long made us know that thou desirest nothing in the world but the salvation of our souls ... ' (Le Clercq, *New relation*, 434; translation 310).

82 'In course of time we hoped to pacify them, and to put an end to the wars which they

wage against one another, in order that in the future we might derive service from them, and convert them to the Christian faith' (Biggar, *Works of Champlain* I: 272).

83 '[As for those] who are nomadic and divided, they must be made sedentary by the cultivation of the land, thus obliging them to stay in one place' (*Jesuit relations* I 86–90; translation, 87).

84 'Two families of Christian Savages, composed of sixteen persons, were during last year settled in this place ... a third, more numerous, came to find us at the beginning of September, on purpose to enjoy the same blessing; and some others have promised to follow this one as soon as possible' (*Jesuit Relations* XXX, 126; translation, 127). Biard, *Relation*, 98–9.

85 'The wandering and vagabond life of these peoples ... [is] unquestionably one of the chief obstacles to their conversion ... ' (Le Clercq, *New relation*, 388–9; translation, 205). Donation of land by Richard Denys, 13 Aug. 1685, AC. C^{IID}, I, ff.188–91; Baillargeon, *Séminaire de Québec*, 231–9; William Francis Ganong, 'Richard Denys, Sieur de Fronsac, and his settlements in northern New Brunswick,' New Brunswick Historical Society *Collections* VII (1907): 28–9.

86 Morrison, 'People of the Dawn,' 116.

87 Ibid., 108–14; Bailey, *Conflict of cultures*, 130–1; *Jesuit relations* LXII: 258–67.

88 In the course of time, the construction of dikes by the Acadians might well have had a detrimental effect upon the Micmac fishery, but this was certainly not evident to contemporaries. See McGee, 'Micmac Indians,' 25.

89 Report of François-Marie Perrot, 9 Aug. 1686, AC, C^{IID}, 2, f.20.

90 See Bailey, *Conflict of cultures*, 112–13; Clark, *Acadia*, 128–9; Conkling, 'Legitimacy and conversion,' 7; Clarence J. d'Entremont, 'Claude Petitpas,' *DCB* II: 524; Naomi E.S. Griffiths, 'The Acadians,' in *DCB* IV:xvii–xviii.

91 *Jesuit relations* XXXVII: 76. 'I was sent to the countries of the Abnaquiois and of the English, who are their neighbors, to ask them for assistance against the Iroquois. I obeyed those who sent me, but my journey was in vain. The Englishman replies not; he has no good thoughts for us. This grieves me much; we see ourselves dying and being exterminated every day' (ibid., 77).

92 *Jesuit relations* XXXVI: 84, 90. '[He has] a special zeal for the Conversion of the Savages ... ' (ibid., 85). 'The minister, named Master heliot, who was teaching some savages, received me at his house, because night was overtaking me; he treated me with respect and kindness, and begged me to spend the winter with him' (ibid., 91).

CHAPTER 4

1 The coast between the Piscataqua and Ste Croix rivers was also within the bounds of New Netherland, as granted in 1614. See Condon, *New York beginnings*, 23.

2 William Maxwell to Sir John Maxwell, 23 Nov. 1628, in Fraser, *Maxwells of Pollok* II: 199–200. The possibility that the Kirkes had been responsible for the destruction of Port Lomeron has been mentioned on p. 213 above. That they may have continued a small presence there, at the same time as the Alexander colony was in operation at Port Royal, is a further possibility. Certainly the instructions given to Razilly in 1632 spoke of both 'Anglois et Escossois' on the coast of Acadia, though this may have referred to the English on the disputed coast of New England. Convention with the Sieur de Razily, 27 Mar. 1632, AC, C^{11D}, ff.47–8. There is also the report of 14 Aug. 1632 in the *Gazette Renaudot*, discussed on p. 213 above. However, if there was an English presence connected with the Kirkes, it was a small concern. In a later representation to the English crown, the Kirkes claimed no more than to have assisted Alexander in his settlement of New Scotland and to have had possession only of the area on the north bank of the St Lawrence. Representation of Sir Lewis Kirke and John Kirke concerning Acadia or Nova Scotia, [1662], PRO, CO1/16, no. 1.

3 Remembrances concerning the patent granted to Sir William Alexander, George Kirk Esquire, Captain Kirke, William Barkley and Company, [c. 1632], BL, Egerton MSS, 2395, f.25. The patent referred to in the title of this document was that of the English and Scottish Company, from which the Alexanders were now attempting to free themselves: hence the appearance of the name of Sir William Alexander the younger. Alexander's name was, of course, conspicuously absent from the petitions of the Kirkes and Berkeley on this matter. See, for example, Petition of George Kirk, David Kirk, William Barkley, Joshua Gallard, and others, [1633], in HMC, *Cowper MSS* II: 42. The Kirkes continued for many years to press their claims, even though transferring their main activities to Newfoundland. See, for example, Sir David Kirke, William Berkeley, and John Kirke to Sir John Coke, 22 Jan. 1636, PRO, CO1/9, no. 1. See also Moir, 'Sir David Kirke,' *DCB* I: 404–7. Nor did the Kirkes entirely give up their trading interests in the northeastern maritime region. In 1646, they were closely associated with La Tour (following the latter's defeat by d'Aulnay) in a proposal for a trading venture on the Atlantic coast of Acadia 'between the Capes of Sable and Britton,' while they may also have traded with Nicholas Shapleigh of Kittery, Maine. Indenture between La Tour and Sir David Kirke, 14 Jan. 1646, *Suffolk deeds* I: 75–6; *Winthrop's journal* II: 275. On the Shapleigh connection, see Invoyce of goods shipped aboard the David, 8 Sept. 1648, *Documentary history of Maine* VI: 2–4. This last document must be treated with caution, however, as there is no definite indication that the Nicholas Shapleigh referred to is the Maine Shapleigh rather than a man of the same name who resided at Charlestown, Massachusetts.

4 See Malapart, *La prise d'un seigneur escossois*, 3–5, 13–14. 'In this account will be remarked the securing of the fishery for our French fishermen, the destruction of heresy as soon as it had appeared, the establishment of the holy faith of the Roman

Church, and the toppling of a petty tyrant as shamefully as he himself had unjustly unsurped this new country and wickedly treated our French subjects' (author's translation).

5 Lord Ewchiltree's information, [1630], PRO, CO1/5, no. 47.

6 Although Daniel's enterprise met difficulties through illness and internal conflict, he retained an interest in the area for some years thereafter. See Le Blant, 'Compagnies du Cap-Breton,' 81–5.

7 'That the Scotch were not disposed to leave Port Royal, but were making themselves more at home there from day to day; and had brought in some families and cattle, with the intention of peopling this place, which does not belong to them except by their illegal seizure of it ... ' (Bigger, Works of Champlain VI: 199).

8 Report of Jean-Daniel Chaline, 1 Nov. 1632, ACM, B, La Rochelle, B5654, no.21; report of Estienne de Mourron, 15 Mar. 1633, ibid., no.22. These two reports are not in harmony in every detail, but the outline of the episode is clear enough. See also George MacBeath, 'Andrew Forrester,' DCB I: 310–11.

9 Winthrop's journal I: 97–8, 146, 201.

10 See map in Alexander, Encouragement; also Jarvis M. Morse, 'Captain John Smith, Marc Lescarbot, and the division of land by the Council for New England, in 1623,' New England Quarterly 8 (1935): 399–404.

11 Documentary History of Maine VII: 112–13. See also Bradford, Plymouth, 200–2; Burrage, Beginnings, 185–8; and Preston, Gorges, 450–3.

12 Those English who did settle northeast of the Kennebec – and in places such as the Sheepscott plantations the numbers were considerable – faced danger and harassment because of this dispute between English and French. In 1671 a report reached Quebec that they would be willing to accept French rule if stability could be thus assured. See Jean Talon to Jean-Baptiste Colbert, 11 Nov. 1671, AC, C^{11A}, 3, ff. 187–8. As a parallel to the pragmatism of the Acadians in their response to English rule, this is further discussed in chap. 7. The exact size and nature of the English settlements in this area will be established only when archaeological evidence is brought to light. See Robert L. Bradley, Maine's first buildings: the architecture of settlement, 1604–1700 (Augusta, Me. 1978), 15.

13 This paragraph is largely based on Bradford, Plymouth, 178, 184–6, 193, 197, 202, 219–20, 232–3, 244, 386. For the Muscongus patent, see Documentary history of Maine VII: 125–8. On Vines' involvement and his patent, see Winthrop's journal II: 128–30; and Documentary history of Maine VII: 121–5.

14 Bradford, Plymouth, 244–5, 262–8. See also Bailyn, New England merchants, 23–6; Gordon E. Kershaw, 'Gentlemen of large property and judicious men': the Kennebeck proprietors, 1749–1775 (Somersworth, N.H. 1975), 7–10; Moloney, Fur trade in New England, 28–9.

15 Bradford, Plymouth, 246. Bradford includes this incident under the year 1631, but the facts that Winthrop more definitely dates it in the following year and that

Bradford's account was a later insertion into his manuscript suggest that 1632 was the true date. *Winthrop's journal* I: 82.

16 Bradford, *Plymouth*, 245. Many years later, in 1643, La Tour would avow that his intention had been to invite the English to leave Machias peacefully, and that the killing of the two men had been an accident. This, however, was in the context of his efforts to secure Massachusetts' assistance in his conflict with d'Aulnay. See *Winthrop's journal* II: 128–30.

17 *Winthrop's journal* I: 145–6.

18 Bradford, *Plymouth*, 245.

19 Ibid., 275–6.

20 Ibid., 277–9; *Winthrop's journal* I: 159.

21 Thomas Cammock to Robert Trelawny, 23 July 1632, *Documentary history of Maine* III: 19.

22 G.B., PRO, *Calendar of state papers, 1574–1660*, 170–1.

23 Edward Trelawny to Robert Trelawny, 10 Jan. 1636, *Documentary history of Maine* III: 78.

24 Winter to Trelawny, 23 June 1636, Ibid., 86. See also the anonymous contemporary account of New England which described the French in Acadia as 'justlie seated to prove ill neighbours' to northern New England. Charles Edward Banks, ed., 'Relation concerning the estate of New-England, about 1634,' *New England Historical and Genealogical Register* 40 (1886): 70.

25 See also Douglas Edward Leach, *Arms for empire* (New York 1973); 48–9.

26 *Winthrop's journal* I: 157, 163.

27 Ibid., 159; extract from letter to Sir Henry Vane, 28 July 1636, PRO, CO1/9, no. 19. The writer was probably Vane's son, the younger Henry Vane, as is suggested in G.B., PRO, *Calendar of state papers, 1574–1660*, 239.

28 Bradford, *Plymouth*, 279; on Shurt's activities, see *Winthrop's journal* II: 180.

29 Rogers, *Stirling's register* II: 527–8.

30 Petition of William Claiborne, March 1677, enclosing copy of commission, 16 May 1631, PRO, CO1/39, nos. 44, 44 (vi); for details of Claiborne's colonial career, see Nathaniel C. Hale, *Virginia venturer: a historical biography of William Claiborne, 1600–1677* (Richmond, Va. 1951), especially 137–47.

31 Trudel, *Beginnings*, chaps 14 and 16; Campeau, *Finances publiques*, chap. 2.

32 'The Savages, who alone journey over these lands or sail in their little gondolas upon these Rivers, occasionally bring us news of these more distant settlements' (*Jesuit relations* IX: 134; translation, 135.)

33 *Documentary history of Maine* VII: 88.

34 *MCR* I: 342.

35 *Winthrop's Journal* II: 267.

36 Ibid., I: 100–1, 104–5.

37 See chap. 2.

38 John Noble, ed., *Records of the Court of Assistants of the colony of the Massachusetts Bay, 1630–1692* (3 vols, Boston 1901–28), II: 28, 61–2; *Winthrop's journal* II: 266–7.

39 Thomas Gorges to John Winthrop, 23 Feb. 1641, *Winthrop papers* VII: 334.

40 Richard Vines to John Winthrop, 25 Jan. 1641, Ibid., 340–1; Thomas Jenner to John Winthrop, 4 Feb. 1641, Ibid., 355. For a further example of the recruitment of a minister from Massachusetts by a Maine community, the calling of Thomas Rashleigh to Agamenticus, see Inhabitants of Accomenticus to the church in Boston, 28 Aug. 1641, Moody, *Gorges letters*, no. 22.

41 *Winthrop's journal* I: 69, 95, 98, 101–2.

42 Thomas Gorges to John Winthrop, 28 June 1643, in Thomas Hutchinson, ed., *Collection of original papers relative to the history of the colony of Massachusetts Bay* (Boston 1769), 114; see also a letter written a few days later in similar vein, Thomas Gorges to Sir Ferdinando Gorges, 7 July 1643, Moody, *Gorges letters*, no. 77.

43 Edward Howes to John Winthrop, Jr, 28 Nov. 1632, *Winthrop papers* VI: 485.

44 Noble, *Records of the Court of Assistants* II: 55; on Wannerton's later death, see Burrage, *Beginnings*, 275.

45 Thomas Gorges to Joseph Godwin, [19 July] 1640, Moody, *Gorges letters*, no. 2; Hugh Peter to John Winthrop, [c. 1640], *Winthrop papers* VI: 106. The strong aspirations of the nascent Maine communities towards stability are further discussed in Edwin A. Churchill, 'The founding of Maine, 1600–1640: a revisionist interpretation,' *Maine Historical Society Quarterly* 18 (1978): 21–54. A close parallel can be drawn with the communities of New Hampshire, which came under the direct influence of Massachusetts earlier, see David Earl Van Deventer, *The emergence of provincial New Hampshire, 1623–1741* (Baltimore 1976), 9–16, 182.

46 Sir Ferdinando Gorges to Sir Henry Vane, John Winthrop, and others, 23 Aug. 1637, *Winthrop papers* VII: 329–31; *Winthrop's journal* I: 224. On the circumstances of the two requests, see Charles Edward Banks, 'The administration of William Gorges, 1636 to 1637,' in Maine Historical Society *Collections* ser. 2, I (1890): 129–31.

47 Gorges to Winthrop, 26 Mar. 1640, *Winthrop papers* VII: 331–2; *Winthrop's journal* II: 8.

48 Gorges and Godfrey to Winthrop, 1 Mar. 1641, *Winthrop papers* VII: 335–6. Further evidence of Gorges's determination to ensure the probity of all immigrants into Maine can be found in his emphasis on the importance of this in a private letter to his father. Thomas Gorges to Henry Gorges, [August 1641], in Moody, *Gorges letters*, no. 25.

49 Edward Godfrey and Basil Parker to John Winthrop and Richard Bellingham, 5 Nov. 1648, appendix to Charles Edward Banks, 'Edward Godfrey: his life, letters,

and public services, 1584–1664,' in Maine Historical Society *Collections* ser. I,
IX (1887): 337–8.

50 See Clark, *Eastern frontier*, 37–47; and Van Deventer, *Provincial New Hampshire*, chap. I.

51 *Winthrop's journal* II: 99. Until finally renamed 'York' in 1652 when Maine was
annexed by Massachusetts, the settlement usually known as 'Agamenticus' in the
earlier period was also referred to by a number of other names. It was occasionally
known as 'Bristol,' though the origin of this is unclear; in 1641, it was chartered as
the city of 'Gorgeana' and designated the seat of government of the Province of
Maine, though still more usually known as 'Agamenticus.' See Charles Edward
Banks, *History of York, Maine* (2 vols; Boston 1931–5), I: 76, 123–6; and
Winthrop's journal II: 8.

52 *Winthrop's journal* II: 267.

53 Thomas Gorges to Sir Ferdinando Gorges, [c. September 1641], in Moody,
Gorges letters, no. 38; Edward Godfrey to John Winthrop, 20 July 1647, *Winthrop
papers* VII: 378–9; Carroll, *Timber economy*, 105–7.

54 Shurt to Winthrop, 28 June 1636, *Winthrop papers* VI; 571; *Winthrop's journal* I:
201.

55 On matters relating to Massachusetts attitudes towards the French, this section has
benefited from the following works: George Alexander Rawlyk, *Nova Scotia's
Massachusetts: a study of Massachusetts-Nova Scotia relations, 1630 to 1784*
(Montreal 1973), chap. I; Wall, *The crucial decade*, 65–73; Ronald Dennis
Cohen, 'New England and New France, 1632–1651: external relations and internal
disagreements among the Puritans,' *Essex Institute Historical Collections* 108
(1972): 252–71; Denis Charles Brian Doherty, 'Oliver Cromwell, Robert Sedgwick, John Leverett, and the Acadian adventure of 1654' (MA thesis, Queen's
University 1969), chap. I; and Buffinton, 'Policy of the northern colonies,' chap.
2. For treatment of Acadia-Massachusetts relations in a comparative diplomatic
context, see Max Savelle with assistance of Margaret Anne Fisher, *The origins of
American diplomacy: the international history of Angloamerica, 1492–1763* (New
York 1967), 173–8.

56 *Winthrop's journal* II: 43.

57 Ibid., 85, 88.

58 Ibid., 43, 85, 88.

59 Ibid., 88.

60 See Rawlyk, *Nova Scotia's Massachusetts*, 10; Wall, *The crucial decade*, 48; and
Cohen, 'New England and New France,' 259–60. In Maine, Thomas Gorges took
a nervous view of the flirtation with La Tour, fearing with justification that
'D'Aulnay will revenge himself on us and our parts.' Thomas Gorges to Sir
Ferdinando Gorges, 7 July 1643, in Moody, *Gorges letters*, no. 77.

61 *Winthrop's journal* II: 106.

62 Ibid., 107. Agreements between La Tour and Edward Gibbons and Thomas Hawkins, 30 June 1643, *Suffolk deeds* I: 7–9.

63 Richard Saltonstall *et al.* to Winthrop, 14 July 1643, in Hutchinson, *Collection of papers*, 115–19. The partnership of Hawkins and Gibbons, and the involvement of the younger Winthrop, have already been mentioned in chap. 2 above.

64 *Winthrop's journal* II: 136–7. See also the accounts of the battle by Capuchin missionaries at Port Royal, AC, C^{IID}, I, f.70; and by the sea captains Estienne de Mouron and Hipollite Bourget who fortuitously and somewhat unwillingly found themselves on opposite sides, in ACM, B, La Rochelle, B5656.

65 *Winthrop's journal* II: 275; Indenture between La Tour and Kirke, 14 Jan. 1646, *Suffolk deeds* I: 75–6; Acknowledgement by La Tour, 19 Jan. 1646, Ibid., 76.

66 'Notwithstanding whatever resistance may be put up by the foreign Protestants who have usurped the lands of Acadia from France, through the negligence or the weakness of the Frenchmen who were my predecessors here' (author's translation). D'Aulnay to Pierre Séguier, chancellor of France, 10 Sept. 1647, BN, Fonds français, 17387, no. 21, f.218.

67 D'Aulnay to governor of Massachusetts, 31 Mar. 1645, MA, 2, ff.486–8.

68 Governor and council of Massachusetts to d'Aulnay, 1644, MA, 2, ff.482–3.

69 D'Aulnay to the magistrates of Massachusetts, 21 Oct. 1644, MA, 2, ff.478–81.

70 La Tour to the Massachusetts General Court, 27 Oct. 1644, MA, 2, ff.484–5; on the Penobscot transaction, see Edward Winslow to William Bradford, Thomas Prence, *et al.*, 31 Aug. 1644, in Massachusetts Historical Society *Proceedings* XVI (1878): 111.

71 For the identity of this envoy, I am indebted to Professor Marcel Trudel.

72 Hutchinson, *Collection of papers*, 146–7; partial translation in *Winthrop's journal* II: 203.

73 D'Aulnay to Winthrop, 3 Nov. 1645, MA, 2, f.491; *Winthrop's journal* II: 284–6; see also Cohen, 'New England and New France,' 266–7.

74 *Winthrop's journal* II: 325–6.

75 'Monsieur de Rasilly was considered a very great Captain, not only among the French and English, but also in the estimation of all the Tribes of his Country' (*Jesuit relations* IX: 134; translation, 135).

76 Ibid XII: 168. For a discussion of the role of the discovery and exploration of America in the invalidation of the term 'Christendom' and in its replacement by the term 'Europe,' see Denys Hay, *The medieval centuries* (London 1964), 163–6.

77 'He visits seven or eight English settlements, at all of which he was received with a cordiality all the more extraordinary since it was little expected' (*Jesuit relations* XXXI: 186; translation, 187).

78 Massachusetts State Archives, Massachusetts Council records, 4 Dec. 1650, n.p.; see also Cohen, 'New England and New France,' 268–9. The General Court in the event took no action on the trade proposal.

79 *Jesuit relations* XXXVI: 108–10.
80 'And likewise the union of hearts and minds between your colonies and ours ...';
'An offensive and defensive alliance with you against the Iroquois' (author's
translations). Council of Quebec to the New England commissioners, 20 June
1651, AC. C^{IID}, 1, ff.84–5. For the identity of Godefroy, I am indebted to
Professor Marcel Trudel.
81 See New Plymouth Colony, *Records of the Colony of Plymouth in New England*,
ed. Nathaniel Bradstreet Shurtleff and David Pulsifer (12 vols, Boston 1855–61),
IX: 202–3.
82 'That the general sentiment of the citizens of boston is, that, if the republic will not
resolve upon this aid against the Irocquois by public authority, private volunteers
are ready for that expedition, upon the mere permission of that request, – just as, by
favor of Monsieur Guebins in behalf of Monsieur latour, some troops went against
the late Monsieur daunay' (*Jesuit relations* XXXVI: 100; translation, 101). New
Plymouth Colony, *Records* IX: 202.
83 '[He] of his own free impulse asks me for a simple certificate of the peace and
friendly understanding between New France and New England, – that he might
proceed to isle percee, about the month of April or May, with thirty tons of indian
corn, besides other commodities' (*Jesuit relations* XXXVI: 96–8; translation, 99).
84 *MCR* IV (i): 146.
85 Burrage, *Beginnings*, 202–4; Noyes *et al.*, *Genealogical dictionary*, 614.
86 Winslow to Bradford, Prence, *et al.*, 31 Aug. 1644, Massachusetts Historical
Society *Proceedings* XVI: 111; Godfrey to Winthrop, 20 July 1647, *Winthrop
papers* VII; 378–9; Noyes *et al.*, *Genealogical dictionary*, 330.
87 Winthrop made this remark in 1639 in the context of a refusal by Massachusetts to
accept jurisdiction in the Sagadahoc region. *Winthrop's journal* I: 306.

CHAPTER 5

1 Denys, *Description*, 480–2; Declaration of Jacques Bourgeois, 31 July 1699, AC,
C^{IID}, 3, ff.191–2; George MacBeath, 'Isaac de Razilly,' *DCB* I: 567–9. An
example of the specific manner in which Razilly sought to exploit the fishery, by
hiring vessels in France on condition that the Razilly company would control the
marketing of the catch, can be found in Charter-party, Menou-Maynard, 31 Mar.
1634, ACM, E, Minutes Juppin, registre 1632–4, f.324. Discussion of this point
will also be found in an article upon which portions of this chapter are based: John
G. Reid, 'Styles of colonisation and social disorders in early Acadia and Maine: a

comparative approach,' Société historique acadienne, *Cahiers* 7 (1976): 106–17.

2 Denys, *Description*, 474, 476.

3 Convention between Claude de Razilly, Jehan Cendre, and Pierre Gaborit, saltmakers, 1 Mar. 1636, ACM, E, Minutes Juppin, registre 1635–6, f.207.

4 Certification, 27 Dec. 1687 (copied from an earlier original), AC, C^{11D}, 2, ff.85–6; Razilly's comments were made in a letter of 16 Aug. 1634 to Marc Lescarbot, reported in an anonymous memorandum, [1634], BN, Fonds français, 13423, f.350.

5 'Two hundred men, including soldiers, labourers, and craftsmen, without counting the women and children, the Capuchin fathers, or the little savage children who have to be maintained in the seminary established for that purpose. There are also twenty French married couples who came over with their families to start peopling these lands, to which the sieur d'Aulnay would have brought over many more if he had had the means.' (Author's translation.) Memorandum [*c*. 1643], BN, Fonds français, 18593, ff.386–9. See also Geneviève Massignon, *Les parlers français d'Acadie: enquête linguistique* (Paris 1962), 18–20.

6 'From the time when the sieur de Menou became sole proprietor of Acadia, he caused to be built at Port Royal the existing fort, a church, a convent, some mills, and many dwellings; he also caused the clearing of a considerable number of *arpents* of land, so as to make up three large farms, which cost him more than 150,000 *livres*' (author's translation). Declaration of the Le Borgne heirs, n.d., AC, C^{11D}, 1, f.68.

7 Lease, 20 Mar. 1649, AC, E, dossier 12. In this concession, the grantee was obliged to pay *cens* at the rate of 4 *deniers* per *arpent*, *rentes* at the rate of a 'demi-chapon' per *arpent*, and also to present d'Aulnay with an elaborate 'gâteau des rois' each year at Epiphany. I am indebted to Professor Marcel Trudel for assistance in the interpretation of this document; for details of grants in Canada for comparison, see Trudel, *Debuts du régime seigneurial*, 174–88. The possibility that earlier grants by d'Aulnay had been based on *métayage* tenure is speculative, but is corroborated by further circumstantial evidence in the form of Nicolas Denys's observation that d'Aulnay never allowed his tenants to make any profit. Denys, *Description*, 483. On this form of tenure elsewhere in New France, see Séguin, *Civilisation traditionelle de l'habitant*, 221–7, and Trudel, *Débuts du régime seigneurial*, 226–34. Our understanding of the whole matter of the early seigneurial system at Port Royal is hampered by lack of documentation; see the remarks by Trudel, 49. The account by Edme Rameau de Saint-Père in *Une colonie féodale en Amérique: L'Acadie, 1604–1710* (Paris 1877), 80–1, has been followed by other historians, but it was based only on inferences from sources relating to the seigneurial structure in Canada and its precision is probably more apparent than real.

8 Letter of Father Ignace de Paris, 6 Aug. 1653, *Collection de manuscrits* I: 136–9;

Ignace de Paris, 'Letter,' PAC *Report, 1904*, 333–41; J.-Roger Comeau, 'Ignace de Paris,' *DCB* I: 379–80. Madame de Brice, the mother of two of the Capuchins at Port Royal, ran a school there for selected Indian pupils and also taught d'Aulnay's children; René Baudry, 'Madame de Brice,' *DCB* I: 129.

9 See Massignon, 'Seigneurie de d'Aulnay,' 477. A genealogical treatment of early Acadian families can be found in Bona Arsenault, *Histoire et généalogie des Acadiens* (2 vols, Quebec 1965).

10 The relationship of Wells to the proprietorial system was more complex than that of the others and is discussed further later in this chapter.

11 Minutes of the Council for New England, 22 Mar. 1638, PRO, CO1/6, no. 29, p.38. Among the examples of Godfrey's sub-grants is the grant to Thomas Waye on 16 Feb. 1651, which involved an annual payment of two days of labour. Maine Historical Society, *York deeds* I, pt 1, f.13. See also Banks, *York* I: 48–9; and Clark, *Eastern frontier*, 18.

12 Grant of Sir Ferdinando Gorges to Thomas Gorges, 4 Mar. 1642, Maine Historical Society, *York deeds* I, Part 2, ff.5–6. For a small sub-grant made on Gorges' behalf, see Deed, Richard Vines on behalf of Thomas Gorges to John Wadlow and Edmond Littlefield, 20 Nov. 1645, Ibid., f.13.

13 Deed, Thomas Gorges to Peter Weare, 15 July 1643, Ibid. II, f.179; Deed, Thomas Gorges to Thomas Withers, 1 Mar. 1643, Ibid. I, pt 1, f.24.

14 Josselyn, *Two voyages*, 348–9. On the magistrate-patentees, see Reid, *Maine, Charles II, and Massachusetts*, 6–11.

15 *Winthrop's journal* I: 129, 190.

16 Thomas Gorges to Henry Gorges, 19 July 1640, in Moody, *Gorges letters*, no. 1; see also Robert Earle Moody, *A proprietary experiment in early New England history: Thomas Gorges and the Province of Maine* (Boston 1963), 28.

17 Winter to Trelawny, 10 July 1639, *Documentary history of Maine* III: 171; Trelawny to the governor and counsell of the Province of New Somersettshire [Maine], 29 June 1641, Ibid., 275–7.

18 'Just so long as there is no order there, and one is not assured of the enjoyment of his concessions, the country will never be populated, and will always be the prey of the enemies of France' (Denys, *Description*, 499; translation, 203–4.)

19 Sir Ferdinando Gorges to Sir Francis Windebank, 28 Jan. 1640, PRO, CO1/10, no. 55; *PCR* I: 36–41; Preston, *Gorges*, 330–1.

20 Thomas Gorges to Henry Gorges, 19 July 1640, in Moody, *Gorges letters*, no, 1; *PCR* I: 42–3.

21 *PCR* I: 3.

22 Ibid., 2; Sir Ferdinando Gorges to Sir Henry Vane, John Winthrop, *et al.*, 23 Aug. 1637, *Winthrop papers* VII: 329–30; see also Banks, 'The administration of William Gorges,' 129–31.

23 *PCR* I: 68–9, 73–7. Thomas Gorges intended to proceed to a division of Maine into

four counties, but his return to England forestalled this measure. Thomas Gorges to Sir Ferdinando Gorges, 29 June 1642, in Moody, *Gorges letters*, no. 58.

24 *PCR* I: 58–64, 72.

25 Winter to Trelawny, 19 Oct. 1640, *Documentary History of Maine* III: 252–3; see also the comments of Thomas Gorges to Winter, [October 1640], in Moody, *Georges letters*, no. 8.

26 John Winter's recognisance, 1 Apr. 1641, *Documentary history of Main* III: 255–7; Winter to Trelawny, 29 July 1641, Ibid., 279.

27 Petition of John Winter, 25 June 1641, Ibid., 262–3; Robert Jordan to Trelawny, 31 July 1641, Ibid., 315–19.

28 Trelawny to Winter, 29 June 1641, Ibid., 273.

29 Thomas Gorges to Sir Ferdinando Gorges, 29 June 1642, in Moody, *Gorges letters*, no. 58; Jordan to Trelawny, 31 July 1641, Documentary history of Maine III: 315.

30 For further discussion of this case, see Burrage, *Beginnings*, 293–9; Joseph Henry Smith, *Appeals to the Privy Council from the American plantations* (New York 1950), 50–1.

31 See Le Blant, 'Compagnie de la Nouvelle-France et la restitution,' 88; also Azarie Couillard-Després, 'Aux sources de l'histoire de l'Acadie,' in Royal Society of Canada, *Proceedings and Transactions* 3rd ser., 27 (1933): section 1, 80–1.

32 'His disposition and that of his council was to reign ... ' (Denys, *Description*, 483; translation, 151). Trudel, *Beginnings*, 198.

33 Memorandum, [c.1643], BN, Fonds français, 18593, ff.377–8. The subject of these disputes is not entirely clear but probably concerned fur-trading profits. See Trudel, *Beginnings*, 198.

34 Memorandum, [c.1643], BN, Fonds Français, 18593, ff.379–81. I am indebted to Professor Marcel Trudel for clarification of the point that the La Tour family did not in fact hold a seigneury at Pentagouet: the 'Vieux-Logis' seigneury, often placed at Pentagouet, was located near Cap de Sable.

35 'The others, the most seditious, were hanged in order to serve as a reminder and an example to posterity' (author's translation). Proceedings and documents in relation to the rebellion of the Sieur de la Tour, 10 May 1645, AC, C^{11D}, 1, ff.72–4; Denys, *Description*, 472. An earlier victim had been Hippolite Bourget, sea captain, who was hired by Emmanuel Le Borgne in 1643 to carry supplies to d'Aulnay at Port Royal, pressed into service in the blockade of the St John, and wounded in the battle of that year at Port Royal. Deposition of Hippolite Bourget, 9 Jan. 1644, ACM, B, La Rochelle, B.5656, f.14.

36 Denys, *Description*, 68, 499; Account of the surrender of fort Saint-Pierre on 4 Sept. 1647, AC, C^{11D}, 1, f.81; Trudel, *Beginnings*, 203; Baudry, 'Charles d'Aulnay,' 232–3 and passim.

37 *Winthrop's journal* I: 65.

38 *Documentary history of Maine* VII: 133–6; Charles Edward Banks, 'Colonel Alexander Rigby,' *Maine Historical and Genealogical Recorder* 2 (1885): 1–23, 64–8, 147–9.

39 Edward Godfrey to Robert Trelawny, 22 Sept. 1640, *Documentary history of Maine* III: 240; Richard Vines to John Winthrop, 25 Jan. 1641, *Winthrop papers* VII: 343.

40 Thomas Gorges to John Winthrop, 8 July 1643, in Moody, *Gorges letters*, no. 82.

41 *PCR* I: 89, 93; see also Preston, *Gorges*, 341–3.

42 See Burrage, *Beginnings*, 327–30; also *PCR* I: 88.

43 *MCR* II: 41. See also George Cleeve to John Winthrop and Edward Gibbons, 2 Feb. 1644, *Winthrop papers* VII: 365–6; and *Winthrop's journal* II: 157–8.

44 Richard Vines to John Winthrop, 9 Jan. 1644, *Winthrop papers* VII: 346–8; George Cleeve to John Winthrop, 27 Jan. 1644, Ibid., 363–5.

45 Thomas Jenner to John Winthrop, [28 Mar. 1646], Ibid., 358.

46 George Cleeve *et al.*, to governor, deputy governor, and assistants of Massachusetts, 18 Feb. 1646, Ibid., 371–3.

47 Thomas Jenner to John Winthrop, 6 Apr. 1646, Ibid., 359–61.

48 [Governor, deputy governor, and Court of Assistants of Massachusetts] to George Cleeve *et al.*, 5 Mar. 1646, draft by John Winthrop, Ibid., 374.

49 Thomas Jenner to John Winthrop, [28 Mar. 1646], Ibid., 358.

50 *Winthrop's journal* II: 267.

51 *Documentary history of Maine* VII: 136. The date given in the document is 27 Mar. 1646, but the fact that Winthrop records news of the decision in late 1647 suggests that the date 1646 was a clerical error, easily made just two days after the new year in the English calendar. See *Winthrop's journal* II: 338. The date 1647 is also adopted in Burrage, *Beginnings*, 339.

52 *PCR* I: 100.

53 Ibid., 171; see also Moody, 'Maine frontier,' 73.

54 *PCR* I: 133–4; Petition of the Maine magistrates to Council of State, 5 Dec. 1651, Maine Historical Society, *York deeds* I, part 1, ff.23–4.

55 *PCR* I: 160; Noyes *et al.*, *Genealogical dictionary*, 512, 576.

56 Confirmation of the government of Acadia to La Tour, 27 Feb. 1651, AC, C^{11D}, 1, ff.82–3.

57 Razilly to Marc Lescarbot, 16 Aug. 1634, reported in Memorandum, [c.1634], BN, Fonds français, 13423, f.349; Ferdinando Gorges, 'Of the Province of Maine,' epilogue to Gorges, 'Brief narration,' 71.

58 'Although it has been believed that my principal object in all my enterprises in these parts has always been the trading in furs with the Indians, I have never considered that as anything other than an accessory which could serve in some measure to

make capital for that which might be done in the country, which is the settlement fishery and the cultivation of the land...' (Denys, *Description*, 481–2; translation, 146).

59 'For I built two forts and he burned one of them, and if he built nothing himself nor cleared more than seven or eight arpents of land, he also burned the church and the monastery contrary to his instructions, which had enjoined him to install men in these establishments who would be responsible for them and so would conserve them' (author's translation). La Tour to Massachusetts General Court, 27 Oct. 1644, MA, 2, ff.484–5. La Tour's claim to have had more than purely commercial aims in Acadia is borne out by the wide-ranging appeal for colonists which he had launched in 1633, offering grants of land to those who would accompany him to Cap de Sable. *Gazette Renaudot*, 1633, 104. See also Clarence-J. d'Entremont, 'Le Cap-Sable: ses établissements avant la dispersion,' *Société historique acadienne, Cahiers* 2 (1967): 165. For an earlier exploration of the notion of geographical fragmentation in Acadia, see J.B. Brebner, *New England's outpost: Acadia before the conquest of Canada* (New York 1927), 45–7.

60 Charles Edward Banks, ed., 'Relation concerning the estate of New England, about 1634,' *New England Historical and Genealogical Register* 40 (1886): 73. Banks suggests strongly that the author of this relation was Walter Neale, a prominent employee of the Laconia Company, who lived on the Piscataqua River at this time and was familiar with the Maine settlements.

61 Richard Vines *et al.* to [General Court of Massachusetts], 20 Oct. 1645, Maine Historical Society Archives, Willis papers, P, no. 6.

62 The La Tour-d'Aulnay struggles in particular have often been described by historians in this way. Just one example is Robert Rumilly, *Histoire des Acadiens* (2 vols, Montreal 1955), in which chap. 6 is entitled 'Luttes féodales.'

63 See, for example, Elizabeth A.R. Brown, 'The tyranny of a construct: feudalism and historians of medieval Europe,' *American Historical Review* 79 (1974): 1063–88; Henry Alfred Cronne, *The reign of Stephen, 1135–1154: anarchy in England* (London 1970), 4–8; H.G. Richardson and G.O. Sayles, *The governance of medieval England from the Conquest to Magna Carta* (Edinburgh 1963), 30–2; though on this last discussion, see also the comments in Brown, 'Tyranny of a construct,' 1066–7.

64 This discussion of the pressures upon the initial land structures in Maine and Acadia has benefited from the analysis by Marcel Trudel of the reasons for the persistence of the seigneurial system in Canada: Trudel, *Débuts du régime seigneurial*, 271–2. For further discussion of the fundamental importance of land and land tenure in the settlements of this time, see Reid, *Maine, Charles II, and Massachusetts*, 1–11.

65 Denys, *Description*, 483.

66 See, for example, the reference to complaints against La Tour by the Acadians Germain Doucet, Isaac Pesselay, and Guillaume Trahan, in Royal order, 6 Mar. 1644, Massachusetts Historical Society, Parkman papers, 32, ff.125–31.

67 Declaration of the Le Borgne Heirs, n.d. [the date 1642 on this document is clearly
an error, and the earliest possible date would be 1685, as mention is made of
Charles II of England as the 'feu Roi'], AC, C^{11D}, 1, f.68. The travails of the Le
Borgnes are discussed more fully in chaps 6 and 7. On the growing complexity and
vigor of Acadian society, see Naomi E.S. Griffiths, *The Acadians: creation of a
people* (Toronto 1973), 13–14.

68 Champernowne is the only one of the patentees whose financial position is reliably
indicated by surviving record; see Reid, *Maine, Charles II, and Massachusetts*, 11.
See also Bailyn, *New England merchants*, 102.

69 *Winthrop's journal* I: 92; Petition of Edward Godfrey to Massachusetts General
Court, 30 Oct. 1654, MA, 3, f.235; Banks, 'Godfrey,' 304–6. Godfrey's house was
described in Lucy Downing to John Winthrop, Jr, 17 Dec. 1648, in Massachusetts
Historical Society *Collections* ser. 5, I (1871): 37.

70 Deed, Thomas Withers to Nicholas Shapleigh and John Shapleigh, 25 Mar. 1681,
Maine Historical Society, *York deeds* III, f.91; see also Reid, *Maine, Charles II,
and Massachusetts*, 13, 23, 222–3.

71 See Harris, *Seigneurial system*, 41.

72 Thomas Jenner to John Winthrop, [28 Mar. 1646], *Winthrop papers* VII: 358.

73 The Massachusetts town is discussed in general terms in McManis, *Colonial New
England*, 53–63. More detailed studies include Powell, *Puritan village*; Greven,
Four generations; Lockridge, *A New England town, the first hundred years*; and
Michael Zuckerman, *Peaceable kingdoms: New England towns in the eighteenth
century* (New York 1970). The foundation of a town on the Massachusetts model
did not necessarily abolish tenancy for ever. It has recently been shown that the
town of Springfield, Mass., in the second half of the seventeenth century, had over
one-third of its adult males renting some or all of their lands, housing, or livestock.
What the town system did do, however, was to guarantee freehold tenure to those
men who were already part of the community, and to ensure that if tenancy
reappeared in the town, the landlord or landlords would be persons of genuine
economic and social strength in the community (such as John Pynchon of
Springfield) rather than having only the external sanction of patents originating from
Europe. See Stephen Innes, 'Land tenancy and social order in Springfield, Massachusetts, 1652 to 1702,' *William and Mary Quarterly* 3rd ser., 35 (1978): 33–56.

74 Van Deventer, *Provincial New Hampshire*, 9–18.

75 Thomas Gorges noted in a letter of late 1640 a preliminary approach from Wheelwright for permission to settle thirty families in Maine. Thomas Gorges to Richard
Bernard, 9 Oct. 1640, in Moody, *Gorges letters*, no. 6.

76 Thomas Gorges to Sir Ferdinando Gorges, 5 Dec. 1641, Ibid., no. 45.

77 Grant of Thomas Gorges to John Wheelwright, Henry Boade, and Edward Rishworth, 14 July 1643, Maine Historical Society, *York deeds* I, pt 2, f.9. Evidence of
the internal workings of Wells is scanty, partly because of the destruction of the

town's earliest records in a fire in 1657. See Clark, *Eastern frontier*, 37–9, 46–7, and Edward E. Bourne, *History of Wells and Kennebunk from the earliest settlement to the year 1820* (Portland 1875), 10–13, 24–5.

78 Thomas Jenner to John Winthrop, 4 Feb. 1641, *Winthrop papers* VII; 355–6; Richard Vines to John Winthrop, 25 Jan. 1641, Ibid., 340–2.

79 On Druillettes's visit to New England, see *Jesuit relations* XXXVI: 86–102. Particularly striking is the friendship which quickly sprang up between Druillettes and the minister John Eliot, who invited Druillettes to spend the winter at his house.

80 Thomas Gorges to Joseph Godwin, [19 July] 1640, in Moody, *Gorges letters*, no. 2; Thomas Gorges to Sir Ferdinando Gorges, [c. September 1641], Ibid., no. 26; see also Moody, *A proprietary experiment*, 18–20.

81 Thomas Gorges to Sir Ferdinando Gorges, [c. September 1641], in Moody, *Gorges letters*, no. 36; Grant by Thomas Gorges to Town of Gorgeana, 18 July 1643, Maine Historical Society, *York deeds* IV, f.46. 'Gorgeana' was a name briefly applied to Agamenticus at this time in honour of Sir Ferdinando Gorges.

82 Record of town meeting, 16 July 1648, Kittery Town Records, 1, [p. 1].

83 Record of Town meeting, 21 Oct. 1651, Ibid., 1, p. 2; Grant to Thomas Withers, 24 May 1652, Ibid., 1, p. 3.

84 Robert Jordan to Robert Trelawny, 31 July 1642, *Documentary history of Maine* III: 314.

85 Godfrey to Trelawny, 22 Sept. 1640, Ibid., 241; Godfrey to Winthrop, 20 July 1647, *Winthrop papers* VII: 379.

86 John Winthrop, Jr, to Lord Forbes, 23 Dec. 1644, *Winthrop papers* VI: 519.

CHAPTER 6

1 See the account of his death by the Capuchin Father Ignace, *Collection de manuscrits* I: 139. Emile Lauvrière, *La tragédie d'un peuple: histoire du peuple acadien de ses origines à nos jours* (3rd ed., 2 vols, Paris 1922), I: 80, hints that La Tour may have planned d'Aulnay's death, but this seems an unlikely supposition.

2 See Massachusetts State Archives, Massachusetts Council records, 1 (1650–6), June 1651, n.p.

3 Decree, 14 Nov. 1650, ACM, B, Guyenne, B. 197; Confirmation of the government of Acadia to La Tour, 27 Feb. 1651, AC, C^{11D}, 1, ff.82–3.

4 'The usurpation committed by Charles de Turgis, called St Estienne de la Tour ... of the fort and habitation on the river St John' (author's translation). Contract of association between the duc de Vendosme and the widow Charnisay, 18 Feb. 1652, AC, C^{11D}, 1, ff.87–90.

5 'Seignior of all that country as creditor of the Sieur d'Aunay' (Denys, *Description*, 465; translation, 99); Rawlyk, *Nova Scotia's Massachusetts*, 20–1; these episodes are further discussed in Doherty, 'Acadian adventure of 1654,' 27–35.

6 '[The] principal object of their intended marriage, which is the peace and tranquility of the country, and the harmony and union of the two families ...' (author's translation). La Tour-Motin marriage contract, 24 Feb. 1653, CÉA, Fonds Placide Gaudet, 1.46–14.

7 See Council decree, 15 Oct. 1655, printed in Denys, *Description*, 67–70.

8 Concession of the Compagnie de la Nouvelle-France, 3 Oct. 1653, AC, C^{11D}, 1, ff.93–4; Denys, *Description*, 61–7, 465–7.

9 Massachusetts State Archives, Massachusetts Council records, 1 (1650–6), June 1651, n.p.

10 *MCR* III: 304; IV (i): 120–1, 146, 157; see also Doherty, 'Acadian adventure of 1654,' 37–41.

11 For a summary of the grounds of this claim, see chap. 4 above.

12 *MCR* IV (i): 70; Petition of Maine magistrates to council of state, 5 Dec. 1651, Maine Historical Society, *York deeds* I, pt I, ff.23–4.

13 Massachusetts State Archives, Massachusetts Council records, 1 (1650–6), September 1651, n.p.

14 See Godfrey Davies, *The early Stuarts, 1603–1660* (2nd ed., Oxford 1959), 220–2; and Charles McLean Andrews, *The colonial period of American history* (4 vols, New Haven 1934–8), IV: 22–49.

15 *MCR* IV (i): 165.

16 See Paul Chrisler Phillips, *The fur trade* (2 vols, Norman, Okla. 1961), I: 145.

17 Carroll, *Timber economy*, 105–7, 110.

18 The full dimensions of this remarkable operation at Arrowsick are currently being revealed by archaeological work under the direction of James S. Leamon, sponsored by Bates College. See Bradley, *Maine's first buildings*, 14–15. Thomas Lake became a close associate of Thomas Temple, governor of Nova Scotia, as is discussed later in this chapter.

19 Carroll, *Timber economy*, 105–6; Bailyn, *New England merchants*, 102–3; see also Kershaw, *Kennebeck proprietors*, passim

20 *MCR* IV (i): 70. The events described in this section are more fully discussed in Reid, *Maine Charles* II, and Massachusetts, 11–22.

21 Edward Rawson to Edward Godfrey, 12 June 1652, Maine Historical Society, *York deeds* I, pt I, f.21.

22 Edward Godfrey *et al.* to Massachusetts commissioners, 9 July 1652, MA, 3, f.184.

23 Edward Godfrey to Edward Rawson, 9 July 1652, Ibid., ff.185–6.

24 Return of Massachusetts commissioners, 20 Nov. 1652, Ibid., ff.189–90, 195.

25 Return of Massachusetts commissioners, 24 Nov. 1652, Ibid., ff.198, 206–7.

26 Petition of Henry Boade, 6 May 1653, Ibid., f.211; Petition of Thomas Wheelwright, 11 May 1653, Ibid., f.213.

27 Proceedings of Massachusetts commissioners, 5 July 1653, Ibid., ff.218–32. The commissioners' proceedings, as well as the petition of Henry Boade, indicate that Wells at this time was torn by religious disputes which were seriously threatening

the coherence of the community, but they give scant evidence of the precise nature of the conflicts. These disputes may help to explain the absence of a number of the prominent inhabitants of Wells from a 1656 petition to Oliver Cromwell in favour of the annexation. Petition of the inhabitants of York, Kittery, Wells, Saco, and Cape Porpoise, [1656], MA, 3, f.242; Bourne, *History of Wells and Kennebunk*, 35–44.

28 Ratification of commissioners' return, 5 Sept. 1653, MA, 3, f.233; Masschusetts General Court to George Cleeve, 5 Sept. 1653, Ibid., f.234; Proceedings of Massachusetts commissioners, 13 July 1658, Ibid., ff.246–7. See also William Scott Southgate, 'History of Scarborough,' in Maine Historical Society *Collections* ser. 1, III (1853): 44–8.

29 Answer of Massachusetts commissioners to Edward Godfrey, 23 Nov. 1652, MA, 3, f.192. Even as late as 1674, the Massachusetts General Court was adhering to this commitment in connection with a dispute in Scarborough, by declaring that 'the eldest grants of land in the county of Yorkshire, whither by patent or grants from the Generall Courts, shall take place before any others.': *MCR* V: 12.

30 *PCR* II: 11, 19, 24, 361, 369; see also *MCR* IV (i): 360.

31 Grant to the town of Kittery, 20 Nov. 1652, MA, 3, ff.204–5.

32 Community studies of the Maine towns, similar to those done on several Massachusetts towns, would be of great assistance in the investigation of issues such as this.

33 York, Town records, 1, p. 8 and passim.

34 Petition of Edward Godfrey, [30 Oct. 1654], MA, 3, f.235.

35 Report of committee, 20 Apr. 1655, Ibid., f.238; Order of General Court, 26 May 1655, Ibid., f.239.

36 Petition of Edward Godfrey *et al.*, [c. 1659], PRO, CO1/13, no. 79; Queries and objections against the Massachusetts encroaching power on several other proprieties, [c. 1659], BL, Egerton MSS, 2395, ff.199–201; Banks, *York* I: 239.

37 Kittery, Town records, 1, pp. 6, 8, 19, 25; Byron Fairchild, *Messrs William Pepperrell: merchants at Piscataqua* (Ithaca, N.Y. 1954), 7; Charles Wesley Tuttle, *Captain Francis Champernowne, the Dutch conquest of Acadie, and other historical papers* (Boston 1889), 110, 121, 335–7; Reid, *Maine, Charles II, and Massachusetts*, 17–18.

38 Remonstrance of Kittery against Richard Leader, 20 Dec. 1652, MA, 3, ff.208–9. For a full discussion of this episode, see Reid, *Maine, Charles II, and Massachusetts*, 18.

39 Petition, 30 May 1660, MA, 3, f.248. For more detail see Reid, *Maine, Charles II, and Massachusetts*, 21.

40 Petition of the inhabitants of York, Kittery, Wells, Saco, and Cape Porpoise, [1656], MA, 3, f.242; Edward Rishworth to Governor John Endicott, 14 Aug. 1656, Ibid., f.243.

41 Robert Sedgwick to Oliver Cromwell, 1 July 1654, in Thomas Birch, ed., *A collection of the state papers of John Thurloe Esq.* (7 vols, London 1742), II: 418-19.

42 John Leverett to Oliver Cromwell, 4 July 1654, Ibid., 425-6; Mark Harrison to the navy commissioners, 1 July 1654, PRO, CO1/32, no. 8.

43 Denys, *Description*, 466; John Leverett to Oliver Cromwell, 5 Sept. 1654, in Birch, *Thurloe state papers* II: 584; Mark Harrison to the commissioners of the Admiralty, 21 July 1654, PRO, CO1/32, no. 9; Mark Harrison to the commissioners of the Admiralty, 30 Aug. 1654, Ibid., no. 11; Mark Harrison to the navy commissioners, 31 Aug. 1654, Ibid., no. 12.

44 See Ignace de Paris, 'Letter,' PAC *Report, 1904*, 337.

45 John Leverett to Oliver Cromwell, 5 Sept. 1654, in Birch, *Thurloe state papers* II: 584. 'Provided that they shall be two to three leagues removed from the fortress' (author's translation). Capitulation of Port Royal, 16 Aug. 1654, AC, C^{11D}, 1, f.97. In practice, this concession was not long adhered to, and a Capuchin source even asserts that the superior of the Port Royal mission, Léonard de Chartres, was deliberately put to death by the English some time after the conquest. Ignace de Paris, 'Letter,' PAC *Report, 1904*, 337; see also G.-M. Dumas, 'Léonard de Chartres,' *DCB* I: 468-9.

46 Order of the Council of State, 22 Feb. 1655, Massachusetts Historical Society, Gay transcripts, Sedgwick papers, p.5.

47 Bordeaux to Mazarin, 31 Dec. 1654, AAÉ Correspondance politique, Angleterre, 64, f.298.

48 Bordeaux to Mazarin, 18 Feb. 1655, AAÉ, Correspondance politique, Angleterre, 64, f.363.

49 Bordeaux to Henri-Auguste de Loménie, Comte de Brienne, 25 Feb. 1655, AAÉ, Correspondance politique, Angleterre, 65, f.58.

50 Bordeaux to Brienne, 1 Apr. 1655, AAÉ, Correspondance politique, Angleterre, 65, f.88.

51 See Doherty, 'Acadian adventure of 1654,' chap. 3.

52 Petit to Bertherret, 5 Apr. 1655, AAÉ, Correspondance politique, Angleterre, 66, ff.40-1; Article xxv of treaty, 13 Nov. 1655, AAÉ, Correspondance politique, Angleterre, 66, f.181.

53 Order of the Council of State, 29 May 1656, G.B., PRO, *Calendar of state papers*, 1574-1660, 441. See also Huia Ryder *et al.*, 'Sir Thomas Temple,' *DCB* I: 636-7, 'William Crowne,' Ibid., 241-2.

54 Warrant, 14 July 1656, PRO, CO1/13, no. 4; Patent, 9 Aug. 1656, PRO, CO1/13, no. 11.

55 Indenture, 20 Sept. 1656, *Suffolk deeds* III (Boston 1885): 325-30.

56 Michel Dantez to Colbert, 6 Nov. 1663, BN, Mélanges de Colbert, 118, ff.153-4.

57 In 1657, Temple and Crowne agreed to divide their interests, with Crowne obtain-

ing exclusive commercial rights in the area from Machias to the border of New
England, including Penobscot. Articles of agreement, 12 Sept. 1657, and
Confirmation, 15 Feb. 1658, *Suffolk deeds* III: 108–12. For discussion of Crowne's
later career and further treatment of the relationships among him, Temple, and La
Tour, see *DCB* I: 241–2; Doherty, 'Acadian adventure of 1654,' 86–8; and
Rawlyk, *Nova Scotia's Massachusetts*, 26–7.

58 Articles of agreement, 6 Oct. 1629, BL,, Egerton MSS, 2395, f.17.

59 By late 1658, Temple was laying claim to the entire extent of Nova Scotia, 'as it
lyes in the Lord Sterling's patent.' Temple to [Lord Fienes *et al.*], 27 Dec. 1658,
PRO, CO1/13, no. 58. Ten years later, under pressure of a royal order to restore
Acadia to France under the terms of the treaty of Breda, he had resorted to the
expedient of distinguishing between 'Nova Scotia' and 'Acadia.' Morillon Du
Bourg to Compagnie des Indes Occidentales, 9 Nov. 1668, PRO, CO1/23, no. 77.
For a careful discussion of the historiography of this confusion over the boundaries
of Acadia/Nova Scotia, and of its role in the negotiations leading to the treaty of
Utrecht in 1713, see Corinne Laplante, 'Le traité d'Utrecht et l'Acadie: une étude
de la correspondance sécrète et officielle qui a entouré la signature du traité
d'Utrecht' (MA thesis, Université de Moncton 1974), 19–27 and passim.

60 See Rawlyk, *Nova Scotia's Massachusetts*, 24.

61 Instructions of the General Court to John Leverett, 23 Nov. 1655, Hutchinson,
Collection of papers, 272–4.

62 Thomas Lake to John Leverett, 2 Sept. 1657, MA, 2, ff.504–5. See also Arthur
Howland Buffinton, 'Sir Thomas Temple in Boston: a case of benevolent assimilation,' Colonial Society of Massachusetts *Publications* XXVII (1932): 308–19.

63 'The lack of attention paid by the English to establishing themselves in these parts
… [and] that they have sent settlers only on a token basis, and without making the
slightest improvement' (author's translation). Memorandum regarding Acadia,
1667, AAÉ, Correspondance politique, Angleterre, 89, f.118.

64 Copy of letter by Thomas Temple, 27 Dec. 1658, PRO, CO1/13, no. 59. Thomas
Lake was the man who was joint owner of the trading post and industrial installation
at Arrowsick, on the Kennebec River; Walker was a prominent citizen of Lynn and
by 1670 was acting as deputy for Temple in Nova Scotia. The connection between
them can be exemplified by the fact that Walker appointed Lake as his attorney in
1666 when he was departing on a sea voyage. *Records and files of the Quarterly
Courts of Essex County, Massachusetts* (8 vols, Salem 1911–21), III: 307. See also
C. Bruce Fergusson, 'Richard Walker,' *DCB* I: 666–7.

65 Thomas Temple to Lord Fienes, 29 Dec. 1659, PRO, CO1/13, no. 77.

66 See the extensive correspondance in Massachusetts Historical Society, Sedgwick
papers, especially pp.33–4. Leverett had also maintained a general supervision to
prevent unauthorized trade in Nova Scotia through an agent, Captain John Allen,
who was retained by Temple in 1657 as one of his own officials. Allen to Leverett,

27 Apr. 1655, Suffolk court files, no. 209; Commission to Captain Thomas Breedon, 28 Apr. 1657, *Suffolk deeds* III: 26.

67 Thomas Lake to John Leverett, 2 Sept. 1657, MA, 2, ff.504–5.

68 Temple to Fienes, 29 Dec. 1659, PRO, CO1/13, no. 77; Thomas Povey to Temple, 3 Apr. 1660, BL, Additional MSS, 11411, ff.27–8; Account of what Samuel Wilson knows of the matter of Acadie in Nova Scotia, 1672, PRO, CO1/29, no. 80 (i); Buffinton, 'Temple in Boston,' 314–15. Temple also built a fort and trading-post at Jemseg, some fifty miles up the St John. Examples of Temple's indebtedness can be found in two mortgages of his property for amounts of £5,500 and £5,000 respectively: Bond and mortgage to Thomas Breedon, Thomas Bell, and John Breedon, 24 June 1665, *Suffolk deeds* IV (Boston 1888); 308–11; Mortgage to Hezekiah Usher and Samuel Shrimpton, 30 Nov. 1668, *Suffolk deeds* V (Boston 1890): 508–10.

69 Petition of William Crowne, 28 May 1666, MA, 39, f.254; Petition of Thomas Elliott, [19 July 1660], PRO, CO1/14, no. 21; Papers about captain Breedon, August 1678, PRO, CO1/42, no. 120; see also Rawlyk, *Nova Scotia's Massachusetts*, 29.

70 Petition of Sir Lewis Kirke, John Kirke, and Francis Berkeley, [19 July 1660], PRO, CO1/14, no. 22; Minute of Committee for Plantations in America, 30 July 1660, PRO, CO1/14, no. 28; Petition of Colonel John Blount and the daughters of the late Earl of Stirling, December 1660, PRO, CO1/14, no. 60; Petition of Sir Lewis Kirke, John Kirke, and Francis Berkeley, 11 Dec. 1660, PRO, CO1/14, no. 61; The case of Henry, Earl of Stirling, [c. 1660], PRO, CO1/14, no. 66.

71 Warrant to the attorney general, 5 Apr. 1662, PRO, CO1/16, no. 42; Bounds of Sir Thomas Temple's patent of Novia [sic] Scotia, July 1662, PRO, CO1/16, no. 86; Warrant to the attorney general, 7 July 1662, PRO, SP44/7, p. 148.

72 See Temple to Secretary Lord Arlington, 2 Mar. 1669, PRO, CO1/24, no. 20.

73 For examples of Le Borgne's contracts with military officers, see Convention, Le Borgne Du Coudray–Jean Périer, 17 Jan. 1658, ACM, E, Minutes Teuleron, 1658, f.6; Convention, Le Borgne–Jean-Baptiste Fernaud, 17 Jan. 1658, ACM, E, Minutes Teuleron, 1658, ff.6–7; Convention, Le Borgne–René Coulon, 17 Jan. 1658, ACM, E, Minutes Teuleron, 1658, f.7. On the battle itself, see Articles against Monsieur Laborne, on behalf of Colonel Temple, [1658], PRO, CO1/13, no. 52; and Denys, *Description*, 467.

74 Denys, *Description*, 467. Le Borgne's proposal was made at a negotiating session held in London in late 1658 at the instance of Bordeaux and of Temple's patron William Fienes, Viscount Saye and Sele; Minutes of a debate, [1658], PRO, CO1/13, no. 54. On the assault of 1659, see Temple to Fienes, 6 Sept. 1659, PRO, CO1/13, no. 71. Nicolas Denys stated that he took no part in these conflicts, and indeed he had enough trouble on his hands at this time in defending his territories against a rival colonizer in the person of Charles Baye, Sieur de La Girodière, who claimed to settle near Canso by right of a grant from the Compagnie de la Nouvelle-France

to his powerful kinsman, Charles de Conigan, Sieur de Cangé. La Girodière's establishment eventually succumbed to an English raid, probably by the forces of Temple, in 1668. See Denys, *Description*, 486–7; Nomination of Sieur de Cangé as royal governor, 2 July 1659, Archives du séminaire de Québec, Polygraphie 4, no. 31; and Robert Le Blant, *Les officiers bretons du 'Marquis de Cangé' au sud du Saint-Laurent (1658–1666)* (Paris 1969, reprint from *Actes du quatre-vingt-onzième congrès national des Sociétés savantes, 1966*), 237–46. On the pressures upon Le Borgne in France, see Memorandum of the La Tour descendants, [*c.* 1699], AC, E, dossier 12.

75 Temple to Fienes, 29 Dec. 1659, PRO, CO1/13, no. 77.

76 Notes relating to America, [*c.* 1667], PRO, CO1/21, no. 174.

77 Deed, Plymouth Colony to Tyng *et al.*, 27 Oct. 1661, Suffolk court files, no. 672; Charter party, 27 Aug. 1664, and Deposition of James Harris, 27 July 1666, Suffolk court files, no. 754; Kershaw, *Kennebeck proprietors*, 13–14; Reid, *Maine, Charles II, and Massachusetts*, 238–9, 243. Tyng's son, also Edward, resided at Falmouth, Maine, in the 1680s and in 1690 was briefly appointed governor of Nova Scotia; he was captured by the French in 1691 and died in captivity at La Rochelle. See C. Bruce Fergusson, 'Edward Tyng,' *DCB* I: 654, and Noyes *et al.*, *Genealogical dictionary*, 701.

78 *MCR* IV (i): 355–6; IV (ii): 74–5, 323.

79 Rawson to Arlington, 20 May 1669, PRO, CO1/24, no. 62.

80 Breedon stated in the petition that he had been sent to England by Temple to represent the troubles of Nova Scotia. Petition of Thomas Breedon, [1659], PRO, CO1/13, no. 66.

81 Daigle, 'Nos amis les ennemis,' 66–8, 71.

82 'The residents who were lodged near the fort have for the most part abandoned their houses and have gone to settle on the upper part of the river' (Denys, *Description*, 474; translation, 123).

83 Declaration of the Le Borgne heirs, n.d., AC, C^{11D}, 1, f.68. For the attempts of Alexandre Le Borgne to reimpose the seigneurial system after 1670, see chap. 7.

84 Memorandum of Le Borgne Du Coudray, 23 Nov. 1665, AC, C^{11D}, 1, f.118.

CHAPTER 7

1 Commissioners of customs to Sir Philip Warwick, 12 Feb. 1661, PRO, CO1/15, no. 16.

2 As the Jesuit superior, Father Hierosme Lallement, reported in 1659, only the northern part of Acadia was left to the French, 'dont les noms principaux sont Miscou, Rigibouctou, et le Cap Breton.' *Jesuit relations* XLV: 58.

3 Royal commission to Emmanuel Le Borgne, 10 Dec. 1657, AC, E, dossier 266. This commission gave Le Borgne the command of the entire territory from Canso to

the (undefined) New England border, and noted that this same territory had been granted to him 'en fief et Seigneurie' by the Compagnie de la Nouvelle-France. The commission was to last nine years, specifically superseding that given to La Tour in 1651, and carried a monopoly of the fur trade. However, in 1664 the Compagnie de la Nouvelle-France was suppressed in favour of the new Compagnie des Indes occidentales, which three years later limited Le Borgne's territory to the Acadian peninsula from Canso to the Minas Basin, reserving to itself the land from Minas to the New England border. Commission to Le Borgne, 17 Dec. 1667, AC, E, dossier 266.

4 Louis XIV to Bordeaux, 30 Jan., 11 Oct. 1658, AC, C^{11D}, 1, ff. 115, 116. The circumstances of Alexandre Le Borgne's release from captivity in London are not clear, but he was certainly back in Acadia by 1662.

5 Minutes of a debate, [1658], PRO, CO1/13, no. 54; English proposals, [1658], PRO, CO1/13 no. 55; Petition of Captain Thomas Breedon, [1659], PRO, CO1/13, no. 66; Temple to Fiennes, 6 Sept. 1659, PRO, CO1/13, no. 71.

6 Temple to Thomas Povey, 6 Sept. 1659, PRO, CO1/13, no. 72.

7 Order of Massachusetts council on complaint of Thomas Temple, 4 Mar. 1662, MA, 2, f.509.

8 Le Borgne's capture in 1663 was attributed by his father to the treachery of a Huguenot, 'nommé Rivredoux.' Emmanuel le Borgne to Colbert, 28 Oct. 1663, BN, Mélanges de Colbert, 117, ff.997–8. Rivedoux is a shadowy figure, who was involved in a fishing voyage from Boston to Cape Sable in 1660 and was at that time residing in Boston. Charter party, 28 May 1660, Suffolk court files, no. 507; see also Denys, *Description*, 559. The documentation concerning Le Borgne's captivity in Boston and his escape may be found in Suffolk court files, nos. 514, 826. See also Temple's comments in a letter to the Earl of Clarendon, 21 Aug. 1663, Public Archives of Nova Scotia [hereafter PANS], RG1, 1, no. 43.

9 Memorandum of Le Borgne Du Coudray, 23 Nov. 1665, AC, C^{11D}, 1, f.118. See also the elder Le Borgne's appeal to the Compagnie des Indes occidentales to support his son's efforts. Le Borgne to Compagnie des Indes occidentales, 27 Dec. 1664, AC, E, dossier 266.

10 Charles II to Temple, 22 Feb. 1666, PRO, CO1/20, no. 18.

11 Temple to Arlington, 2 Mar. 1669, PRO, CO1/24, no. 20.

12 Claim by the French ambassador, [*c*. 1662], PRO, CO1/16, no. 14; Destrades to Louis XIV, 22 Aug. 1661, AAÉ, Correspondence politique, Angleterre, 75, ff.127–9.

13 Answer to the ambassador of France, 7 Feb. 1662, PRO, CO1/16, no. 15.

14 Answer to the French ambassador's claim, [1662], PRO, CO1/16, no. 24.

15 Order in council, 7 Mar. 1662, BL, Egerton MSS, 2395, f.341.

16 Warrant to the attorney-general, 5 Apr. 1662, PRO, CO1/16, no. 40; Warrant to the attorney-general, 7 July 1662, PRO, SP44/7, p. 148; Bounds of Sir Thomas Temple's patent of Novia Scotia, July 1662, PRO, CO1/16, no. 86.

17 'In order to obtain news of the sieur de la Tour, who is assumed still to be there, and to gain information on the state of the forces and establishment which he and the English may have, not only at Port Royal, but also on the river St John and at the place called Pentagouet' (author's translation). Order and Instruction to the Sieur de La Rochette Gargot, captain of the Marine, 4 May 1663, CÉA, Fonds Placide Gaudet, 1.1–23. See also J.-Roger Comeau, 'Nicolas Gargot de La Rochette,' *DCB* I: 323–4.

18 '[Charles II] shall without delay cause to be restored ... the forts of Pentacoet, St John and Port Royal in America, occupied by the English.' 'It is public knowledge that the French possessed the whole of Acadia, Canada, and all the other neighbouring countries for more than eighty years ... and that the English expelled them thence by force and violence.' (Author's translations). Louis XIV to Commenges, 17 July, 7 Oct. 1663, AAÉ, Correspondance politique, Angleterre, 78, ff.189–90, 397–8.

19 Commenges to Louis XIV, 22 Oct. 1663, and Hugues de Lionne to Commenges, 24 Dec. 1664, AAÉ, Correspondance politique, Angleterre, 80, ff. 102–3; 84, f.101.

20 Godfrey to Nicholas, 15 July 1660, PRO, CO1/15, no. 20.

21 Petition of divers persons who have been sufferers in New England, [1661], PRO,CO1/15, no. 31,p.1.

22 Petition of Ferdinando Gorges, [4 Apr. 1661], PRO, CO1/15, no. 31, pp.7–8.

23 Report of Council for Foreign Plantations, April 1661, PRO, CO1/15, no. 42; Minutes of Council for Foreign Plantations, 13 May 1661, PRO, CO1/14, no. 59, p.29; Order in council, 17 May 1661, PRO,CO5/903, pp.1–3.

24 Result of an agitation at a meeting held at Wells, 27 Dec. 1661, PRO, CO1/15, no. 96; see also Reid, *Maine, Charles II, and Massachusetts*, 46–7.

25 Letter of Richard Waldron, 13 Dec. 1662, MA, 3, f.262.

26 Will of Jonas Balie, 11 Nov. 1663, in William Mitchell Sargent, ed., *Maine wills* (Portland 1887), 15.

27 Godfrey to John Winthrop, Jr, 5 Oct. 1661, *Winthrop papers* VII: 380; Godfrey to Thomas Povey, 7 Apr. 1663, PRO, CO1/17, no. 17.

28 Charles II to governor of Massachusetts, 28 June 1662, PRO, CO1/16, no. 66; Charles II to governor and council of Massachusetts, 23 Apr. 1664, PRO, CO1/18, no. 53.

29 Report of Sir Geoffrey Palmer, 8 June 1664, PRO, CO1/18, no. 70.

30 Charles II to the inhabitants of the Province of Maine, 11 June 1664, PRO, CO1/18, no. 72; *PCR* I: 200–2.

31 Samuel Maverick to Secretary Sir William Coventry, 21 July 1664, PRO, CO1/18, no. 86. See in addition the Duke of York's patent, MA, 3, ff.303–5. See also the instructions, both open and secret, to the royal commissioners: Instructions, 23 Apr. 1664, PRO, CO1/18, no. 51; Secret instructions, 23 Apr. 1664, PRO, CO1/18, no. 52. The whole question of the royal commission is more fully discussed in Reid, *Maine, Charles II, and Massachusetts*, 54–123.

32 *PCR* I: 202; see also Reid, *Maine, Charles* II, *and Massachusetts*, 81–3.
33 *PCR* I: 204–5, 208.
34 York, Town records, I, p.27; *PCR* II: 162–3.
35 Answer of Massachusetts council to the magistrates of Gorges, 30 Nov. 1664, MA, 3, f.265.
36 George Cartwright to Richard Nichols, 30 Jan. 1665, PRO, CO1/19, no. 11.
37 *MCR* IV (ii): 151.
38 Warrant, 21 June 1665, MA, 3, f.267.
39 Commission to Maine justices of the peace, 23 June 1665, PRO,CO1/19, no. 75; Sir Robert Carr, George Cartwright, and Samuel Maverick to Arlington, 26 July 1665, PRO, CO1/19, no. 82; see also Reid, *Maine, Charles* II, *and Massachusetts*, 86–92.
40 Charles II to the colonies of New England, 10 Apr. 1666, PRO, CO1/20, no. 44; Clarendon to Nichols, 13 April 1666, PRO, CO1/20, no. 56; see also Reid, *Maine, Charles* II, *and Massachusetts*, 95–8.
41 Petition of the inhabitants of Maine, [c. May 1668], PRO, CO1/22, no. 98(i).
42 *MCR* IV(ii): 370–3; Petition of Cape Porpoise, 28 Apr. 1668, MA, 3, f.275; Petition of Wells, 30 Apr. 1668, MA, 3, f.276.
43 Maine justices to Richard Nichols, July 1668, PRO, CO1/23, no. 11; Declaration of the Maine justices, 7 July 1668, PRO, CO1/23, no. 11(i); *PCR* II: 163–5; see also Reid, *Maine, Charles* II, *and Massachusetts*, 110–13.
44 The royal commissioners had noted in 1665 that there was conflict between the patents of Temple and the Duke of York, but the restitution of 1670 obviously made this conflict unimportant. George Cartwright to [Arlington], 14 Dec. 1665, PRO, CO1/19, no. 143.
45 See Kershaw, *Kennebeck proprietors*, 7–16. A copy of the deed of sale can be found in Suffolk court files, no. 672.
46 This statement is based not on direct evidence but is inferred from what few indications have survived. The scanty sources are reviewed in Burrage, *Beginnings*, 143, 198, 218, 249. Archaeological evidence is the most promising source of new knowledge on this region, as has been proved at Pemaquid and should be further demonstrated at Sheepscott. See Camp, *Pemaquid*, passim.
47 Samuel Maverick, 'A briefe description of New England,' BL, Egerton MSS, 2395, f.397. Maverick's statement is, of course, vague, and some secondary sources have estimated as many as 84 English families by 1630 in the Kennebec-Penobscot area. Such estimates, however, are excessive. See the discussion of this point in Edwin A. Churchill, introduction to Camp, *Pemaquid*, x.
48 *PCR* I: 244–5; Cartwright to [Arlington], 14 Dec. 1665, PRO, CO1/19, no. 143.
49 Maverick, 'Description,' f.397; Josselyn, *Two voyages*, 345.
50 General Court to John Leverett, [c. 1658], Hutchinson, *Collection of papers*, 320–2.
51 'An effect of the fear which they have of French neighbourhood, or of a true desire to come under the rule of His Majesty' (author's translation). Report of Grandfon-

taine, [1671], AC, C^{11D}, 1, f. 139; Talon to Colbert, 2 Nov., 11 Nov. 1671, AC, C^{11A}, 3, ff.161, 187–8.

52 Report of Granfontaine, [1671], AC, C^{11D}, 1, f.139.

53 Petition, 18 May 1672, Suffolk court files, no. 1117; Edward Rawson to Thomas Gardner and Silvanus Davis, 17 June 1672, Suffolk court files, no. 1118; Proceedings of the Massachusetts commissioners, 22 July 1674, MA, 3, ff.306–8.

54 Brunet's letters and his logs of voyages are preserved in BN, Collection Clairambault, 864. See Journal of a voyage from La Rochelle to Plaisance and Acadia, 1673, in vol. 864, pt 1, ff. 39, 42; Brunet to Grandfontaine, 4 Feb. 1675, in vol. 864, 2, f.71. Extracts from Brunet's letters and an account of his career may be found in Louis-André Vigneras, 'Letters of an Acadian trader, 1674–1676,' *New England Quarterly* 13 (1940): 98–110.

55 *MCR* V: 30, 87. Lake was killed in the Abenaki war in 1676. For Brunet's hopeful remarks, see Brunet to the Compagnie du Nord, 13 Oct. 1674, BN, Collection Clairambault, 864, pt 2, f.60. In true mercantilist style, Brunet excoriated the practice of allowing New Englanders to trade in Acadia but was keen to expand his own trade in New England.

56 John Evelyn, *The diary of John Evelyn*, ed. Esmond Samuel Beer (6 vols, Oxford, 1955), III: 582.

57 Proposals of William, Earl of Stirling, Ferdinando Gorges, and Robert Mason to the king, [20 Mar. 1674], PRO, CO1/31, no. 22. Although Stirling's first name was given as William in this document, drafted by Mason, it seems clear that this was an error for Henry Alexander, 4th Earl. Stirling's claim, while antecedent to that of Temple, had for all practical purposes been superseded.

58 John Collins to John Leverett, 16 Feb. 1675, Hutchinson, *Collection of papers*, 470.

59 Charles II to Temple, 22 Feb. 1666, PRO, CO1/20, no. 18; Charles II to Temple, 1666 [a draft of a letter sent later than that of 22 February], PRO, CO1/20, no. 19; Temple to Arlington, 24 May 1667, PRO, CO1/21, no. 49.

60 Temple to [Arlington], 10 Dec. 1667, PRO, CO1/21, no. 155.

61 Charles II to Temple, November 1667, PRO, CO1/21, nos. 150, 153. Both of these documents are endorsed to the effect that they were never sent.

62 Memorandum of Sir Joseph Williamson, [1667], PRO, CO1/21, no. 159.

63 Charles II to Temple, 31 Dec. 1667, PRO, CO1/21, no. 168.

64 Temple to Privy Council, 24 Nov. 1668, PRO, CO1/23, no. 86.

65 'Incoherent and unfounded difficulties and ambiguities, in order to make me lose time' (author's translation). Du Bourg to Colbert de Terron, 27 Nov. 1668, AC, C^{11D}, 1, ff.126–7; Charles II to Temple, 1 Aug. 1668, PRO, CO1/23, no. 32; Du Bourg to Le Borgne de Belle-Isle, [1668] PRO, CO1/23, no. 102(iv).

66 '[That he was] a rogue ... and that he would by all means make him obey' (author's translation). Charles II to Temple, 8 Mar., 6 Aug. 1669 PRO, CO1/24, no. 26,

CO5/903, pp.20–1; Colbert de Terron to Louis XIV, 24 Jan. 1669, AAÉ, Correspondance politique, Angleterre, 94, ff.28–9.

67 Royal authorization to the Sieur de Grandfontaine, 22 July 1669, AC, B, 1, f.158; Royal order to the Chevalier de Grandfontaine, 20 Feb. 1670, Archives de la Marine, B², 10, pp.38–9. For the terms of the surrender, see Treaty between the Sieurs de Grandfontaine and Temple, 7 July 1670, AAÉ, Mémoires et documents, Amérique, 5, ff.277–8. The specific acts of surrender for Pentagouet, Jemseg, and Port Royal are in *The memorials of the English and French commissaries concerning the limits of Nova Scotia or Acadia* (2 vols, London 1755), I: 604–13.

68 Temple to Charles II, 10 Jan. 1671, PRO, CO1/26, no. 4; Talon to Colbert, 2 Nov. 1671, AC, c^{IIA}, 3, f.160; Report of Sieur de Patoulet, 25 Jan. 1672, AC, C^{IIA}, 3, f.276; Colbert to Talon, 4 June 1672, AC, B, 4, f.60; Certificate of the governor and council of Massachusetts touching Sir Thomas Temple, 9 May 1673, PRO, CO1/30, no. 34. Temple awarded to Thomas Lake and three others the doubtful privilege of being executors of his will, which they tried unsuccessfully to decline. As the Suffolk County Court rightly judged, 'the saide Estate will prove insolvant.' Records of the Suffolk County Court, in Colonial Society of Massachusetts, *Publications* (XXIX and XXX, Boston 1933), XXIX: 476–7.

69 Memorandum regarding Acadia, 1667, AAÉ, Correspondance politique, Angleterre, 89, f.118.

70 Memorandum on the state of the country of Acadia, [*c.* 1668], AC, C^{IID}, 1, ff.11–15.

71 'If it would not be more advantageous to revoke and annul all the gifts and concessions which have been made in that country, and at the same time to send somebody there who could build a good fort on the river which marks the partition from the English, with a view to sending a number of men there every year and working gradually to build up population.' (author's translation). Dispatch to Colbert de Terron, 26 Aug. 1669, Archives de la Marine, B², 9, pp.340–2.

72 '[Acadia would prove] not only in a condition to sustain itself, but also to supply to the French West Indies some portion of the commodities which they need for the subsistence of the inhabitants there and for their other needs' (author's translation). Colbert to Talon, 11 Feb. 1671, AC, B, 3, ff.23–4; Instructions to Grandfontaine, 5 Mar. 1670, AC, B, 2, ff.57–61.

73 '[To be] in a condition to supply salt meats to the Antilles' (author's translation). Talon to Colbert, 11 Nov. 1671, AC, C^{IIA}, 3, ff.184–5. The year 1671 also saw the first in the series of Acadian censuses, showing a population total of 392. Archives nationales, Section Outre-mer, G^1, 466, nos.8,9.

74 'To break off, without violence, the trade which the English conduct with the king's subjects living at Port Royal, from whom they obtain every year a quantity of meat in exchange for woollen cloth and other fabric materials made in Boston; my feeling is that this could be accomplished easily enough by sending out to Port

Royal, from France or from here [Quebec], some small amount of cloth to supply the more immediate needs' (author's translation). Talon to Colbert, 11 Nov. 1671, AC, C^{11A}, 3, ff.184–5. In a later memorandum, Talon also revealed a direct contact between Maine and Acadia in naming 'major chapelay,' Nicholas Shapleigh of Kittery, as one of the English traders on the coast of Acadia. Memorandum of Jean Talon, 1673, AC, C^{11A}, 4, f.42.

75 See Clark, *Acadia*, chap. 5; also Hynes, 'Demography of Port Royal,' 4–5.

76 See Denys, *Description*, introduction by W.F. Ganong, 14–17; and Pothier, 'Nicolas Denys,' 62–7.

77 Report of Perrot, 9 Aug. 1686, AC, C^{11D}, 2, f.21. For d'Entremont's seigneurial grant, see CÉA, Fonds Placide Gaudet, 1.1–16A. See also Clément Cormier, 'Philippe Mius d'Entremont,' *DCB* I: 510; Clarence-J. d'Entremont, 'Le manoir et les armoiries de la famille Mius-d'Entremont d'Acadie,' Société historique aca-dienne, *Cahiers* 6 (1964): 19–24; d'Entremont, 'Le Cap Sable,' 166.

78 Memorandum of Jean Talon, 1673, AC, C^{11A}, 4, ff.41–2; Clark, *Acadia*, 113–21.

79 'This land, such as and even better than I represent it, in order to become useful to our own has need of those very fortunate influences with which it has pleased Your Majesty to look upon its neighbours' (Denys, *Description*, 455; translation, 88).

80 Dudouyt to Laval, 1677, Archives du séminaire de Québec, Lettres N, no. 48, pp.10,15. See also Eccles, *France in America*, 65–6; and Daigle, 'Nos amis les ennemis,' 46–7.

81 Report of Grandfontaine, [1671], AC, C^{11D}, 1, f.139. The same report also indicated that Le Borgne had been responsible for the deaths of a Negro and an Indian. Unfortunately, details are lacking, and the individuals concerned in these incidents are unknown. The circumstances in which a black became a resident of Port Royal and then met his death would be especially interesting.

82 Report of Perrot, 9 Aug. 1686, AC, C^{11D}, 2, f.15.

83 Meneval to Seignelay, 31 Oct. 1689, AC, C^{11D}, 2, f.125.

84 Declaration of the Le Borgne heirs, n.d., AC, C^{11D}, 1, f.68; Memorandum of the Le Borgnes, n.d., AC, E, dossier 266.

85 On the convocation of an assembly of the inhabitants of the parish of St. Jean Baptiste of Port Royal, 18 June 1673, AC, E, dossier 277. As far as is known, the request went unheeded.

86 'Or because of the divisions among them, or lastly because of some English and parliamentary leaning inspired by the contact and trade which they have with the Bostonians ...'; 'To hold public celebrations of the glorious conquests which Your Majesty made last year' (author's translation). Frontenac to Louis XIV, 6 Nov. 1679, AC, C^{11A}, 5, f.16. Frontenac may have had in mind the holding of parish meetings such as the one in 1673 cited above, which bore the names of 'la majeure par desdits habitants' and addressed itself to the questions of weights and measures and unruly animals, as well as to the building of the parish church. It is unfortunate

that records of other such meetings have not survived.

87 'In all matters [to maintain] good relations with the English of Boston ... [and at your discretion] to supply all your needs from thence' (author's translation). Colbert to Grandfontaine, 11 Mar. 1671, AC, B, 3, ff.41–4.

88 '[He had] even traded a cannon belonging to the king to the savages' (author's translation). Grandfontaine to Governor Richard Bellingham, 12 Jan. 1672, MA, 2, f.511. See also a 1672 legal case in which William Waldron sued Christopher Smith for his share of the proceeds of two fur-trading voyages to the Bay of Fundy in 1671; records of the Suffolk County Court, Colonial Society of Massachusetts *Publications* XXIX: 135–9.

89 'The miserable condition in which Monsieur le chevalier de grand fontaines ... informed Monsieur Talon that he found himself and his garrison' (author's translation). Frontenac to Colbert, 2 Nov. 1672, AC, C^{IIA}, 3, f.243.

90 Report of Grandfontaine, [1671], AC, C^{IID}, 1, f.139; Talon to Louis XIV, 2 Nov. 1671, AC C^{IIA}, 3, f.159.

91 'It will be well to make it understood that His Majesty has not given approval that one should enter into such a relationship with foreigners, who have superior forces to our own since their settlements are older and better supplied than our settlements' (author's translation). Instructions to the Sieur de La Tour, 1673, Archives de la Marine, C^7, dossier 169. For further discussion of Grandfontaine's dilemma, see Daigle, 'Nos amis les ennemis,' 84.

92 Commission to Sieur de Chambly, 5 May 1673, AC, C^{IID}, 1, f.141; Frontenac to Colbert, 16 Feb. 1674, AC, C^{IIA}, 4, f.52.

93 See the reports of Henri Brunet on this episode: Brunet to Jacques Godefroy, 7 Nov. 1674, BN, Collection Clairambault, 864, pt 2, f.56; Brunet to [Colbert de Terron], 7 Nov. 1674, BN, Collection Clairambault, 864, pt 2, ff.57–8. For a full discussion, see John Clarence Webster, *Cornelis Steenwyck: Dutch governor of Acadie* (Shediac, N.B. 1929).

94 A death sentence on Rhoades was never carried out. Extensive documentation of the case may be found in MA, 61, ff.60–122.

95 'I was powerless to send help to Acadia, even if I had had the supplies necessary to do so; I had to be satisfied with sending some men with canoes to try to find out in what condition they had left the fort, and whether they might not have made an attempt on Port Royal' (author's translation). Frontenac to Colbert, 14 Nov. 1674, AC, C^{IIA}, 4, f.78.

96 'His Majesty was surprised to learn [of the Dutch raid] ... and cannot persuade himself that there was not some degree of negligence on the part of the Sieur de Chambly' (author's translation). Colbert to Frontenac, 15 Mar. 1675, *Collection de manuscrits* I: 232.

97 See Memorandum of William Vaughan *et al.*, 1685, PRO, CO5/940, p.149.

CHAPTER 8

1 Ignace de Paris, 'Letter,' PAC *Report, 1904*, 338.

2 *Jesuit relations* XLV: 58, XLVII: 62–4, '[The Jesuit Fathers] seeing that there was nothing more to be done with these people, whom the frequentation of the ships kept in perpetual drunkenness' (Denys, *Description*, 603; translation, 446).

3 See Dudouyt to Laval, 1677, Archives du séminaire de Québec, Lettres N, no. 48, pp.5, 15.

4 Laval to Seignelay, 10 Nov. 1683, Archives du séminaire de Québec, Lettres O, no. 61, p.2. See also Baillargeon, *Séminaire de Québec sous Laval*, 145–7, 230–9; Casgrain, *Les Sulpiciens*, 22–4. Thury's mission on the Miramichi marked the first entry of the Séminaire de Québec into purely missionary work, rather than pastoral and missionary work combined.

5 See Seignelay to Laval, 10 Apr. 1684, AC, B, 11, ff.34–6; also Casgrain, *Les Sulpiciens*, 49.

6 See Casgrain, *Les Sulpiciens*, 51–5; and *Jesuit relations* LXII: 258–66, XLIII: 26–138.

7 Morrison, 'People of the Dawn,' 434; see also 108-16, on which this paragraph is largely based.

8 Baron de Lahontan, *New voyages to North-America*, ed. Reuben Gold Thwaites (Chicago 1905), 328; see also Pierre Daviault, *Le Baron de Saint-Castin: chef abénaquis* (Montreal 1939), 21–8; and Le Blant, *Baron de St-Castin*, chap. 3.

9 'A gentleman ... who has neither cleared land nor done anything' (author's translation). Report of Perrot, 9 Aug. 1686, AC, C¹¹D, 2, f.20. Saint-Castin's unorthodox way of life was also mentioned disapprovingly in the French government's instructions to Perrot's successor, Des Friches de Meneval. Instructions to Meneval, 5 Apr. 1687, AC, C¹¹D, 2, f.83.

10 See Morrison, 'People of the Dawn,' 411–12; and Casgrain, *Les Sulpiciens*, 70–1.

11 'That is to say to be Catholics, to procure land and to work like Frenchmen' (author's translation). Memorandum, 1686, AC, C¹¹D, 2, f.34.

12 Thomas Gardner to John Leverett, 22 Sept. 1675, *Documentary history of Maine* VI: 91–3. See also John O. Noble, Jr, 'King Philip's War in Maine' (MA thesis, University of Maine 1970), 10–14; and Washburn, 'Seventeenth-century Indian wars,' *HNAI* 15: 93.

13 Noble, 'King Philip's War in Maine,' passim; Morrison, 'People of the Dawn,' 123–8; Morrison, 'Dawnland decisions,' 94, 116–21; Reid, *Maine, Charles II, and Massachusetts*, 155–62. Once again, the role of the Penacooks on the York and Piscataqua rivers is less than clear; it is likely that their small numbers kept them out of the conflict, despite their affinities with the peoples further south, and that it was Abenaki raiding parties which brought the war to the southernmost English settlements of Yorkshire.

14 See Morrison, 'People of the Dawn,' 128, 135–6; Noble, 'King Philip's War in Maine,' 35–6, 50–2; Sévigny, *Les Abénaquis*, 122–5.
15 Noble, 'King Philip's War in Maine,' 6–7.
16 Order of Richard Waldron, 6 Oct. 1675, *Documentary history of Maine* IV: 348–9; Order of Massachusetts council, 9 Dec. 1675, MA, 68, f.89.
17 Massachusetts council to Joshua Scottow, 16 Nov. 1675, MA, 68, f.59.
18 Letter of Richard Waldron *et al.*, 19 Oct. 1676, MA, f.71.
19 Petition of Edward Rishworth *et al.*, 27 May 1677, MA, 69, f.126; Petition of Joshua Scottow on behalf of ... the inhabitants of Scarborough, [18 Oct. 1677], MA, 69, f.160. For further treatment of the impact of the Abenaki war on English settlement, see Reid, *Maine, Charles II, and Massachusetts*, 157–62.
20 James Axtell, 'The vengeful women of Marblehead: Robert Roules's deposition of 1677,' *William and Mary Quarterly* 3rd ser., 31 (1974): 647–52.
21 See Douglas Edward Leach, *Flintlock and tomahawk: New England in King Philip's War* (New York 1966), 245; see also Nash, *Red, white, and black*, 121–7.
22 See Massachusetts council to Brian Pendleton and Richard Waldron, 9 Mar. 1678, MA, 69 f.185; also Mather, *Magnalia Christi Americana* II: 584.
23 Kennebec sachems to Massachusetts governor, 1 July 1677, MA, 30, ff.241–2.
24 See Andrews, *British committees*, 111–12; Winfred Trexler Root, 'The Lords of Trade and Plantations, 1675–1696,' *American Historical Review* 23 (1917–18): 23; Alison Gilbert Olson, *Anglo-American politics, 1660–1775* (Oxford 1973), 57–61. This whole episode is further discussed in Reid, *Maine, Charles II, and Massachusetts*, 162–72.
25 Petition of Robert Mason and Ferdinando Gorges, [9 Jan. 1678], PRO, CO1/42, no. 15(vii).
26 Robert Mason to Committee for Trade and Plantations, 25 Mar. 1678, PRO, CO1/42, no. 38.
27 Early copies of the deeds exist in the Suffolk court files, nos. 1697, 2128. They are available in printed form in Maine Historical Society *Collections* ser. 1, II (1847): 257–64.
28 See Report of General Court committee, 8 Oct. 1678, MA, 3, ff.333–4; *MCR* V: 195–6, 226, 263; *PCR* III: 3.
29 *MCR* V: 326.
30 *PCR* III: 30.
31 Ibid., 18, 46; *MCR* V: 326–7.
32 See *MCR* V: 391–2, 441–2, 490; see also Edward Randolph to Sir Leoline Jenkins, 30 Apr. 1681, PRO, CO1/46, no. 130.
33 For the land transfer, see Trust deeds, 26 July 1684, Noyes *et al.*, *Genealogical dictionary*, 6.
34 Address of General Assembly of Maine to Charles II, 30 June 1680, MA, 3, ff.343–4; Petition of inhabitants of Maine to Charles II, [1680], PRO, CO1/46, no.

14. See also Reid, *Maine, Charles II, and Massachusetts*, 184–94; Van Deventer, *New Hampshire*, 44–51.

35 Commission to Chambly, 20 May 1676, AC, C^{11D}, 1, f.143; Dudouyt to Laval, 1677, Archives du séminaire de Québec, Lettres N, no. 48, p.10; Frontenac to Louis XIV, 6 Nov. 1679, AC, C^{11A}, 5, ff.15–16.

36 Louis XIV to Frontenac, 12 May 1678, AC, B, 7, ff.159–61; Jean Daigle, 'Michel Le Neuf de La Vallière, seigneur de Beaubassin et gouverneur d'Acadie' (MA thesis, Université de Montréal 1970), 41.

37 'I have the honour to inform Your Majesty that last year I sent the Sieur de La Vallière to command in Acadia, after the death of the Sieur de Marson and pending Your Majesty's orders in regard to the Sieur de Chambly, who I understand has been given another command in the West Indies.' (author's translation). Frontenac to Louis XIV, 6 Nov. 1679, AC, C^{11A}, 5, ff.15–16; Summary of documents, 1678–84; AC C^{11D}, 1, f.148.

38 J.-Roger Comeau, 'Michel Leneuf de La Vallière de Beaubassin,' *DCB* II: 409–11; Daigle, 'La Valliere,' 21–3, 35–8.

39 Ordinance of La Barre, 22 Mar. 1683, AC, F^3, 6, ff.34–5; Seignelay to La Barre, 10 Apr. 1684, *Collection de manuscrits* I: 324–5.

40 See Daigle, 'La Vallière,' 79–82.

41 'The Sieur de La Valiere is a very honourable gentleman who is conducting himself extremely well' (author's translation). La Barre to Seignelay, [1682], AC, C^{11A}, 6, f.61.

42 See Frontenac to Louis XIV, 2 Nov. 1681, AC, C^{11A}, 5, f.387; and Order of La Vallière, 22 Oct. 1682, PRO, CO1/55, no. 37(v).

43 '[That] without the aid of the English, who have always brought essential supplies there, that country would have been abandoned' (author's translation). La Barre to La Vallière, 4 Oct. 1683, PRO, CO1/55, no. 37(ii).

44 Journal of Committee for Trade and Plantations, 21 June 1679, PRO, CO391/3, p.28. The context was a continuation of Temple's dispute with William Crowne.

45 Order of La Vallière, 22 Oct. 1682, PRO, CO1/55, no. 37(v); Rawlyk, *Nova Scotia's Massachusetts*, 35–6, 42–3.

46 Frontenac to Massachusetts council, 3 Nov. 1681, MA, 2, f.518; Frontenac to Massachusetts governor, 2 Aug. 1682, MA, 2, ff.520–1; Order of Massachusetts General Court, 17 Oct. 1682, MA, 2, f.522; *MCR* V: 373–4. See also Arthur Howland Buffinton, 'John Nelson's voyage to Quebec in 1682: a chapter in the fisheries controversy,' Colonial Society of Massachusetts, *Publications* XXVI (1927): 427–37.

47 See Daigle, 'Nos amis les ennemis,' 74, 94–7.

48 Journal of the Committee for Trade and Plantations, 8 Apr. 1678, PRO, CO391/2, 244.

49 'Since there has been no governor in that place for a long time, and since the Sieur de la Valiere has fulfilled the governor's role without commission for two years,

His Majesty wishes him to investigate whether the said la Valiere is fit for the position ...' (author's translation). Instructions to La Barre, 10 May 1682, AC, B, 8, f.104; Louis XIV to La Barre, 5 Aug. 1683, AC, B, 9, f.3; Summary of documents, 1678–84, AC, C¹¹D, 1, ff.148–9.

50 See Donald H. Pennington, *Seventeenth century Europe* (London 1970), 29–32.

51 New York council minutes, 9 June 1677, in Franklin B. Hough, ed., 'Pemaquid papers,' Maine Historical Society *Collections* ser. 1, V (1857); 14–15.

52 New York council minutes, 11 Sept. 1677, Ibid., 18–19.

53 New York council minutes, 12 June 1678, Ibid., 29–31; on Alden's later activities, see Rawlyk, *Nova Scotia's Massachusetts*, 62, 68, 73–5.

54 Acts of Massachusetts council regarding Pemaquid, August 1680, MA, 3, ff.345–6. For Andros' version of these incidents, see his letters in Colonial Williamsburg, Inc., Blathwayt papers, 3.

55 Anthony Brockholst to Henry Jocelyn, 24 Aug. 1682, Hough, 'Pemaquid papers,' 58–9; Saint-Castin to Meneval, 15 Sept. 1687, *Collection de manuscrits* I: 403.

56 New York council minutes, 22 Nov. 1683, Hough, 'Pemaquid papers,' 80.

57 Journal of the Committee for Trade and Plantations, 8 Apr. 1678, PRO, CO391/2, pp.233–7; Andros to Blathwayt, 16 Sept., 12 Oct. 1678, 25 March 1679, PRO, CO1/42 nos. 124, 131, CO1/43, no. 38; Abstract of Andros letters, 25 Feb. 1680, PRO, CO1/44, no. 31; Blathwayt to Andros, 10 Feb., 15 July 1679, 21 Feb. 1680, Colonial Williamsburg, Inc., Blathwayt papers, 3. On the career of William Blathwayt, see Gertrude Ann Jacobsen, *William Blathwayt: a late seventeenth century English administrator* (New Haven 1932); and Stephen Saunders Webb, 'William Blathwayt, imperial fixer: from popish plot to glorious revolution,' *William and Mary Quarterly* 3rd. ser., 25 (1968): 3–21.

58 See Michael G. Hall, *Edward Randolph and the American colonies, 1676–1703* (Chapel Hill, N.C. 1960), chap. 1 and passim.

59 Answer of Edward Randolph regarding the present state of New England, 12 Oct. 1676, PRO, CO1/37, no. 70.

60 Randolph to Committee for Trade and Plantations, 30 Dec. 1682, in Robert Noxon Toppan and Alfred Thomas Scrope Goodrick, eds, *Edward Randolph; including his letters and official papers from the New England, middle, and southern colonies in America, with other documents relating chiefly to the vacating of the royal charter of the colony of Massachusetts Bay, 1676–1703* (7 vols, Boston 1898–1909; hereafter Toppan and Goodrick, *Randolph letters*), III: 219; Extract from Suffolk County Court record, 30 Jan. 1683, PRO, CO1/51, no. 22.

61 Articles of high misdemeanour exhibited against Thomas Danforth, [11 Mar. 1681], PRO, CO1/46, no. 111(ii).

62 Concession to the Bergier company, 28 Feb. 1682, AC, C¹¹D, 1, ff.150–1; Dudouyt to Laval, 9 Mar. 1682, Archives du séminaire de Québec, Lettres N, no. 61, pp.24–5.

63 'That the coast [of Acadia] would be entirely ruined by the English if a prompt

remedy were not applied, and that this situation had been caused by the right of entry to our ports given to them [the English] for money by the man named La Valière from Quebec, which he did on his own authority and without any orders from His Majesty' (author's translation). Paper addressed to Seignelay, [1682], AC, C^{11D}, 1, f.162. See also the anonymous complaints against La Vallière on behalf of Bergier's company, in PANS, RG1, 4, no.5.

64 Order of Louis XIV, 14 Apr. 1684, AC, C^{11D}, 1, ff.183–4; Louis XIV to La Barre, 10 Apr. 1684, AC, C^{11A}, 6, f.249. On La Vallière's subsequent actions, see Daigle, 'Nos amis les ennemis,' 105.

65 Anonymous letter, 15 Sept. 1684, PRO, CO1/55, no. 37; Petition of William Vaughan *et al.*, [c. Dec. 1684], PRO, CO1/55, no. 105; Answer of the French regarding the fishery, [16 Jan. 1686], PRO, CO1/59, no. 10; Memorandum of the Compagnie de la Pêche sédentaire, 1685, AC, C^{11D}, 1, f.193.

66 'A large and strong establishment on the coast' (author's translation). Report of Perrot, 9 Aug. 1686, AC, C^{11D}, 2, f.22. '[John Nelson], who has always traded on this coast, and who has done much good among the inhabitants through the large loans which he has made to them in their greatest need' (author's translation). Letter of Perrot, 29 Aug. 1686, AC, C^{11D}, 2, f.14. See also Perrot's Plan for Acadia, [c. 1686], AC, C^{11D}, 2, f.24; Memorandum of the Compagnie de la Pêche séden-taire, [c. 1686], AAÉ, Correspondance politique, Angleterre, 151, ff.222–3; see also Daigle, 'Nos amis les ennemis,' 106–7.

67 'If Bergier had not embroiled us with the English, Chedabouctou would have been able to carry on … ' (author's translation). A. Augustin-Thierry, ed., *Un colonial au temps de Colbert: mémoires de Robert Challes, écrivain du roi* (Paris 1931), 274.

68 '[A] man of integrity and courage, and one known to be uninfluenced by self-interest' (author's translation). Memorandum of the Compagnie de la Pêche sédentaire, [c. 1686], AAÉ, Correspondance politique, Angleterre, 151, f.223.

69 'To have the fort at Port Royal repaired, or to construct a new one at whatever place shall be found most suitable' (author's translation). Instructions to Meneval, 5 Apr. 1687, AC, C^{11D}, 2, ff.78–83; see also the discussion in Rawlyk, *Nova Scotia's Massachusetts*, 51–3.

70 Donald G. Pilgrim, 'France and New France: two perspectives on colonial secur-ity,' *Canadian Historical Review* 55 (1974): 387–96; Daigle, 'Nos amis les ennemis,' 112–16.

71 See letters of Meneval, September 1689, AC, C^{11D}, 2, ff.112–18.

72 Memorandum as to the Province of Maine, November 1684, PRO, CO1/56, no. 84.

73 See Viola Florence Barnes, *The Dominion of New England* (New Haven 1923), 47–9, 69–72. The King's Province was a small area in the Narragansett Bay region, so named by the royal commissioners in 1665.

74 *PCR* III and IV.

75 See Theodore Burnham Lewis, 'Land speculation and the Dudley council of 1686,' *William and Mary Quarterly* 3rd. ser., 31 (1974): 255–72.

76 See Reid, *Maine, Charles II, and Massachusetts*, 201–3.

77 See George Norman Clark, *The later Stuarts* (2nd ed., Oxford 1955), chaps 4, 6.

78 See Pilgrim, 'France and New France,' 396–8.

79 '[It would be] very useful for the commercial advantage of the two nations that new orders should be sent to the respective governors of Acadia and New England for the full implementation of the treaty of Breda' (author's translation). Usson de Bonrepaux to Seignelay, 7 Jan. 1686, AAÉ, Correspondance politique, Angleterre, 160, f.8. Paul Barillon, Marquis de Branges, was also involved in these negotiations as French ambassador in London.

80 Bonrepaux to Seignelay, 17 Jan. 1686, AAÉ, Correspondance politique, Angleterre, 160, ff.33–4; Barillon to Seignelay, 18 Feb. 1686, AAÉ, Correspondance politique, Angleterre, 160, ff.107–8; Pilgrim, 'France and New France,' 399–401.

81 'In all the places in America which in either case are or shall be possessed [by the opposite party]' (author's translation). *Édits, ordonnances royaux, déclarations et arrêts du Conseil d'État du roi concernant le Canada ...* I (Quebec 1803): 258.

82 'There shall always there be a true and firm peace and neutrality between the said peoples of France and Great Britain, just as if such a rupture in Europe had not occurred' (author's translation). Printed in *Édits* I: 261.

83 See Pilgrim, 'France and New France,' 401.

84 '[There was no other way] than to regulate the limits of the lands which each of the two nations should possess ... '; 'experience has shown that those who command act more often according to their own particular interest than according to the general good and the advantage of the colonies' (author's translations). Memorandum of the French commissioners to James II, 7 Nov. 1687, PRO, CO5/1113, 168.

85 Governor Denonville of New France to Governor Dongan of New York, 2 Oct. 1687, PRO, CO1/63, no. 39.

86 See Bruce Tiebout McCully, 'The New England-Acadia fishery dispute and the Nicholson mission of August, 1687,' *Essex Institute Historical Collections* 96 (1960): 285–7, 289.

87 Randolph to Blathwayt, 28 July 1686, Toppan and Goodrick *Randolph letters* IV: 98.

88 Randolph to John Povey, 21 June 1688, Ibid., 224–5; Andros to Blathwayt, 4 June 1688, Colonial Williamsburg, Inc., Blathwayt papers, 3; Andros to James II, 9 July 1688, PRO, CO1/65, no. 20

89 Francis Nicholson to [?Blathwayt], 31 Aug. 1688, PRO, CO1/65, no. 51; see also Augustin-Thierry, *Mémoires de Challes*, 272–3.

90 Nicholson to [?Blathwayt], 31 Aug. 1688, PRO, CO1/65, no. 51; Andros to Committee for Trade and Plantations, 7 July 1688, PRO, CO1/65, no. 19.

91 Anonymous letter, 15 Sept. 1684, PRO, CO1/55, no. 37; Edward Tyng to Andros, 18 Aug. 1688, *Documentary history of Maine* VI: 419–20; Mather, *Magnalia Christi Americana* II: 584; Samuel Sewall, *The diary of Samuel Sewall, 1674– 1729*, Massachusetts Historical Society *Collections* 5th ser., v (Boston 1878), 225; Morrison, 'People of the Dawn,' 154, 159–60, 165–7.

92 Randolph to Committee for Trade and Plantations, 29 May 1689, PRO, CO5/855, no. 8; Letter transmitted to Committee for Trade and Plantations by John Usher, 10 July 1689, PRO, CO5/855, no. 16; see also Morrison, 'People of the Dawn,' 181–3; and *PCR* III: introduction, li. On the revolution, see David Sherman Lovejoy, *The Glorious Revolution in America* (New York 1972), chaps 12 and 13.

93 Benjamin Church, *The history of the eastern expeditions of 1689, 1690, 1692, 1696, and 1704 against the Indians and French* (Boston 1716), 65; Letter of Thomas Newton, 26 May 1690, PRO, CO5/1081, no. 138; see also *PCR* III: introduction, liii.

94 Petition of Robert Nelson [father of John Nelson], [c. 1689], PRO, CO5/855, no. 51; Massachusetts State Archives, Records of the General Court of Massachusetts, 6 (1689–98), pp.96–97.

95 Journal of Sir William Phips, 1690, PRO, CO5/855, no. 109, pp.6–7.

96 Ibid., p.15.

97 Cotton Mather to the Reverend James Brown, 30 Apr. 1690, HMC, *Ninth report, part II: appendix and index* (London 1884), MSS of Alfred Morrison Esq., 462.

98 'That which I have always had reason to fear, ever since I have been here, has eventually come about, Monseigneur' (author's translation). Meneval to Seignelay, 29 May 1690, *Collection de manuscrits* II: 10.

99 Report of Jean Bochart de Champigny, 1690, Ibid. II: 29.

100 Villebon to the Marquis de Chevry, 1690, in John Clarence Webster, ed., *Acadia at the end of the seventeenth century* (Saint John, N.B. 1934), 24.

101 See Proposal of Villebon to the French crown, February 1691, AC, C^{11D}, 2, ff.172–3. See also Villebon's journals and other documents in Webster, *Acadia*.

CONCLUSION

1 See Stephen E. Patterson, 'In search of the Massachusetts-Nova Scotia dynamic,' *Acadiensis* 5 (spring 1976): 138–43.

2 See *L'Évangéline* (Moncton), 27 Apr. 1976, 5. Just over two years later, in June 1978, an entire issue of the periodical *L'Action nationale* was devoted to discussion of this concept of 'une nouvelle Acadie.' *L'Action nationale* 67 (1978): 789–896.

Bibliography

MANUSCRIPT SOURCES

Manuscript sources are listed according to the country in which each collection is located. However, all the French sources cited are available in the form of transcripts or microfilms at the Public Archives of Canada, and in many cases also at the Centre d'études acadiennes of the Université de Moncton.

Canada

Archives du Séminaire de Québec. Lettres N; Lettres O; Polygraphie 4
Public Archives of Nova Scotia. Nova Scotia records, RGI, I–4
Université de Moncton, Centre d'études acadiennes. Collection Émile Lauvrière; Fonds Placide Gaudet: Fonds René Baudry

France

Archives départementales de la Charente-Maritime. Série B; Série E, Minutes Juppin, Minutes Teuleron (PAC, MG6, A2)
Archives du ministère des Affaires étrangères. Correspondance politique, Angleterre (PAC, MG5, A1); Mémoires et documents, Amérique (PAC, MG5, B1)
Archives nationales
    Archives de la Marine. Série B (PAC, MG2)
    Archives des Colonies. Séries B; C^{11A}; C^{11D}; E; F3 (PAC, MGI)
    Section Outre-Mer. Série G^1 (PAC, MGI)
Bibliothèque Nationale. Collection Clairambault, 864 (PAC, MG7, IA5); Fonds français, 13423, 17387, 18593, 28927 (PAC, MG7, IA2); Mélanges de Colbert, 118 (PAC, MG7, IA6); Nouvelles acquisitions françaises, 5131, 9281 (PAC, MG7, IA3)

Great Britain

British Library. Additional MSS, 11411; Egerton MSS, 2395
National Library of Scotland. Hawthornden MSS, MS2061
Public Record Office. Series CO1; CO5; CO391; SP16; SP44; SP78
Scottish Record Office. Series GD17; PS5

United States of America

Kittery, Maine. Town records, 1
Maine Historical Society Archives. Willis papers, P
Massachusetts State Archives. Massachusetts Archives, 2, 3, 30, 39, 61, 67–9, 100;
   Massachusetts Council records, 1650–6; Records of the General Court, 6
Massachusetts Historical Society. Gay transcripts, Sedgwick papers; Parkman papers,
   32
Suffolk County, Massachusetts. Suffolk court files
York, Maine. Town records, 1

PRINTED PRIMARY SOURCES

Alexander, Sir William. *An encouragement to colonies*. London 1624
Augustin-Thierry, A., ed. *Un colonial au temps de Colbert: mémoires de Robert
   Challes, écrivain du roi*. Paris 1931
Banks, Charles Edward, ed. 'Relation concerning the estate of New England, about
   1634.' *New England Historical and Genealogical Register* 40 (1886): 66–73
Bede. *Ecclesiastical history of the English people*. Edited by Bertram Colgrave and
   R.A.B. Mynors. Oxford 1969
Biard, Pierre. *Relation de la Nouvelle France, de ses terres, naturel du païs, et de ses
   habitations*. Lyons 1616
Biggar, Henry Percival, ed. *The voyages of Jacques Cartier*. Ottawa 1924
– *The works of Samuel de Champlain*. 6 vols. Toronto 1922–36
Birch, Thomas, ed. *A collection of the state papers of John Thurloe*. 7 vols. London
   1742
Bradford, William. *Of Plymouth plantation*. Edited by S.E. Morison. New York 1952
Brown, Alexander, ed. *Genesis of the United States*. 2 vols. New York 1890
Burrage, Henry Sweetser, ed. *Gorges and the grant of the province of Maine*. Portland
   1923
Campeau, Lucien, ed. *Monumenta Novae Franciae, vol. 1: La première mission
   d'Acadie*. Quebec and Rome 1967
Church, Benjamin. *The history of the eastern expeditions of 1689, 1690, 1692, 1696,
   and 1704 against the Indians and French*. Boston 1716

Collection de manuscrits contenant lettres, mémoires, et autres documents historiques relatifs à la Nouvelle-France recueillis aux Archives de la province de Québec ou copiés a l' étranger. 4 vols. Quebec 1883–5

Colonial Society of Massachusetts. *Publications,* XXIX, XXX. Records of the Suffolk County Court. Boston 1933

Denys, Nicolas. *The description and natural history of the coasts of North America (Acadia).* Edited by William F. Ganong. Toronto 1908. First published in 1672 as *Description géographique et historique des costes de l' Amérique septentrionale. Avec l' histoire naturelle du pais*

Deschamps, Léon. *Un colonisateur du temps de Richelieu, Isaac de Razilly, biographie, mémoire inédit.* Paris 1887. Extract from *Revue de géographie*

Dièreville Sieur de. *Relation of the voyage to Port Royal in Acadia or New France.* Edited by John Clarence Webster. Toronto 1933. First published in 1708 as *Relation du voyage du Port Royal de l' Acadie, ou de la Nouvelle France*

Documentary history of the State of Maine. Edited by William Willis *et al.* Maine Historical Society Collections, ser. 2. 24 vols. Portland and Cambridge, Mass. 1869–1916.

III: *The Trelawny papers.* Edited by James Phinney Baxter

IV, VI: *The Baxter manuscripts.* Edited by James Phinney Baxter

VII: *The Farnham papers, 1603–1688.* Compiled by Mary Frances Farnham

Édits, ordonnances royaux, déclarations et arrêts du Conseil d' État du roi concernant le Canada ... Vol. I. Quebec 1803

Evelyn, John. *The diary of John Evelyn.* Edited by E.S. de Beer. 6 vols. Oxford 1955

Fraser, William, ed. *Memoirs of the Maxwells of Pollok.* 2 vols. Edinburgh 1863

– *The red book of Menteith.* 2 vols. Edinburgh 1880

Gordon of Lochinvar, Sir Robert. *Encouragements for such as shall have the intention to be under-takers in the new plantation of Cape Briton, now New Galloway in America.* Edinburgh 1625

Gorges, Sir Ferdinando. 'A brief narration of the original undertakings for the advancement of plantations in America.' Maine Historical Society *Collections,* ser. I, II. Portland 1847

Great Britain, Historical Manuscripts Commission. *Ninth report, part II: appendix and index.* London 1884

– *Twelfth report, appendix: the manuscripts of the Earl Cowper, K.G., preserved at Melbourne Hall, Derbyshire.* 3 vols. London 1888–9

Great Britain, Privy Council. *Acts of the Privy Council of England; colonial series.* Edited by W.L. Grant and James Munro. 6 vols. London 1908–12

Great Britain, Public Record Office. *Calendar of state papers, colonial series, America and West Indies, 1574–1660.* Edited by W. Noel Sainsbury. London 1860

Hakluyt, Richard. *A discourse on western planting ...* Edited by Charles Deane. Cambridge, Mass. 1877

Hough, Franklin B., ed. 'Pemaquid papers.' Maine Historical Society *Collections*, ser. I, V. Portland 1857

Hubbard, William. *The history of the Indian wars in New England from the first settlement to the termination of the war with King Philip in 1677*. Edited by Samuel G. Drake. 2 vols. Roxbury, Mass. 1865

Hutchinson, Thomas, ed. *Collection of original papers relative to the history of the colony of Massachusetts Bay*. Boston 1769

The Jesuit relations and allied documents: travels and explorations of the Jesuit missionaries in New France, 1610–1791. Edited by Reuben Gold Thwaites. 73 vols. Cleveland 1896–1901

Johnson, Edward. *Wonder-working providence of Sion's saviour in New England*. Edited by J. Franklin Jameson. New York 1910

Josselyn, John. *An account of two voyages to New-England*. Massachusetts Historical Society *Collections*, 3rd ser., III. Boston 1833

Lahonton, Louis-Armand de Lom d'Arce, Baron de. *New Voyages to North-America ...* Edited by Reuben Gold Thwaites. Chicago 1905. First published in French and in English in 1703

Laing, David, ed. *Royal letters, charters, and tracts relating to the colonisation of New Scotland and the institution of the order of Knights Baronets of Nova Scotia, 1621–1638*. Edinburgh 1867

Le Blant, Robert, and René Baudry, eds. *Nouveaux documents sur Champlain et son époque*. Vol. I. Ottawa 1967

Le Clercq, Chrestien, *New Relation of Gaspesia, with the customs and religion of the Gaspesian Indians*. Edited by William F. Ganong. Toronto 1910. First published in 1691 as *Nouvelle relation de la Gaspésie, qui contient les mœurs et la religion des sauvages Gaspesiens porte-croix, adorateurs du soleil, et d'autres peuples de l'Amérique septentrionale, dite le Canada*.

Lescarbot, Marc. *The history of New France ...* Edited by W.L. Grant. 3 vols. Toronto 1907–14. First published in 1618 as *Histoire de la Nouvelle-France ...*

Levermore, Charles Herbert, ed. *Forerunners and competitors of the Pilgrims and Puritans*. New York 1912

Maine Historical Society. *Collections*. 1st ser., II, Portland 1847; V, Portland 1857
– *York deeds*. 18 vols. Portland and Bethel, Me 1887–1910

Malapart, André. *La prise d'un seigneur escossois et de ses gens qui pilloient les navires pescheurs de France. Ensemble le razement de leur fort, et l'establissement d'un autre pour le service du roy, et l'asseurance des pescheurs françois en la Nouvelle France*. Rouen 1630

Massachusetts. *Records of the governor and company of the Massachusetts Bay in New England*. Edited by Nathaniel Bradstreet Shurtleff. 6 vols. Boston 1853–54. This series is numbered I, II, III, IV(i), IV(ii), V.

Massachusetts Historical Society. *Proceedings*. 1st ser., XVI. Boston 1878

Mather, Cotton, *Magnalia Christi Americana, or the ecclesiastical history of New England* ... London 1702; 2 vols., New York 1852

The memorials of the English and French commissaries concerning the limits of Nova Scotia or Acadia. 2 vols. London 1755

Moody, Robert Earle, ed. *The letters of Thomas Gorges, deputy governor of the province of Maine, 1640–1643.* Portland 1978

Morse, William Inglis, ed. *Pierre Du Gua, sieur de Monts: records, colonial and 'Saintongeois.'* London 1939

New Plymouth Colony. *Records of the colony of Plymouth in New England.* Edited by Nathaniel Bradstreet Shurtleff and David Pulsifer. 12 vols. Boston 1855–61

Noble, John, ed. *Records of the Court of Assistants of the colony of the Massachusetts Bay, 1630–1692. 3 vols. Boston 1901–28*

Province and court records of Maine. Edited by Charles Thornton Libby *et al.* 6 vols. Portland 1928–75

Public Archives of Canada. *Report ... for the year 1904.* Ottawa 1905

Purchas, Samuel. *Hakluytus posthumus or Purchas his pilgrimes ...* 20 vols. Glasgow 1905–7

Records and files of the Quarterly Courts of Essex County, Massachusetts. 8 vols. Salem 1911–21

Renaudot, Théophraste. *Recueil des gazettes, nouvelles, relations et autres choses memorables de toute l' année 1632.* Paris 1633

– *Recueil des gazettes, nouvelles, et relations de toute l' année 1633.* Paris 1634

Rogers, Charles, ed. *The Earl of Stirling's register of royal letters relative to the affairs of Scotland and Nova Scotia from 1615 to 1635.* 2 vols. Edinburgh 1885

Sargent, William Mitchell, ed. *Maine wills, 1640–1760.* Portland 1887

Scotland. *The Acts of the Parliament of Scotland.* Edited by Cosmo Innes *et al.* 12 vols. Edinburgh 1844–75

– *The register of the great seal of Scotland.* [Vol. VIII] *A.D. 1620–1633.* Edited by John Maitland Thomson. Edinburgh 1894

– Privy Council. *The register of the Privy Council of Scotland.* Edited by John Hill Burton *et al.* 38 vols. Edinburgh 1877–1970

Sewall, Samuel. *The diary of Samuel Sewall, 1674–1729.* Massachusetts Historical Society *Collections*, 5th ser., v. Boston 1878

Skene, William Forbes, ed. *Memorials of the family of Skene of Skene.* Aberdeen 1887

Slafter, Edmund E., ed. *Sir William Alexander and American colonization.* Boston 1873

Suffolk County, Massachusetts. *Suffolk deeds.* Vols. I–V. Boston 1880–90

Thayer, Henry O., ed. *The Sagadahoc colony.* Portland 1892

Toppan, Robert Noxon, and Goodrick, Alfred Thomas Scrope, eds. *Edward Randolph; including his letters and official papers from the New England, middle and southern colonies in America, with other documents relating chiefly to the vacating of the*

royal charter of the colony of Massachusetts Bay, 1676–1703. 7 vols. Boston
1898–1909

Vigneras, Louis-André, ed. 'Letters of an Acadian trader, 1674–1676.'*New England Quarterly* 13 (1940): 98–110

Webster, John Clarence, ed. *Acadia at the end of the seventeenth century: letters, journals and memoirs of Joseph Robineau de Villebon, commandant in Acadia, 1690–1700, and other contemporary documents*. Saint John, N.B. 1934

Winship, George Parker, ed. *Sailors' narratives of voyages along the New England coast, 1524–1624*. Boston 1905

Winthrop, John. *Winthrop's journal*. Edited by James Kendall Hosmer. 2 vols. New York 1908

Winthrop papers. Massachusetts Historical Society *Collections*, 4th ser., VI, VII; 5th ser., I. Boston 1863–71

Wodrow, Robert, ed. *Collections upon the lives of the reformers and most eminent ministers of the Church of Scotland*. 2 vols. Glasgow 1834–45

SECONDARY SOURCES: BOOKS AND PAMPHLETS

Andrews, Charles McLean. *British committees, commissions and councils of trade and plantations, 1622–1675*. Baltimore 1908

– *The colonial period of American history*. 4 vols. New Haven 1934–8

Arsenault, Bona. *Histoire et généalogie des Acadiens*. 2 vols. Quebec 1965

Bailey, Alfred Goldsworthy. *The conflict of European and eastern Algonkian cultures, 1504–1700: a study in Canadian civilization*. 2nd ed. Toronto 1969

Baillargeon, Noel. *Le Séminaire de Québec sous l' épiscopat de Monseigneur de Laval*. Quebec 1972

Bailyn, Bernard. *The New England merchants in the seventeenth century*. Cambridge, Mass. 1955

Banks, Charles Edward. *History of York, Maine*. 2 vols. Boston 1931–5

Barnes, Viola Florence. *The Dominion of New England*. New Haven 1923

Baxter, James Phinney. *Christopher Levett of York*. Portland 1893

Berkhofer, Robert F., Jr. *The white man's Indian: images of the American Indian from Columbus to the present*. New York 1978

Biggar, Henry Percival. *The trading companies of New France: a contribution to the history of commerce and discovery in North America*. Toronto 1901

Bolton, Charles Knowles. *The real founders of New England*. Boston 1929

Bolton, Herbert Eugene, and Thomas Maitland Marshall, *The colonization of North America, 1492–1783*. New York 1920

Bond, Beverley Waugh. *The quit-rent system in the American colonies*. New Haven 1919

Bourne, Edward E. *History of Wells and Kennebunk from the earliest settlement to the year 1820*. Portland 1875

Boxer, Charles R. *The Portuguese seaborne empire, 1415-1825*. London 1969

Bradley, Robert L. *Maine's first buildings: the architecture of settlement, 1604-1700*. Augusta, Me 1978

Brebner, John Bartlet. *New England's outpost: Acadia before the conquest of Canada*. New York 1927

Burrage, Henry Sweetser. *The beginnings of colonial Maine, 1602-1658*. Portland 1914

Camp, Helen B. *Archaeological excavations at Pemaquid, Maine, 1965-1974*. Augusta, Me 1975

Campbell, Douglas F., ed. *Banked fires: the ethnics of Nova Scotia*. Port Credit, Ont. 1978

Campeau, Lucien. *Les Finances publiques de la Nouvelle-France sous les Cent-Associés*. Montreal 1975

Candide de Nant. *Pages glorieuses de l'épopée Canadienne: une mission capucine en Acadie*. Montreal, 1927.

Carroll, Charles Francis. *The timber economy of Puritan New England*. Providence, R.I. 1973

Carroll, Peter N. *Puritanism and the wilderness: the intellectual significance of the New England frontier, 1629-1700*. New York 1969

Casgrain, Henri-Raymond. *Les Sulpiciens et les prêtres des Missions-Étrangères en Acadie (1676-1762)*. Quebec 1897

Cell, Gillian T. *English enterprise in Newfoundland, 1577-1660*. Toronto 1969

Clark, Andrew Hill. *Acadia: the geography of early Nova Scotia to 1760*. Madison, Wis. 1968

Clark, Charles E. *The eastern frontier: the settlement of northern New England, 1610-1763*. New York 1970

Clark, George Norman. *The later Stuarts, 1660-1714*. 2nd ed. Oxford 1955

Cole, Charles Woolsey. *Colbert and a century of French mercantilism*. 2 vols. New York 1939

Condon, Thomas J. *New York beginnings: the commercial origins of New Netherland*. New York 1968

Couillard-Després, Azarie. *Charles de Saint-Étienne de La Tour, gouverneur, lieute-nant-général en Acadie, et son temps, 1593-1666*. Arthabaska, Que. 1930

Cowan, William, ed. *Papers of the ninth Algonquian conference*. Ottawa 1978

– *Papers of the tenth Algonquian conference*. Ottawa 1979

Cox, Bruce, ed. *Cultural ecology*. Toronto 1973

Dagnaud, G. *L'Administration centrale de la Marine sous l'ancien régime*. Nancy 1912

Daviault, Pierre. *Le baron de Saint-Castin, chef abénaquis*. Montreal 1939

Davies, Godfrey. *The early Stuarts, 1603-1660*. 2nd ed. Oxford 1959

Davies, Kenneth Gordon. *The North Atlantic world in the seventeenth century*. Minneapolis 1974

Day, Clarence Albert. *A history of Maine agriculture, 1604-1860*. Orono, Me 1954

Demos, John. *A little commonwealth: family life in Plymouth colony*. New York 1970

Dictionary of Candian biography. Edited by George W. Brown *et al*. 6 vols to date. Toronto 1965–

Donaldson, Gordon. *Scotland: James V to James VII*. Edinburgh 1965

– *The Scots overseas*. London 1966

Duchêne, Albert. *La Politique coloniale de la France: le ministère des Colonies depuis Richelieu*. Paris 1928

Eccles, W.J. *France in America*. New York 1972

Eckstorm, Fannie Hardy. *Indian place names of the Penobscot Valley and the Maine coast*. Orono, Me 1941

Fairchild, Byron. *Messrs William Pepperrell: merchants at Piscataqua*. Ithaca, N.Y. 1954

Flinn, Michael, *et al*. *Scottish population history*. Cambridge 1977

Gibson, Charles. *Spain in America*. New York 1966

Greven, Philip J., Jr. *Four generations: population, land, and family in colonial Andover, Massachusetts*. Ithaca, N.Y. 1970

Griffiths, Naomi E.S. *The Acadians: creation of a people*. Toronto 1973

Hale, Nathaniel C. *Virginia venturer: a historical biography of William Claiborne, 1600–1677*. Richmond, Va 1951

Hall, Michael G. *Edward Randolph and the American colonies, 1676–1703*. Chapel Hill, N.C. 1960

Hanke, Lewis. *The Spanish struggle for justice in the conquest of America*. Philadelphia 1949

Harris, Richard Colebrook. *The seigneurial system in early Canada: a geographical study*. Madison, Wis. 1966

Hill, George. *An historical account of the plantation of Ulster at the Commencement of the seventeenth century, 1608–1630*. Belfast 1877

Hulbert, Archer Butler. *Soil: its influence on the history of the United States*. New Haven 1930

Innis, Harold Adams. *The cod fisheries: the history of an international economy*. Revised edition. Toronto 1954

– *The fur trade in Canada: an introduction to Canadian economic history*. Revised edition. Toronto 1970

Insh, George Pratt. *Scottish colonial schemes, 1620–1686*. Glasgow 1922

Jacobsen, Gertrude Ann. *William Blathwayt: a late seventeenth century English administrator*. New Haven 1932

Jaenen, Cornelius J. *Friend and foe: aspects of French-Amerindian cultural contacts in the sixteenth and seventeenth centuries*. Toronto 1976

Jenness, Diamond. *Indians of Canada*. Ottawa, 1932.

Jennings, Francis. *The invasion of America: Indians, colonialism, and the cant of conquest*. Chapel Hill, N.C. 1975

Johnson, Douglas Wilson. *The New England-Acadian shoreline*. New York 1925

Johnson, Frederick, ed. *Man in northeastern North America*. Andover, Mass. 1946

Kershaw, Gordon E. *'Gentlemen of large property and judicious men': the Kennebeck proprietors, 1749-1775*. Somersworth, N.H. 1975

La Morandière, Charles de. *Histoire de la pêche française de la morue dans l'Amérique septentrionale (des origines à 1789.)* 2 vols. Paris 1962

Lanctot, Gustave. *L'administration de la Nouvelle-France: l'administration générale*. Paris 1929

Lapsley, Gaillard Thomas. *The county palatine of Durham: a study in constitutional history*. New York 1900

Lauvrière, Émile. *La tragédie d'un peuple: histoire du peuple acadien de ses origines à nos jours*. 2 vols. 3rd ed. Paris 1922

Leach, Douglas Edward. *Arms for empire*. New York 1973

– *Flintlock and tomahawk: New England in King Philip's War*. New York 1966

LeBlant, Robert. *Les officiers bretons du 'Marquis de Cangé' au sud du Saint-Laurent (1658-1666)*. Paris 1969

– *Une figure légendaire de l'histoire acadienne: le baron de St-Castin*. Dax, [1934]

Lemon, James T. *The best poor man's country: a geographical study of early southeastern Pennsylvania*. Baltimore 1972

Linton, Ralph, ed. *Acculturation in seven American Indian tribes*. New York, 1940; Gloucester, Mass. 1963.

Lockridge, Kenneth Alan. *A New England town, the first hundred years: Dedham, Massachusetts, 1636-1736*. New York 1970

Lounsbury, Ralph Greenlee. *The British fishery at Newfoundland, 1634-1763*. New Haven 1934

Lovejoy, David Sherman. *The Glorious Revolution in America*. New York 1972

Lythe, S.G.E. *The economy of Scotland in its European setting*. Edinburgh 1960

McCusker, John J. *Money and exchange in Europe and America, 1600-1775: a handbook*. Chapel Hill, N.C. 1978

McGrail, Thomas H. *Sir William Alexander, first Earl of Stirling: a biography*. Edinburgh 1940

Mackenzie, William Cook. *History of the Outer Hebrides*. Paisley 1903

McManis, Douglas R. *Colonial New England: a historical geography*. New York 1975

Martin, Calvin. *Keepers of the game: Indian-animal relationships and the fur trade*. Berkeley 1978

Massignon, Geneviève. *Les parlers français d'Acadie: enquête linguistique*. 2 vols. Paris [1962]

Moloney, Francis X. *The fur trade in New England, 1620-1676*. Cambridge, Mass. 1931

Moody, Robert Earle. *A proprietary experiment in early New England history: Thomas Gorges and the province of Maine*. Boston 1963

Morison, Samuel Eliot. *The European discovery of America: the northern voyages,*
    A.D. *500–1600.* New York 1971
Nash, Gary B. *Red, white and black: the peoples of early America.* Englewood Cliffs,
    N.J. 1974
Noyes, Sybil, *et al. Genealogical dictionary of Maine and New Hampshire.* Portland
    1928–39
O'Gorman, Edmundo. *The invention of America.* Bloomington, Ind. 1961
Olson, Alison Gilbert. *Anglo-American politics, 1660–1775.* Oxford 1973
Parry, John H. *The age of reconnaissance.* London 1963
– *The Spanish seaborne empire.* London 1966
Patterson, E. Palmer, II. *The Canadian Indian: a history since 1500.* Don Mills, Ont.
    1972
Pennington, Donald H. *Seventeenth century Europe.* London 1970
Phillips, Paul Chrisler. *The fur trade.* 2 vols. Norman, Okla. 1961
Porter, H.C. *The inconstant savage: England and the North American Indian, 1500–
    1660.* London 1979
Powell, Sumner Chilton. *Puritan village: the formation of a New England town.*
    Middletown, Conn 1963
Preston, Richard Arthur. *Gorges of Plymouth Fort.* Toronto 1954
Quinn, David B. *North America from earliest discovery to first settlements: the Norse
    voyages to 1612.* New York 1977
– *The Elizabethans and the Irish.* Ithaca, N.Y. 1966
Rameau de Saint-Père, Edme. *Une colonie féodale en Amérique (L'Acadie, 1604–
    1710).* Paris 1877
Rawlyk, George Alexander. *Nova Scotia's Massachusetts: a study of Massachusetts-
    Nova Scotia relations, 1630 to 1784.* Montreal 1973
Reid, John Graham. *Maine, Charles II, and Massachusetts: governmental relationships
    in early northern New England.* Portland 1977
Rumilly, Robert. *Histoire des Acadiens.* 2 vols. Montreal, 1955.
Rutman, Darrett B. *Winthrop's Boston: a portrait of a Puritan town, 1630–1649.*
    Chapel Hill, N.C. 1965
Sanger, David. *Cow Point: an archaic cemetery in New Brunswick.* Ottawa 1973
Savelle, Max. *Empires to nations: expansion in America, 1713–1824.* Minneapolis
    1974
– with assistance of Margaret Anne Fisher. *The origins of American diplomacy: the
    international history of Angloamerica, 1492–1763.* New York 1967
Scott, William Robert. *The constitution and finance of English, Scottish and Irish
    joint-stock companies to 1720.* 3 vols. Cambridge 1912
Séguin, Robert-Lionel. *La civilisation traditionelle de l''Habitant' au 17ᵉ et 18ᵉ siècles:
    fonds matériel.* Montreal 1967

Sévigny, P.-André. *Les Abénaquis: habitat et migrations (17ᵉ et 18ᵉ siècles)*. Montreal 1976

Smith, James Morton, ed. *Seventeenth century America: essays in colonial history*. Chapel Hill, N.C. 1959

Smith, Joseph Henry. *Appeals to the Privy Council from the American plantations*. New York 1950

Speck, Frank Gouldsmith. *Penobscot man: the life history of a forest tribe in Maine*. Philadelphia 1940

Trigger, Bruce G. *The children of Aataentsic: a history of the Huron people to 1660*. 2 vols. Montreal 1976

– ed. *Handbook of North American Indians, volume 15, northeast*. Washington 1978

Trudel, Marcel. *Histoire de la Nouvelle-France: le comptoir, 1604–1627*. Ottawa 1966

– *Histoire de la Nouvelle-France: les vaines tentatives, 1524–1603*. Montreal 1963

– *Les débuts du régime seigneurial au Canada*. Montreal 1974

– *The beginnings of New France, 1524–1663*. Toronto 1973

Tuttle, Charles Wesley. *Captain Francis Champernowne, the Dutch conquest of Acadia, and other historical papers*. Boston 1889

United States, Bureau of the Census. *The statistical history of the United States from colonial times to the present*. Stamford, Conn. 1965

Upton, L.F.S. *Micmacs and colonists: Indian-white relations in the Maritimes, 1713–1867*. Vancouver 1979

Van Deventer, David Earl. *The emergence of provincial New Hampshire, 1623–1741*. Baltimore 1976

Vaughan, Alden T. *The New England frontier: Puritans and Indians, 1620–1675*. Boston 1965

Ver Steeg, Clarence L. *The formative years, 1607–1763*. New York 1964

Wall, Robert Emmet. *Massachusetts Bay: the critical decade, 1640–1650*. New Haven 1972

Wallerstein, Immanuel. *The modern world-system: capitalist agriculture and the origins of the European world economy in the sixteenth century*. New York 1974

Washburn, Wilcomb E. *The Indian in America*. New York 1975

Webster, John Clarence. *Cornelis Steenwyck: Dutch governor of Acadie*. Shediac, N.B. 1929

Zavala, Silvio. *New viewpoints on the Spanish colonization of America*. New York 1943

– *The colonial period in the history of the new world*. Abridged in English by Max Savelle. Mexico City 1962

– *The defence of human rights in Latin America (sixteenth to eighteenth centuries)*. Paris 1964

Zuckerman, Michael. *Peaceable kingdoms: New England towns in the eighteenth century*. New York 1970

SECONDARY SOURCES: ARTICLES

Axtell, James. 'The ethnohistory of early America: a review essay.' *William and Mary Quarterly* 3rd ser., 35 (1978): 110–44
– 'The vengeful women of Marblehead: Robert Roules's deposition of 1677.' *William and Mary Quarterly* 3rd ser., 31 (1974): 647–52
– 'The white indians of colonial America.' *William and Mary Quarterly* 3rd ser., 32 (1975): 55–88
Banks, Charles Edward. 'Colonel Alexander Rigby.' *Maine Historical and Genealogical Recorder* 2 (1885): 1–23, 65–77, 145–62
– 'Edward Godfrey: his life, letters, and public services, 1584–1664.' Maine Historical Society *Collections* 1st ser., IX (1887): 295–384
– 'The administration of William Gorges, 1636–1637.' Maine Historical Society *Collections* 2nd ser., I (1890): 125–31
Barkham, Selma. 'The Basques: filling a gap in our history between Jacques Cartier and Champlain.' *Canadian Geographical Journal* 96 (1978): 8–19
Baudry, René. 'Charles d'Aulnay et la Compagnie de la Nouvelle-France.' *Revue d'histoire de l'Amérique française* 11 (1957–8): 218–41
Bentley, P.A., and E. C. Smith. 'The forests of Cape Breton in the seventeenth and eighteenth centuries.' Nova Scotian Institute of Sciences, *Proceedings and Transactions* 24 (1954–5): 1–15
Bolton, Herbert Eugene. 'The epic of greater America.' *American Historical Review* 38 (1932–3): 448–74
Bourinot, Sir John G. 'Builders of Nova Scotia, an historical review.' Royal Society of Canada, *Proceedings and Transactions* 2nd ser., V (1899): section 2, 1–198
Bourque, Bruce J. 'Aboriginal settlement and subsistence on the Maine coast.' *Man in the Northeast* 6 (1973): 3–20
Brown, Elizabeth A.R. 'The tyranny of a construct: feudalism and historians of medieval Europe.' *American Historical Review* 79 (1974): 1063–88
Buffinton, Arthur Howland. 'John Nelson's voyage to Quebec in 1682: a chapter in the fisheries controversy.' Colonial Society of Massachusetts, *Publications* XXVI (1927): 427–37
– 'Sir Thomas Temple in Boston: a case of benevolent assimilation.' Colonial Society of Massachusetts, *Publications* XXVII (1932): 308–19
Canny, Nicholas P. 'The ideology of English colonization: from Ireland to America.' *William and Mary Quarterly* 3rd ser., 30 (1973): 575–98
Churchill, Edwin A. 'The founding of Maine, 1600–1640: a revisionist interpretation.' *Maine Historical Society Quarterly* 18 (1978): 21–54
Cohen, Ronald Dennis. 'New England and New France, 1632–1651: external relations and internal disagreements among the Puritans.' *Essex Institute Historical Collections* 108 (1972): 252–71

Condon, Thomas J. 'Early America: old views and present possibilities.' Canadian Association for American Studies, *Bulletin* I (1966): 3–14

Conkling, Robert. 'Legitimacy and conversion in social change: the case of French missionaries and the northeastern Algonkian.' *Ethnohistory* 21 (1974): 1–24

Cooper, John M. 'Is the Algonkian family hunting ground system pre-Columbian?' *American Anthropologist* new ser., 41 (1939): 66–90

Couillard-Després, Azarie. 'Aux sources de l'histoire de l'Acadie.' Royal Society of Canada, *Proceedings and Transactions* 3rd ser., XXVII (1933): section I, 63–81

Day, Gordon M. 'The Indian as an ecological factor in the northeastern forest.' *Ecology* 34 (1953): 329–46

Debien, Gabriel. 'Engagés pour le Canada au XVIIᵉ siècle vus de la Rochelle.' *Revue d'histoire de l'Amérique française* 6 (1952–3): 177–220

Delafosse, M. 'La Rochelle et le Canada au XVIIᵉ siècle,' *Revue d'histoire de l'Amérique française* 4 (1950–1): 469–511

D'Entremont, Clarence-J. 'Le Cap-Sable: les établissements acadiens avant la dispersion.' Société historique acadienne, *Cahiers* 2 (1967): 161–76

– 'Le manoir et les armoiries de la famille Mius-D'Entremont d'Acadie.' Société historique acadienne, *Cahiers* 6 (1964): 19–24

– 'Nicolas Denys, historien veridique.' Société historique acadienne, *Cahiers* 10 (1979): 147–55

Devine, T.M., and S.G.E. Lythe. 'The economy of Scotland under James VI: a revision article.' *Scottish Historical Review* 50 (1971): 91–106

Diamond, Sigmund. 'An experiment in "feudalism": French Canada in the seventeenth century.' *William and Mary Quarterly* 3rd ser., 18 (1961): 3–34

– 'From organization to society: Virginia in the seventeenth century.' *American Journal of Sociology* 63 (1957–8): 457–75

Dickason, Olive P. 'The concept of *l'homme sauvage* and early French colonialism in the Americas.' *Revue française d'histoire d'outre-mer* 64 (1977): 5–32

Ganong, William Francis. 'Richard Denys, sieur de Fronsac, and his settlements in northern New Brunswick.' New Brunswick Historical Society, *Collections* VII (1907): 7–54

– 'The vegetation of the Bay of Fundy salt and diked marshes: an ecological study.' *Botanical Gazette* 36 (1903): 161–86, 280–302, 346–67, 429–55

Hallowell, A. Irving. 'The size of Algonkian hunting territories: a function of ecological adjustment.' *American Anthropologist* new ser., 51 (1949): 35–45

Hynes, Gisa I. 'Some aspects of the demography of Port Royal, 1650–1755.' *Acadiensis* 3 (Autumn 1973): 3–17

Innes, Stephen. 'Land tenancy and social order in Springfield, Massachusetts, 1652 to 1702.' *William and Mary Quarterly* 3rd ser., 35 (1978): 33–56

Jaenen, Cornelius J. 'Amerindian views of French culture in the seventeenth century.' *Canadian Historical Review* 55 (1974): 261–91

Kupperman, Karen Ordahl. 'English perceptions of treachery, 1583–1640: the case of the American "savages".' *Historical Journal* 20 (1977): 263–87

Larrabee, Edward M. 'Recurrent themes and sequences in North American Indian-European contact.' American Philosophical Society, *Transactions* new ser., 66 (1976): pt 7, 3–52

Le Blant, Robert. 'La compagnie de la Nouvelle-France et la restitution de l'Acadie, 1627–1636.' *Revue d'histoire des colonies* 42 (1955): 69–93

– 'La première compagnie de Miscou, 1635–1645.' *Revue d'histoire de l'Amérique française* 17 (1963–4): 363–70

– 'L'avitaillement du Port-Royal d'Acadie par Charles de Biencourt et les marchands rochelais, 1615–1618.' *Revue d'histoire des colonies* 44 (1958): 138–64

– 'Le commerce compliqué des fourrures canadiennes au début du XVIIᵉ siècle.' *Revue d'histoire de l'Amérique française* 26 (1972–3): 53–66

– 'Les compagnies du Cap-Breton, 1629–1647.' *Revue d'histoire de l'Amérique française* 16 (1962–3): 81–94

Lewis, Theodore Burnham. 'Land speculation and the Dudley council of 1686.' *William and Mary Quarterly* 3rd ser., 31 (1974): 255–72

Lockridge, Kenneth Alan. 'Land, population, and the evolution of New England society, 1630–1790.' *Past and Present* 39 (1968): 62–80

McCully, Bruce Tiebout. 'The New England-Acadia fishery dispute and the Nicholson mission of August 1686.' *Essex Institute Historical Collections* 96 (1960): 277–90

Massignon, Geneviève. 'La seigneurie de Charles de Menou d'Aulnay, gouverneur de l'Acadie, 1635–1650.' *Revue d'histoire de l'Amérique française* 16 (1962–3): 469–501

Miller, Virginia. 'Aboriginal Micmac population: a review of the evidence.' *Ethnohistory* 23 (1976): 117–27

Morgan, Edmund S. 'The labor problem at Jamestown, 1607–18.' *American Historical Review* 76 (1971): 595–611

Morse, Jarvis M. 'Captain John Smith, Marc Lescarbot, and the division of land by the council for New England in 1623.' *New England Quarterly* 8 (1935): 399–404

Nash, Gary B. 'The image of the Indian in the southern colonial mind.' *William and Mary Quarterly* 3rd ser., 29 (1972): 197–230

Nichols, G.E. 'The hemlock–white pine–northern hardwood region of eastern North America.' *Ecology* 16 (1935): 403–22

Patterson, Stephen E. 'In search of the Massachusetts-Nova Scotia dynamic.' *Acadiensis* 5 (spring 1976): 138–43

Penhallow, David Pierce. 'A contribution to our knowledge of the origin and development of certain marsh lands on the coast of New England.' Royal Society of Canada, *Proceedings and Transactions* 3rd ser., 1 (1907): section IV, 13–55

Pilgrim, Donald G. 'France and New France: two perspectives on colonial security.' *Canadian Historical Review* 55 (1974): 381–407

Pothier, Bernard. 'Nicolas Denys: the chronology and historiography of an Acadian hero.' *Acadiensis* I (autumn 1971): 54–70

Preston, Richard Arthur. 'The Laconia Company of 1629: an English attempt to intercept the fur trade.' *Canadian Historical Review* 31 (1950): 125–44

Reid, John Graham. 'Styles of colonisation and social disorders in early Acadia and Maine: a comparative approach.' Société historique acadienne, *Cahiers* 7 (spring 1976): 106–17

– 'The Scots crown and the restitution of Port Royal, 1629–1632.' *Acadiensis* 6 (spring 1977): 39–63

Rich, Edwin Ernest. 'Trade habits and economic motivation among the Indians of North America.' *Canadian Journal of Economics and Political Science* 26 (1960): 35–53

Root, Winfred Trexler. 'The Lords of Trade and Planatations, 1675–1696.' *American Historical Review* 23 (1917–18): 20–41

Sanger, David. 'Passamaquoddy Bay prehistory: a summary.' Maine Archaeological Society, *Bulletin* 11 (1971): 14–19

Snow, Dean Richard. 'Wabanaki "family hunting territories".' *American Anthropologist* new ser., 70 (1968): 1143–51

Southgate, William Scott. 'History of Scarborough.' Maine Historical Society *Collections* 1st ser., III (1853): 1–237

Speck, Frank Gouldsmith, and Loren C. Eiseley. 'Significance of hunting territory systems of the Algonkian in social theory.' *American Anthropologist* new ser., 41 (1939): 269–80

Trigger, Bruce G. 'Champlain judged by his Indian policy: a different view of early Canadian history.' *Anthropologica* 13 (1971): 85–114

Webb, Stephen Saunders. 'William Blathwayt, imperial fixer: from popish plot to glorious revolution.' *William and Mary Quarterly* 3rd ser., 25 (1968): 3–21

SECONDARY SOURCES: THESES

Bear, Andrea Jeanne. 'The concept of unity among Indian tribes of Maine, New Hampshire, and New Brunswick: an ethnohistory.' Senior scholar's paper, Colby College 1966

Buffinton, Arthur Howland. 'The policy of the northern colonies towards the French to the peace of Utrecht.' PH D thesis, Harvard University 1925

Comeau, Roger. 'Pêche et traite en Acadie jusqu'en 1713.' PH D thesis, Université d'Ottawa 1949

Daigle, Jean. 'Michel Le Neuf de La Vallière, seigneur de Beaubassin et gouverneur d'Acadie.' MA thesis, Université de Montréal 1970

– 'Nos amis les ennemis: relations commerciales de l'Acadie avec le Massachusetts, 1670–1711.' PH D thesis, University of Maine 1975

Doherty, Dennis Charles Brian. "Oliver Cromwell, Robert Sedgwick, John Leverett, and the Acadian adventure of 1654.' MA thesis, Queen's University 1969

Hoffman, Bernard Gilbert. 'Historical ethnography of the Micmac of the sixteenth and seventeenth centuries.' PH D thesis, University of California 1955

Laplante, Corinne. 'Le traité d'Utrecht et l'Acadie; une étude de la correspondance sécrète et officielle qui a entouré la signature du traité d'Utrecht.' MA thesis, Université de Moncton 1974

Leacock, Eleanor. 'The Montagnais "hunting territory" and the fur trade.' PH D thesis, Columbia University 1952

McGee, Harold F., Jr. 'Ethnic boundaries and strategies of ethnic interaction: a history of Micmac-white relations in Nova Scotia.' PH D thesis, Southern Illinois University 1974

Moody, Robert Earle. 'The Maine frontier, 1607–1763.' PH D thesis, Yale University 1933

Morrison, Alvin Hamblen. 'Dawnland decisions: sixteenth century Wabanaki leaders and their responses to the differential contact stimuli in the overlap area of New France and New England.' PH D thesis, State University of New York at Buffalo 1974

Morrison, Kenneth Myron. 'The People of the Dawn: the Abnaki and their relations with New England and New France, 1600–1727.' PH D thesis, University of Maine 1975

Noble, John O., Jr. 'King Philip's War in Maine.' MA thesis, University of Maine 1970

Index

Abbadie de Saint-Castin, Jean-Vincent d'
77–8, 166, 172, 175, 180–1
Abenaki 6, 77, 78, 99, 130; territory 3;
relations with English 18, 30, 62–9,
70, 166–9, 181–2; relations with
French, 165–6; population 223 n24;
see also Native people
Acadia
– to 1630: concept of xiv; native
peoples 3–6, 58–60; natural resources
5–10; patent of 1603 14; de Monts
colony 14, 16, 18; under Poutrincourt,
Biencourt, and La Tour 19, 29–30, 33
– from 1630 to 1650: settlement xv,
103–4; question of restitution (to 1632)
38–40; under Razilly 40–1, 43–4;
economy 43–9 passim; French-
Scottish relations 81–2; French-
English relations 82–7, 94–102; and
Canada 88–90; internal divisions
109–10, 115–16, 118–19; as marginal
colony 122–4
– from 1650 to 1690: internal divisions
127–30; Sedgwick conquest 135–6;
under Temple 137–41, 144–7; question of restitution (to 1670) 157–63;

French-Indian relations 164–6; under
La Vallière 171–4; conflict with New
England 175–7, 180–1; Phips raid
182–3; as marginal colony 184–90
passim
Acadians: and Indians 77–8; settlement
103–4; landholding 104, 118–19,
141, 160; sense of community 118–
19; and Sedgwick conquest 136; under
Temple 140–1, 154; and Le Borgnes,
141, 160, 172; population 158–9; and
Massachusetts 160–1, 173, 177;
under La Vallière 171–2; after Phips
raid 182–3; later developments 190
Acomenticus, see Agamenticus
Aernoutsz, Jurriaen 162
Agamenticus 3n, 93, 105, 106, 108, 113,
117, 119, 121, 122, 132, 232 n40; see
also Bristol, Gorgeana, York
agriculture: Indian 3, 4, 5–6, 167;
Acadian 7–8, 103–4, 118, 157–8; in
Maine 7–8, 49, 92, 105; northeast of
Kennebec River 153
Alden, John, 174
Alexander, Henry, Earl of Stirling 155,
252 n57

Alexander, William, Earl of Stirling 42,
46, 51, 70, 82, 88, 114, 137, 139, 153,
187, 188, 252 n57; hopes for New
Scotland 7, 21–2; organizes New
Scotland scheme 23–5, 27–8; estab-
lishes colony 26, 30–3; and restitution
of 1632 38–40; and Council for New
England 50, 83; bankruptcy 50, 56;
and the Kirkes 80–1
Alexander, Sir William, the younger
31–2, 37, 46, 50, 229 n3
Algonkians, see Native people
Allen, John 138n
Allerton, Isaac 84–5
Andigné de Grandfontaine, Hector d'
153, 154, 157–61 passim, 166
Andrewes, Edmond 45
Andros, Sir Edmund 174–5, 178, 180–1
Androscoggin: native people 167; see
also Native people
Argall, Samuel 19
Arlington, Earl of, see Bennett
Arrowsick 130–1, 155, 246 n64
Ashley, Edward 84
Augier, René 38–9
Aulnay, see Menou

Bagnall, Walter 67, 92, 217 n37
Baie Françoise, see Bay of Fundy
Balie, Jonas 148
Barbados 111, 156
Barillon, Paul, Marquis de Branges 179
Barnstaple 13
Basques 8
Baye, Charles, Sieur de La Girodière 247
n74
Bay of Fundy 8, 52, 77, 82, 103, 117,
118, 137
Bayonne 13
Beaubassin 159, 165, 171–2

Bede 74
Bellingham, Richard 93, 96
Bennett, Henry, Earl of Arlington 152
Bergier, Clerbaud 176–7
Béthune, Maximilien de, Baron de
Rosny, Duc de Sully 15, 18
Biard, Pierre 4, 5, 19, 20–1, 22, 63–4,
72–6
Biencourt de Poutrincourt et de Saint-Just,
Jean de 19, 43
Biencourt de Saint-Just, Charles de 19,
20, 29, 43, 73, 211 n114
Biencourt, Jacques de 29, 211 n114
Bigot, Jacques 78
Black Point 89, 91, 111, 132, 175; see
also Scarborough
Blathwayt, William 175, 180
Blue Point 132, 148; see also Scarbor-
ough
Boade, Henry 112, 120, 243 n27
Bonnèfre, Pierre 45
Bonrepaux, Usson de 179
Bonython, John 107–8, 116–17
Bonython, Richard 108, 112
Bordeaux 13
Bordeaux, Antoine de 136, 145
Boston 66, 83, 91–100 passim, 106,
113, 127, 131, 132, 135, 143, 145,
149, 152, 153, 155, 158, 161, 167–72,
175–82 passim; economic influence
47–8, 90, 130; La Tour in 47–8, 55,
96–7, 110; merchant interests 47–8,
96, 101, 129, 138–40, 162, 174; Tem-
ple in 138–40; see also Massachusetts
Bay Colony
Bouildron, Jacques 45
Bourbon, César de, Duc de Vendôme
128
Bourgeois, Jean 45
Bourget, Hippolite 238 n35

Bradford, William 30, 85, 86, 87
Breda, treaty of (1667) 147, 155, 156, 179, 180, 246 n59
Breedon, Thomas 139, 140, 146
Bristol (England) 9, 23, 41, 45, 106
Bristol (Maine) 233 n51; see also Aga-menticus, Gorgeana, York
Brown, John 65
Brunet, Henri 154–5, 166
Buade, Louis de, Comte de Frontenac et de Palluau 160–1, 162, 169, 171, 172–3
Bulkeley, Peter 169
Burdett, George 108
Burridge, Avis 45
Burridge, John 45

Cabot, John 12, 81
Cammock, Thomas 86
Canada xv, 119, 156, 180; Alexander and Kirke claims 31, 39, 80–1; restitution of 1632 38–9; Indian missions 77, 165, 167; relations with Acadia 88–90, 123, 162, 169, 171–2, 173; relations with New England 78, 99–101, 172–3; reorganized (1663) 144, 159, 177, 186
Canso (Canceau) 40, 52, 69, 129, 181, 247 n74, 248 n3
Cap de Sable 19, 33, 40, 51, 53, 82, 85, 99, 110, 115, 137, 140, 156, 157, 159, 213 n126, 214 n135
Cape Breton Island 11, 14, 31, 45, 56, 76, 81–2, 110, 115, 128, 171, 189, 190, 211 n108
Cape Cod 85
Cape Porpoise 111, 114, 132, 152
Cap Fourchu 33, 137
Cape Sable, see Cap de Sable

Cap Nègre 19, 211 n114
Capuchins, see Religious orders
Carleton, Dudley, Viscount Dorchester 38–9
Cartier, Jacques 6, 12n, 58, 59
Cartwright, George 150, 153
Casco 30, 66, 107, 108, 112, 113, 132; see also Falmouth
Casco Bay 6, 65, 105, 140, 182
Cecil, Robert, Earl of Salisbury 15, 18
Chaleur Bay 89
Chaline, Jean-Daniel 82
Challes, Robert 176
Chambly, Jacques de 161–2, 171
Champernowne, Sir Arthur 14
Champernowne, Francis 14, 119, 134
Champlain, Samuel de 5–6, 10, 17, 32, 59, 69, 76
Charles I, king of Scotland and England 21, 24, 32, 37–40, 41, 49–50, 51, 81, 88, 113
Charles II, king of Scotland and England 88, 136, 144, 146, 147, 148, 155, 157, 169
Charnisay, see Menou
Châteauneuf, Marquis de, see L'Aupe-spine
Chaudière River 77, 165
Chauvin de Tonnetuit, Pierre de 16
Chedabouctou 176, 181, 183
Chevery, Martin de 104
Chignecto Isthmus 159, 171, 183
Church, Benjamin 182
Church of England 91, 112, 121
Church of Scotland 72
Claiborne, William 88
Clarendon, Earl of, see Hyde
Clarke, Thomas 130, 155
Cleeve, George 57, 106–9 passim, 111–13, 116, 122, 132, 133, 134, 219 n73

Cleeve-Trelawny dispute 106, 107, 108–9, 111–14, 134

Cloven Cape, see Cap Fourchu

Coke, Sir John 86

Colbert de Terron, Charles 157

Colbert, Jean-Baptiste 144–5, 158, 159–60, 162, 186

colonies: capitalization of 15–17, 18, 20, 23–6, 42–4; communal xiv, 17, 19–20, 24, 29, 32, 33, 44, 59–60, 82, 114, 122, 187

Commenges, Comte de 147

commerce, see Fisheries, Fur trade, Timber trade

Communauté des Habitants 89–90

Compagnie de la Nouvelle-France (Compagnie des Cent-Associés) 29, 30, 31, 45, 51, 80, 82, 83, 129; capitalization 18–19, 25; composition 25–6; and seigneurial system, 28, 210 n105; La Tour and 33, 43, 51–2; Razilly and 40, 43, 109; d'Aulnay and 43–4, 56, 110; religious purpose 70–1; surrenders trade monopoly 89; suppression of 249 n3

Compagnie des Indes occidentales 249 n3

Conigan, Charles de, Sieur de Cangé 248 n74

Connecticut 149, 178

Council for New England 18, 21, 51, 64, 80, 107, 203 n35, 207 n81; composition 22–3, 26; capitalization 23; land grants 27, 30, 41, 44, 50, 83, 84, 86, 90, 105, 111, 116, 120, 153, 211 n111; resignation of patent 41, 53; religious purpose 70

Cromwell, Oliver 135, 136–7, 146, 186, 244 n27

Cromwell, Richard 140

Cronder, Anne 93

Crowne, William 137–9 passim, 146

Cushnoc 84

Danforth, Thomas 170–1, 175, 177, 178

Daniel, Charles 31–2, 81–2, 85

Dartmouth 13

Daumont de Saint-Lusson, Simon-François 154

Davis, Silvanus 154

Dennison, Daniel 161

Denys de Fronsac, Richard 76, 159, 171

Denys, Nicolas 76, 127, 171, 236 n7; with Razilly in Acadia 40, 46, 103; commercial interests 43–5, 89, 110, 128–9, 159; quoted 46–7, 106–7, 109, 115, 118, 139, 141, 165; hopes for colonization 103, 115–16

Dermer, Thomas 4

Des Friches de Meneval, Louis-Alexandre 160, 177, 182, 183

Desjardins Du Val, Guillaume 43, 45, 47, 55

Desportes, Pierre 45

De Vic, Henry 38–9

Devon, county of (England) 22, 119

Devon, county of (New England) 154–5

dikes 104, 118, 228 n88; see also Acadians, Agriculture

disease, European: effects on native people 4, 11, 60, 64, 73, 224 n44

Dominion of New England 83, 177–8, 181, 183, 186

Dorchester, Viscount, see Carleton

Dover, treaty of (1670) 152, 178

Druillettes, Gabriel 78, 99–100, 121, 242 n79

Du Bourg, Morillon 157

Duchesneau de La Doussinière et d'Ambault, Jacques 171

Dudley, Joseph 177–8

Dudouyt, Jean 159–60

Du Gua de Monts, Pierre 7, 14–19
   passim, 24
Dumbarton 31
Du Plessis, Armand-Jean, Cardinal de
   Richelieu 22, 25, 30, 40–1, 51, 52,
   56, 186
Durham, bishopric of 55
Dutch xi, xii, 18, 86, 130, 156, 161–2,
   171, 208 n84; see also New Netherland

Eden, Peter 63
Eliot, John 72, 78, 242 n79
Elliott, Thomas 139, 146
Endicott, John 96, 97
England: crown and government of 13,
   41–2, 53–5, 117, 144, 146–9, 155,
   156–7, 169, 174–80 passim, 186–7;
   civil war 44, 48, 56, 111, 113; revolution of 1688–9 181
English: and fur trade 6, 58, 84–5; and
   timber trade 7; and fisheries 8–9, 12–
   13, 44; approaches to colonization 14–
   18, 21–3, 26–8; in New England 17–
   18, 30, 90–4, 105–24 passim, 129–35,
   149–55, 169–70; relations with native
   people 17–18, 60–72, 78–9, 164,
   166–9, 174, 180–2, 185, 188; relations
   with French in America 19, 29, 83–7,
   94–102, 129, 135–41 passim, 145–6,
   155–7, 160–1, 172–3, 176, 178–83,
   189; relations with Scots in America
   31, 80–1; in Nova Scotia, 135–41,
   145–7, 156–7
English and Scottish Company 31, 80–1
Entremont, see Mius
environment: influence on colonization
   5–11, 115–17
Essex, county of (Massachusetts) 47, 96
Etchemin, see Malecite
Euramericans 118, 122, 133, 135, 141–

3, 154, 162–3, 164, 169–74 passim,
   178, 183, 184, 185, 188
Europeans: and American colonization
   xi–xvi; perceptions of America 10–11;
   establish overseas empires 11–12, 20;
   and native peoples 58–62, 62–3, 70–
   1; and territorial claims in America 80;
   and northeastern maritime colonies
   123–4, 162–3, 184–90
evangelization, Christian: as purpose of
   European colonization 6, 15, 20, 21,
   26, 61, 70–1; in New England 71–2,
   78; in Acadia 72–7, 123, 164–6; in
   Canada 165–6; see also Religious
   orders, Séminaire de Québec
Exeter (England) 23
Exeter (New Hampshire) 120
Exmouth 13

Falmouth (England) 13
Falmouth (Maine) 132, 134, 168, 175,
   181; see also Casco, Spurwink
féodalité 27–8, 104–5, 117–19; see also
   Proprietary system, Seigneurial system
Fienes, William, Viscount Saye and Sele
   137, 247 n74
fisheries 23, 25, 49, 77, 108, 121, 135,
   144, 145, 153, 154, 158, 163, 174,
   178, 181, 187, 188, 189; Newfoundland 8–9, 12–13, 19; English 8–9,
   12–13, 30, 44–6, 92, 105, 116, 119;
   French 8–9, 12–13, 19, 32, 44–6,
   56, 81, 103–4, 115, 176–7; Scottish
   202 n34, 204 n42; Indian, 10, 228 n88;
   sedentary 44–6, 121, 176–7; New
   England based 48, 140, 172–3, 176–
   7; and treaty of Whitehall 179
Fléché, Jessé 72
Forrester, Andrew 82, 85
France: crown and government of 14–15,
   38–40, 47, 49, 51–3, 55–7, 117, 142,

144–7, 157, 159–61, 163, 176, 178–80, 186–7

French: and fur trade 6, 58; and timber trade 7; and fisheries 8–9, 12–13, 176–7; approaches to colonization 14–21, 22, 25–8; in Acadia 17–19, 29–30, 40–1, 103–4, 109–10, 114–24 passim, 127–9, 157–62, 171–4, 176–7, 182–3; relations with English in America 19, 29–30, 83–7, 94–102, 129, 135–41 passim, 144–7, 154–5, 156–7, 172–3, 176–7, 178–83, 189; in Canada 38, 88–90, 99–100, 171; merchant interests 43–9 passim, 154–5; relations with native people 69–70, 72–9, 164–6, 180–3, 185, 188; relations with Scots in America 81–2; relations with Dutch in America 161–2

François-Marie de Paris 98, 99

Frontenac, see Buade

Frost, Nicholas 91

fur trade 19, 25, 50; effects on native culture 4–5, 59–60, 199 n5; in sixteenth century 6, 13, 187; in northeastern maritime region 17–18, 30, 40, 42–51 passim, 67, 84–6, 87, 99, 103, 109, 115–16, 119, 130, 138, 140, 159, 188; and European-Indian relations 58–60, 77, 78

Gardner, Thomas 70, 154, 166, 167

Gaspé 3, 6, 23, 27, 31, 75, 80, 129, 165, 177

Georges, Samuel 19, 43

Gibbons, Edward 47–8, 50, 96, 98, 100, 101, 112

Gibson, Mary 108

Gibson, Richard 108

Gilbert, Bartholomew 58

Gilbert, Sir Humphrey 13, 203 n41

Gilbert, Raleigh 18, 63

Godefroy de Lintot, Jean 100

Godfrey, Edward 93, 105, 111, 114, 119, 122, 131–4, 142, 147, 148

Goodyear, Moses 44

Gordon of Lochinvar, Sir Robert 10, 31, 211 n108

Gorgeana 233 n51; see also Agamenticus, Bristol, York

Gorges, Ferdinando 66, 114, 152, 160, 162, 187; petitions for restitution of Maine 148–9, 155; names commissioners 150–1; sells patent 169–70

Gorges, Sir Ferdinando 84, 90, 91, 93, 103, 113, 117, 123, 132, 162, 178, 187, 188, 189; quoted 10, 15, 18; promoter of north Virginia colony 15–18; and New Scotland 21, 49–50; and Council for New England 21–3, 26–7, 41; and Laconia Company 30, 41, 44; designated governor of New England 41, 50, 53–4; and Laud 41–2; and Massachusetts 53–4, 90, 93; lord proprietor of Maine 54–5, 56, 105–7, 109, 120, 121; attitude to native people 64, 71–2; occupied by civil war 111; death 114

Gorges, Robert 23, 30, 65, 107

Gorges, Thomas: receives manorial grant at Ogunquit 105, 120, 210 n105; and native people 67–8, 72, 166, 219 n66; governor of Maine 56, 93, 105–9, 116, 117, 121; quoted 91, 92; returns to England 111

Gorges, William 41, 93, 107

Gosnold, Bartholomew 58

Graham, William, Earl of Menteith 32, 46

Grandfontaine, see Andigné

Gregory the Great, Pope 74

Guercheville, Madame de, see Pons

Guignard, Gilles 110

Guppy, Reuben 93

Hakluyt, Richard 63, 205 n48
Harrison, Mark 135–6
Hawkins, Narias 67
Hawkins, Thomas 47–8, 50, 96, 98, 101
Henri IV, king of France 15, 128
Hill, Valentine 101
Hocking, John 84
Holland, John 92
Home, Sir George 14, 46
Hudson, Henry 64
Hudson Bay 179, 180
Hudson River 149
Huguenots 176, 203 n41, 249 n8
Hunt, Thomas 64
Huron 89
Hutchinson, Anne 120
Hyde, Edward, Earl of Clarendon 152
Hyde, Laurence, Earl of Rochester 179

Ignace de Paris 164
Île Percée 101
Île Royale 190; see also Cape Breton
    Island
Île Sainte-Croix 6, 17
Île Saint-Jean 190
Ireland 13–14, 22, 46, 63–4, 73, 144
Iroquois 78, 89, 99, 100
Isles of Shoals 116

Jacquelin, Françoise-Marie (Saint-
    Étienne de La Tour) 110
James VI and I, king of Scotland and
    England 13, 14, 15
James VII and II, king of Scotland and
    England: as Duke of York 83, 149,
    153–4, 169, 174–5, 187; as king 83,
    178–9
Jamestown 17, 206 n59
Jamin, Pierre 52

Jemseg 171, 183, 247 n68, 253 n67
Jenner, Thomas 91, 112–13, 119, 120–1
Jesuits, see Religious orders
Jocelyn, Henry 91, 111, 113, 132
Jordan, Robert 112, 113, 121–3, 132,
    134
Josselyn, John 5, 105, 111, 153
Jouvency, Joseph 75
Joybert de Soulanges et de Marson, Pierre
    de 161–2, 171

Kennebec River 70, 83, 108, 168, 180,
    189; as boundary 27, 41, 50, 111,
    117, 149, 153, 158, 174–5, 178, 187;
    New Plymouth colonists and 84, 86,
    87, 140, 153, 212 n116; native people
    59, 63–5, 70, 166–7, 169; English
    settlements on 99, 153–5, 166, 181
Kennebec-Ste Croix territory: granted to
    Alexanders 50, 83, 153; fur trade in
    83–6, 116; and French-English rela-
    tions 83–7, 154–5, 178, 180–1; and
    New Plymouth colonists 83–7, 153;
    and Duke of York 83, 149, 153, 174–
    5, 187; and Massachusetts 153–5; see
    also Abbadie de Saint-Castin, Devon,
    James VII and II, Kennebec River,
    Pemaquid, Ste Croix River
Kennebunk River 108
Keyes, Henry 46
King Philip's War 167–8, 186
King's Province 177
Kirke, Gervase 26
Kirke brothers 13n, 26, 31, 32, 38, 80–
    1, 88, 97, 139, 204 n42
Kittery 14, 68, 101, 105, 113, 114, 117,
    119, 121, 122, 129–30, 132, 134, 182,
    204 n42
knights-baronetcies of Scotland 24–5,
    27–8, 32–3, 39, 137, 139, 146

La Barre, *see* Le Febvre
labour: in early colonies 17, 45–6
Laconia Company 30, 33, 41, 44–6, 49, 90, 92, 105, 119, 121, 240 n60
La Croix de Chevrières de Saint-Vallier, Jean-Baptiste de 165
La Hève 19, 40, 45, 52, 77, 82, 87, 103–5, 109, 117, 139, 145, 157
Lake, Thomas 130, 138–9, 140, 155, 246 n64, 253 n68
land tenure 27–8, 66, 104–5, 118–22, 131, 133–4, 141, 148, 150–2, 158, 160, 170, 178; *see also* Féodalité, Proprietary system, Seigneurial system
La Rochelle 13, 16, 19, 43, 44, 45, 47, 139, 176
La Rocque de Roberval, Jean-François de 203 n41
Las Casas, Bartolomé de 61, 63, 64, 71, 73
La Tour, *see* Saint-Étienne
La Tour–d'Aulnay conflict 47–8, 52–3, 55–6, 70, 73, 92, 95–9, 109–10, 111, 128, 219 n74
Laud, William 41–2, 53, 54, 56, 186
Launay-Rasilly, Claude de 40, 43, 45, 52, 122
L'Aupespine, Charles de, Marquis de Châteauneuf 38–9
Laval, François de 159, 165
La Vallière, *see* Leneuf
Leader, Richard 134
Le Borgne de Belle-Isle, Alexandre 127, 139, 141, 145, 160, 172
Le Borgne Du Coudray, Emmanuel 139, 145
Le Borgne, Emmanuel 204 n42; creditor of d'Aulnay 44, 47, 104, 110, 127, 187; efforts to gain control of Acadia 110, 127, 128–9, 135, 139, 140, 142, 145–6, 157; family of, claims in Acadia 118, 141, 160–2, 172, 187

Le Clercq, Chrestien 5, 10, 74–6, 165
Le Creux Du Breuil, Nicolas 69
Le Febvre de La Barre, Joseph-Antoine 172, 173
Le Jeune, Paul 89, 99
Leneuf de La Vallière, Michel 169, 171–4, 176, 177
Lescarbot, Marc 6, 7, 9, 15, 17, 20, 69, 76
Les Mines 159
Leverett, John 101, 131, 135–6, 138, 152, 155
Levett, Christopher 30, 58, 64–5, 66, 166
Lewis, Thomas 107
liquor trade 60, 165, 166
Lomeron, Daniel 43
Lomeron, David 43, 206 n70
London, 13, 26, 29, 38, 44, 84, 92, 119, 136, 139, 142, 145, 147, 148, 151, 155, 156, 157, 162, 169, 175, 179, 182
Louis XIII, king of France 22, 29, 52
Louis XIV, king of France 56, 128, 144, 145, 147, 159, 161, 179
Lygonia 111–13, 132–3

Macain, Jean 19
Machias 84–5, 246 n57
Mackworth, Arthur 112
Maine
– to 1630: concept of xiv; native peoples 3–6, 58–60, 62–5; natural resources 5–10; Sagadahoc colony 15–18; first province of (1622) 27, 28; settlement attempts 30
– from 1630 to 1650: settlement xv, 49, 92, 103, 105–6, 120; province of New Somersetshire 41, 54, 67, 107; economy 43–9 passim, 90, 94, 101; government 53–7, 107–9; province of Maine charter (1639) 54–5, 83; under Thomas Gorges 56, 105–9; internal

divisions 57, 106–9, 111–14, 116–
22; English-Indian relations 62–9,
71–2, 78–9; and Massachusetts 90–4,
101–2; and province of Lygonia 111–
13; as marginal colony 122–4
– from 1650 to 1690: English-Indian
hostility xv, 66, 68–9, 166–9, 181–3;
annexation by Massachusetts 129–33;
as county of Yorkshire 133–5, 142–3,
147–9; natural resources and economy
130–1, 144; colonists 133–5, 148,
150–3, 168, 170–1, 178, 182; internal
conflicts 133–4; claim of Ferdinando
Gorges 148–9, 155, 169; and royal
commission of 1664–6 149–52;
county of Yorkshire re-established
(1668) 152–3; purchase of charter by
Massachusetts 169–70; encroachment
of Sir Edmund Andros 175; integration in Dominion of New England
177–8; as marginal colony 184–90
passim; later development 189–90
Malecite 3, 52, 77, 223 n24; see also
Native people
Marblehead 168
marshland xv, 8, 41, 77, 103–4, 105,
118, 120, 123, 134, 141
Marson, see Joybert
Martin, Pierre 47
Martire d'Anghiera, Pietro 63
Mason, John 27, 30, 44, 106, 120
Mason, Robert 155, 169, 170, 175
Massachusetts Bay Colony
– in seventeenth century: population and
economy xv, 47–9, 90–1, 115, 130–
1, 143; religious character 10, 65, 72,
91, 120–1; and English government
41–2, 53–5, 57, 148–50, 152, 155,
169, 177–8, 181; and native people
61, 65–6, 67, 68, 72, 78, 167–9;
relations with Canada 78, 99–101,
172–3; town system 119; annexation

of New Hampshire 90, 93, 94, 119–
20; and Sir Edmund Andros 175, 178,
181
– and Acadia/Nova Scotia: merchant
interests in Acadia 47–8, 50–1, 87,
95–101 passim, 129, 158, 161, 172–3,
177, 182; and La Tour 47–8, 55, 95–
9, 110; relations with Acadia (1630–
50) 85–7, 94–9, 122–3; and d'Aulnay
95–9, 185; relations with Acadia
(1650–54) 127, 129; attitude to Sedgwick conquest 137–8; and Temple
138–40, 145, 187; merchant interests
in Temple's Nova Scotia 138–41;
relations with Acadia (from 1670)
158, 160–1, 172–3; and Acadian
fishery 172–3, 176–7; support of
Phips raid 182–3
– and Kennebec-Ste Croix territory 153–
5, 175
– and Maine: merchant interests in Maine
48, 94, 101, 130–1; relations with
Maine (1630–50) 90–4, 112–13, 122;
annexes Maine 129–35, 187; and royal
commission of 1664–6 149–52; re-
annexes Maine 152–3; and Abenaki
wars 167–9, 181–2; purchase of
Maine charter 169–70; Danforth
government 170–1, 175, 177
Massé, Énemond 72
Mather, Cotton 182
Maverick, Samuel 153
Maxwell, William 31
Mayhew, Thomas 72
Mazarin, Jules 136, 186
Membertou, Henri 72, 75
Meneval, see Des Friches
Menou d'Aulnay, Charles de 100, 184;
connections with Razilly family 40,
43, 122; merchant connections 43–4,
45, 47, 109; debts to Le Borgne 47,
48–9, 187; conflict with La Tour

47–8, 52–3, 55, 73, 92, 95–7,
109–10, 115–16; supported by French
government 52–6 passim; commissions as governor 52, 56, 90, 117; and
native people 70; and New England
83, 85–7, 94–9, 102; treaty with
Massachusetts (1644) 98, 162, 179,
185; and settlement of Port Royal
103–4, 118–9; as seigneur 104, 117,
118, 122; conflict with Denys 106–7,
110, 115–16; conflict with Cent-
Associés 110; death 114, 123, 127;
family 136, 139
Menou d'Aulnay, Jeanne de, see Motin
Menou de Charnisay, René de 47, 127,
129
Menteith, Earl of, see Graham
Merrimack River 27, 90
Micmac: territory 3; population 4, 73,
223 n24; relations with French 6, 10,
59, 62, 69, 73–7 passim, 123, 165;
relations with Scots 32, 58; see also
Native people
Middlesex, county of (Massachusetts) 96
Minas Basin 77; see also Les Mines
Miramichi 76, 165
Mirliquesh 33, 137, 145
Miscou 43, 56, 76, 106, 110
missionaries, see Evangelization, Chris-
tian; Religious orders
Mius d'Entremont, Philippe 159
Mohawk, see Iroquois
Monmouth, Duke of, see Scott
Montagnais 165
Montaigne, Michel de 61
Montreal 89, 173, 176
Monts, see Du Gua
Motin, Jeanne (Menou d'Aulnay; Saint-
Étienne de La Tour) 110, 127–9
passim

Muscongus, 84, 101, 137, 153

Nantes 13
native people: aboriginal culture and
economy xiii, 3–6, 10–11, 68, 165–6;
effects of European contact xiii, 4–5,
11, 59–61, 64, 68–9, 73–4, 76–8,
164–9, 183, 185–6, 189; attitudes to
European colonists xv, 58–79 passim,
123, 164–9, 185, 219 n66; peoples of
northeastern maritime region, defined
3; lands 4, 60, 64–8, 164, 181, 185;
religion 4, 6, 60, 73–6, 165–6; and
Christian missionaries 5, 70–9, 164–
6; relations with English 17–18, 60–
72, 164, 166–9, 174, 180–2, 185;
relations with Scots 32, 58; as perceived by Europeans 58–79 passim,
185; population 64; warfare 68–9,
75, 167–9, 181–3; relations with
French 69–70, 72–9, 164–6, 180–3,
185, 188; see also Disease, European;
Evangelization, Christian
Navigation Acts 130, 144, 186
Naxouat 183
Neale, Walter 90, 92, 240 n60
Nelson, John 172–3, 175, 176, 182, 189
Nepisiquit 75, 76
Neutrality, treaty of, see Whitehall, treaty
of
New England, see Council for New Eng-
land, Dominion of New England, Eng-
lish
New England towns xii, 92, 119–22
passim, 131–5
Newfoundland 8–9, 12–13, 19, 24, 97,
147, 154, 205 n49, 229 n3
New France, see Acadia, Canada, Com-
pagnie de la Nouvelle-France, French
New Hampshire 90, 93, 94, 101, 119–

20, 130, 155, 168, 169, 170–1, 177, 180, 232 n45

New Netherland xv, 26, 123, 135, 149, 228 n1; *see also* Dutch, New York

New Plymouth 23, 30, 65, 71, 92, 99, 100, 101, 149, 178; and fur trade in Kennebec–Ste-Croix territory 83–7, 94, 98, 153, 212 n116; land holdings on Kennebec 83–4, 140, 153

New Scotland
– to 1630: concept of xiv, 21–2; native peoples 3–6, 32, 58; natural resources 5–10; plans of Alexander 21–2, 23–5, 26, 27–8, 70, 72; and Kirke brothers 26, 31, 80–1; settlements 30–3
– from 1630 to 1650: Port Royal settlement 37–8, 46, 58, 81–2, 103; question of restitution (1632) 37–40; evacuation of 1632 40, 42, 82, 88; Scottish claim, after evacuation 49–51, 57, 81; as marginal colony 122–4
– from 1650 to 1690: concept of 136–7, 138, 146, 149, 163, 173; grant to La Tour, Temple, and Crowne 137; under Temple 138–41, 145–7, 154, 155–7; rival claims 139, 146, 155; question of restitution (to 1670) 146–7, 155–7; restored to France (1670) 157; claimed by Nelson 172, 182; Phips raid 182–3; as marginal colony 184–90 passim; *see also* Alexander; knights-baronetcies of Scotland; Scots

New Somersetshire, *see* Maine

New Spain xv, 11–12, 21, 61, 123; *see also* Spanish

New York 149, 174–5, 178, 180, 182; *see also* James VII and II, New Netherland

Nicholas, Sir Edward 147

Nichols, Richard 149, 152

Nicholson, Francis 180–1

Norfolk, county of (Massachusetts) 96

North Virginia 14–18; *see also* Maine, Sagadahoc

Nova Scotia, *see* New Scotland

Ochiltree, Lord, *see* Stewart

Ogunquit 105, 120

Oporto 44, 103

Palmer, Sir Geoffrey 149

Paris 13, 19, 20, 25, 171

Pascataquack, *see* Piscataqua

patentees, Maine 86, 91, 93, 105, 107–9, 111–14, 116, 119–22, 133–4, 147, 151, 210 n105

Paul III, Pope 71

Pemaquid 65, 70, 83, 85, 87, 92, 94, 95, 98, 153, 154, 166, 167, 174–5, 180, 181, 182

Penacook: territory 3; relations with English 68, 256 n13; *see also* Native people

Penobscot 3, 64, 68, 70, 77–8, 166–7

Penobscot: river 3, 10, 82, 84–6, 168, 181, 246 n57; bay 9, 153; English trading-posts and settlements 84–6, 94, 98, 101, 153, 154, *see also* Pentagouet

Pentagouet 76, 139, 147, 154, 202 n32; river 19, 87, 115, 161; d'Aulnay at 52, 69–70, 87, 92, 98, 110; and Sedgwick conquest 135–6; Grandfontaine at 153, 157–9 passim; Saint-Castin at 78, 166, 175, 180–1; *see also* Penobscot

Perrot, François-Marie 77, 159, 160, 166, 176–7

Peter, Hugh 93

Petit, Louis 165, 166
Phips, William 182–3
Pigiguit 159
Piscataqua River 3, 84, 94, 101, 116, 120, 129, 130, 136, 175, 181; as boundary xiv, 41, 80, 90, 93, 108, 117, 153; English settlements on 30, 46, 86, 92, 105, 106, 121, 149, 240 n60; native people of 68, 256 n13; see also Kittery, Portsmouth (New Hampshire)
Plymouth (England) 13, 15, 22, 44, 45, 108
Plymouth (New England), see New Plymouth
Pons, Antoinette de, Marquise de Guercheville 19, 73
Popham, George 15, 18, 63
Popham, Sir John 16, 18
Port aux Baleines 31
Port Lomeron 19, 29, 33, 213 n126, 229 n2
Port Mouton 7
Port Rossignol 44, 45, 145
Port Royal 9, 10, 14, 76, 77, 85, 88, 98, 109, 115, 116, 147, 162, 165, 166, 175, 184, 187, 190; settlement of de Monts 17–18; settlement of Poutrincourt 19, 20; under Alexander 31–2, 37–9, 46, 50, 58, 82; surrendered to Razilly 39–40, 81, 82–3, 213 n126; under d'Aulnay 41, 52, 103–4, 118–19, 122; attacked by La Tour 96–7, 110; colonists 104, 118–19, 123, 140–1, 158–9, 160–1, 172; after death of d'Aulnay 127–8; and Sedgwick conquest 135–6, 164; under Temple 141, surrendered by Temple 157; and Le Borgne 160; under Meneval 177; and Phips raid 182–3; see also Acadia, Acadians

Portsmouth (England) 46
Portsmouth (New Hampshire) 130
Portuguese xi, 8, 11–12, 14, 20
Poutrincourt, Jean de, see Biencourt
Prince Edward Island, see Île Saint-Jean
Pring, Martin 9
proprietary system 55, 103, 104–6, 114, 116, 118, 119–22, 142, 144, 148, 150–2, 170, 184, 188, see also Féodalité
Protestantism 64, 78, 95, 205 n48; see also Church of England; Church of Scotland; Evangelization, Christian

Quebec 17, 26, 38, 39, 48, 55, 78, 88–90, 97, 100, 154, 159–60, 165, 173, 181; see also Canada

Raleigh, Sir Walter 13–14, 203 n41
Randolph, Edward 170–1, 175, 180, 181
Rashleigh, Thomas 232 n40
Rawson, Edward 131–2, 140
Razilly, Isaac de 42, 69, 73, 87, 94, 99, 114; memorandum of 1626 22, 25, 187; seigneury 28, 40, 51; takes surrender of Port Royal 40, 82, 213 n126; as lieutenant general 40, 51, 89, 123; at La Hève 40, 46, 82, 103–4, 105; merchant connections 40–1, 43–4; death 41, 52, 109
Razilly (Razilly/d'Aulnay) company 43–4, 45, 109
Recollets, see Religious orders
Religious orders: Capuchins 72, 97–8, 104, 136, 164; Jesuits 4, 19, 25, 71–9 passim, 89, 99, 121, 165, 207 n79; Recollets 4, 5, 29, 73, 74, 82, 165; Sulpicians 165
Rendell, Margery 114
Restigouche 76

Rhoades, John 162
Rhode Island 149, 178
Richelieu, Cardinal de, *see* Du Plessis
Richmond's Island 44–8 passim, 67, 86, 92, 108, 116
Rigby, Alexander 111–13
Rishworth, Edward 120
Rivedoux, Monsieur 249 n8
Roberval, *see* La Rocque
Robinau de Villebon, Joseph 183
Rochester, Earl of, *see* Hyde
Rogers, Christopher 106
Roman Catholicism 64, 71, 72, 74, 178; *see also* Evangelization, Christian; Religious orders; Séminaire de Québec
Rosier, James 9
Rossignol, Jean 58
Rouen 13, 16
Rowles 68
Royal Commission of 1664–6 149–53, 155, 186

Sable Island 40, 52, 87, 140
Saco 105, 112, 117, 181; river 3; native people 58, 67, 167; English settlement 67, 84, 91, 107–8, 120, 122, 132, 134
Sagadahoc 23, 65, 91, 111; English colony at (1607–8) 15, 17–18, 58, 59, 63–4, 187
Saint-Castin, *see* Abbadie
St Christopher 147, 156–7
Ste Croix River 3, 23, 28, 40, 50, 51–2, 80, 83–4, 115, 117, 149, 153, 175, 178, 180, 187, 189
Saint-Étienne de La Tour, Charles de 159; commander in Acadia (1620s) 29–30, 213 n126; and New Scotland 32–3, 82, 137; and Compagnie de la Nouvelle-France 33, 43, 82, 109; commissions as lieutenant general 40, 51, 52–3, 57, 85, 88, 109, 114, 128;

and Razilly 40, 51–2, 109; merchant connections 43, 45, 87, 94, 109, 229 n3; conflict with d'Aulnay 47, 52, 55, 70, 73, 95–7, 109–10, 115, 118; and Massachusetts 47–8, 55, 92, 95–9; defeat by d'Aulnay 55, 96, 110; flees to Quebec 55, 89–90, 97; returns to Acadia 110, 128; captured by Sedgwick 135–6; Nova Scotia grant (1656) 137, 138; and Temple's Nova Scotia 137, 146, 147; death 137
Saint-Étienne de La Tour, Claude de 32–3
Saint-Étienne de La Tour, Françoise-Marie de, *see* Jacquelin
Saint-Étienne de La Tour, Jeanne de, *see* Motin
Saint-François-de-Sales 165
St George River 174
Saint-Germain-en-Laye, treaty of (1632) 39, 42, 81, 82, 88–9
Saint-Jean-de-Luz 9, 16
St John River 3, 29, 58, 73, 85, 115, 159, 165, 171, 183; La Tour's post 40, 47, 51, 52, 82, 95, 96, 109, 110, 128, 135; post taken by d'Aulnay 55, 96, 110; and Sedgwick raid 135–6; under Temple 139, 147, 157; Dutch raid 161
St Lawrence: gulf of xiv, 56, 89, 115, 117, 137; river xiv, 13, 16, 23, 25, 26, 28, 31, 80–1, 89, 137, 157, 180
Saint-Lusson, *see* Daumont
Saint-Malo 13, 16
Saint-Sauveur 19, 20, 73, 207 n79
Saint-Vallier, *see* La Croix
Salem 96, 168
Salisbury, Earl of, *see* Cecil
Samoset 65
Saunders, Robert 45
Sauvaget, Jean 45

Savalet, Captain 9
Sawyer, Sir Robert 177
Saye and Sele, Viscount, see Fienes
Scarborough: 132, 134, 148, 168, 244
   n29; see also Black Point, Blue Point
Scotland: crown and government of 13–
   14, 37–40, 49–51, 57, 88, 146, 186
Scots: and fur trade 6; and timber trade
   7; and fisheries 202 n34; of Highlands
   and Islands 13, 22; approaches to
   colonization 21–2, 23–5, 26–8, 188–
   9, 205 n49; in New Scotland 30–3,
   37–9, 50, 58, 82; relations with
   French in America 31–3, 81–2; relations with native people 32, 58; and
   surrender of Port Royal 39–40, 82;
   relations with English in America 80–
   1, 88
Scott, James, Duke of Monmouth 155
Scottow, Joshua 101
Sedgwick, Robert 135–6, 137–8, 141,
   164
Segipt 32
seigneurial system 28, 103–4, 106, 114,
   116, 118–19, 122, 140–1, 142, 159,
   160, 172, 184, 188, 210 n105; see also
   Féodalité
Séminaire de Québec 72–3, 160, 165;
   see also Evangelization, Christian
Sahpleigh, Nicholas 121, 134, 204 n42,
   229 n3
Sheepscott 153, 230 n12
Shurt, Abraham 70, 87, 94
Sillery 77, 165, 167
Smith, John 6, 7, 12, 20
Spanish xi, xii, xiv, 6, 8, 11–12, 14, 61,
   63, 65, 70, 71, 78
Spurwink 107, 108, 132; see also Fal-
   mouth
Squando 167
Stephens, Benjamin 45

Stewart, Andrew, Lord Ochiltree 14
Stewart of Killeith, James, Lord Ochiltree
   14, 31–2, 81–2
Stirling, Earl of, see Alexander
Stoughton, William 169
Strachey, William 17–18
Suffolk, county of (Massachusetts) 96
Sully, Duc de, see Béthune
Sulpicians, see Religious orders
Suza, treaty of 31–2, 38
Swedes xi

Tadoussac 16, 26, 31, 88
Talon, Jean 154, 157–9, 161
Temple, Sir Thomas: Nova Scotia grant
   (1656) 137; governor of Nova Scotia
   138–41, 146–7, 153, 154; and Massachusetts 138–40, 187; rival claimants to Nova Scotia 139, 146; conflicts
   with Le Borgnes 139, 142, 145–6,
   157, 160; and English crown 146–7,
   149, 156–7; and restitution of Acadia
   155–7; death 157; claims taken up by
   Nelson 172, 182
Thomas, Jean 69
Thomson, David 30
Thury, Louis-Pierre 73, 76, 165
timber trade 7, 43, 45, 94, 101, 115, 121,
   130, 135–6, 144, 154, 155, 175
Tordesillas, treaty of 11
Trelawny, Edward 46, 86
Trelawny, Robert 44–8 passim, 67,
   106–9 passim, 111, 116, 121–2
Treworgie, John 204 n42
Trois-Rivières 89
Tucker, Richard 112
Tuffet, Jean 45
Tyng, Edward 140

United Colonies of New England 93, 99,
   100

Usher, John 170

Utrecht, treaty of (1713) 246 n59

Vendôme, Duc de, *see* Bourbon

Verrazzano, Giovanni da 6, 12, 58

Villebon, *see* Robinau

Vines, Richard 84, 91, 111–12, 116, 119, 120–1

Virginia xv, 15, 19, 22–3, 26, 52, 56, 65–6, 68, 86, 88

Waldron, Richard 168

Walker, Richard 138

Wannerton, Thomas 92–3

Waymouth, George 9, 71

Weare, Peter 105

Wells 105, 113–14, 117, 120, 122, 132, 134, 148, 152, 168, 182

Welsh, John 72

West Indies 12, 121, 147, 156, 158, 171, 179

Wheelwright, John 120

Whitehall, treaty of 179–82, 185, 187

Wiggin, Thomas 92

William of Orange 179, 181

Williamson, Sir Joseph 140, 157

Winslow, Edward 72, 78, 84

Winslow, John 78

Winter, John 44–8 passim, 67, 86, 106–9 passim, 111, 112, 116, 121–2

Winthrop, John 65–6, 67, 83, 87, 90–7 passim, 106, 111–13, 121

Winthrop, John, Jr 50, 57, 92, 96, 98, 101, 123

Wise, Thomas 67

Withers, Thomas 105, 119, 121

York, Duke of, *see* James VII and II

York (Maine) 132, 133–4, 150, 151, 152–3, 168, 170, 182; *see also* Agamenticus, Bristol, Gorgeana

Yorkshire, county of, *see* Maine